W9-AUD-516

Social Innovation

Social Innovation: Comparative Perspectives investigates socioeconomic impact. Since it is hard to establish causality and to measure social properties when investigating impact, especially at the level of society, the book narrows down impact to one priority aspect: social innovation—understood as organisations' capacity to generate novel ideas, ways and means of doing things, and of addressing public and social problems of many kinds.

This volume's primary assertion is that the third sector, specifically through stimulating civic involvement, is best placed to produce social innovation, outperforming business firms and state agencies in this regard. By investigating actor contributions to social innovation across seven fields of activity, *Social Innovation: Comparative Perspectives* develops our understanding of why and how the third sector is central to functioning, cohesive and viable societies.

This volume is based on contributions of the project "ITSSOIN— Impact of the Third Sector as Social Innovation" funded by the European Commission under the 7th framework programme. It will be of insight across disciplines, in particular to the growing social innovation community, innovation researchers more generally and to non-profit scholars. The practical relevance of the book will be of interest to European and national policy makers and practitioners across different sectors.

Helmut K. Anheier is the academic director of the Centre for Social Investment at the University of Heidelberg, Germany, past president of the Hertie School of Governance, Berlin, Germany, and holds adjunct professorial positions at the London School of Economics and UCLA.

Gorgi Krlev is a research associate at the Centre for Social Investment at the University of Heidelberg, Germany.

Georg Mildenberger is head of research at the Centre for Social Investment at the University of Heidelberg, Germany.

Routledge Studies in Social Enterprise & Social Innovation

Series Editors: Jacques Defourny, Lars Hulgård, and Rocio Nogales

A Social Enterprise seeks to achieve social, cultural, community, economic or environmental outcomes whilst remaining a revenue generating business. A Social Innovation is said to be a new idea or initiative to a social problem that is more effective, efficient, sustainable, or just than the current process and which sees the society it is operating in receive the primary value created rather than a private organization or firm.

Routledge Studies in Social Enterprise & Social Innovation looks to examine these increasingly important academic research themes as a central concept for social theories and policies. It looks to examine and explore the activities of social participation among civil society organisations, SMEs, governments and research institutions, publishing the breakthrough books of the new frontiers of the field as well as the state-of-the-nation-defining books that help advance the field.

Social Entrepreneurship and Social Enterprises
Nordic Perspectives
Edited by Linda Lundgaard Andersen, Malin Gawell, and Roger Spear

Social Enterprise and Special Events
Market-Based Approaches to Mission-Driven Gatherings
Edited by Julie Cencula Olberding

Co-design and Social Innovation: Connections, Tensions and Opportunities
Garth M. Britton

Social Regeneration and Local Development
Cooperation, Social Economy and Public Participation
Edited by Silvia Sacchetti, Asimina Christoforou, and Michele Mosca

The Growth of Italian Cooperatives
Innovation, Resilience and Social Responsibility
Piero Ammirato

Social Innovation
Comparative Perspectives
Edited by Helmut K. Anheier, Gorgi Krlev, and Georg Mildenberger

Social Innovation
Comparative Perspectives

**Edited by Helmut K. Anheier,
Gorgi Krlev, and
Georg Mildenberger**

Routledge
Taylor & Francis Group

NEW YORK AND LONDON

First published 2019
by Routledge
52 Vanderbilt Avenue, New York, NY 10017

and by Routledge
2 Park Square, Milton Park, Abingdon, Oxon, OX14 4RN

Routledge is an imprint of the Taylor & Francis Group, an informa business

© 2019 Taylor & Francis

The right of Helmut K. Anheier, Gorgi Krlev, and Georg Mildenberger to
be identified as the authors of the editorial material, and of the authors
for their individual chapters, has been asserted in accordance with
sections 77 and 78 of the Copyright, Designs and Patents Act 1988.

The Open Access version of this book, available at www.taylorfrancis.com,
has been made available under a Creative Commons Attribution-Non
Commercial-No Derivatives 4.0 license.

Trademark notice: Product or corporate names may be trademarks
or registered trademarks, and are used only for identification and
explanation without intent to infringe.

Library of Congress Cataloging-in-Publication Data
A catalog record for this book has been requested

ISBN: 978-1-138-06836-0 (hbk)
ISBN: 978-1-315-15802-0 (ebk)

Typeset in Sabon
by Apex CoVantage, LLC

Contents

Preface

The third or non-profit sector has received growing policy recognition as well as academic attention in recent years. Researchers have analysed non-profit organisations from different angles, usually emphasising specific roles the sector is hypothesised to perform (Anheier, 2014). The most prominent among them are: (1) service providing role: in the wake of government failure non-profits are seen as either complement or substitute for public service systems (Ben-Ner & van Hoomissen, 1991; Hansmann, 1980, 2006; Weisbrod, 1975, 1998; Young & Steinberg, 1995); and (2) role as advocates and value guardians: research has also focussed on the extent to which non-profits engage in advocacy and either protect or advance the position and welfare of those who would otherwise find little or no attention and "give voice" to those otherwise unheard. This function was found to vary by the civic culture and civic-mindedness of local populations (Almond & Verba, 1963; Halman & Nevitte, 1996; Putnam, 2000; Putnam, Leonardi, & Nanetti, 1993).

In addition to the identification of the sector's functions, it has been mapped both conceptually and empirically, most notably in the The Johns Hopkins Comparative Non-profit Sector project (Anheier & Salamon, 1997) and the United Nation's Handbook on "Non-profit Institutions in the System of National Accounts"(United Nations Statistical Division, 2003). While these efforts have contributed to a better understanding of the sector in its economic and social foundations, a major gap remains, which the book will address: the sector's impact and the longer-term outcomes achieved or involved. Evidence on impact is rare because of methodological difficulties to evaluate non-profit programmes (i.e., the attribution problem in matching cause and effect in complex social settings) and a long-standing emphasis on simple cost and revenue accounting that stressed input measures (thus efficiency) rather than effectiveness or contributions to policy or programme outcomes (Drummond, Stoddart, Torrance, & George, 1998; Kendall & Knapp, 2000; McCrone & Knapp, 2007). In the past many efforts to gauge the impact of the sector as a whole, in particular fields, or of single organisations have led to rather inconclusive results, focussing on the same areas of measurement contained in the statistical accounts referred to previously, such as employment, contributions to the economic value added, etc. (see, e.g., Flynn & Hodgkinson, 2001).

This points to a certain degree of intractability: the existence of non-profits is linked to conditions where it is easier to monitor cost behaviour and distributional aspects than actual performance. We take non-profit status as an indicator of trustworthiness (Hansmann, 1980) because measured and accounted performance is difficult to establish, if not nearly absent. Yet the inconclusive record of previous research on empirical non-profit performance does not suggest the questions about impact are impossible to answer or irrelevant. We suggest to the contrary that research has emphasised conventional, steady-state or standard performance compared to other forms of performance which are both conceptually as well as policy relevant and more feasible: one such aspect is social innovation, understood as the capacity of organisations to generate novel ideas, ways and means of doing things, and of addressing public and social problems of many kinds (Crepaldi, Rosa, & Pesce, 2012; The Young Foundation, 2012). The basic claim of the book is that non-profits are "better" at social innovations than governments and markets due to a variety of organisational properties. Thus, "Impact of the Third Sector as Social Innovation" (ITSSOIN) is the name of the project this book is based on.

The book examines the claim as follows. It draws on two strands of research: (1) performance measurement in non-profit organisations (Davies & Knapp, 1994; Kaplan, 2001; Kendall & Knapp, 2000; Rosenbaum et al., 2011); and (2) technological innovation theories (Abernathy & Clark, 1985, pp. 22–23; Archibugi & Iammarino, 2002; Henderson & Clark, 1990) and the emergent theory on social innovation (Nicholls & Murdock, 2012; Zapf, 1989). These two anchors are used to derive a focus on the stimulation of social innovation by non-profit organisations as a measure of their ultimate performance, that is their social impact. In the empirical testing of this claim, the book relies on cross-national and multi-field case study research (Eisenhardt, 1989) of recognised social innovation streams (SI streams) across Europe. 'SI stream' refers to new approaches, principles of action, governance forms or modes of organisation that have fundamentally affected a field of activity, and already for a certain period of time (at least for five years back from 2015, when the empirical work was initiated) and across national borders, so that they are not geographically restricted. The transformative effects of the SI streams, which have been identified by means of expert consultation, range from gradual to 'disruptive' (Christensen, 2000).

The innovation streams are analysed by means of a retrospective 'process tracing' (Collier, 2011; George & Bennett, 2005) to find out which (types) of organisations have contributed to their emergence and how they have done so. The research approach is open to spotting innovation actors from the third sector as well as the state and the market. The actors involved in promoting these innovations are studied in the context of the 'strategic action fields' (Fligstein & McAdam, 2012) they inhabit, with a view to their power positions, functions and mission. Results are synthesised across fields of activity with the aim of distilling which (types of) actors have played a role in making the social innovation happen, and which traits have enabled them to act in that role. This yields a set of conditions which are likely causal for the emergence of social innovations.

The empirical research of the book covers nine European countries: the Czech Republic, Denmark, France, Germany, Italy, the Netherlands, Spain, Sweden and the United Kingdom. And it relates to seven fields of activity: Arts & Culture, Social Services, Health Care, Environmental Sustainability, Consumer Protection, Work Integration, and Community Development. One social innovation stream per field is compared across three to four countries. The field-country combinations have been chosen by (1) the rationale of representing European diversity, (2) the relevance of the respective SI stream and the field as a whole within the respective countries and (3) variations in national institutional context conditions.

References

Abernathy, W. J., & Clark, K. B. (1985). Innovation: Mapping the winds of creative destruction. *Research Policy, 14*(1), 3–22. https://doi.org/10.1016/0048-7333(85)90021-6

Almond, G. A., & Verba, S. (Eds.). (1963). *The civic culture revisited.* Newbury Park: Sage Publications.

Anheier, H. K. (2014). *Nonprofit organizations: Theory, management, policy* (expanded and revised 2nd ed.). Oxford, New York, NY: Routledge.

Anheier, H. K., & Salamon, L. (Eds.). (1997). *Defining the nonprofit sector.* Manchester: Manchester University Press.

Archibugi, D., & Iammarino, S. (2002). The globalization of technological innovation: Definition and evidence. *Review of International Political Economy, 9*(1), 98–122.

Ben-Ner, A., & van Hoomissen, T. (1991). Nonprofit organizations in the mixed economy: A demand and supply analysis. *Annals of Public and Cooperative Economics, 4,* 519–550.

Christensen, C. M. (2000). *The innovator's dilemma: When new technologies cause great firms to fail. The management of innovation and change series.* Boston, MA: Harvard Business School Press.

Collier, D. (2011). Understanding process tracing. *PS: Political Science & Politics, 44*(4), 823–830. https://doi.org/10.1017/S1049096511001429

Crepaldi, C., Rosa, E. de, & Pesce, F. (2012). *Literature review on innovation in social services in Europe: Sectors of health, education and welfare services.* Report from Innoserv.

Davies, B. P., & Knapp, M. (1994). Improving equity and efficiency in British community care. *Social Policy & Administration, 28*(3), 263–285.

Drummond, M. F., Stoddart, G. L., & Torrance, G. W. (1998). *Methods for economic evaluation of health care programmes* (2nd ed.). Oxford, New York, NY, Toronto: Oxford University Press.

Eisenhardt, K. M. (1989). Building theories from case study research. *Academy of Management Review, 14*(4), 532–550.

x *Preface*

Fligstein, N., & McAdam, D. (2012). *A theory of fields*. Oxford, New York, NY: Oxford University Press.

Flynn, P., & Hodgkinson, V. A. (2001). *Measuring the impact of the nonprofit sector*. New York, NY: Kluwer Academic/Plenum Publishers.

George, A. L., & Bennett, A. (2005). *Case studies and theory development in the social science*. Cambridge: MIT Press.

Halman, L., & Nevitte, N. (1996). *Political value change in western democracies: Integration, values, identification, and participation. European values studies*. Tilburg, The Netherlands: Tilburg University Press.

Hansmann, H. (1980). The role of nonprofit enterprise. *The Yale Law Journal, 89*(8), 835–902.

Hansmann, H. (2006). Economic theories of non-profit organizations. In W. W. Powell & R. Steinberg (Eds.), *The nonprofit sector: A research handbook*. New Haven, London: Yale University Press.

Henderson, R. M., & Clark, K. B. (1990). Architectural innovation: The reconfiguration of existing product technologies and the failure of established firms. *Administrative Science Quarterly, 35*(1), 9–30. https://doi.org/10.2307/2393549

Kaplan, R. S. (2001). Strategic performance measurement and management in nonprofit organizations. *Nonprofit Management and Leadership, 11*(3), 353–370. https://doi.org/10.1002/nml.11308

Kendall, J., & Knapp, M. (2000). Measuring the performance of voluntary organizations. *Public Management Review, 2*(1), 105–132.

McCrone, P., & Knapp, M. (2007). Economic evaluation of early intervention services. *British Journal of Psychiatry, 191*(51), 19–22.

Nicholls, A., & Murdock, A. (Eds.). (2012). *Social innovation: Blurring boundaries to reconfigure markets*. Houndmills, Basingstoke, Hampshire, New York, NY: Palgrave Macmillan.

Putnam, R. D. (2000). *Bowling alone: The collapse and revival of American community*. New York, NY: Simon & Schuster.

Putnam, R. D., Leonardi, R., & Nanetti, R. (1993). *Making democracy work: Civic traditions in modern Italy*. Princeton, NJ: Princeton University Press.

Rosenbaum, M. S., Corus, C., Ostrom, A. L., Anderson, L., Fisk, R. P., Gallan, A. S., . . . Williams, J. D. (2011). Conceptualization and aspirations of transformative service research. *Journal of Research for Consumers, 19*, 1–6.

United Nations Statistical Division. (2003). *Handbook on non-profit institutions in the system of national accounts: Studies in methods. Series F: Vol. 91*. New York, NY: United Nations.

Weisbrod, B. A. (1975). Toward a theory of the voluntary nonprofit sector in a three-sector-economy. In E. S. Phelps (Ed.), *Altruism, morality, and economic theory* (pp. 171–195). New York, NY: Russell Sage Foundation.

Weisbrod, B. A. (1998). *To profit or not to profit: The commercial transformation of the nonprofit sector*. Cambridge, New York, NY: Cambridge University Press.

The Young Foundation. (2012). *Social innovation overview: Part I—defining social innovation*. A Deliverable to the Project "The Theoretical, Empirical and Policy Foundations for Building Social Innovation in Europe" (DG Research). Brussels.

Young, D. R., & Steinberg, R. (1995). *Economics for nonprofit managers*. New York, NY: Foundation Center.

Zapf, W. (1989). Über Soziale Innovationen. *Soziale Welt, 40*(1–2), 170–183.

Acknowledgements

The results of the ITSSOIN project, for which we gratefully acknowledge the funding from the European Commission, have been produced as a collaborative effort at its best. We would like to express our heartfelt gratitude to the many colleagues who have participated in realising the research and writing the deliverables which form the basis for the chapters in this book. Their contribution is acknowledged explicitly in the corresponding sections.

We would also like to highlight the significant assistance in coordinating and executing the research, and in preparing this book, from Lea Heyer and in particular from Ute Bongertz.

In addition we want to stress the role of those whose comments have been pivotal to advancing the project, although they have not been directly involved in the production of this part of the research. Our thanks go to Anker Brink Lund, Arjen de Wit, Filip Wijkström, Kevin André, Paul Dekker, René Bekkers and Stina Preuss from the ITSSOIN consortium; Lesley Hustinx (University of Ghent), Jonathan Michie (University of Oxford) and Zeke Hasenfeld (UCLA) from the ITSSOIN advisory board; and Patrick Kenis (Tilburg University/WU Vienna), the commentator of our concluding conference.

At Routledge we would like to thank our editors Brianna Ascher, David Varley, Mary del Plato and Megan Smith, as well as Jennifer Bonnar at Apex CoVantage, for their embracement of this book and their swift and effective support in the production process.

Contributors

Dr. Begoña Alvarez García is a lecturer in the Department of Business at the University of La Coruña (Spain), where she teaches several courses in the area of finance. She has also been a lecturer at the University of Paris IX-Dauphine (France) and the coordinator of the master's program in Banking and Finance at the University of La Coruña. She holds a PhD in Economy and Management from the University of La Coruña and she was given an Extraordinary Doctorate Award. She has completed several research stages at the Universities of Paris-Dauphine and the Massachusetts Institute of Technology (MIT), being awarded a grant by institutions such as UNESCO. She has participated in several European and national research projects, including the project called Marine Safety and Environmental Protection: Social Acceptance Criteria for the Spanish Ports of Refuge (funded by the Spanish Ministry of Science and Innovation), and the project called Integrated System for Energy Optimization and Reduction of the CO_2 Footprint in Buildings (funded by the Spanish Ministry of Economy and Competitiveness). She has published several books related to financial topics. The most recent (published in 2017 by Esic Editorial) is entitled *The Reform of the Spanish Post-trading System: Major Causes and Consequences*. She has attended numerous international conferences and has published several research articles. She is currently working on two lines of research: the first one focuses on financial topics such as the evaluation and selection of investment projects, and the second one focuses on social topics such as social innovations.

Dr. Luis Ignacio Álvarez-González is an associate professor of marketing at the School of Economics and Business, University of Oviedo, Spain. His research focuses on not-for-profit organisations management, corporate social responsibility, and social innovation. He has published in academic journals such as *International Journal of Nonprofit and Voluntary Sector Marketing, European Journal of Marketing, International Review on Public and Nonprofit Marketing, Annals of Public and Cooperative Economics* and *The Foundation Review*. Recently, Prof. Álvarez-González has been the lead researcher of the project entitled Marketing and Social

Innovation: Consequences of Business-Nonprofit Partnerships on Social Well-being. The main objective of this project, promoted by the Ministry of Economy and Competitiveness of Spain, was to analyse the role played by so-called "stakeholder marketing" in order to promote social innovations in firms and not-for-profit organisations (NPOs).

Dr. Helmut K. Anheier is the academic director of the Centre for Social Investment at the University of Heidelberg, Germany, past president of the Hertie School of Governance, Berlin, Germany, and holds adjunct professorial positions at the London School of Economics and UCLA.

Annette Bauer is a research fellow at the Personal Social Services Research Unit (PSSRU) at the London School of Economics, UK. Annette's research is concerned with (mental) health policy and systems, and economic evaluations of preventative interventions at the interface between sectors. Annette has published her work in high-impact academic journals and presents at national and international conferences and events. Her work on the costs of perinatal mental illness had a major impact on policy and practice in the UK and beyond. Annette's interests are on generating robust real-world evidence that is meaningful to people with lived experience and can be used in decision making.

Dr. Giulia Cancellieri is an assistant professor in the Management Department at Ca' Foscari University of Venice, Italy. She was a visiting researcher at the University of Michigan and a post-doctoral researcher at Bocconi University and LUISS Guido Carli. Her research interests are in the fields of strategic management and marketing in cultural organisations, cultural entrepreneurship, and social innovation. She is the author of several articles and working papers on these topics. Her works have been published in the *International Journal of Arts Management* and awarded by the International Conference on Arts and Cultural Management (AIMAC). She presented her works at several premier international conferences including the Academy of Management Annual Meeting (AOM), the Strategic Management Society Annual Conference (SMS), and the International Conference on Arts and Cultural Management.

Lucia Čemová, MA (Masaryk University, Czech Republic) has a background in psychology. She is currently a PhD candidate, working on community integration of migrants, and works as a social worker.

Dr. Aurélie Sara Cognat currently works as a university lecturer at the University Paris-Est Marne La Vallée (IRG Lab), France. She holds master's degrees in Management from Paris X University. In 2013, she submitted her PhD in management, focusing on managerial identity work. Her current projects, in partnership with several European universities, examine the economic and social integration of migrants in France compared to various other European countries.

Dr. Torbjörn Einarsson is a researcher at Stockholm Center for Civil Society Studies, Stockholm School of Economics, Sweden. He is a business and management scholar. His research covers ongoing and historical changes in Swedish civil society. His work also covers membership and governance in complex federative organisations.

Ana Felgueiras is the European Projects Manager in Cluster Alimentario de Galicia (Spain). She has served as a policy officer and chief of the department of international relations and policies in the field of youth policies and youth work at national and international level third-sector organisations, as well as a consultant at private firms and international institutions. For the last few years, she has been researching social sciences in fields such as the third sector, philanthropy, social services and social responsibility, and innovation, participating in research projects and in international congresses and publications.

Dr. Maria Figueroa is an assistant professor in business and societal innovation for climate and sustainability at the Department of Management Society and Communication at Copenhagen Business School, Denmark. Her research and teaching intersect with the scholarship of urban sustainability science, the politics of climate mitigation, and multi-sectoral transformative social and policy innovation. Her research focuses on identifying design principles for innovative, fair and inclusive social pathways toward a systemic low carbon transition. Maria is involved in several European and international case studies to assess the potential of new sustainability models, such as sharing economy, circular economy, and smart digital solutions in cities and the transport sector. She was one of the lead authors in the Working Group III of the Intergovernmental Panel of Climate Change - Fifth Assessment Report on Mitigation Options (2014). She is currently the lead coordinator of a multi-disciplinary academic initiative between three Danish universities to teach and research on sustainability and Smart City challenges, led by Copenhagen Business School.

Dr. Vladimír Hyánek is director and researcher at the Center for Nonprofit Sector Research at Masaryk University in Brno, Czech Republic. He studied public economics and deals mainly with public policy towards the non-profit sector, financing of non-profit organisations, and social entrepreneurship in a post-communist society.

Dr. Gorgi Krlev is a research associate at the Centre for Social Investment at the University of Heidelberg, Germany. He is a business and management scholar and holds a DPhil from the University of Oxford (Kellogg College). Currently his main research subjects are organisational hybridity, social innovation, and impact.

Dr. Jeanet Kullberg (1961, geographer) is a senior researcher at the Netherlands Institute of Social Research in Den Haag. Her research mostly centres on housing and the residential environment. The bulk of her publications are in Dutch with the inclusion of a summary in English. She was until recently a member of the editorial and advisory board of the *International Journal of Housing Studies* and wrote for various Dutch housing journals.

Dr. Bernard Leca is a professor in management control at ESSEC Business School in Paris, France. His broad interest is in the evolution of capitalism. His research focuses on the impact of organisations on society and government and how actors initiate, implement, or resist change.

Vanessa Mato-Santiso is a PhD candidate in economics and business analysis at the University of A Coruña (Spain). She conducts her research on omni-channel strategies used by non-profit organisations and the effects of these strategies on their key stakeholders. She made a collaboration grant for a research project on spatial econometrics (University of A Coruña). Currently she is the technical secretary of the Inditex Chair on Sustainability.

Dr. Wouter Mensink (Netherlands Institute for Social Research, the Netherlands) has a background in public administration and philosophy. He now works as a researcher, focusing on grassroots initiatives, fair trade activism, and social support.

Dr. Georg Mildenberger is head of research at the Centre for Social Investment at the University of Heidelberg, Germany. He has led several project teams working on social innovation in the European context and in addition to this has focused on researching social investment, impact measurement and volunteering. He holds a doctoral degree from Darmstadt University and a master's degree in Philosophy and Political Science from Tübingen University.

Dr. Jiří Navrátil is an assistant professor at the Faculty of Economics and Administration, Masaryk University, Czech Republic. He focuses on the study of collective action, civic engagement, and political networks. He has published in *Democratization*, *Studies in Social Justice* and *Social Movement Studies*.

Dr. Anne-Claire Pache is a chaired professor in social innovation and philanthropy at ESSEC Business School in Paris, France. Her research interests lie at the intersection of organisational theory and social innovation, with a particular emphasis on pluralistic environments, hybrid organisations, and scaling-up processes in organisations. She has conducted qualitative studies in the fields of social enterprises, corporate philanthropy, and private foundations. She has authored several books and articles, published in the *Academy of Management Review* and *Academy of Management Journal*, *Journal of Business Ethics*, *California Management Review*, and *Leadership Quarterly*. Before embarking on an academic career, Prof. Pache was part of the co-founding team of Unis-Cité, a French non-profit organisation that pioneered youth civil service in France.

Dr. Klára Placier is an independent lecturer and researcher formerly working at several Czech and Mexican universities (Brno University of Technology, Masaryk University, Universidad Regiomontana). She has a background in economics and her research interests include corporate social responsibility, the non-profit sector, and social innovation.

Dr. Marta Rey-Garcia (PhD, Complutense University, Madrid, Spain; MBA, Columbia University, New York, USA) is an associate professor in the Management Department of the School of Economics and Business at the University of A Coruña (UDC), Spain. Since 2011 she has been the director of the Inditex-UDC Chair on Sustainability and its graduate course on Sustainability and Social Innovation. She has authored over 50 publications on her fields of interest, such as governance and management of civil society and non-profit organisations, philanthropy, corporate social responsibility and sustainability, and social innovation. Her publications include articles in peer-reviewed journals such as *Nonprofit and Voluntary Sector Quarterly*, *American Journal of Evaluation*, *American Behavioral Scientist*, *Management Decision*, *VOLUNTAS*, and *Nonprofit Management & Leadership*.

Dr. Elisa Ricciuti (Centre for Research on Health and Social Care Management (CeRGAS), Bocconi University, Italy) is responsible for the Nonprofit Management and Philanthropy research area of the Centre. She holds a PhD in global health and development from the London School of Hygiene and Tropical Medicine (LSHTM). Her main areas of interest include global philanthropy and giving, non-profit management, social impact evaluation, and social innovation.

Noelia Salido-Andres is an assistant professor in marketing, Department of Business, and vice-dean for students and communication at the School of Economics and Business at the University of A Coruña (UDC), Spain. Within the context of her PhD, she conducts research on the influence of technological innovation on social innovation within the scope of relations between civil society and the non-profit sector. She has been a visiting fellow at the School of Management and Technology of the Polytechnic Institute of Porto, the School of Economics and Business of the University of Oviedo, the Communication and Media Research Institute of the University of Westminster, and Sheffield Hallam University. As an author as well as co-author, she has published on technological socialisation topics within the scope of citizens' participation. She has both teaching and researching experience, held different positions in companies and social organisations, and currently belongs to the research team of the INDITEX–UDC Chair of Sustainability.

Dr. Sarah Sandford is a research fellow at the ESSEC Philanthropy Chair, Paris, France. Sarah holds master's degrees in mathematics and economics from Cambridge and the London School of Economics (LSE). In 2014, she submitted her PhD in economics, focusing on intrinsic motivation at work, to the LSE. Sarah's research examines the influence donors have on their recipients' missions and objectives, and the influence that charities' core costs have on giving behaviour and the efficiency of the non-profit sector. Before starting her PhD, Sarah worked as an analyst and advisor to UK-based donors at New Philanthropy Capital.

Dr. María José Sanzo Perez is a professor of marketing at the University of Oviedo (Spain), whose research works, mainly related to relationship marketing and non-profit management, have been published in journals such as *Industrial Marketing Management, Supply Chain Management–An International Journal, Journal of Business and Industrial Marketing, Journal of Business Research, Journal of Business-to-Business Marketing, British Food Journal, Technovation, European Journal of Marketing, International Small Business Journal, VOLUNTAS: International Journal of Voluntary and Nonprofit Organizations, The Service Industries Journal, Service Business: An International Journal*, and *Nonprofit and Voluntary Sector Quarterly*. She has been deputy director of the Department of Business Administration of the University of Oviedo, coordinator of the PhD program in Business Administration, and vice-dean for quality assurance at the School of Economics and Business of the University of Oviedo.

Dr. Alex Turrini (PhD in management, Bocconi University, Milan, Italy) is an associate professor at the Department of Social and Political Science at Bocconi University and visiting chair of the Division of Arts Management and Arts Entrepreneurship at SMU Meadows School for the Arts, Dallas, USA. His research activities centre on public policies and management in the arts and cultural sector and public sector leadership and change. Turrini is the author of numerous books and papers on these topics. His works have been published in *International Journal of Arts Management*; *Journal of Arts Management, Law, and Society*; *International Journal of Cultural Policy*; *Public Administration Review*; *Public Administration*; and *American Behavioral Scientist*, among others. He serves as a reviewer of some national and international journals and is associate editor in management for *the International Journal of Arts Management*.

Dr. Gerald Wistow is a visiting professor at the London School of Economics and honorary professor at the London School of Hygiene and Tropical Medicine, UK. He was previously co-director of the Centre for Research in Social Policy at Loughborough University and director of the Nuffield Institute for Health at Leeds University. His current research includes implementing integrated care and pooled budgets; the future funding of adult social care in England; improving integrated care for older people in the EU; and the role of prevention across health and social care.

Chapter Summaries

Part I (Chapters 1–3) provides the theoretical conception of the book and develops its main claim and hypothesis. It lays out the methods by which the claim and hypothesis are tested.

Chapter 1 reviews recent developments in assessing third sector impact and the challenges they face. As a result of the latter, it proposes a focus on social innovation as one of the main impacts, in particular when regarding the sector as a whole. It discusses how the traditional research on technological innovation relates to the emergent interest in social innovation and how the third sector is connected to it.

Chapter 2 builds on the previous chapter and develops a systems based approach to the study of social innovation. It outlines an open research approach that aims to investigate social innovation neutral to sector affiliation, departing from the innovation as the unit of analysis to then identify involved actors and their properties. Field theory is introduced as the analytic lens to narrow down fields of activity and to study actor constellations and interplay.

Chapter 3 outlines the method used in the empirical work to test the main claim that social innovation is one of the key impacts of third sector organisations: process tracing. Process tracing is a method from political science, which is used to analyse policy making, be it political programmes and agendas, or legislation. In retrospect investigators try to follow a process backwards to uncover milestones and pivotal actors in its development. This very same approach is applied to several SI streams, one in each of seven fields of activity the book will analyse. Each SI stream is studied across three to four European countries. It also provides the rationale for choosing specific fields of activity and field-country combinations. By the cross-national setup the book helps condense (1) the actors most strongly promoting the respective social innovation stream and (2) the traits that have enabled them (or not) to do so. This effort is performed in the empirical Chapters 4–10 in Part II.

Part II (Chapters 4–10) contains the empirical evidence of the book. Each chapter refers to one specific field of activity and traces an SI stream within the respective field and across three to four countries. All chapters are connected by the common structure and methodology, outlined in Chapter 3, but all of them are thematically distinct.

Chapter 4 is located in the field of Arts & Culture and examines the SI stream 'urban spatial regeneration for higher social cohesion by means of cultural initiatives.' The stream is investigated across Italy, Spain, France and the Netherlands.

Chapter 5 is located in the field of Social Services and examines the SI stream 'collaborative efforts in governing social service provision for vulnerable segments of the population.' This includes processes of citizen empowerment. The stream is investigated across Spain, Italy, Sweden and the UK.

Chapter 6 is located in the field of Health Care, more specifically in that of mental health care, and examines the SI stream of 'the recovery approach' as a manifestation of the social model of disability. The stream is investigated across the UK, the Czech Republic, Denmark and France.

Chapter 7 is located in the field of Environmental Sustainability and examines the SI stream 'sharing public spaces for the promotion of bicycle use.' The stream is investigated across Denmark, the Czech Republic, Italy and Germany. The scope of the research is geographically restricted to one major city in the countries to enable a greater depth in the investigation. The selected cities are Copenhagen, Brno, Milan and Frankfurt.

Chapter 8 is located in the field of Consumer Protection in finance, more specifically alternative financial services outside the traditional banking system, and examines the SI stream of 'consumer protection by means of online financial education.' The stream is investigated across the Czech Republic, Spain and Denmark.

Chapter 9 is located in the field of Work Integration and examines the SI stream of 'cross-sector partnerships for (re)integrating vulnerable citizen groups into the labour market.' The stream is investigated across France, Germany, Spain and the Czech Republic.

Chapter 10 is located in the field of Community Development with an explicit link to refugees and examines the SI stream of 'self-organisation as a means for community integration.' The stream is investigated across the Netherlands, Italy, the UK and the Czech Republic.

Part III (Chapters 11–12) provides a synthesis of insights derived across Chapters 4–10 and gives conclusions about the overall learnings achieved through the book on the role third sector organisations play for social innovation relative to others and the enabling organisational properties necessary for driving social innovation. The synthesis itself is performed in Chapter 11, while Chapter 12 illustrates how the book has advanced our knowledge with regard to third sector impact, (social) innovation theory and organisational capabilities for the promotion of social innovation. It summarises what researchers, practitioners and policy makers can learn from it and how the issues examined can be explored in future research.

Part I

The Question

Who Are the Innovators and How to Find Them? (Conceptual Foundations)

1 Introduction

Social Innovation—What Is It and Who Makes It?

*Gorgi Krlev, Helmut K. Anheier, and
Georg Mildenberger*[1]

Impact of the Third Sector as Social Innovation

The third sector or non-profit sector[2] has increasingly gained, in recent years, policy recognition and attracted academic attention. Researchers have analysed non-profit organisations from different perspectives, usually emphasising specific roles this set of institutions is assumed to perform (Anheier, 2014). The most prominent among them are:

1. **Service-providing role:** In the wake of government failure, non-profit organisations are seen as complementary or substitutional elements in the public service systems. As governments with limited resources seek to serve the average voter under conditions of demand heterogeneity for public and quasi-public goods and services, non-profit organisations meet a broad range of minority preferences (Ben-Ner & van Hoomissen, 1991; Weisbrod, 1975, 1998). In response to market failures, non-profits signal trustworthiness in terms of service delivery under conditions of information asymmetries that make profiteering likely and monitoring expensive (Hansmann, 1980, 2006; Young & Steinberg, 1995).

   Comparative research has shown that tendencies towards government and market failure depend on the type of welfare regime (Esping-Andersen, 1990), the variant of capitalism involved (Amable, 2003; Hall & Soskice, 2001; Schneider & Paunescu, 2012), and correspond to different non-profit regimes (Anheier, 2014; Anheier & Salamon, 1997; Salamon & Anheier, 1992). Such patterns and tendencies also vary over time, especially in terms of state capacity in respect of an effective regulation (Anheier, 2014; Hansmann, 1996; Hertie School of Governance, 2013).

2. **Advocates and value guardians:** Apart from investigating the non-profit organisations' service-providing role, research has focussed on the issue of to what extent non-profits engage in advocacy activities to protect or advance the position in society and welfare of people needing help, e.g., disabled or poor persons or members of neglected communities. Non-profit organisations are hypothesised to be an important element

of social self-organisation, to 'give voice' to those otherwise unheard, and to support those who would otherwise find little or no attention.

The research on the topic has explored cross-national differences as to the advocacy and the values-related role of the non-profit sector, and observed that—just as the service-providing role mentioned previously— they not only vary by the kind of welfare regime but also by the kind of democratic and administrative system and, more generally, the civic culture and civic-mindedness of local populations (see, e.g., Almond & Verba, 1963; Halman & Nevitte, 1996; Putnam, 2000; Putnam, Leonardi, & Nanetti, 1993).

By implication, third sector service provision and advocacy are often linked in ways that go beyond combining the economic with the social, as it has traditionally been the case in social economy organisations such as cooperatives, mutual and employee-owned enterprises (Borzaga & Spear, 2004; Pestoff, 2012). By contrast, non-profits are co-producers and engage in product bundling as they combine service provision and values (Anheier, 2014; James, 1989), which are social values, of course, but frequently also religious, political or humanitarian values in a profound sense. They are "likely to seek out and include the target population for purposes of value formation, and long-term commitment and loyalty" (Anheier, 2005, p. 213). Thus, non-profits deliver services with a 'plus' (Salamon, Hems, & Chinnock, 2000, p. 23).

In addition to the identification of the sector's functions it has been mapped, both conceptually and empirically: The Johns Hopkins Comparative Non-profit Sector project (CNP) has made a seminal contribution to mapping the sector in an international perspective with a special emphasis on its scale, scope, structure and financing (Salamon & Anheier, 1999). This effort has been followed up by the United Nations' *Handbook on Non-profit Institutions in the System of National Accounts*, developed by Anheier, Tice and Salamon with the UN Statistics Division, which resulted in a satellite account on non-profit organisations (SNA) that has since then been adopted by a growing number of countries.

While all these efforts have contributed to a better understanding of the sector in its economic and social foundations, a major gap remains: the sector's impact and the longer-term outcomes achieved or involved. This book has evolved against the background of a call for proposals issued by the European Commission targeting these very results of third sector activity.

In this book, we seek to explore this issue and propose a novel way to approach the capturing of the third sector's impact. We start with reviewing the tradition of performance measurement in relation to the third sector, specifically from an economic and management perspective. Performance in the wider sense (including, for instance, the reliability or quality of service provision) can thereby be regarded as a proxy for impact. In the more narrow sense (effectuated targeted change as well as externalities for a range of beneficiaries), it can be seen as a synonym for impact. Social impact is denoted in the standard way of the 'logic model' of programme evaluation (Weiss, 1998) as the change caused within a 'social system' (outcomes that result from outputs delivered by an intervention) minus the change that would have happened anyway ('deadweight') (Clark, Rosenzweig, Long, & Olsen, 2004; see also Ebrahim & Rangan, 2014 or Nicholls, 2009 for the underlying connections).

In the second step we will outline the challenges that evolve in assessment of performance. Against these methodological and conceptual challenges and despite the major advances that have been made in promoting performance measures in the third sector, we will propose another, more timely, policy relevant, and feasible way of assessing third sector impact: a focus on social innovations and the question as to how the third sector is likely to play a key role in their emergence, nurturing and spreading.

To establish this link, it will be necessary to review a variety of traditions that exist in innovation research and to posit how social innovations take a particular position therein, specifically in view of today's societies' challenges. Subsequently, we will establish a tight link to the third sector and provide some key rationales for its socially innovative capacity giving the project which this book is based on its name: Impact of the Third Sector as Social Innovation (ITSSOIN). While an explicit definition of social innovation will follow, we can forestall that social innovations come in different outfits and there are recent as well as historical examples of what they are. Contemporary examples range from new employment models built on a *special* ability image of *disability*, to (decentralised) renewable energy production. Historical examples comprise social housing, public fresh water supply, or mutual and co-operative movements.

In the chapters following the introduction we will systematically gauge the socially innovative capacity of the third sector by introducing a research design on social innovation that examines the actors involved from a neutral position, that is targets non-profits, public agencies and firms alike to study their relative contributions.

Performance, Impact and the Third Sector

The growing role of performance measurement and impact assessments in the third sector is linked to both, its enhanced position in taking on state-funded service provision and its critical role as an advocate for many causes. The third sector is arguably likely to be able to achieve social welfare benefit in certain areas but also less likely to be able (and sometimes willing) to demonstrate it. In a context of rapidly escalating health and social care demands alongside public expenditure restraints, performance measurement becomes ever more important. There is an extensive literature in economics concerned with valuing the quality of life, the fulfilment of needs and related matters. Economics has contributed to the theoretical and policy debate about the different alternatives for measuring social welfare and also to the discussion of strategies for enhancing social wellbeing. Economists have been providing foundations for normative theorising and developing different methodologies or approaches to meet the challenges of analysis in a complex and continuously changing environment.

To get a better understanding of welfare in the context of long-term care needs and services, Davies and Knapp (1981) pioneered a simple organising framework known as 'The Production of Welfare Framework' which "seeks to make explicit the interrelationships between key elements [in the system], and then exploits the parallels with, for example, parts of the economics literature to enter hypotheses, structure empirical investigations and interpret findings" (Davies & Knapp, 1994, p. 264). The framework provides a useful conceptual foundation for performance evaluation which stems from economics but is also influenced by other disciplines (Davies & Knapp, 1981; Knapp, 1984). The framework encourages various theoretical concepts, approaches, objectives and stakeholders' goals. Its main features rely on the description of elements and relations under an economic approach; the relevance of the purposes and processes within a specific context, and finally on its explanatory and predictive capacity (Kendall & Knapp, 2000). The framework has found to be useful in helping identify relevant evaluative criteria based on economy, effectiveness, efficiency and equity.

Economy refers to cost minimisation pursued to lever action capacity in view of scarce resources. Effectiveness refers to the relationship between service provision (or prevention and other policy strategies) and enhanced final outcomes relevant to the overarching aim of increasing welfare. Because measuring the comparative effect on final outcomes is often difficult, intermediate outputs are often used which are simpler but more short-sighted. Despite being insufficient to provide an estimation of their impact on the welfare of individuals and communities, intermediate outputs may offer information about performance in the shape of rough estimation about recipient-related consequences. Efficiency, in a broad sense, refers to the combination of resource inputs and effectiveness of service provision, aiming to maximise ends from given means or to minimise the means needed to achieve given ends (Knapp, 1984, pp. 10–11). It can be improved when reducing the cost of producing a certain level of service or good, or improving the level of effectiveness given a certain cost. Equity in economic research has been used as a concept of fairness or justice, which is a subjective matter and requires value judgement. Although the terms equity and equality are often used interchangeably, they are not the same: equity is concerned with ensuring that everyone has a fair share whilst equality tries to give everyone the same share. Assessing whether an organisation, community or individual is 'meeting needs' in an equitable manner is to assess how far the agents are (more) capable of living a better or good life (capability approach; Sen, 1985).

This trend has been complemented by broader performance ratings and incentives relating to quality of life, wellbeing and happiness. The most prominent among them could be the increasing spread of quality-adjusted-life year (QALY) analysis, in particular in Anglo-Saxon health care contexts (going back to Fanshel & Bush, 1970; Torrance, Thomas, & Sackett, 1972; Weinstein & Stason, 1977). It combines the additional number of years granted to a person by a medical treatment with the quality of life that person will enjoy during these years. Some of the tools used to measure QALYs have been criticised for their inability to measure all aspects of life that matter to people, and for being insensitive to changes in broader wellbeing (Tsuchiya & Dolan, 2005). Partly in response to this, new measures have been developed to capture different aspects of quality of life: A happiness measure has been developed which encompasses experiences of mood and evaluations of life satisfaction and is now employed in population surveys in Europe (Dolan, 2011).

The Remaining Gaps

It is probably impossible to develop one outcome tool that is able to capture all aspects of life that matter to different people in different situations. The attractiveness of employing the small range of generic measures presented earlier is that resource allocation decisions can be made within department budgets (such as departments responsible for health and social care). In the following we outline how performance measurement is used in third sector practice and which particular challenges are caused by third sector characteristics in such kinds of measurement. This will mark the point of transition from performance measures to other ways of assessing impact, one of which—and the most effective, as ITSSOIN argues—is a focus on the third sector's contribution to social innovation.

The Limits of Economic (E)valuation Practices

Economic evaluation is a comparative analysis of costs and outcomes associated with the goals of increasing social welfare and making best use of limited resources. Although the method could be too resource-intensive to be repeated frequently as part of regular performance management processes, economic evaluations present a theoretical foundation of performance measurement and set the context in which performance measurement takes place. The contribution of involved analysts refers to

> all stages of the evaluation process including: helping to clarify objectives and convert these into outcomes that are measurable; drawing a clear distinction between processes, inputs, outputs and outcomes; encouraging a more systematic and rigorous assessment of costs and outcomes, with a particular emphasis on generating statistically valid

results; highlighting the need to consider what would have happened in the absence of the intervention being evaluated; adopting a societal perspective or multiple perspectives, thus ensuring a more comprehensive assessment of a programme's impact.

(Byfold & Sefton, 2003)

Whilst these authors refer in their report to the application of economic evaluation in social welfare—and to social care in particular—these principles apply to all sectors, including those where the third sector may play an important role.

There are different methods to value costs and outcomes depending on the nature of the research question asked. Cost-minimisation analysis is used where outcomes are certain and similar across the alternatives to be evaluated, which is rare. All other approaches to economic evaluation incorporate outcomes explicitly in the analysis, but they do it in different ways. In areas where there is an accepted generic measure that is thought to capture all relevant effects, one can employ cost-effectiveness analysis. If this measure is a preference-weighted measure of utility (such as the QALY), the evaluation is often called (in health care contexts, at least) a cost-utility analysis. Recommendations about investments are then based on lowest cost per unit of outcome gained. Finally, the so-called cost-benefit analysis requires both costs and benefits to be measured in monetary units, and findings are presented in form of a net benefit or return on investment; it is particularly useful when making an economic case to donors or commissioners.

There are methodological challenges, however, when trying to assign a monetary value to some outcomes, and although there are methodological innovations, in practice most cost-benefit analyses have focussed on those consequences that translate directly into savings (e.g., reductions in hospital admissions). A particular form of cost-benefit analyses has evolved from third sector practice and received much political attention, namely the Social Return on Investment (SROI) analysis, which has an explicit focus on involving stakeholders and using monetary proxy-indicators with the specific aims to value all benefits, including intangible ones. However, the SROI method lacks sufficiently rigorous theoretical foundations so that the way values are derived can appear rather arbitrary and subject to (unwanted and not disinterested) manipulation. Besides, the study of more genuine social effects (which are hardest or impossible to monetise) is found to be unsatisfactory to date (Krlev, Münscher, & Mülbert, 2013). These deficits and the challenges lying behind are partly of methodological nature, and partly grounded in the nature of third sector activity (see Krlev, 2018 for more on this).

Third Sector Properties and Performance Challenges

Economic theory can be used to explain third sector activity through the existence of market failure. Although based on many assumptions, it contributes to a useful understanding of many challenges of performance measurement in the third sector, four of which are cardinal:

First, externality characteristics leave many third sector activities unpriced or with market-generated prices that do not reflect true social value (for example, volunteering or unpaid care); information asymmetries and some transaction costs would usually be high for these goods or services, which are often provided remotely from the donor over long time periods and which are difficult to assess or monitor, mainly due to the limited ability of the user or donor to assess their quality in advance or sometimes even afterwards ('experience goods'). They explain why users and donors may rely more on non-profit organisations in whom they have greater trust. It is argued that for these reasons third sector organisations find it easier to enter the market and even develop monopoly power over time. For example, Kendall et al. (2006, pp. 423–425) argue that the proportionately large role of the third sector in social care (compared with many other areas of public investment/activity) is explained by relatively low start up and entry costs (help with shopping, advice, befriending can be provided by individuals without formal qualification), lack of economies of scale (because services are highly individualised), lack of opportunities to sustain large profits and a greater ability to recruit a greater supply of volunteer labour. All of these conditions have made it less likely for the public or private sectors to enter these fields.

Second, governments at the same time rely (arguably increasingly) heavily on third sector provision and in most countries the third sector receives large amounts of public money through a number of different channels, including service contracts and grants. One could argue that with that also comes accountability, the need for transparency of third sector activities and a responsibility to demonstrate that money is well spent. Third sector organisations are different from the public sector in that they are constitutionally independent from the state and are different from the private sector in that they do not distribute profits. Their governance arrangements are much more complicated and their accountability is towards multiple stakeholders, including funding bodies. The latter may change frequently and incorporate different forms of accountability through, for example, contracts, service level agreements and grant agreements as well as less formalised forms of accountability to donors and regulators. Perhaps unsurprisingly, performance measurement in third sector organisations has been patchy and inconsistent, with different third sector organisations employing different tools (Harlock, 2013).

Insecure, short-term funding often also means short-term reporting and many individuals employed or volunteering in third sector programmes have lacked enthusiasm for performance measurement, which is perceived as a time consuming burden imposed by governments (or donors):

> In terms of measuring voluntary sector performance, there is a belief that there is still a great deal of paternalism, with the UK Government

believing it can demand information from the voluntary sector and have
control over how money is spent.

(Little, 2005, p. 833)

Data collection capacity of most of the small projects is very limited and
the informal nature of their activities also means that it is more difficult to
get reliable data for users; for example Moxham and Boaden (2007, p. 837)
reported that "all case organisations offered confidential activities [. . .]
where the beneficiaries are not known".

Third, any narrow interpretation of performance measurement is likely to
be unhelpful and could even have adverse effects on the sector if it changes
the way that third sector organisations operate and disincentivises organisations to innovate. Also, the ability of third sector organisations to advocate and criticise could be influenced by the role that is placed on them
and may be reduced if government bodies have too much control over the
activities of third sector organisations. Knapp (2013, p. 5) writes, "professional rivalry, narrowly framed performance measures and simply the slow
churn of bureaucracy" can constrain an organisation's freedom to innovate and thereby remove one of the earliest and strongest arguments for a
third sector, and for individuals involved—the benefits of organising one's
own cause. This has been recognised by some government departments and
donors, who in turn have developed broad frameworks and simple tools
such as the so called 'logic model approach' that give a stronger priority to
learning and development of third sector organisations rather than on monitoring them (Harlock, 2013; Whitman, 2008). The aim of those approaches
is to support the organisation in reflecting on their own purpose, what they
set out to achieve and identify mechanisms to bring the organisation back in
line where it deviates from its original purpose and vision.

Fourth, as in the case of volunteering and informal or unpaid care, there
may be a risk that some third sector activities remain invisible and at risk
of not being well supported because their value is not measured or appreciated. Even for organisations which themselves do not have the capacity to
apply their own performance measures, evaluations may be carried out by
researchers who would understand the potential value of small third sector
organisations (Knapp, Bauer, Perkins, & Snell, 2013). Larger organisations
which are contracted to provide publicly funded services are likely to have
the capacity and obligation for more extensive performance measurement,
and which might—by virtue of the contracts underpinning their work—
need to evidence costs and outcomes.

Extended Performance Frameworks

The preceding challenges seem to be better catered by broader performance
concepts for third sector activities. A performance measurement framework
was developed by Kendall and Knapp (2000). It represents an extended

version of the Production of Welfare Framework introduced earlier and specifically addresses some of the third sector particularities. Kendall and Knapp incorporate meso-level (stakeholder networks) and macro-level (policy processes at an institutional level) perspectives. Performance is no longer limited to the organisation (and no longer assumes everything else being constant) but is embedded in the environment of the organisation with interdependent relationships with its context. In addition to efficiency, effectiveness and equity, Kendall and Knapp introduce three domains of third sector activity: advocacy, participation and innovation. These concepts are arguably both a means to an end and ends themselves, and should each be measured. For example, an increase in participation or volunteering has immediate benefits to the altruistically motivated individual (Le Grand, 2003), a direct impact on resources and can be linked (as shown in longitudinal studies) to intermediate and final outcomes for the volunteer such as self-confidence, skills and employability, health and wellbeing.

The amount of volunteering resources available also strongly depends on contextual factors such as labour market conditions, welfare entitlements and the ways in which government encourages and supports volunteering, which is only one example of relevant advocacy. The impact of advocacy is particularly difficult to measure because of the strong interdependencies with contextual factors: some advocacy (such as campaigning or lobbying) might have as their primary goal changes to the contextual factors themselves so that iterative loops need to be taken into account.

In addition to the choice of type of evaluation and indicators, other methodological complications arise in the analysis of third sector activities. The particular characteristics of the third sector suggest certain requirements for evaluation (many of which are similar to the ones for complex interventions in the statutory sector social welfare and prevention field). Typically in third sector programmes there are different groups of beneficiaries including volunteers, users, their family members (including unpaid carers) and other participants. It is also likely that a third sector programme will achieve multiple and diverse outcomes for some of these groups and one single tool is unlikely to capture all of them. In addition, outcomes will not always be known in advance (because of the complex and personalised pathways often leading from resource inputs to outputs, intermediate and final outcomes) so that a process needs to be incorporated into the evaluation design which first establishes the objectives of the third sector programme and then leads to selecting some important outcomes and choosing tools how those can be best measured.

Finally, following the principle of opportunity costs, economic evaluations are comparative in nature and costs and outcomes are compared against what is likely to have happened in the absence of the programme ('the counterfactual'). As argued before, third sector activity is more likely to occur in areas where there is no alternative public or private sector provision and the alternative might be to 'do nothing', leaving it to individuals and the community to provide this kind of support or to simply not have this type of support available. Having a comparison group could in some situations be seen as unethical and there are many other reasons why it might be difficult to recruit individuals into a study. Techniques are available to make up for this deficiency, one of which is called decision modelling. It helps "tracing pathways through care for individuals with particular characteristics or needs" (Knapp et al., 2013, p. 6). The method can also be used to extrapolate outcomes beyond the time horizon of the study. This benefits interpreting the long-term impact and helps in meeting the problem that "the time horizon constraint on government contrasts with the ability of some voluntary bodies to specialise in activities which confer benefits only over many years" (Knapp, Robertson, & Thomason, 1990).

While there have been significant advances recently on how some of these issues can be dealt with in view of a single organisation, even better a single intervention (see Krlev, 2018), we remain at a loss for ways of dealing with the problems when we think about broader organisational populations.

Focus on Innovation as a Way Out

The preceding reasoning illustrated the leaps performance measurement has made forward in a third sector context. We have learnt that a number of promising approaches—addressing neglected dimensions more or less comprehensively—exist that pay tribute to the complexity of impacts involved and the inherent particularities of the sector. This has resulted in a significantly improved capability of assessing third sector outcomes and impacts, at least in specific fields or for certain stakeholders.

Despite this advancement, it has also become evident that a thorough capturing of third sector impact is only about to emerge and that methodological challenges impede an encompassing assessment. Some of the discussed tools for capturing impact (at least partly) conflict with the very essence of third sector organisations. Although being subject to limited resources and thus to a cost savings rationale, the organisations' inherent value consists in providing services and exerting advocacy where simple input-output models under the rationale of output maximisation per unit of input are not easily applied. In principle, one of the central concerns of third sector organisations is optimal effectiveness as defined previously, which is yet usually superordinated by the efficiency principle (also described previously) that determines public economics and is thereby transformed into a policy directive. The resulting inherent tension between the organisations' purpose and mission on the one hand, and policy principles of economical provision on the other, is partly mediated by the emergent focus on equity and related concepts.

A case at hand illustrating the extension of the measurement perspective is the study of service provision under the angle of its 'transformative power', including the effects on the wellbeing of recipients and their wider surroundings (Rosenbaum et al., 2011). Generally, a significant extension of the range of approaches that are available to third sector organisations with respect to performance and impact assessments can be observed. We can thereby detect a tendency moving from standard performance tools such as the Balanced Scorecard (Kaplan, 2001) to (quasi-experimental) outcome and impact assessments that include a focus on mission-related impact, which is central to the existence of third sector organisations (Liket, Rey-Garcia, & Maas, 2014; see also Rey-Garcia, Álvarez González, & Bello Acebrón, 2013). Yet, even if measurement frameworks incorporate a broader perspective on impacts, they remain more suitable for service-providing organisations, rather than for 'advocates and value guardians'. In addition to welfare and quality of life as final outcomes, it is characteristic of third sector organisations that they strive for symbolic outcomes or abstract ideals such as equality, freedom of speech and expression, or preservation of nature and culture. These outcomes do not translate directly into welfare units.

There is another issue concerning economic approaches to impact, specifically where they involve 'pricing'. For instance, there is a critical counter-argument against assessing the monetary value of volunteering involved in third sector service provision: the negative consequence for volunteer motivation arising from attaching a monetary value to volunteer work. There is a lot of (yet inconclusive) research on crowding-out of intrinsic motivation (Frey, 2017 finding evidence for it and Fiorillo, 2011 against it). It remains that it is difficult to find a balance between valuing volunteering as a 'good beyond prices' and its economic counterpart, which we arrive at if we simply assume services otherwise provided by people working for free would have to be provided by paid staff. Thus, in economic valuation there is a struggle between leaving the virtue of altruistic action untouched and making volunteer labour more visible in accounts of productivity.

These issues affect insights into impact generated by specific interventions or organisations—they become exponential when we try to understand the contribution of the third sector at the regional or national level more broadly. Thus, classical economic rationales can serve as a point of departure but have to be complemented so as to include the contextual environment comprising opinions, attitudes and ideologies as well as field specifics and outcomes pinpointed at beneficiaries. As Kendall and Knapp conclude in relation to their extended third sector performance framework "performance measurement may have to rely on indirect measures of actual effects, or subjective impressions of impact, or even simply (but uninformatively) measures of resources allocated to this activity" (Kendall & Knapp, 2000, p. 112). There is "no single criterion of performance upon which to rely, particularly in the view of the multiple-stakeholder context", and no "simple or uncontroversial way to aggregate indicators across domains" (Mook, Richmond, & Quarter, 2003, p. 129).

We suggest that all issues combined indicate a critical degree of intractability: the existence of non-profits is linked to conditions where it is easier to monitor cost behaviour and distributional aspects as determinants of performance than outcomes and impact. We regard the non-profit status as an indicator of trustworthiness because measured and accounted performance is extremely difficult to establish. Yet, does the inconclusive record of previous research on empirical non-profit performance suggest that questions about impact are impossible to answer, even irrelevant? We suggest to the contrary that research may have emphasised the conventional, steady-state or standard performance compared to other forms of performance, which are conceptually and policy relevant, and more feasible—in particular at this very point in time. One such aspect is innovation, understood as the capacity of non-profits to generate novel ideas as well as new ways and methods of acting or of implementing objectives, and of addressing diverse public and social problems.

The basic underlying idea of ITSSOIN was that non-profits are 'better' at social innovations than governments and markets. To judge this claim we first define what social innovation is and then why there is reason to think socially innovative capacity to be more profound in non-profit organisations than in public agencies or firms, before we go on to test the claim.

What is Social Innovation? Characteristics of an Emergent Concept

The concept of social innovation can be traced back to Max Weber, who reflected on the impact of 'abnormalities' in social behaviour that lead to social change, affecting the general social order (compare to Bureau of European Policy Advisers (BEPA), 2011). It can also be related to the discussion about the piecemeal strategy of 'social engineering' that had challenged the grand designs of social reforms (Popper, 1966). First targeted research on the topic, however, only emerged in the late 1980s and early 1990s (see, for instance, Zapf, 1989). Since 2000 it has attracted the attention of institutional and organisational research and contributed to a growing body of literature. It has also gained attention of policy makers, since social innovations are seen as an option to find solutions for problems emerging in the wake of the financial crisis, especially societal problems concerning the welfare state (Borzaga & Bodini, 2012, p. 3).

In view of this broad interest in and the extensive hopes that are connected with social innovations, clear definitions that grasp the essence of this concept are difficult to find. Most definitions include a multitude of aspects that are relevant for social innovations. The European Commission, for instance, describes social innovation in its *Guide to Social Innovation* as follows:

> Social innovation can be defined as the development and implementation of new ideas (products, services and models) to meet social needs

and create new social relationships or collaborations. It represents new responses to pressing social demands, which affect the process of social interactions. It is aimed at improving human well-being. Social innovations are innovations that are social in both their ends and their means. They are innovations that are not only good for society but also enhance individuals' capacity to act.

(European Commission, 2013a, p. 6)

Researchers proposed to treat social innovation as a 'quasi-concept', just as is the case with 'social cohesion', for example. A quasi-concept is characterised by its approximating character and inherent definitional looseness, which is beneficial for a phenomenon's use in a research and a policy context (Hollanders & Es-Sadki, 2014; Jenson, 2010, both as referred to in European Commission, 2013b). We are generally supportive of the idea, since it tries to remove ambiguity while taking seriously the complexity of the subject and rejecting a too narrow focus. However, a quasi-concept of social innovation is not useful, if it is not built on empirical and conceptual accounts of what constitutes and differentiates distinct kinds of innovations so as to derive a more detailed understanding. Only by doing so can we move on to assess actor contributions to social innovation. In order to arrive at an improved understanding of social innovation, it is useful to embed it within established innovation theory, with a particular focus on how innovation is supposed to affect social outcomes.

In the following, we will disregard more fine-grained types of innovation, which are field-specific or 'theme'-specific, such as 'green-innovation' (Cuerva, Triguero-Cano, & Córcoles, 2014, p. 105). Although helpful in studying specific fields or themes, such differentiation would lead to unnecessary conceptual confusion. Although 'eco-innovation' generally refers to contributions that reduce environmental harm, its function can differ from social innovation. It may refer to a technological innovation that reduces employment or resources in order to improve production efficiency and primarily serves a commercial function, but has social side effects. In contrast, successful advocacy in favour of renewable energy production by mobilising a diverse community of actors would qualify as social innovation.

The long-standing differentiation by Schumpeter of what we refer to as 'innovation objects', which is what definitional category the innovation occurs in, has been restructured and complemented over time. A non-exclusive list of innovation objects includes: ideas, products, services, processes, structures, behaviours and practices (Cuerva et al., 2014, p. 105). From the viewpoint of technological innovations some of these can be illustrated by innovation in industrial production: the car (product), assembly line production (processes), lean manufacturing (structure) and outsourcing (practice). Notwithstanding variations in intensity, innovation objects can occur in every innovation type. That is why despite their relevance to the subsequent empirical investigations presented in this book, we refrain from addressing them explicitly herein.

Technological or Business Innovation

New technologies shaped the last century more strongly than any other time before. Some of the most salient examples of innovation are information and communication technologies, biotechnology or new materials (Archibugi & Iammarino, 2002). Though technologies are often relevant in their transformed shape of an 'end-product', opening up new opportunities for customers by using new gadgets, technological innovation in its fundamental outfit can be understood as a significant shift in production techniques that triggers economic productivity. Salter (1969) and other scholars have shown how these shifts have increased productivity by decreasing the costs of production processes or increasing output. The introduction of such technologies has typically led to organisational, institutional and infrastructural change (Archibugi & Iammarino, 2002, p. 99, in relation to Freeman, 1994) and even to 'revolutions' (Perez, 2010, employing a techno-economic paradigm in recourse to Schumpeter).

Spencer et al. (2008, p. 9), for instance, examined how high-tech start-ups in micro and nano technologies have "redefined the electronics industry, deconstructed the mainframe computer industry and are redefining the pharmaceutical industry today". The idea has also been taken up in more popular writing claiming that certain technological innovations have contributed to "flatten the world" (Friedman, 2005). Traditionally, research and development have been central to both, studying and promoting innovation. While the two aspects of research and development used to be treated as a homogeneous couple affecting organisations' innovative capacity in one and the same way, meanwhile more fine-grained investigations have emerged (Barge-Gil & Lopez, 2014). Independent of their specific function research and development department(s) ascribe to, they point at a certain tractability and manageability of technological innovation, despite the general acknowledgement of the increasingly complex nature of innovation (Rothwell, 1994).

In this, some firms are the spearhead of innovation, whereas others are regarded as 'followers'. These particularities translate into the regional and national level. Mate-Sanchez-Val and Harris (2014) compared innovation in Spain and the UK and found the UK in the former position, Spain in the latter position. Innovation is seen as an important source of improved overall economic performance and as a key variable to the prosperity of a country. Technology, as Ramstad (2009, p. 533) pointed out, is a central element in this "innovation-driven growth approach" (see also Furman, 2002). While in the case of these two countries differences in innovation in fact translate into differences in economic prosperity, it is less clear where the innovation imperative originates from at the organisational level. One of the most prominent factors, also mentioned earlier, is the struggle for organisational survival against competition (Salaman & Storey, 2002).

To summarise, we can say that technological innovations are characterised according to three fundamental perspectives: First, their motivational character is grounded in competitiveness. Second, their underlying image of innovation is of a dynamic nature, yet innovation is seen as manageable and specific structures are built to enable it. Third, their primary impact consists in increasing overall economic productivity, but even more so in transforming organisational fields.

Social Innovation

First it has to be mentioned that there is yet no general consensus as to what social innovation is (see, for instance, Klein et al., 2014). Nonetheless, a variety of unifying elements across studies and definitional propositions can be identified. Based on the experience of several major research projects on social innovation, our summary helps to further refine the 'quasi-concept' of social innovation.

The intensified practical and policy discussion on social innovation mainly arose from the dissatisfaction with the technological emphasis in economic innovation literature and innovation policy (The Young Foundation, 2012, p. 5). Secondly, social innovations are seen as a solution for growing social, environmental and demographic challenges and as a result of the failure of conventional market capitalism, resource scarcity, climate change, ageing population and the associated care and health costs, globalisation and mass urbanisation. Consequently, a number of authors (see, for instance, Nicholls & Murdock, 2012) stated that social innovation differs in many ways from core characteristics of technological innovations and the systems they are generated by.

First of all and most importantly, social innovation is per definition 'socially oriented' and thus person-related, although it can involve non-human actors (for instance, the natural environment). As a consequence of this person-centeredness, social innovation is fundamentally geared to serving social needs in unprecedented ways—this is a definitional criterion that appears not only in the definition of the European Commission cited in the introduction (see also Borzaga & Bodini, 2012, p. 5; Crepaldi, Rosa, & Pesce, 2012; European Commission, 2013a; Pol & Ville, 2009; The Young Foundation, 2012). According to Phills et al. (2008, p. 39), social innovation "becomes important as a way to fill needs that would not otherwise be met and to create value that would not otherwise be created". This points at the fact that social innovations (more) often relate to immaterial aspects whereas technological innovation mostly involves some material aspects (Borzaga & Bodini, 2012, p. 5; Howaldt & Schwarz, 2010).

In relation to the serving of needs we can take on a functionalist and a transformationalist perspective (Crepaldi et al., 2012, p. 23): From the functionalist perspective social innovations literally serve demands which neither the state nor markets would or can meet. By contrast, the transformationalist approach understands social innovation as a process that provokes an institutionalisation of new practices, standards and rules, founded on values inherent to solidarity. The functionalist perspective is close to the one of technological innovation, while the transformationalist perspective is of increasing yet still minor significance, as discussed earlier. In any case, social innovation is obviously not (primarily) driven by the profit motive. Thus, financial support may help socially innovative ideas to stand on their own feet but is unlikely to serve as the primary prompt (Pol & Ville, 2009).

Furthermore, social innovation is more preoccupied both with the actions of involved actors and the effects on them. This has two general consequences:

First, social innovation is of an open, collaborative character where people engage without normal market structures and mechanisms. This involvement and the social needs orientation give social innovation a strong influence on social relationships and capabilities (The Young Foundation, 2012, p. 23). This is further related to the circumstance that social innovation involves a higher degree of grass roots and bottom-up involvement than other innovation types. Actors and initiative are often dispersed to the periphery (The Young Foundation, 2012, p. 23). In consequence, participatory elements and civil society as well as cultural and social movements as sources for the revitalisation of self-organisation and new social solidarities should receive careful consideration, but are currently neglected in innovation studies (Evers, Ewert, & Brandsen, 2014).

Second, this circumstance makes social innovation vulnerable. Unlike technological innovation that can lead to disruptive change by generating demand on the market which guarantees a stable financial inflow, in the case of (pure) social innovation the beneficiaries often differ from its funders. Therefore, financial stability has to be created artificially. If a system is not prepared to do so, viability gaps emerge that threaten the survival of the social innovation concerned (compare to the argument on the viability of social entrepreneurial organisations in Krlev, 2013). In view of this situation, social innovation is often dependent on the assertive engagement of its proponents and because it typically lacks high political power it is likely to need more time to evolve and sustain.

When interrelated, both aspects of the grounding of social innovation point at the critical importance of legitimacy as a core determinant of the success of social innovation, and thus of performance and ultimately impact. Unlike technological innovations, social innovations cannot compensate for legitimacy deficits by creating demand on markets. Thus, legitimacy as a licence to operate has not only proven essential to a successful diffusion of innovations in general (Rogers, 2003, pp. 223–229), but social innovation is more prone of the danger of self-inflicted presuppositions that block its natural evolvement and development (compare to Nicholls, 2010, on the legitimacy of social entrepreneurship).

To conclude we can describe social innovation in relation to the definitional elements used for technological innovation.

> Social innovations are characterised by: first, their motivational character consists in meeting neglected social needs; second, their underlying image of innovation combines functionalist and transformationalist aspects; third, their primary impact is on the well-being of the beneficiaries as well as the actors involved, the borders between them being reshuffled and blurred by the underlying mechanisms of social innovation.

In addition to this, we formulate the traits of social innovation as follows:

> Social innovations involve a higher degree of bottom-up and grass-roots involvement than technological innovation. This can make their impact broader and more sustainable, but social innovations will typically take longer to evolve and sustain than other types of innovation. The most critical moderator (beyond the very survival of the innovation) will be their ability to gain legitimacy in a socially grounded negotiation process.

Relating the Types of Innovation

Technological innovation is mainly preoccupied with economic productivity by being linked to commercial performance. Social innovation relates more strongly to social problems and challenges and is thus a moderator of social productivity or performance. It is worth mentioning that types of innovation do not occur in an isolated way and are intertwined. It might well be that a social innovation is technology-based, for instance in the case of assistive technologies for people with disabilities. Technological innovations in turn can be based on social interactions as is the case with online communication platforms.

For reasons of completeness it is also worth mentioning that there are other types of innovation which are discussed in the literature and that contain further potential overlaps. Governance innovations for instance refer to shifts in the relative actor constellations involved in practices, to the involvement of new parties or the application of new tools utilised to achieve specific policy goals (compare to Anheier & Korreck, 2013). An example is the emergence of modern accounting that is actively promoted by the state as a means of regulation and self-control across fields and sectors (Burchell, Clubb, Hopwood, Hughes, & Nahapiet, 1980, in relation to Hopwood, 1978; Gandhi, 1976)—which, however, remains vulnerable to malpractice.

Pestoff relates governance innovations more directly to public benefit activities and understands it as "innovations in public services [that] are not just new ideas, techniques or methods, but also new practices, and they do not only involve physical artifacts, but can also include changes in the relationships between the service providers" (Pestoff, 2012, p. 1104). Wise et al. (2014, 106f.) point out that the two main reasons behind the increased interest in governance innovations is the "decline of the capacity of the state in regulation and the emergence of new public problems and governance challenges". Instead of having a pronounced interest in the constituent players of a system and the roles these players assume, governance innovations take a specific look at the mechanisms employed, i.e., the interface of innovation. In consequence, governance innovation also refers, for instance, to new forms of citizen engagement or the expansion of democratic involvement in public services (Pestoff, 2012, p. 1104).

Compared to social and technological innovations, governance innovations have a different focus: First, their motivational character is related to policy directives and modes of political steering. Second, their underlying image of innovation is focussed on principles and interfaces rather than actors and roles. Third, their primary impact is on regulatory performance but it is not restricted to public administration. For the fact that the study of governance innovations is even more recent than that of social innovations and because of ambiguities that might arise through potential overlaps between the concepts, we will not focus on governance innovations as a separate category in the following.

The Link Between Social Innovation and the Third Sector

We can see the potential role of the third sector in social innovation not only in the cases of revolutions and radical social movements such as the feminist, green or peace movements (Kelly, 1994), but also in less contentious and less disruptive civil society activities and grass-roots associations that advocate and realise actions in the interests of various social groups. For instance, we can discern the innovative capacity of the third sector when observing non-governmental organisations that significantly influence multinational corporations to be more environmentally or socially responsible, thus contributing to the evolvement of new standards and practices (de Bakker, den Hond, King, & Weber, 2013). We can also observe social innovation in connection with social entrepreneurs' activities (Seelos & Mair, 2017), foundations supporting medical research, and international development organisations seeking to improve the standards of living of the poor (Chowdhury & Bhuiya, 2004). All these examples outline third sector activities as highly driven by the objective to establish social innovation. Therefore social innovation is seen as an impact that can be attributed to a great extent to the third sector.

This, however, does not mean that we disregard the role of contentious politics in advancing social innovations. There is, for instance, a global movement (promoted by the World Bank and the International Monetary Fund) focussing on justice and 'good governance' and aiming at changing the way multinationals and international institutions around the world act (Mkandawire, 2007). Another example is the 'global compact' initiated by the United Nations and driven by the commitment of 'responsible-minded' businesses (Brinkmann & Pies, 2003; Cetindamar, 2007; McIntosh, Waddock, & Kell, 2017). Our investigation aims exactly at analysing all actors involved in relevant social innovation processes, with a focus on countries within the European Union. Our initial examples only serve to showcase why the idea of a pronounced role of third sector activities in social innovation has emerged. In relation to the further examples given, one might argue that pressure from civil society to promote the 'good governance' agenda or social responsibility was the element to spark innovation and businesses' engagement and that the political agenda was just the result—another prompt for the underlying claim that this book intends to discuss and challenge.

If, indeed, the desired impact of social innovations by third sector organisations consists in better meeting social needs by means of creative solutions, it is only natural to ask whether these innovations actually have this impact, and in which conditions the impact is larger or smaller. 'Impact' is used here in a loose sense, referring to changes in social innovation. Kendall and Knapp (2000) warn that while innovation is often regarded as a part of third sector organisations' performance, it is almost impossible to determine the impact of the third sector on innovation, because, in the first place, it is impossible to measure innovation. We do not use the term 'impact' in a causal sense. It does not refer to the causal influence of the existence or activities of third sector organisations or its determinants. An adequate counterfactual is lacking because it is impossible to observe what would happen to society if third sector organisations were non-existent. Therefore, the question as to whether third sector organisations actually spur social innovation in the scientific sense of cause and effect is almost impossible to answer.

We can, however, examine what seems to make third sector organisations particularly suitable to contribute to social innovations in a major way, especially with regard to other players. This is a comprehensive effort that tries to combine and move beyond more fine-grained investigations on specific capabilities, such as professionalism, or the use of information and communication technology, which can enhance social innovativeness in third sector organisations (see Sanzo Pérez, Álvarez González, Rey-Garcia, & García Rodríguez, 2014, as one of the rare studies that link organisational properties and practices to social innovation). Because of the (current) lack of tractability, ITSSOIN did not apply a quasi-experimental research design but we studied the underlying mechanisms and enabling factors on the basis of in-depth cases studies of social innovations and associated actor involvement by means of 'process-tracing' (Ford, Schmitt, Schechtman, Hults, & Doherty, 1989; Tansey, 2007) to be laid out in the following chapters. Before we do that we want to briefly review the evidence that could lead us to support or deny the claim that third sector organisations will be particularly important for social innovations.

Supportive Evidence

As an organisational manifestation of the commitment to change, the third sector is often viewed as an important force in social innovation. Judith Maxwell of the Canadian Policy Research Networks (in Goldenberg, 2004, p. iii) claimed: "In communities, the non-profit sector plays a vital role in social innovation". This is particularly evident in post-communist societies. Although citizens were engaging in voluntary action and social innovation even before 1989, after the collapse of communism third sector organisations emerged in a much more visible way (Juknevičius & Savicka, 2003). Poole (2003, p. 1) argues:

> Through innovation nonprofit organisations find ways to use scarce resources more wisely, capture new resources, and enhance the quality of their services. Effective innovation is one key to the nonprofit sector's ability to improve our quality of life and the health of the polity.

Beckmann (2012, pp. 250–251) describes the promise of social enterprises, which are typically regarded as part of the third sector, as follows:

> the public sector has preference for the status quo—solutions already known and tested. Social entrepreneurs, in contrast, are able to test much riskier and innovative approaches. Once these solutions demonstrate their effectiveness and deliver the 'proof of concept', other actors, including the public sector, can adopt them.

Picciotto (2013) for instance looks at social entrepreneurs transforming confiscated mafia properties in Italy in their projects. This is one of the examples where an unusual organisational mission coincides with such organisations' increased ability to draw on uncommon and otherwise inaccessible resources (mafia properties).

So there is a lot of praise for the capacities of third sector actors. But why exactly are third sector organisations likely to have an effect on social innovation? We suggest that there are structural as well as values-based properties of third sector organisations that make them very likely to play a key role in social innovation.

The first characteristic social innovation and third sector organisations have in common is their social needs orientation, which is, in fact, an indispensable prerequisite for their work (Nock, Krlev, & Mildenberger, 2013). The fact that third sector organisations give voice to minority groups and point out societal problems (Osburg, 2013) is constantly emphasised. This is not only bound to their advocacy function, which plays a critical role in communicating and lobbying needs, third sector organisations are also well positioned for detecting these needs: "The change potential of civil society stems from its structural location: close to the grassroots and the local level, civil society actors are usually the first to become aware of social problems of many kinds" (Anheier & Korreck, 2013, p. 85). It is the proximity to target groups that sensitises the sector, not only for problems but potential solutions (Neumayr et al., 2007). What is more, existing research stresses that persistent multi-stakeholder setups, which third sector organisations possess, allow a multiplicity of signals to reach the sector and to disseminate innovative pilots (The Young Foundation, 2012). The sector thus exhibits a 'receiving' as well as a 'sending function', both of which together can be seen as characteristic of organisational openness, which has been identified as a critical moderator of innovation in a broad range of innovation studies (Hogan & Coote, 2014).

The positioning of the third sector within society is not only relevant as a detecting device, but also important in terms of stakeholder mobilisation. It is supposed that the reason why third sector organisations can accomplish tasks the state and the market cannot (in particular with regard to social innovation), is that they are accepted as the organisational embodiment of civil society: "NPOs encourage social interaction and help to create trust and reciprocity, which leads to the generation of a sense of community" (Donoghue, 2003, p. 8). They build connections "between groups of individuals and the larger society" and integrate those "groups into that society", thereby contributing to the "initiation of change, and the distribution of power" (see Kramer, 1981, p. 194; also Prewitt, 1999). Studies have shown that third sector organisations contain a high degree of social capital as a result of civic engagement and the positioning described previously (Evers et al., 2014; Ranci, Costa, Sabatinelli, & Brandsen, 2012). Third sector organisations are, indeed, described as "facilitators of social learning" (Valentinov, Hielscher, & Pies, 2013, p. 372). This in turn increases acceptance of innovations and thus serves as a significant variable in building and maintaining the legitimacy, which as discussed previously is crucial for any innovation's viability, sustainability and ultimately impact (Rogers, 2003).

Furthermore, the service and advocacy function of third sector organisations introduced at the beginning are regarded as compatible, even mutually reinforcing in third sector analysis (Valentinov et al., 2013, p. 367). Due to this reinforcing relationship between the two functions, third sector organisations are likely to be able to cater to both the functionalist and the transformationalist aspects of social innovation. Valentinov et al. (2013, p. 368) see the third sector's "main mechanism of societal problem-solving in implementing institutional and ideational innovations that help to overcome dysfunctional discrepancies". With respect to the functional perspective concerning innovation, the fact that third sector organisations are not subject to the same pressure as commercial organisations is interpreted as beneficial: "[N]ot beholden to the ballot box and market expectations, civil society actors enjoy a degree of independence neither public agencies nor corporations may have" (Anheier & Korreck, 2013, p. 85). This comes along with the (relative) freedom to test new approaches or advocate new issues. The non-distribution constraint (Hansmann, 1980) is a critical moderator in this. It encourages longer-term approaches and enhances third sector organisations' ability to 'endure', a trait which is crucial with regard to the longer time needed for establishing sustained social innovation in comparison to technological innovation, where market pull can accelerate the process—a mechanism that third sector organisations largely lack. A lack of pressure also promotes 'tinkering', which has a stimulating function on innovation, as outlined by Saxenian (1994) in relation to Silicon Valley. However, how and to what extent this reflects third sector reality remains open. More economically orientated research approaches to innovation in non-profit organisations, for instance, don't see any integration of the functionalist and the transformationalist perspective. They argue that market orientation and competition are the driving forces of innovation and regard innovation as an important means for organisational survival (Choi, 2012; Fonseca & Baptista, 2013). Market orientation and competition are present in third sector organisations but certainly less so than in firms. Which of these aspects will matter (more) for social innovation will have to be examined.

Moving from the system and organisational level to the individual one, we can expect that third sector organisations are likely to necessitate skills of a more versatile and therefore more complex nature than competencies that can simply be defined as 'high-tech skills' (see, for instance, Bornstein, 2007 on the variety of skills involved in social entrepreneurship). Against the background of this requisite, we suppose that the work done by volunteers, their ideas, motivation, and variety of expertise, may represent a useful resource in fostering social innovation. Examining innovation conditions at the organisational level, we identified that access to a large set of knowledge inputs is beneficial for the emergence of innovation (see Rogers, 2003; Vedres & Stark, 2010). Moreover, in addition to providing knowledge, volunteers establish a link between non-profits and other communities and sectors, and therefore contribute to the previously mentioned organisational openness. However, this will have to be specified, and the question as to who will act as 'knowledge and exchange broker', which has proved to be a significant variable in transforming knowledge into innovation (Fleming, Mingo, & Chen, 2007; Obstfeld, 2017) is still unanswered. Innovation research finally suggests that executives may play a significant role therein. 'Transformational leadership' has been pronounced as a driving force of innovation (Gumusluoglu & Ilsev, 2009; Jung, Chow, & Wu, 2003; Sarros, Cooper, & Santora, 2008). Although organisational variations will exist, the often 'utopian' agendas of third sector organisations (Crossley, 1999) qualify for nurturing such transformational leadership. This and the pronounced presence of values (Scheuerle, Schmitz, & Hoelz, 2013) could have a strong effect on organisational culture and the commitment of involved actors.

Counterevidence

There is some evidence on relations between the third sector and social innovation that contrast or relativise our reasoning as presented earlier. For instance, the crossing of borders as an important part of innovation can also be seen in research on innovation compiled by third sector organisations. Some findings, however, may make some of our assumptions appear doubtful. In a study on third sector organisations in the United Kingdom, Osborne (1998) found that their innovative capacity was not a function of their organisational characteristics, but rather a result of the interaction with local and central government. Despite changes in the following ten years after Osborne's study, a new wave of research essentially brought the same result (Osborne, Chew, & McLaughlin, 2008a, 2008b). The study "emphasises the need to understand the innovative capacity of VCOs [voluntary and community organisations] as a variable organisational capacity, with its key contingencies in the institutional environment rather than an inherent element of these organisations 'per se'". In the discussion of their results, Osborne et al. (2008a) issue "a warning to VCO managers and staff not to attach too great a significance to the sectoral rhetoric of innovative capacity".

In a study on innovations including 17 local authorities in the UK, Damanpour, Walker and Avellaneda (2009) found that a strong focus on innovation is actually detrimental to performance. Sirianni and Friedland (2001) argue that civic innovation—defined as the "mobilisation of social capital to build the civic capacities of communities and institutions to solve problems [. . .] through policy designs that foster self-government" is an extended learning process for engaged citizens, community organisers, and professional practitioners. They mention congregation-based community organising, community development corporations, and neighbourhood associations as three types of organisational forms that spurred social innovation in the United States of America in the 1980s and 1990s. The study is consistent with the findings of Osborne for the UK in the sense that local and state government institutions and funding are described as key factors that shape the scope and nature of civic innovation. These studies provide important insights. We will have to carefully consider the conclusions of this research in our subsequent investigations.

However, these studies also have some quite distinct properties, which we have to take into account when assessing their findings. First, in the studies by Osborne et al., innovation is examined in a quite technocratic sense, using new or old client groups and new or old services as definitional variables for types of innovation. The discussion on social innovation has shown that the properties we would have to take into account when assessing the third sector's capacity to promote social innovation would have to be significantly broader.

Second, the primary mode of investigation applied by Osborne et al. was a survey-based quantitative one. Case studies were used as a complementary research strategy with the aim of triangulation. Moreover, the research was executed with a focus on organisations. The following chapter, however, will show that a systems-based perspective of innovation processes (see Nicholls, 2013), rather than an analysis of single actors, will likely be more fruitful for developing our understanding of social innovation. Such an approach necessitates detailed in-depth case work that allows for tracing processes rather than a clear-cut quantitative approach. The results of Osborne et. al. indicating that the innovation process depends on the interactions between VCOs and their institutional environment supports this argument. However, the observation alone that interaction is more crucial than organisational properties or culture does not tell us much about who set specific innovative impulses in this interaction, who exactly the actors involved were, or who was not participating in this interactive process at all.

Third and finally, the previous investigations have studied innovation in the third sector, without taking particular account of differences between fields of activity. In consequence, there may exist a levelling out of effects across these fields. Certainly, some fields will generally be more innovative than others. We have outlined previously that innovation is to be expected where organisations typically have a strong motivational vocation in performing advocacy (values-driven field such as disability rights; Dahl et al., 2014) and/or where there is a strong service component to their activity (quasi-market-driven field such as renewable energy). But the third sector also comprises other fields, of course. Recreational associations, for instance, could be suspected to display less innovative behaviour.

Conclusions

The preceding sections have illustrated why there is good reason to relate social innovation to the third sector as its core contribution to socio-economic impact and why we presume that the third sector is better positioned to stimulate, create and develop social innovation than the market or the state. However, we have also seen that this reasoning is faced with critique and that insights on this particular issue are still quite ambiguous. Generally, we will move from these presumptions to an empirical design based on in-depth case studies across seven organisational fields: Arts &

Culture, Social Services, Health Care, Environmental Sustainability, Consumer Protection, Work Integration, and Community Development. The rationale for selecting these particular fields will be elaborated on later.

The question we will address is: How much and what kind of social innovation happens through the activities of the three sectors? In other words, as part of a multi-pronged approach, the project and this book aim to show the mechanisms and processes that are at work in social innovation.

Notes

1. We would like to acknowledge substantial inputs by Annette Bauer, Martin Knapp, Gerald Wistow, A. Hernandez and Bajo Adelaja to the sections on performance.
2. Here used as a generic description for the various national and international usages to refer to the set of organisations operating at the intersection of the market and the state.

References

Almond, G. A., & Verba, S. (Eds.). (1963). *The civic culture revisited*. Newbury Park: Sage Publications.

Amable, B. (2003). *The diversity of modern capitalism*. Oxford: Oxford University Press.

Anheier, H. K. (2005). *Nonprofit organisations: Theory, management, policy*. New York, NY: Routledge.

Anheier, H. K. (2014). *Nonprofit organizations: Theory, management, policy* (expanded and revised 2nd ed.). Oxford, New York, NY: Routledge.

Anheier, H. K., & Korreck, S. (2013). Governance innovations. In Hertie School of Governance (Ed.), *The governance report 2013* (pp. 83–116). Oxford: Oxford University Press.

Anheier, H. K., & Salamon, L. (1997). Towards a common definition. In H. Anheier & L. Salamon (Eds.), *Defining the nonprofit sector* (pp. 29–51). Manchester: Manchester University Press.

Archibugi, D., & Iammarino, S. (2002). The globalization of technological innovation: Definition and evidence. *Review of International Political Economy*, 9(1), 98–122.

Barge-Gil, A., & Lopez, A. (2014). R versus D: Estimating the differentiated effect of research and development on innovation results. *Industrial and Corporate Change*, 24(1), 93–129. https://doi.org/10.1093/icc/dtu002

Beckmann, M. (2012). The impact of social entrepreneurship on societies. In C. K. Volkmann, K. O. Tokarski, & K. Ernst (Eds.), *Social entrepreneurship and social business: An introduction and discussion with case studies*. Wiesbaden: Springer Gabler.

Ben-Ner, A., & van Hoomissen, T. (1991). Nonprofit organizations in the mixed economy: A demand and supply analysis. *Annals of Public and Cooperative Economics*, 4, 519–550.

Bornstein, D. (2007). How to change the world: social entrepreneurs and the power of new ideas (Updated ed.). Oxford: Oxford Univ. Press.

Borzaga, C., & Bodini, R. (2012). *What to make of social innovation? Towards a framework for policy development*. Working Paper (No. 36). Trento, Italy: Euricse.

Borzaga, C., & Spear, R. (2004). *Trends and challenges for co-operatives and social enterprises in developed and transition countries*. Trento: Edizioni 31.

Brinkmann, J., & Pies, I. (2003). Der Global Compact als Beitrag zu Global Governance: Bestandsaufnahme und Entwicklungsperspektiven. In R. M. Czada & R. Zintl (Eds.), *Politische Vierteljahresschrift. Sonderheft: 34, 2003. Politik und Markt* (Vol. 34, pp. 186–206). Wiesbaden: VS Verlag für Sozialwissenschaften. https://doi.org/10.1007/978-3-322-80517-1_10

Burchell, S., Clubb, C., Hopwood, A. G., Hughes, J., & Nahapiet, J. (1980). The role of accounting in organizations and society. *Accounting, Organizations and Society, 5*(1), 5–27.

Bureau of European Policy Advisers (BEPA). (2011). *Empowering people, driving change: Social innovation in the European Union*. Luxemburg: Publications Office of the European Union.

Byfold, S., & Sefton, T. (2003). Economic evaluation of complex health and social care interventions. *National Institute Economic Review, 186*, 98–108.

Cetindamar, D. (2007). Corporate social responsibility practices and environmentally responsible behavior: The case of the United Nations global compact. *Journal of Business Ethics, 76*(2), 163–176. https://doi.org/10.1007/s10551-006-9265-4

Choi, S. (2012). Learning orientation and market orientation as catalysts for innovation in nonprofit organization. *Nonprofit and Voluntary Sector Quarterly, 43*(2), 393–413.

Chowdhury, A. M. R., & Bhuiya, A. (2004). The wider impacts of BRAC poverty alleviation programme in Bangladesh. *Journal of International Development, 16*(3), 369–386. https://doi.org/10.1002/jid.1083

Clark, C., Rosenzweig, W., Long, D., & Olsen, S. (2004). *Double bottom line project: Assessing social impact in double bottom line ventures*. Working Paper Series. Berkeley: Center for Responsible Business, UC Berkeley.

Crepaldi, C., Rosa, E. de, & Pesce, F. (2012). *Literature review on innovation in social services in Europe: Sectors of health, education and welfare services*. Report from Innoserv.

Crossley, N. (1999). Working Utopias and social movements: An investigation using case study materials from radical mental health movements in Britain. *Sociology, 33*(4), 809–830. https://doi.org/10.1177/S0038038599000516

Cuerva, M. C., Triguero-Cano, Á., & Córcoles, D. (2014). Drivers of green and non-green innovation: Empirical evidence in low-tech SMEs. *Journal of Cleaner Production, 68*(0), 104–113. https://doi.org/10.1016/j.jclepro.2013.10.049

Dahl, H. M., Eurich, J., Fahnøe, K., Hawker, C., Krlev, G., Langer, A., . . . Pieper, M. (2014). *Promoting innovation in social services: An agenda for future research and development*. Summary Findings and Key Recommendations.

Damanpour, F., Walker, R. M., & Avellaneda, C. N. (2009). Combinative effects of innovation types and organizational performance: A longitudinal study of service organizations. *Journal of Management Studies, 46*(4), 650–675.

Davies, B. P., & Knapp, M. (1981). *Old people's homes and the production of welfare* (6th ed.). London: Routledge & Kegan Paul.

Davies, B. P., & Knapp, M. (1994). Improving equity and efficiency in British community care. *Social Policy & Administration, 28*(3), 263–285.

De Bakker, F. G. A., den Hond, F., King, B., & Weber, K. (2013). Social movements, civil society and corporations: Taking stock and looking ahead. *Organization Studies, 34*(5–6), 573–593. https://doi.org/10.1177/0170840613479222

Dolan, P. (2011). Thinking about it: Thoughts about health and valuing QALYs. *Health Economics, 20*, 1407–1416.

Donoghue, F. (2003). *Nonprofit organisations as builders of social capital and channels of expression: The case of Ireland.* ISTR Conference 2002 Working Paper Series, Baltimore, MD.

Ebrahim, A., & Rangan, V. K. (2014). What impact? A framework for measuring the scale and scope of social performance. *California Management Review, 56*(3), 118–141.

Esping-Andersen, G. (1990). *The three worlds of welfare capitalism* (Pbk. ed.). Cambridge: Polity Press.

European Commission. (2013a). *Guide to social innovation.* Brussels. Retrieved from http://ec.europa.eu/regional_policy/sources/docgener/presenta/social_innovation/social_innovation_2013.pdf

European Commission. (2013b). *Social innovation research in the European Union: Appraoches, findings and future directions.* Brussels: European Commission.

Evers, A., Ewert, B., & Brandsen, T. (2014). *Social innovations for social cohesion: Transnational patterns and approaches from 20 European cities.* Retrieved from www.wilcoproject.eu/downloads/WILCO-project-eReader.pdf

Fanshel, S., & Bush, J. W. (1970). A health status index and its application to health services outcomes. *Operations Research, 18*(6), 1021–1066.

Fiorillo, D. (2011). Do monetary rewards crowd out the intrinsic motivation of volunteers? Some empirical evidence for Italian volunteers. *Annals of Public and Cooperative Economics, 82*(2), 139–165. https://doi.org/10.1111/j.1467-8292.2011.00434.x

Fleming, L., Mingo, S., & Chen, D. (2007). Collaborative brokerage, generative creativity, and creative success. *Administrative Science Quarterly, 52*(3), 443–475. https://doi.org/10.2189/asqu.52.3.443

Fonseca, S., & Baptista, A. (2013). Market orientation, organization, organizational learning, innovation and performance: Keys to the sustainability of non-profits. *European Scientific Journal, 9*(19).

Ford, J. K., Schmitt, N., Schechtman, S. L., Hults, B. M., & Doherty, M. L. (1989). Process tracing methods: Contributions, problems, and neglected research questions. *Organizational Behavior and Human Decision Processes, 43*, 75–117.

Freeman, C. (1994). The economics of technical change. *Cambridge Journal of Economics, 18*(5), 463–514.

Frey, B. (2017). Policy consequences of pay-for-performance and crowding-out. *Journal of Behavioral Economics for Policy, 1*(1), 55–59.

Friedman, T. L. (2005). *The world is flat: A brief history of the twenty-first century* (1st ed.). New York: Farrar, Straus and Giroux.

Furman, J. L., Porter, M. E., & Stern, S. (2002). The determinants of national innovative capacity. *Research Policy, 6*(31), 899–933.

Gandhi, N. M. (1976). The emergence of the post-industrial society and the future of the accounting function. *Journal of Management Studies, 13*(3), 199–212. https://doi.org/10.1111/j.1467-6486.1976.tb00899.x

Goldenberg, M. (2004). *How the non-profit sector serves Canadians . . . and how it can serve them better.* Research Report W|25 Work Network. Retrieved from www.urbancentre.utoronto.ca/pdfs/elibrary/CPRN_Non-Profit-Sector-in-C.pdf

30   *Gorgi Krlev et al.*

Gumusluoglu, L., & Ilsev, A. (2009). Transformational leadership, creativity, and organizational innovation. *Journal of Business Research*, 62(4), 461–473. https://doi.org/10.1016/j.jbusres.2007.07.032

Hall, P. A., & Soskice, D. W. (Eds.). (2001). *Varieties of capitalism: The institutional foundations of comparative advantage.* Oxford, New York, NY: Oxford University Press.

Halman, L., & Nevitte, N. (1996). *Political value change in western democracies: Integration, values, identification, and participation. European values studies.* Tilburg, The Netherlands: Tilburg University Press.

Hansmann, H. (1980). The role of nonprofit enterprise. *The Yale Law Journal*, 89(8), 835–902.

Hansmann, H. (1996). *The ownership of enterprise.* Cambridge, MA: The Belknap Press of Harvard University Press.

Hansmann, H. (2006). Economic theories of non-profit organizations. In W. W. Powell & R. Steinberg (Eds.), *The nonprofit sector: A research handbook.* New Haven, London: Yale University Press.

Harlock, J. (2013). *Impact measurement practice in the UK third sector: A review of emerging evidence* Third Sector Research Centre Working Paper (No. 106), Birmingham.

Hertie School of Governance. (Ed.). (2013). *The governance report 2013.* Oxford: Oxford University Press.

Hogan, S. J., & Coote, L. V. (2014). Organizational culture, innovation, and performance: A test of Schein's model. *Journal of Business Research*, 67(8), 1609–1621. https://doi.org/10.1016/j.jbusres.2013.09.007

Hollanders, H., & Es-Sadki, N. (2014). *Regional innovation scoreboard 2014.* Brussels: European Commission, DG Enterprise.

Hopwood, A. G. (1978). Towards an organizational perspective for the study of accounting and information systems. *Accounting, Organizations and Society*, 3(1), 3–13. https://doi.org/10.1016/0361-3682(78)90003-X

Howaldt, J., & Schwarz, M. (2010). *'Soziale Innovation' im Fokus: Skizze eines gesellschaftstheoretisch inspirierten Forschungskonzepts* (1st ed.). Bielefeld: Script.

James, E. (1989). *The nonprofit sector in international perspective: Studies in comparative culture and policy. Yale studies on nonprofit organizations.* Oxford, New York, NY: Oxford University Press.

Jenson, J. (2010). *Defining and measuring social cohesion: Social policies in small states series: Vol. 1.* London: Commonwealth Secretariat.

Juknevičius, S., & Savicka, A. (2003). From restitution to innovation: Volunteering in postcommunist countries. In P. Dekker & L. Halman (Eds.), *Nonprofit and civil society studies: The values of volunteering: Cross-cultural perspectives.* New York, NY: Kluwer Academic/Plenum Publishers.

Jung, D. I., Chow, C., & Wu, A. (2003). The role of transformational leadership in enhancing organizational innovation: Hypotheses and some preliminary findings. *The Leadership Quarterly*, 14(4–5), 525–544. https://doi.org/10.1016/S1048-9843(03)00050-X

Kaplan, R. S. (2001). Strategic performance measurement and management in nonprofit organizations. *Nonprofit Management and Leadership*, 11(3), 353–370. https://doi.org/10.1002/nml.11308

Kelly, P. K. (1994). *Thinking green! Essays on environmentalism, feminism, and nonviolence*. Berkeley, CA: Parallax Press.

Kendall, J., & Knapp, M. (2000). Measuring the performance of voluntary organizations. *Public Management Review, 2*(1), 105–132.

Kendall, J., Knapp, M., & Forder, J. (2006). Social care and the nonprofit sector in the western developed world. In W. W. Powell & R. Steinberg (Eds.), *The nonprofit sector: A research handbook* (pp. 415–431). New Haven, London: Yale University Press.

Klein, J. L., Laville, J. L., & Moulaert, F. (Eds.). (2014). *L'Innovation sociale: Repères introductifs*. Collection sociologie économique. Toulouse: Erès.

Knapp, M. (1984). *The economics of social care: Studies in social policy*. Basingstoke: Palgrave Macmillan.

Knapp, M. (2013). Prevention: Wrestling with new economic realities. *Tizard Learning Disability Review, 18*(4), 186–191. https://doi.org/10.1108/TLDR-03-2013-0029

Knapp, M., Bauer, A., Perkins, M., & Snell, T. (2013). Building community capital in social care: Is there an economic case? *Community Development Journal, 48*, 313–331.

Knapp, M., Robertson, E., & Thomason, C. (1990). Public money, voluntary action: Whose welfare. *The Third Sector*, 183–218.

Kramer, R. M. (1981). *Voluntary agencies in the welfare state*. Berkeley: University of California Press.

Krlev, G. (2013). Framework conditions for social entrepreneurship: A spotlight on legal and financial issues. *Trusts & Trustees, 19*(6), 526–534.

Krlev, G. (2018). *Measuring social impact: The conceptual and empirical advancement of an emergent concept* (DPhil Dissertation). University of Oxford, Oxford.

Krlev, G., Münscher, R., & Mülbert, K. (2013). *Social Return on Investment (SROI): State-of-the-art and perspectives: A meta-analysis of practice in Social Return on Investment (SROI) studies published 2000–2012*. CSI Report. Retrieved from www.csi.uni-heidelberg.de/downloads/CSI_SROI_Meta_Analysis_2013.pdf

Le Grand, J. (2003). *Motivation, agency, and public policy: Of knights & knaves, pawns & queens*. Oxford: Oxford University Press.

Liket, K. C., Rey-Garcia, M., & Maas, K. (2014). Why aren't evaluations working and what to do about it: A framework for negotiating meaningful evaluation in nonprofits. *American Journal of Evaluation, 35*(2), 171–188.

Little, W. (2005) Charities ready to play with the big boys but say 'let's be fair'. *Health Service Journal*, 14–15.

Mate-Sanchez-Val, M., & Harris, R. (2014). Differential empirical innovation factors for Spain and the UK. *Research Policy, 43*(2), 451–463. https://doi.org/10.1016/j.respol.2013.10.013

McIntosh, M., Waddock, S., & Kell, G. (Eds.). (2017). *Learning to talk: Corporate citizenship and the development of the UN global compact*. Sheffield: Taylor and Francis.

Mkandawire, T. (2007). 'Good governance': The itinerary of an idea. *Development in Practice, 17*(4–5), 679–681. https://doi.org/10.1080/09614520701469997

Mook, L., Richmond, B., & Quarter, J. (2003). Integrated social accounting for nonprofits: A case from Canada. *VOLUNTAS: International Journal of Voluntary and Nonprofit Organizations, 14*, 283–297.

Moxham, C., & Boaden, R. (2007). The impact of performance measurement in the voluntary sector: Identification of contextual and processual factors. *International Journal of Operations & Production Management, 27*(8), 826–845.

Neumayr, M., Schneider, U., Meyer, M., Pospíšil, M., Skarabelová, S., & Trávníčková, D. (2007). *Nonprofits' functions in old and new democracies: An integrative framework and empirical evidence for Austria and the Czech Republic.* Working Paper, WU Vienna.

Nicholls, A. (2009). 'We do good things, don't we?': 'Blended Value Accounting' in social entrepreneurship. *Accounting, Organizations and Society, 34*(6–7), 755–769. https://doi.org/10.1016/j.aos.2009.04.008

Nicholls, A. (2010). The legitimacy of social entrepreneurship: Reflexive isomorphism in a pre-paradigmatic field. *Entrepreneurship Theory and Practice, 34*(4), 611–633.

Nicholls, A. (2013). The Social Entrepreneurship-Social Policy Nexus in Developing Countries. In R. Surender, & R. Walker (Eds.), *Social policy in a developing world.* Cheltenham: Edward Elgar.

Nicholls, A., & Murdock, A. (Eds.). (2012). *Social innovation: Blurring boundaries to reconfigure markets.* Houndmills, Basingstoke, Hampshire, New York, NY: Palgrave Macmillan.

Nock, L., Krlev, G., & Mildenberger, G. (2013). *Soziale Innovationen in den Spitzenverbänden der Freien Wohlfahrtspflege: Strukturen, Prozesse und Zukunftsperspektiven.* Retrieved from www.bagfw.de/uploads/media/2013_12_17_Soziale_Innovationen_Spitzenverbaenden_FWp.pdf

Obstfeld, D. (2017). *Getting new things done: Networks, brokerage, and the assembly of innovative action.* Stanford, CA: Stanford Business Books, an imprint of Stanford University Press.

Osborne, S. P. (1998). Naming the beast: Defining and classifying service innovations in social policy. *Human Relations, 51*(9), 1133–1154.

Osborne, S. P., Chew, C., & McLaughlin, K. (2008a). The innovative capacity of voluntary and community organisations: Exploring the organisational and environmental challenges. In S. P. Osborne (Ed.), *The third sector in Europe: Prospects and challenges* (pp. 134–156). London: Routledge.

Osborne, S. P., Chew, C., & McLaughlin, K. (2008b). The once and future pioneers? The innovative capacity of voluntary organisations and the provision of public services. *Public Management Review, 10*(1), 51–70. https://doi.org/10.1080/14719030701763187

Osburg, T. H. (Ed.). (2013). *Social innovation: Solutions for a sustainable future.* Berlin, Heidelberg [u.a.]: Springer.

Perez, C. (2010). Technological revolutions and techno-cconomic paradigms. *Cambridge Journal of Economics, 34*(1), 185–202. https://doi.org/10.1093/cje/bep051

Pestoff, V. (2012). Co-production and third sector social services in Europe: Some concepts and evidence. *VOLUNTAS: International Journal of Voluntary & Nonprofit Organizations, 23*(4), 1102–1118.

Phills, J. A., Deiglmeier, K., & Miller, D. T. (2008, Fall). Rediscovering social innovation. *Stanford Social Innovation Review,* 34–43.

Picciotto, L. (2013). *Social entrepreneurship and confiscated mafia properties in Italy.* (No. LG13–73). Retrieved from EMES Network website www.emes.net/uploads/media/Picciotto_ECSP-LG13-73.pdf

Pol, E., & Ville, S. (2009). Social innovation: Buzz word or enduring term? *The Journal of Socio-Economics*, *38*, 878–885.

Poole, M. S. (2003). Innovation in nonprofit organisations: A selective review and introduction. In H. Kaplan (Ed.), *Organisational innovation: Studies of program change in community agencies* (pp. 1–12). New York, NY: Kluwer Academic/ Plenum Publishers.

Popper, K. R. (1966). *The open society and its enemies*. Princeton, NJ: Princeton University Press.

Prewitt, K. (1999). The importance of foundations in an open society. In Bertelsmann Stiftung (Ed.), *The future of foundations in an open society* (pp. 17–29). Gütersloh: Bertelsmann Foundation Publishers.

Putnam, R. D. (2000). *Bowling alone: The collapse and revival of American community*. New York, NY: Simon & Schuster.

Putnam, R. D., Leonardi, R., & Nanetti, R. (1993). *Making democracy work: Civic traditions in modern Italy*. Princeton, NJ: Princeton University Press.

Ramstad, E. (2009). Expanding innovation system and policy: An organisational perspective. *Policy Studies*, *30*(5), 533–553.

Ranci, C., Costa, G., Sabatinelli, S., & Brandsen, T. (2012). *Measures of social cohesion: Comparative report*. A result of the WILCO project. EMES Working Paper Series (No. WP no. 12/02). Retrieved from www.wilcoproject.eu

Rey-Garcia, M., Álvarez González, L. I., & Bello Acebrón, L. (2013). The untapped potential of marketing for evaluating the effectiveness of nonprofit organisations: A framework proposal. *International Review on Public and Nonprofit Marketing*, *10*(2), 87–102.

Rogers, E. M. (2003). *Diffusion of innovations* (5th ed.). New York, NY: Free Press.

Rosenbaum, M. S., Corus, C., Ostrom, A. L., Anderson, L., Fisk, R. P., Gallan, A. S., . . . Williams, J. D. (2011). Conceptualization and aspirations of transformative service research. *Journal of Research for Consumers*, *19*, 1–6.

Rothwell, R. (1994). Towards the fifth-generation innovation process. *International Marketing Review*, *11*(1), 7–31. https://doi.org/10.1108/02651339410057491

Salaman, G., & Storey, J. (2002). Managers' theories about the process of innovation. *Journal of Management Studies*, *39*(2), 147–165. https://doi.org/10.1111/1467-6486.00286

Salamon, L. M., & Anheier, H. K. (1992). In search of the non-profit sector I: The question of definitions. *VOLUNTAS: International Journal of Voluntary and Nonprofit Organizations*, *3*(2), 125–151.

Salamon, L. M., & Anheier, H. K. (1999). *Der Dritte Sektor: Aktuelle Internationale Trends: Eine Zusammenfassung*. The Johns Hopkins Comparative Nonprofit Sector Project, Phase II. Gütersloh: Verl. Bertelsmann-Stiftung.

Salamon, L. M., Hems, L. C., & Chinnock, K. (2000). *The nonprofit sector: For what and for whom?* Working Paper (No. 37). Baltimore: Johns Hopkins University.

Salter, W. E. G. (1969). *Productivity and technical change: Department of applied economics monographs*: Cambridge University Press.

Sanzo Pérez, M. J., Álvarez González, L. I., Rey-Garcia, M., & García Rodríguez, N. (2014). Business-nonprofit partnerships: A new form of collaboration in a corporate responsibility and social innovation context. *Service Business: An International Journal*, *9*(4), 611–636.

Sarros, J. C., Cooper, B. K., & Santora, J. C. (2008). Building a climate for innovation through transformational leadership and organizational culture. *Journal of Leadership & Organizational Studies*, *15*(2), 145–158. https://doi.org/10.1177/1548051808324100

Saxenian, A. L. (1994). *Regional advantage: Culture and competition in Silicon Valley and Route 128*. Cambridge, MA: Harvard University Press.

Scheuerle, T., Schmitz, B., & Hoelz, M. (2013). Governancestrukturen bei Sozialunternehmen in Deutschland in verschiedenen Stadien der Organisationsentwicklung. In S. A. Jansen, R. Heinze, & M. Beckmann (Eds.), *Sozialunternehmen in Deutschland: Analysen, Trends und Handlungsempfehlungen*. [S.l.]: Vs Verlag fuer Sozialwissenschaften.

Schneider, M., & Paunescu, M. (2012). Changing varieties of capitalism and revealed comparative advantages from 1990 to 2005: A test of the Hall and Soskice claims. *Socio-Economic Review*, *10*(4), 731–753.

Seelos, C., & Mair, J. (2017). *Innovation and scaling for impact: How effective social enterprises do it*. Stanford: Stanford University Press.

Sen, A. K. (1985). *Commodities and capabilities*. Oxford India paperbacks. Delhi, New York: Oxford University Press.

Sirianni, C., & Friedland, L. (2001) *Civic innovation in America: Community empowerment, public policy, and the movement for civic renewal*. Berkeley: University of California Press.

Spencer, A. S., Kirchhoff, B. A., & White, C. (2008). Entrepreneurship, innovation, and wealth distribution: The essence of creative destruction. *International Small Business Journal*, *26*(1), 9–26. https://doi.org/10.1177/0266242607084657

Tansey, O. (2007). Process tracing and elite interviewing: A case for non-probability sampling. *Political Science and Politics*, *40*(4), 765–772.

Torrance, G. W., Thomas, W. H., & Sackett, D. L. (1972). A utility maximization model for evaluation of health care programs. *Health Service Research Journal*, *7*, 118–133.

Tsuchiya, A., & Dolan, P. (2005). The QALY model and individual preferences for health states and health profiles over time: A systematic review of the literature. *Medical Decision Making*, *25*(4), 460–467.

Valentinov, V., Hielscher, S., & Pies, I. (2013). The meaning of nonprofit advocacy: An ordonomic perspective. *The Social Science Journal*, 367–373.

Vedres, B., & Stark, D. (2010). Structural folds: Generative disruption in overlapping groups. *American Journal of Sociology*, *115*(4), 1150–1190.

Weinstein, M. C., & Stason, W. B. (1977). Foundations of cost-effectiveness analysis for health and medical practices. *The New England Journal of Medicine*, *296*, 716–721.

Weisbrod, B. A. (1975). Toward a theory of the voluntary nonprofit sector in a threesSector-economy. In E. S. Phelps (Ed.), *Altruism, morality, and economic theory* (pp. 171–195). New York, NY: Russell Sage Foundation.

Weisbrod, B. A. (1998). *To profit or not to profit: The commercial transformation of the nonprofit sector*. Cambridge, MA: Cambridge University Press.

Weiss, C. H. (1998). *Evaluation: Methods for studying programs and policies* (2nd ed.). Upper Saddle River, NJ: Prentice Hall.

Whitman, J. (2008). Evaluating philanthropic foundations according to their social values. *Nonprofit Management and Leadership*, *18*(4).

Wise, R., Wegrich, K., & Lodge, M. (2014). Governance innovation. In Hertie School of Governance (Ed.), *The governance report 2014* (pp. 77–109). Oxford: Oxford University Press.

The Young Foundation. (2012). *Social innovation overview: Part I—defining social innovation.* A Deliverable to the Project "The Theoretical, Empirical and Policy Foundations for Building Social Innovation in Europe" (DG Research). Brussels.

Young, D. R., & Steinberg, R. (1995). *Economics for nonprofit managers.* New York, NY: Foundation Center.

Zapf, W. (1989). Über Soziale Innovationen. *Soziale Welt*, 40(1–2), 170–183.

2 Research Strategy
Identifying the Actors—An Open Approach

Gorgi Krlev, Helmut K. Anheier, and Georg Mildenberger

How to Study (Social) Innovation

The effects of innovation are usually multi-sectoral and trespass theoretically constituted borders between spheres and fields, which explains why there are multi-disciplinary approaches to innovation (Anheier & Fliegauf, 2013, p. 137; Borzaga & Bodini, 2012; Crepaldi, Rosa, & Pesce, 2012, p. 15; The Young Foundation, 2012, p. 4). Literature on innovation can be found in research in economics, public administration, management studies, political science, law, sociology and technology studies. Various conceptual perspectives on innovation are one of the results.

The most common differentiation of innovation was coined by Schumpeter, who distinguishes between product, process (e.g., such that improves the production process), and organisational innovation (e.g., restructuring that is geared to the improved production process), with a particular emphasis on the role of the entrepreneur (Schumpeter, 1934). These schemes were adopted by a large number of authors; in particular, the discussion on process innovation has gained momentum over the last two decades in relation to the discussion on product innovation, which has traditionally been more advanced (Adner & Levinthal, 2001; Davenport, 1993; Ettlie & Reza, 1992) despite the seminal discussion of process innovation by Utterback and Abernathy early on (1975). One of the reasons for increased interest in processes is the complexity of assessing the effects of innovation from a process perspective: as Kendall and Knapp (2000) pointed out, the impact of new goods, services or technologies can be measured by means of their intermediate or final outputs (partly outcomes), whereas process innovation will be more reliant on subjective impressions of impact (varying dependent on stakeholder perspectives) or even the opportunity of impact.

Traditionally, the concept of impact was narrowly defined and impact mostly understood as the effects of an innovation in relation to previous approaches; its wider societal influences were rather not taken into consideration. This applies to the way in which Abernathy and Clark (1985, 22f.) and also Henderson & Clark (1990) studied innovation (discussed in Anheier & Fliegauf, 2013, 140f.). Abernathy and Clark speak of 'niche innovations' that are able to transform markets but leave the general technological knowledge involved largely unaltered; 'architectural innovations' that preserve and enhance knowledge of individual components but change knowledge about the linkages of these components; or of 'regular innovations' that work the other way round and trigger new knowledge on the individual components while maintaining knowledge on the larger system. The already applied terminology implies that innovations will obviously differ in the scope and scale of their impact—architectural innovations are likely to have a higher impact than regular innovations. In principle, however, it should not be neglected that more 'incremental innovations', if aggregated, can have a higher impact than more revolutionary and thus visible 'disruptive innovations' (Christensen, 2000).

In contrast to the rather 'technical' understanding of innovation, which refers to how innovations affect narrowly delineated spheres, an interest in broader innovation outcomes has recently developed. This is in part related to a change in focus from studying single individuals or organisations to a thorough integration of individual and organisational perspectives. 'Entrepreneurial ecosystems' are suggested as a new unit of analysis (Autio, Kenney, Mustar, Siegel, & Wright, 2014) and the examination of 'innovation ecosystems' are meant to embed the innovation event in wider spatial and sectoral innovation environments (Anheier & Fliegauf, 2013, 145f.). Studies at the organisational level and innovation systems approaches have in common that they concentrate on structural elements; the latter however takes specific account of the interaction between structures and actors. At least in theory, the idea of innovation systems is to analyse processes in these clusters to gain insights into innovation interactions and enabling conditions.

Innovation system theory embeds innovations in territorial clusters. Since the 1980s national or regional innovation systems have been discussed (Asheim, Lawon Smith, & Oughton, 2011; Mahroum & Al-Saleh, 2013, p. 321). Understanding innovation as a collective and interactive process, systems of innovation are often defined according to Lundvall (1992) as "elements and relationships which interact in the production, diffusion and use of new, and economic useful knowledge" (as cited in Mahroum & Al-Saleh, 2013, p. 322). Asheim and others emphasise the importance of local aspects and argue that knowledge is more easily shared in local contexts (Asheim et al., 2011). The authors illustratively outline the diversity of actors such systems comprise. In this they identify openness and connectivity of such systems as critical determinants of innovative capacity. They also show that even in times of dynamic transfer and mobility of resources and capital such properties are hard to develop and replicate. This is for instance illustratively outlined by taking the example of Silicon Valley which can hardly be replicated anywhere else around the world (Saperstein & Rouach, 2002; Saxenian, 1994; Rosenberg, 2002). Given such observations, it is not surprising that empirical research on the topic is growing. The study of Rodriguez-Pose and Comptour (2012), for example, examines the conditions under which innovative clusters, the so-called 'regional innovation systems', can strive and eventually contribute to economic growth. Their study finds that more crucial than the mere existence of clustered structures are the socio-economic conditions surrounding them. These conditions include a good level of education, a high skill level, particularly well-developed high-tech skills, and fiscal incentives.

Although the latter approach extends innovation research to context factors, it is likely to become subject to Ramstad's (2009) critique. Ramstad criticised the abstract focus on scientific-driven innovation and the relative disregard of the (dynamic) interplay between structures and actors involved in innovation processes. In relation to Kuhlmann (2003), she draws a picture of the innovation landscape at the intersection of innovation policies and organisational innovation. Ramstad refers to three spheres that are commonly considered in these studies (2009, p. 536): (1) the scientific system comprising a variety of research and education institutions; (2) the economic system mainly focussing on firms; and (3) the political system referring to political actors and administrative bodies. She also addresses formal and informal networks operating at the intersection of these spheres. In all of this, she emphasises the importance of recognising innovation as an organisational process rather than regarding it as an abstract level element within the field of technologies. And Ramstad also calls for targeted responses with regard to the first understanding on a policy level.

Against the background of Ramstad's criticism, we postulate that a proper 'ecosystems' perspective, which takes account of the links between different frameworks, would enhance and advance our knowledge on the moderators and actors of innovation and their interplay. Krlev et al. (2014) have not only recently picked up on this idea, but also extended the scope of innovation studies by compiling a potential indicator suite of social innovativeness on the national level. They distinguish between four frameworks (institutional, political, societal climate, and resources) in which the entrepreneurially or intrapreneurially driven process of innovation is embedded. From this perspective it is vital to comprehend and study innovation in its wider ecology, rather than focus on single organisational entities. This is of as much relevance to social innovation as it is to technological or business innovation: Anheier and Korreck (2013, p. 85) draw on the work of Archiburgi and Iammarino on the "globalisation of technological innovation" (2002) to show that, in general, the relevance of civil society to innovation processes continues to increase.

In the wake of this development, it is becoming evident that innovation in itself is rarely of significance, if not seen in perspective. There is a growing attitude that innovation shall not be sought for its own sake but because innovation can nurture systemic societal renewal and revitalisation just as it can enhance effectiveness. With no clear account of what innovation does— thus without the impact perspective in mind—we miss a large part of the picture that illustrates what values are created and how this happens. This broader understanding of innovation is, for instance, addressed by the study of innovation in relation to international advocacy movements, e.g., with regard to the transformation of national standards in social service provision (Dahl et al., 2014). Consequently, more careful consideration should be given to aspects of advocacy and how innovation and its agents are perceived by their constituents. The thematic interlinkage between innovation and social impact adverts to a critical argument: It is increasingly recognised that innovation is often not a clear-cut phenomenon resembling a jolt running through existing systems and producing traceable effects. Such kind of innovational impact may occur in the context of some technological innovations (for instance, the 'replacement' of analogue cameras by digital ones), but other innovation processes are so diffuse that it is difficult to calculate attributions or deadweight, i.e., to estimate what would have happened in the absence of the innovation. This does not mean, however, that we cannot take account of who has contributed and in which way to the emergence of that innovation.

The considerations on systems, actor interplay and embeddedness inform the way we study actor contributions to social innovation. Instead of focussing on organisational entities to begin with we start off by identifying what we refer to as 'social innovation streams', that is, recognised phenomena that have affected particular fields of activity in a profound way and for some time in order to then trace back how they have come about. Our research approach and the methodological repertoire to be laid out in the following chapters build on this principle. Both are necessarily marked by openness and sector neutrality, since only by being encompassing in terms of sector provenience and the types of actors we study can we confirm or refute our supposition of a pronounced role of the third sector.

The Key Concept and Hypothesis

Our point of departure was an inventory of social innovations that originated, took place or can generally be identified in a particular field of activity and selected using a thorough, systematic search of the literature and relevant documents in addition to expert interviews. The relevant process will be further explained in Chapter 3. The inventories were then vetted using a protocol to yield a set of recognised social innovations. A process-based examination of selected cases against particular innovation incidents, items or field trends was used to specify how the analysed organisations have contributed or responded to pick up and develop innovations. This procedure was used as a valid proxy to judge the investigated organisations' contribution to social innovation and thus their particular form of impact in this regard. This research strategy made sure there is no built-in bias against privileging third sector organisations, over-estimating their innovative capacity. The very notion of a random sample—that is, a sample identified by the open screening for dominant social innovation streams and the actors involved—guards against 'sampling on the positive side only', and the openness of the subsequent process-tracing of social innovation events or episode towards the roles of other organisations protects against 'selecting only third sector successes'.

In this process we were able to judge varying levels of the involved organisations' 'social innovativeness' by the degree to which they had paved the way for and shaped the identified innovations. In recurrence to our definition of social innovation, organisational '*social innovativeness*' refers to:

> The ability to contribute to or create solutions to previously inadequately addressed social needs—this solution shall serve both a functionalist (efficiency & effectiveness) and a transformationalist function (change) and primarily aim at improving the situation for the beneficiaries and actors involved. Increased social innovativeness is marked by a more frequent (overall or within the social innovation process) and more substantial (clearly recognisable or dominant) and more sustainable (lasting) involvement in the development of such solutions.

As regards the question who such actors are and where we can find them we have developed one *main hypothesis*:

> Social innovativeness varies by organisational form and actor involvement in the sense that the properties of third sector organisations and volunteering make its formation particularly likely.

Our advocated shift of defining the social innovation as the unit of analysis and arriving at actors only in the second instance comes with two main advantages. First, social innovations can be studied from the stance of surrounding frameworks, be they institutional, political or perceptual just as it can be with regard to the actors involved in generating innovation and organisational traits enabling them to do so. Second, social innovations, though they might be broad and hard to narrow down, are likely 'well-documented' (leaving traces in all or several of the preceding frameworks) and can be studied cross-nationally as to enabling and hindering factors, with natural occurrence of counter-factuals, namely settings where innovations are developed rudimentarily or not at all while flourishing elsewhere.

Fields and Actors

It should have become evident that studying social innovation in contrast to technological innovation necessitates the embracement of analysing systems that might not be formalised and tracing processes that are influenced by a multitude of actors and potentially in indistinct ways. For this reason it is not particularly useful to adapt a rigid systems approach from technological innovation research that often presupposes traceable processes, clusters of actors and clearly defined institutions governing the field of activity. Instead we decided to rely on theory and conceptualisation that has proved valuable to the study of open social systems and used the theory of 'strategic action fields' (Fligstein & McAdam, 2012a) as a lens to systemise actor positions and influence in our selected fields of activity. The field description we compiled should provide a general insight into the structure characterising the field of activity, meaning central regulative characteristics, important changes within the last 10 years and important actors from the state, market and third sector. Up to this point the use of field theory in our particular setting is no different from any other institutional approach. But instead of focussing only on structural traits, field theory allows in-depth insights on the sub-levels of society by referring to fields as contexts constructed by the specific agendas of actors sharing a common interest in a subject. It enables descriptions of organisations' structures as well as those that exist between organisations, which allow identifying the most important components of the innovation process (Fligstein & McAdam, 2012a). In contrast to alternative approaches such as actor network theory (Latour, 2008), field theory does not only consider those actors that have a relation to each other. Field theory instead simplifies the analysis of actors that engage in the same empirical context and thus have an impact on the object of research (here: the social innovation) but are not directly connected to each other. This is not to say that networks are irrelevant. The contrary is true: The construction of networks is considered a helpful method for empirically researching fields (Owen-Smith & Powell, 2008).

It is to be remarked that 'the field' does not simply equal our seven fields of activity (Arts & Culture, Social Services, Health Care, Environmental Sustainability, Consumer Protection, Work Integration and Community Development), but refers to actor constellations surrounding our particular 'object of interest'. To illustrate this more clearly we link to the empirical chapter on health care, which has first been narrowed down to mental health and then pinpointed at the 'social model of disability' as our object of interest. The social model of disability thereby describes an understanding of health that is marked by complexity and acknowledges that health can only be maintained or restored when the influence of patients' social contexts are taken seriously. The specific social innovation stream within the field was then identified to be the 'recovery approach' in mental health that values and utilises lived experience of ex-patients and tries to stimulate patients' self-healing capacities rather than making them the passive objects of therapies executed by professionals (follow this illustration further in Box 2.1). In the logic of field theory all actors that engage in the 'object of interest' (here: the 'social model of disability' and related sub-topics such as self-help or patient participation initiatives) are to be understood as field members. This follows the central assumption in field theory that actors (here: third sector organisations, social entrepreneurs or social movements, but also policy makers and business firms) construct a field around their 'object of interest'. They employ the resources available to them, be they financial, knowledge-based or relational, to meet their interests. These interests and their pursuit can lead to cooperation between actors, but can also result in conflicts between actors in the field. This creates a common frame of reference for interactions of those actors interested in the said object of interest. Accordingly the empirical description of such constellations allows for a conceptual construction of field structures that consist of institutional settings and power relations (Bourdieu, 1993; DiMaggio & Powell, 1983; Fligstein & McAdam, 2012a). Despite potential struggles between actors it is likely that a common 'field logic' effective for all field members can be found, underlying the actor engagement (Fligstein & McAdam, 2012b; Friedland & Alford, 1991).

Box 2.1   Fields and Objects of Interest

'Strategic action fields' and the 'objects of interest' they surround can be exemplified by relating to the empirical work performed in our seven fields of activity. In a systematic process to be explained in more details later on the field of Community Development, a focus is developed on asylum seekers, refugees and unauthorised migrants. In the field of Environmental Sustainability, in turn, we concentrate on sustainable cities with a particular focus on the aspect of mobility. As mentioned previously, our work on health relates to the 'social model of disability'. The way the latter materialised in the UK should be used to outline how field theory has helped systemise engaged actors and interplay, without establishing a link to the particular social innovation stream we studied at this point.

In relation to the 'social model of disability' and connected themes, such as the promotion of patient autonomy in health care provision, the Royal College of General Practitioners and membership bodies used their professional networks and influence on training and professional development agendas (i.e., knowledge, professional power) to facilitate the introduction of self-management as part of modernised routine health care practice provided to patients. Third sector organisations simultaneously used their resources (in particular their social capital) and the media to advocate for self-management as part of a broader personalised and asset-based approach, in which the treated person moves away from being a passive recipient (patient) towards being an active citizen who takes control of their own health.

This shows how different actors, in their own way and motivated by their own interests, have contributed to the evolvement of a common field logic and related to the same 'object of interest'. Even though both types of actors are in favour of self-management they approach the subject differently due to the different resources at their disposal and interests in capitalising them. On this basis a more detailed analysis can reveal the power relation between said actors and potential synergies as well as tensions in their interplay.

As regards power constellations and potential shifts caused in the field 'self-management' raises expectations among service users, potentially up to a point which health professionals might not want to or be able to carry out. Professionals might perceive this as losing control over service provision and as a threat to their powerful position, which they might want to maintain. In this case professionals are well established incumbents in the field, while users and their advocates act as challengers.

Which results this constellation yielded as regards the promotion of social innovation and how this differed from other countries, due to different historical pathways, actor interests and structures as well as institutional contexts, can be seen in the analysis of the recovery approach social innovation stream.

To account for the power relations of field members, the role of incumbents and challengers is often differentiated. Challengers are said to be new to the field and have relatively little power due to their recent entrance (Fligstein & McAdam, 2011). Researchers assume that challengers are more likely to be interested in changes in the field, because this would improve their position in it (Fligstein, 1996, 2006; Greenwood & Suddaby, 2006; Seo & Creed, 2002). Here we find a parallel to social entrepreneurs as initiators of social innovation through maximising local network embeddedness to meet social needs, thereby building social credibility (Shaw & Carter, 2007). Incumbents in contrast are well established, powerful field actors. They are less likely to foster innovations, since changes in the field may endanger their position of power (Fligstein & McAdam, 2011). However, these are only assumptions and may be contradicted by the empirical evidence, in which case it is of particular interest to find an explanation for the deviation. Helpful for finding such explanations is the understanding of resources as 'sources of power' and differences in actors' ability to apply these resources. The ability to enforce one's interests does not only result from the quantity of resources one actor can dispose of (Bourdieu, 1986). It also depends on the organisations' capacity to use them (Fligstein, 2001). Third sector actors do for example generally not possess a high level of economic capital. But their ability to use other sorts of capital may enable them to substitute these relatively low resources with support of volunteers or by mobilising stakeholders (social capital). Furthermore, the framing of their interest in accordance with effective value sets (cultural capital) can provide legitimacy to the interests of these relatively powerless actors and improve their position in the power structure of the field. Through this, challengers may become more powerful than already incumbent actors in a field. The mechanism just described underlines that strategic action fields are a useful theoretical lens for testing our suppositions about the capacities of third sector actors.

From the stance of the social innovation another concept of field theory should prove useful, namely that of 'episodes of contention' that refer to change processes occurring within a field (McAdam, 2005). Their starting point is a mobilisation of actors in situations where they see a chance to achieve their interests (in the case of social innovation, address unmet social needs). Actor coalitions using 'social skills' are able to establish new routines (Fligstein, 2001). Social movements, which typically obtain their power by a high degree of mobilisation, are a good example for this mechanism (McAdam, 2005; McAdam, Edelman, & Leachman, 2010). 'Episodes of contention' can be triggered by 'exogenous shocks', for instance by "political crises such as war, invasion, serious regime change, [or] economic collapse" (Fligstein & McAdam, 2012a, p. 101). These are likely to be taken up by actors as points of departure for initiating mobilisation in a field. Our research was performed against the background of different exogenous shocks, for instance that of the financial crisis or the refugee crisis which will prove to be relevant moderators in our empirical research.

Conclusion

The considerations on field theory yield a common repertoire of analytical categories when it comes to the analysis of actors and their interplay with regard to the promotion or stymieing of the specific social innovation under investigation. Table 2.1 illustrates these elements in relation to the 'social model of disability'.

It is becoming evident that a mere list of actors and their characteristics is insufficient for understanding the embedding of a social innovation within a field and attributing (again, not in the strict causal sense) actors' influence on that innovation. Instead we need to take careful account of actors' interests and resources and the context they are governed by. Actor relations, cooperation or conflict, sources of power and regulation are important pillars of the analysis to be performed. Only by bringing these elements together can a dynamic analysis unfold, which is necessary to further our understanding of how social innovations come about.

In addition to a theoretical lens that interprets and adapts the 'innovation systems' approach to the specifics of social innovation, we need a tool box

Table 2.1 Exemplary field composition in relation to the 'social model of disability'

Element	Empirical description (e.g., in relation to the 'social model of disability')	Purpose
Actors	Description of all actors engaging in the defined 'object of interest' (e.g., government bodies, public and private health providers, professional associations, research organisations, charities, advocacy organisations, think tanks).	Identification of field members; actors only indirectly engaged have to be understood as actors from other fields with a significant relation to the assessed field.
Actor interests	Description of interests (including the whole variety of motives and aims) actors have in regard to the object of interest (e.g., professional associations might want to prevent shifts in power to service users or patients).	Identification of cooperation and conflicts between actors in the field.
Actor-resources	Description of resources actors dispose of and use to implement their interest in regard to the object of interest: money or influence, support of other actors, knowledge and information with regard to field setting.	Identification of resources as 'sources of power'. Allows for the description of the power structure in the field by positioning actors in relation to their resource endowment.
Field structure	Description of power structure results from relations between actors; further key regulative characteristics that frame field activities need to be described (e.g., dominance of the medical profession based on a biomedical understanding of human illness which is confronted with a more sociological understanding of health that takes account of the specificities of human capacities and behaviour).	Reflection of key regulations and their impact on field structure (e.g., (new) definitions of actors' roles, increases or decreases in resources endowments and power positions, etc.).

of methods to (1) identify relevant social innovations, (2) find meaningful field country combinations and (3) systemise the tracing of social innovations to enable an objective and well-documented examination of their evolution and the roles, functions and contributions of involved actors. Our methodological approach will be portrayed in the next chapter.

References

Abernathy, W. J., & Clark, K. B. (1985). Innovation: Mapping the winds of creative destruction. *Research Policy*, *14*(1), 3–22. https://doi.org/10.1016/0048-7333(85)90021-6

Adner, R., & Levinthal, D. (2001). Demand heterogeneity and technology evolution: Implications for product and process innovation. *Management Science*, *47*(5), 611–628. https://doi.org/10.1287/mnsc.47.5.611.10482

Anheier, H. K., & Fliegauf, M. T. (2013). The contribution of innovation research to understanding governance innovation: A review. In H. K. Anheier (Ed.), *Governance challenges & innovations: Financial and fiscal governance* (pp. 137–170). Oxford: Oxford University Press.

Anheier, H. K., & Korreck, S. (2013). Governance Innovations. In Hertie School of Governance (Ed.), *The governance report 2013* (pp. 83–116). Oxford: Oxford University Press.

Archibugi, D., & Iammarino, S. (2002). The globalization of technological innovation: Definition and evidence. *Review of International Political Economy*, *9*(1), 98–122.

Asheim, B. T., Lawon Smith, H., & Oughton, C. (2011). Regional innovation systems: Theory, empirics and policy. *Regional Studies*, *45*(2), 875–891.

Autio, E., Kenney, M., Mustar, P., Siegel, D., & Wright, M. (2014). Entrepreneurial innovation: The importance of context. *Research Policy*, *43*(7), 1097–1108. https://doi.org/10.1016/j.respol.2014.01.015

Borzaga, C., & Bodini, R. (2012). *What to make of social innovation? Towards a framework for policy development*. Working Paper (No. 36). Trento, Italy: Euricse.

Bourdieu, P. (1986). The forms of capital. In J. G. Richardson (Ed.), *Handbook of theory and research for the sociology of education* (pp. 241–258). New York, NY: Greenwood Press.

Bourdieu, P. (1993). *Soziologische Fragen*. Frankfurt am Main: Suhrkamp.

Christensen, C. M. (2000). *The innovator's dilemma: When new technologies cause great firms to fail. The management of innovation and change series*. Boston, MA: Harvard Business School Press.

Crepaldi, C., Rosa, E. de, & Pesce, F. (2012). *Literature review on innovation in social services in Europe: Sectors of health, education and welfare services*. Report from Innoserv.

Dahl, H. M., Eurich, J., Fahnøe, K., Hawker, C., Krlev, G., Langer, A., . . . Pieper, M. (2014). *Promoting innovation in social services: An agenda for future research and development*. Summary Findings and Key Recommendations.

Davenport, T. H. (1993). *Process innovation: Reengineering work through information technology*. Cambridge, MA: Harvard Business Review Press.

DiMaggio, P., & Powell, W. W. (1983). The iron cage revisited: Institutional isomorphism and collective rationality in organizational fields. *American Sociological Review*, *48*(2), 147–160.

Ettlie, J. E., & Reza, E. M. (1992). Organizational integration and process innovation. *Academy of Management Journal*, *35*(4), 795–827. https://doi.org/10.2307/256316

Fligstein, N. (1996). Markets as politics: A political-cultural approach to market institutions. *American Sociological Review*, *61*(4), 656–673.

Fligstein, N. (2001). Social skill and the theorie of fields. *Sociological Theory*, *19*(2), 105–125.

Fligstein, N. (2006). Sense making and the emergence of a new form of market governance: The case of the European defense industry. *American Behavioral Scientist*, *49*, 949–960.

Fligstein, N., & McAdam, D. (2011). Toward a general theory of strategic action fields. *Sociological Theory*, *29*(1), 1–26.

Fligstein, N., & McAdam, D. (2012a). *A theory of fields*. Oxford, New York, NY: Oxford University Press.

Fligstein, N., & McAdam, D. (2012b). Response to Goldstone and Useem. *Sociological Theory*, *30*(1), 48–50.

Friedland, R., & Alford, R. R. (1991). Bringing society back in: Symbols, practices and institutional contradictions. In W. W. Powell & P. DiMaggio (Eds.), *The new institutionalism in organizational analysis* (pp. 232–263). Chicago: University of Chicago Press.

Greenwood, R., & Suddaby, R. (2006). Institutional entrepreneurship in mature fields: The big five accounting firms. *Academy of Management Journal*, *49*(1).

Henderson, R. M., & Clark, K. B. (1990). Architectural innovation: The reconfiguration of existing product technologies and the failure of established firms. *Administrative Science Quarterly*, *35*(1), 9–30. https://doi.org/10.2307/2393549

Kendall, J., & Knapp, M. (2000). Measuring the performance of voluntary organizations. *Public Management Review*, *2*(1), 105–132.

Krlev, G., Bund, E., & Mildenberger, G. (2014). Measuring what matters—indicators of social innovativeness on the national level. *Information Systems Management*, *31*(3), 200–224. https://doi.org/10.1080/10580530.2014.923265

Kuhlmann, S. (2003). Evaluation of research and innovation policies: A discussion of trends with examples from Germany. *International Journal of Technology Management*, *26*(2–4), 134–149.

Latour, B. (2008). *Reassembling the social: An introduction to actor-network-theory* (Reprint). *Clarendon lectures in management studies*. Oxford [u.a.]: Oxford University Press.

Lundvall, B.-Å. (1992). *National systems of innovation: Towards a theory of innovation and interactive learning*. London, New York, NY: Pinter Publishers; Distributed exclusively in the USA and Canada by St. Martin's Press.

Mahroum, S., & Al-Saleh, Y. (2013). Towards a functional framework for measuring national innovation efficacy. *Technovation*, *33*(10–11), 320–332. https://doi.org/10.1016/j.technovation.2013.03.013

McAdam, D. (2005). Civil society reconsidered: The durable nature and community structure of collective civic action. *American Journal of Sociology*, *111*, 673–714.

McAdam, D., Edelman, L. B., & Leachman, G. (2010). On law, organizations, and social movements. *Annual Review of Law in Social Science*, *6*, 653–685.

Owen-Smith, J., & Powell, W. W. (2008). Networks and institutions. In R. Greenwood, C. Oliver, K. Sahlin, & R. Suddaby (Eds.), *The Sage handbook of organizational institutionalism* (pp. 594–621). Los Angeles, London, Neu Deli, Singapur: Sage Publications.

Ramstad, E. (2009). Expanding innovation system and policy: An organisational perspective. *Policy Studies*, *30*(5), 533–553.

Rodrìguez-Pose, A., & Comptour, F. (2012). Do clusters generate greater innovation and growth? An analysis of European regions. *The Professional Geographer*, 64(2), 211–231.

Rosenberg, D. (2002). *Cloning Silicon Valley: The next generation high-tech hotspots*. London, New York: Pearson Education.

Saperstein, J., & Rouach, D. (2002). *Creating regional wealth in the innovation economy: Models, perspectives, and best practices*. Upper Saddle River, NJ: Financial Times Prentice Hall.

Saxenian, A. L. (1994). *Regional advantage: Culture and competition in Silicon Valley and Route 128*. Cambridge, MA: Harvard University Press.

Schumpeter, J. A. (1934). *The theory of economic development: An inquiry into profits, capital, credit, interest, and the business cycle*. Cambridge, MA: Harvard University Press.

Seo, M-G., & Creed, W. E. D. (2002). Institutional contradictions, praxis, and institutional change: A dialectical perspective. *Academy of Management Review*, 27(2), 222–247.

Shaw, E., & Carter, S. (2007). Social entrepreneurship: Theoretical antecedents and empirical analysis of entrepreneurial processes and outcomes. *Journal of Small Business and Enterprise Development*, 14(3), 418–434. https://doi.org/10.1108/14626000710773529

Utterback, J. M., & Abernathy, W. J. (1975). A dynamic model of process and product innovation. *Omega*, 3(6), 639–656. https://doi.org/10.1016/0305-0483(75)90068-7

The Young Foundation. (2012). *Social innovation overview: Part I—defining social innovation*. A Deliverable to the Project "The Theoretical, Empirical and Policy Foundations for Building Social Innovation in Europe" (DG Research). Brussels.

3 Methods

Identifying and Analysing the Social Innovation Streams

Gorgi Krlev, Helmut K. Anheier, and Georg Mildenberger[1]

The Fields of Activity

In the selection of fields of activity to be studied we were guided by the logic presented in the introduction, which outlined two predominant aspects in non-profit activity but also relates to the functions of government and the business sector: the advocacy function on the one side and the service provision function on the other. We combined these two aspects to denominate areas that embody the functions to a varying degree (see Table 3.1). These span from an almost exclusive focus on advocacy ('advocates') or service provision ('service providers') to a mix between the two, with 'co-producers' denoting fields where the two functions are strongly integrated, whereas 'self-actualisers' marks an area that might only loosely be coupled to any of the two axes. The proposed categories then allowed us to investigate sub-fields that are integrated by the common labels just referred to. These are meant as 'ideal types' and these ideal types are converging or mutually influencing, but they still serve for giving our analysis direction.

Due to reasons of capacity, all but one area ('self-actualisers') of the matrix were examined empirically in two sub-fields of activity. These sub-fields are evidently different from each other in many respects but also share

Table 3.1 Fields by focus on service provision and advocacy

		Service provision	
		Less pronounced	More pronounced
Advocacy	Less pronounced	Arts & Culture (I) *'Self-actualizers'*	Social Services; Health Care (II) *'Service providers'*
	More pronounced	Environment; Consumer Protection (III) *'Advocates'*	Migration (Work Integration); Community Development (IV) *'Co-producers'*

some common threads, which shall be outlined in the following along with a more global reflection on the significance of the fields in relation to social innovation.

Self-Actualisation in Arts & Culture

The cultural sector plays a key role in terms of its social, economic and political implications with a focus on its inclusive role as part of European integration on the European Agenda, in particular as regards (1) cultural diversity and intercultural dialogue and (2) stimulating creativity within the framework European strategies for growth and jobs. Non-profits operating in the cultural field have traditionally played an important role as pioneers in different countries. They have sustained the development of innovative forms of arts and culture, and they have represented the 'stage' upon which new artistic and cultural trends in society could be expressed (Turrini & Irigoyen, 2010). More recently, the limitation of state interventions has paved the way for the transformation of leading public arts organisations (e.g., opera houses, theatres and symphonies) into private foundations and associations. This trend has led to the creation of new forms of partnerships between the public and the private sector, leading to the emergence of new hybrid non-profit organisations (i.e., mixed forms of public/private non-profit organisations) (Merlo & Turrini, 2002; Turrini & Irigoyen, 2010).

It seems that the economic and social crisis has increased the need for more cooperative systems based on interrelations among different actors of society. A synergetic process has been created by the conceptualisation of social enterprises allowing for integrative collaborations and profitable exchanges of expertise (Fiorentini, 2006). These trends in the field of Arts & Culture enhance its potential for explaining which variables exactly contribute to stimulating social innovation. Arts & Culture offers several levels of studying social innovation with a particular focus on civic cultural participation (Dubini & Provera, 2008 and Turrini, 2009): (1) on the level of the governance of cultural organisations, e.g., through studying social and political movements and their links to organisations and their organisational culture; (2) through looking at different models for the cultural inclusion of marginalised people, e.g., rehabilitation theatre for vulnerable populations; or (3) through assessing new technologies and social networks, e.g., web applications or participative cultural websites that aim at spurring cultural exchange and empowerment.

Within all of this it is becoming evident that Arts & Culture is a field of activity where social impact, more than in other fields, depends on the proximity to target groups and where value discourses, norms and virtues play a particularly prominent role in self-actualisation actions that target the individual. As a consequence of its person-related, subjective character and the potentially informal processes involved in the realisation of social innovation, it largely defies the advocacy or service provision aspects established before, although of course it utilises both to some extent.

Service Provision in Social Services and Health Care

Social Services and Health Care are two core fields of service provision and are expected to gain importance facing the main drivers of demographic change. What is more, exactly due to this overarching trend, these sectors are to be investigated with a special emphasis of institutional interrelatedness. They represent settings in which the evolving role of NPOs in society, and their complex and dynamic relationships with the public and business sectors, can be studied. The latter have been approached from a variety of disciplines, ranging from economic theory to political science (Smith & Grønbjerg, 2006; Steinberg, 2006). The roles of NPOs have been characterised as supplementary, complementary or adversarial to government (Young, 2000). NPOs have been approached as independent entities competing to address market and government failures (Hansmann, 1980; Weisbrod, 1977); as publicly funded entities partnering with government to deliver public goods and services as a result of voluntary failures (Salamon, 1995; Vaughan, 2010); as policy influencers and service providers in competition/ partnership with government, businesses and other non-profits and in the context of both neoliberal and welfare state policies (Enjolras, 2009; Hall, 2006; Salamon & Anheier, 1996; Walker, 1991); as vehicles for citizens' interests and values that guarantee pluralism and help to build social capital within civil societies (Clemens, 2006; Coleman, 1988; Giner & Pérez, 1988; Putnam, Leonardi, & Nanetti, 1993); or as relevant participants in the governance of contemporary societies (Newman, 2004; Rhodes, 2001). It is exactly the tension between service provision and other (potentially conflicting) aspects like citizen inclusion, fostering of social capital and new forms of governance that is present in these fields that make them prime places for the empirical investigation of social innovation.

All of this is placed in a highly regulated public environment that bears the threat of hindering innovation as compared to more 'independent' fields like Environmental Sustainability or Consumer Protection in finance. Big differences are also to be expected in comparison to more 'inclusive' service fields like Work Integration or areas that are inherently close to civil society like Community Development—rationales that underline the significant value that lies in our comparative research design.

Advocacy in Environmental Sustainability and Consumer Protection in Finance

Promoting 'sustainable development' has been a key policy objective for the EU, as well as globally, for well over two decades (European Commission, 2009; United Nations, 1987), but with the persistence of many environmental problems, the prospects of climate change and governmental failure in securing a binding global climate agreement, and market failure in changing organisational and public conduct in relationship to sustainable growth, the need for developing new approaches in addressing these grand challenges is pressing (European Commission, 2011). There are numerous sustainability challenges in and across all societal domains: within energy, production, consumption and transport. At the EU level, the persistence of these problems, and the lack of governmental and market success in addressing them, has resulted in increasing calls for a challenge-led approach to innovation in environmental sustainability (European Commission, 2011; Steward, 2012) in which the 'mobilisation of society', based on a more systematic and durable co-operation among different organisational actors—NGOs, social enterprises, firms, local and central government—is allotted a crucial role in changing the course of development. The ongoing economic and social problems in the EU associated with the financial and sovereign debt crises, and a renewed focus on the significance of sustainable growth in the face of mounting ecological concerns, has exacerbated the importance of mobilising public engagement/active citizenship. Although there have been numerous calls over the last two decades to promote this, e.g., in the Rio Declaration (The United Nations Conference on Environment and Development, 1992) and in the ensuing efforts to develop local Agenda21 plans, and there are many citizen-led initiatives (George & Irwin, 2002), the conditions for their success and diffusion are not well understood.

A similar situation is apparent in the field of Consumer Protection in finance: The global financial crisis with its consequences for banking systems, welfare systems or households has, more than other developments, intensified the palpable need for effective tools for protecting citizens against the prevailing lack of knowledge, unfair treatment or fraud on the side of providers of various financial services and markets as well as financial instruments that have large damaging potential if applied in an unregulated fashion (Bertola, Disney, & Grant, 2006). In general, we may define Consumer Protection in finance as activities driven and undertaken by various institutions, policy makers or non-state actors that focus on protecting and promoting the rights of citizens in the area of financial services. Even before the crisis occurred, there was a growing concern in many countries about financial education and capabilities of consumers. Consequently, a large number of initiatives have been developed and various strategies of financial education have been proposed by major international institutions in order to prevent citizens from falling prey to non-transparent strategies of various financial institutions (DG Health and Consumers, 2013; European Commission, 2005; OECD—Organisation for Economic Co-operation and Development, 2006). While policies of consumer protection have slowly been making their way into national and international polities, it seems that organisations are able to respond to the real world more instantly: there have been useful toolboxes for citizens and civic initiatives for a number of years. Thereby they take different attitudes toward the issue—they promote new ideas and principles and advocate the rights of consumers on the political level, or focus on service provision as well as grass-roots educational activities by means that range from 'politics of the street' to lobbying and direct negotiations with policy makers.

The main aim in both fields is to contribute to the study of social innovation in fields that crucially depend on the mobilisation of particular forms of civic engagement and 'active citizenship' spurred mainly if not exclusively through advocacy. The analysis is thus going to be characterised by a 'two-tier' approach, analysing the effects of advocacy efforts stemming from broader civil society on formal, rule setting institutions and organisations to promote innovative development.

Co-Production in Work Integration and Community Development

Trends such as individualisation, the ageing of the population, the corresponding decrease in the proportion of the population active in the labour market and the current economic crisis affect social welfare systems in various ways. Such trends have given cause to a reassessment of the way in which a wide array of (public) services and goods such as education, energy, safety, care and social support are organised in European societies. The manner in which different countries attempt to cope with such questions has led to a variety of institutional frameworks. Especially at the local and community level people come together to face these kinds of challenges in different ways and with models of different scales and reach. Micro examples include so-called 'repair cafés' in countries like the Netherlands and Germany, while 'development trusts' in the UK (Wyler, 2009) and Transition Towns, for instance, in Italy (Smith, 2011) aim at meso or even macro level problem solving. Also, established organisations such as the Mondragon cooperative in Spain (Roelants & Sanchez Bajo, 2011) seem to be well-equipped for dealing with communal and multi-level challenges. Together actors provide a wide array of goods and services spanning from social care (Restakis, 2010) over local currencies for regional development (Curl, 2012, p. 361) and renewable energy (Kelly, 2012, p. 109). What they have in common is a high degree of self-organisation and a blurring between the lines of production and consumption (Verschuere, Brandsen, & Pestoff, 2012). What is more, all of these initiatives, as an explicit aim or a spin-off effect, promote community development.

In addition to these community initiatives all over Europe, the field of Work Integration plays an important role in promoting social inclusion. Within the vast range of activities covered by the social economy, those aiming at the social and professional integration of disadvantaged workers represent only a small part, but one that is of particular interest in view of the vulnerability of marginalised groups of the population. Work Integration

Social Enterprises (WISEs) (Davister, Defourny, & Gregoire, 2004) are private organisations whose primary goal is to help long-term unemployed people transition back into the workforce. To accomplish their mission, WISEs hire unemployed people, who are the beneficiaries of their service. WISEs provide their beneficiaries with training and mentoring that allow them to acquire the skills that are necessary for them to obtain regular jobs. WISE models with high impact can be found today across Europe, including, for example, Beschäftigungsgesellschaften in Germany, empresas de inserção in Portugal, work integration social enterprises in Ireland and the UK, and enterprises d'insertion in France (Cooney, 2011; Garrow & Hasenfeld, 2012; Kerlin, 2009; Spear & Bidet, 2005).

It becomes evident that both fields are affected by an intermingling and blurring of the borders between non-profit and for-profit models, and are subject to strong state regulation or the absence of state intervention respectively. The fields also show a welcome variation in the level of action that most likely promotes social innovation. In this regard the investigation of Work Integration puts a main emphasis on the organisational level, while Community Development initiatives are investigated against the background of (the absence of) political regulation on the one side and informal, individual arrangements on the other.

Field-Country Combinations

Once the seven fields of activity had been identified, we had to determine the country contexts in which the fields were to be investigated. Representing the variety of Europe, the ITSSOIN consortium consisted of partners in nine European countries in different geographic regions: the Czech Republic, Denmark, France, Germany, Italy, the Netherlands, Spain, Sweden and the United Kingdom.

Overall we aimed at executing empirical work on more than 20 'cases', whereby the case (see Ragin & Becker, 1992; Snow & Trom, 2002 on what is a case) refers to the study of a social innovation in each of our seven fields of activity across three to four partner countries. As highlighted several times before, the 'cases' were not meant to portray organisations but explicitly to uncover the mechanisms at play with regard to their contribution to social innovations. This happened against the traits of welfare regimes, the particular activity field the studied organisations were engaged in as well as surrounding policy and perception frameworks. Due to its breadth only part of the work, namely that directly referring to the social innovation, can be presented here. But generally the products of the research that ITSSOIN yielded downright deserved the label *in-depth* case studies. The design just described restricted the number of cases but significantly increased their explanatory potential. We performed the following methodological steps in order to arrive at the provisioned three to four field-country combinations.

To create a comprehensive overview, all partners searched for structural data for their respective country and provided descriptions on central subjects, the actors in the fields and significant changes occurring over time. This information was provided in concise country vignettes, whereby one vignette was compiled for each field in each country, yielding 63 vignettes overall. The aim of the country vignettes was to gain an overview on the specifics of our seven fields of activity across all of the ITSSOIN countries, with a particular focus on identifying the ideal setting for comparatively studying social innovations. Therefore, the focus lay on the description of the following field specifics:

- The **importance of the field** in the respective country (also in respect to other fields of activity; mainly based on a quantitative scoping including economic shares of the field; expenditures; workforce including volunteering; numbers and types of organisations as well as their shares; sources of funding and income).
- Its **actor patterns and variety** (the involvement and interplay of commercial, state and third sector entities).
- Key **regulative characteristics** of the field (especially recent changes in the latter, for instance in legislation).
- The **dynamism of the field** (following the questions: Have there been major reforms? Is it a contested field (both in terms of competition and political or public controversies)? Are there many new entrants or predominantly established players? etc.).
- The **key subjects** shaping the field at present as a first lead to assess the probability to identify prominent and significant social innovations.

As for the time period we considered approximately the last 10 years, but predominantly focussed on the current state of the field. To find the relevant information we screened a wide range of secondary sources. Concerning the structural data (public budgets spent on the field, numbers of organisations, sector provenience of providers/advocates etc.) project partners could draw on sources and inputs we had gathered in order to deliver an update on the mapping of third sector contours in Europe (Anheier, Krlev, Preuss, Mildenberger, & Einarsson, 2014) and complemented them by similar data sources with a particular focus on government and firm activity in the fields.

With regard of the involved actors and their objectives, first insights could be drawn from a media analysis (Brink Lund & Lilleor, 2015) and the policy framing we had performed on social innovation in the partner countries (Krlev, Einarsson, Wijkström, Heyer, & Mildenberger, forthcoming). The insights generated previously at the very least led researchers effectively to further sources. The websites of the responsible ministries for the respective fields were another useful source of information. And policy documents (those we had already analysed and others) often summed up the current central objectives of activities in the field, named the actors involved and pointed to their interplay. The reports of stakeholder meetings or conferences that dealt with current issues in the respective fields of activity were further interesting sources. They could provide a good overview of the currently pressing issues in the field, which we were most interested in against the background of some basic description of field characteristics. Starting from this, the search for statements and press releases issued by involved actors that responded to the most pressing issues were helpful in drafting a comprehensive picture of the developments and debates in the field.

The field-country selection was mainly based on the brief but pointed description of the seven fields in the nine countries, but took two additional aspects into account. First, in the selection of countries, although reduced in number as compared to the project consortium, we sought to maintain a balanced account of European geographic diversity. So we ruled out an exclusive focus on central European countries, for instance. Second, we gauged field-country combinations against three theoretical approaches we had used previously to derive propositions on national capacity for social innovation: Social Origins theory, the Welfare Regimes, and the Varieties of Capitalism approach. The Social Origins theory was used to reflect on the specific role of the third sector in regard to social innovations (Anheier, 2005, 2010; Salamon & Anheier, 1998). Welfare Regimes, by referring to de-commodification and stratification, consider the impact of state involvement on the national level, thus enabling an estimation of the innovative capacity of a country in regard to state activities (Arts & Gelissen, 2002; Esping-Andersen, 1990). Lastly, the Varieties of Capitalism approach reflects on types of market economies in reference to the intensity of innovations to be expected (Hall & Soskice, 2001; Schneider & Paunescu, 2012). Drawing on these insights and against the background of our 'open approach' presented in the previous chapter on research strategy, the roles of the third sector, the market and the state were of special interest for the empirical field descriptions. Accordingly, an explicit account of these spheres was also considered in the country selection.

More particularly, we tried to take into account the proposed effects of the institutional environment on social innovation, whereby one guiding hypothesis had been derived from one of the theoretical approaches and in turn yielding the following:

- Social Origins: 'The larger a nation's third sector and the higher its degree of volunteering, the larger its social innovativeness'.
- Welfare Regimes: 'National social innovativeness will be highest, where stratification is low and de-commodification is moderate'.
- Varieties of Capitalism: 'Coordinated market economy (CME) countries are more likely to foster incremental social innovations, whereas liberal market economy (LME) countries are more likely to foster radical innovation'.

For lack of space we cannot go into further detail here as regards the formulation of these hypotheses, but the conceptualisation is available elsewhere (see Anheier et al., 2014). As our empirical work aimed at explaining the success (or failure) of innovations, it was important to take these theoretical reflections into account in order to arrive at a balanced country composition for each of the seven fields of activity.

Lastly and again based on the vignettes, we performed a comparative discussion of how sector influence generally varied in the fields of activity across countries in order to incorporate some variation on that account too. As for the preceding framework hypotheses, going into further detail would trespass the limits of this book, but the detailed reasoning on sector influence in combination with innovation potential, which will be sketched roughly in the following, is available (see Anheier, Krlev, Mildenberger, & Preuss, 2015 on all criteria for field-country selection). All aspects taken together resulted in the field-country structure displayed in Table 3.2.

As successful social innovations were of particular interest, when conducting the country selection a strong focus was on countries that promised to be especially innovative. This focus is reflected particularly in the country selection in the field of Environmental Sustainability, where the theoretical frameworks suggest a high innovative capacity for three countries (Denmark, Germany and Italy) and low capacity only for one (Czech Republic). In this field a comparison of contexts that are relatively similar in regard to their innovative capacity but different as to the empirical setting could be conducted. The analysis of the field of Arts & Culture also concentrates on countries where social innovations are very likely (the Netherlands) or at least moderately likely (France, Italy and Spain). The selection in Social Services did not have quite such a stress on strong social innovation potential with all located at the medium level (Italy, UK, Spain and Sweden), yet with considerable variation in the countries' assessment depending on the theoretical framework applied. Still, all these country-field combinations are expected to reveal specifics that foster social innovations, since social innovations will depend on various context conditions. To be able to provide counterfactuals for the other fields, countries have been selected that were expected to show degrees of high, medium and low innovativeness: in Health Care the different degrees are covered by the UK (high), Denmark and France (medium) and the Czech Republic (low); in Work Integration, by Germany (high), France and Spain (medium) and the Czech Republic (low); and in Community Development by the Netherlands (high), the UK and Italy (medium) and the Czech Republic (low).

Sometimes the interplay between country level assessments, based on the theoretical frameworks, and assessments on the level of the specific fields of activity, based on the composition of vignettes, was of particular interest. The question as to how an especially innovative capacity on the country

Table 3.2 Field-country combinations

Category	'Self-actualisation'	'Service provision'		'Advocacy'		'Co-production'		SUM
Field-country	Arts & Culture	Social Services	Health Care	Env. Sustainability	Cons. Protection	Work Integration	Com. Development	
Czech Republic			X	X	X	X	X	
Denmark			X	X	X			
France	X		X			X		
Germany				X		X		
Italy	X	X		X			X	
The Netherlands	X						X	
Spain	X	X			X	X		
Sweden		X						
UK		X	X				X	
SUM of cases	4	4	4	4	3	4	4	27
SUM of cases per category	8	8		7		8		

level affects innovative processes in a field less likely to foster innovations (and vice versa) could be addressed. This particularly applies to the field of Consumer Protection, where for Spain and the Czech Republic more innovative potential was detected on the field level than on the country level, whereas in Denmark the country level was a more promising setting for innovations than the field level.

In a nutshell, we sampled on a variety of criteria, among which the most important were (1) representing European diversity; (2) accounting for current developments in the fields of activity; (3) incorporating varying degrees of expected national social innovativeness in relation to framework factors; and (4) covering cross-national variations in sector dominance within the fields of activity. It needs to be highlighted that the feedback of the work package leaders (the lead authors of the empirical chapters in this book, each responsible for one field of activity) was especially important at this point, as they have been entrusted with this task according to their expertise in the respective field. The joint methodological framework enabled a comparable description of similarities and differences of each empirical field across countries and built the base for a description of actor patterns and their variety, with a special focus on the involvement and interplay of market, state and third sector entities. Our approach to define settings for the empirical research was meant to make sure that the role of the third sector, the market and the state could be evaluated to the same extent. Even though we expected third sector organisations to have a particularly strong influence on social innovation processes, the empirical investigation of all social innovation cases drawing on this country selection was fit to reveal the opposite, and/or to qualify the roles of different actors.

In addition to a more static description of the states of the fields, we also took into account key regulative characteristics of the field and the dynamism of the field, rendered visible, e.g., through major reforms, conflicts between actors or the entry of new actors. This focus allowed for spotting outstanding changes in the field which are of special interest for the analysis of social innovations. It also allowed for identifying sub-areas within the fields of activity that seemed particularly salient for the study of social innovations and thus enabled first steps in the identification of the 'objects of interest' promoted in field theory (Bourdieu, 1992; Fligstein & McAdam, 2011). Based on this concept we promoted the reduction of broad and varied fields of activity to more specific areas. The field of Consumer Protection, for instance, was specified by relating explicitly to consumer protection in finance. The field of Community Development in turn was reduced to the topic of integrating asylum seekers, refugees and unauthorised immigrants in communities. And in the field of Environmental Sustainability we saw a salience of urban contexts, which is why we chose to focus on the latter. These first leads were taken further in defining concrete 'social innovation streams' that were identified through expert consultation, which is portrayed in the next section.

The Social Innovation Streams

Instead of studying potentially isolated and unique organisational innovation practices and sampling at the organisational level, we have identified 'social innovation streams' (SI streams) within our seven fields of activity as the anchor for our comprehensive empirical analysis:

> Social innovation stream refers to new approaches, principles of action, governance forms or modes of organisation that have fundamentally affected a field of activity, and already for a certain period of time (at least for five years back from today) and across national borders, so that they are not geographically restricted.

In other words, social innovation streams are not nascent anymore; they are not particular to certain settings or locally restricted. Although we do not challenge that any of the latter might qualify as social innovation, we could not use any of such innovations to perform our comparative, sequential and cross-national analysis. Departing from the state of the innovation at present, we have then applied the 'process tracing' to be presented in the next section to arrive at its origins. The identified SI streams built on the 'country vignettes' and were identified in a two-step expert consultation process that illustrated various social innovation developments within the national settings and eventually led to the most promising one.

The expert consultation was designed as follows. It was conducted by means of semi-structured interviews, mostly by telephone, with up to 10 international experts per field of activity judging recent trends cross-nationally and an additional two to three national experts in each of the three to four pre-selected countries per field, amounting to about 15 interviews in each of the seven ITSSOIN fields. The experts were asked to reflect on the general developments in the fields of activity identified in the composition of the country vignettes. They were then asked to identify what they considered to be social innovations occurring in the field based on our definition. Depending on the sequence of the interviews, they were either finally asked to assess a repertoire of innovations that had emerged in the interview process or re-contacted to give their assessment later on. Overall this did not only enable us to identify the social innovation stream we eventually studied, but also helped put it into perspective and get a general impression of innovativeness in the field, nationally and cross-nationally. Both the vignettes and the final selection of social innovation streams have been reviewed by and discussed with our advisory board as well as with the participants of ITSSOIN's mid-term conference in July 2015 in Paris.

The results of this process were analysed systematically—the key rationales will be described in the sub-sections to follow—in order to identify one social innovation stream per field of activity (see Box 3.1 for an illustration).

Box 3.1 What's 'the Case'?

First and foremost our targeted 'case' is always a social innovation. In the following we use 'crowdfunding' as a *hypothetical example of innovation*. Please note that this is for illustrative purposes only and no profound discussion is provided on whether this is a justified example of innovation more generally or of social innovation more specifically, nor if it may be related or ascribed to one of our seven fields of activity. It can be seen that it appears in some of our fields, but mostly as a means rather than an end in itself.

Our hypothetical scenario: The first question to ask is how have we arrived at 'crowdfunding' as the innovation case to study? The answer builds on the country vignettes in which we have described each of our seven fields of activity covering all ITSSOIN countries and identified the ones where these fields seem to be either most or least dynamic and which by means of comparison seem to offer the highest explanatory potential for our set goal, which is to identify social innovation streams and to process trace them in order to find out which actors have contributed in which way to this social innovation stream. In the analysis of vignettes, 'crowdfunding' may already have appeared (and it may have not) as a first side comment in one of our fields of activity (let's call it X) in one or more of the countries discussed.

We then go on to give a more detailed description of the field of activity, focussing only on the countries we pre-selected. Thereby we consider several social innovation streams of particular importance to the specific fields of activity. Here at the latest, 'crowdfunding' must occur in field X as a social innovation stream with at least a tendency of dominance in or importance to field X. We start to suspect that when we talk about social innovation in field X, 'crowdfunding' as a specific case is likely to play an important role. At this point there are still up to 10 other social innovation streams in field X that we are considering as the one to be studied. We discuss this list of social innovation streams in field X internally but also and more importantly consult external 'experts'. We have already done so in compiling the list of 10 social innovation streams of field X, but we continue to do so (for instance at the mid-term conference, in other stakeholder formats or in one-on-one discussions, potentially re-interrogating the people we talked to earlier). By way of such a discursive back and forth, we finally arrive at 'crowdfunding' as the social innovation stream we wanted to study in field X.

This does not imply that 'crowdfunding' is the most important social innovation stream in X, but that given the selection process, and through the inclusion of a multitude of opinions that we have kept as objective as possible, 'crowdfunding' is a justified case with a high degree of explanatory potential regarding our research question, which is which actors have contributed to its emergence and in which way. To back this up we provide a clear account of our decision rationale relating to the consultation process but also take into account theoretical arguments, such as those that stem from previous empirical research or a regional argument considering context-specific peculiarities. To sum up: We make the case for our case.

Several guiding questions were important in the selection of the SI streams. The newness of the social innovation was of major relevance. We therefore asked: Is the phenomenon to be studied really new or just something that received a different label recently? Does a functional equivalent exist and how is the social innovation different from it? What are the key contextual factors in which the social innovation arose? Equally important was the innovation's suitability for identifying actor and sector influence in the subsequent analysis, meaning that it should at least provide the potential for a diverse set of actors to have engaged in its evolution. Table 3.3 summarises the SI streams that we arrived at in each of the ITSSOIN fields of activity.

Based on our previous country-field combination each social innovation stream was studied across three to four countries, or more narrow regional settings such as cities. Overall we identified 129 organisational entities (some of them networks or informal groups) involved in bringing about the SI stream to be discussed in the empirical chapters, which were therefore analysed as to their role in the process and as regards their characteristics. We traced out organisational traits, constellations and roles that spurred 'social innovativeness', defined initially as referring to a contribution to the creation of solutions to previously inadequately addressed social needs with the effect of increasing efficiency and effectiveness (functionalist aspects) and leading to change (transformational aspects) and with the primary aim of improving the situation for the beneficiaries and actors involved. Degrees of actor contributions were judged along three dimensions whereby high social innovativeness was marked by actors' more frequent (overall or within the social innovation process), more substantial (clearly recognisable or dominant) and more sustainable (lasting) involvement in the development of such solutions.

Before we go on to explain how exactly the SI streams were traced, we will summarise the key rationales that led to the selection of the specific social innovation in each of our seven fields of activity.

Table 3.3 ITSSOIN social innovation streams and country settings

Field of activity	SI stream	Countries
Arts & Culture	Arts for spatial rejuvenation	Spain, Italy, France, the Netherlands
Social Services	New governance arrangements to reach marginalised groups	Spain, Italy, UK, Sweden
Health Care	The recovery approach to mental health	UK, Czech Republic, France, Denmark
Environmental Sustainability	Promotion of bicycle use in urban contexts	Italy, Germany, Czech Republic, Denmark
Consumer Protection	Online financial education	Spain, Czech Republic, Denmark
Work Integration	Cross-sector partnerships	Spain, Germany, Czech Republic, France
Community Development	Self-organised integration of refugees	Italy, UK, Czech Republic, the Netherlands

Why Spatial Rejuvenation in Arts & Culture?

A large number of SI streams had been identified in Arts & Culture, which were located in seven broad areas and can be systemised as to their functions. Some SI streams related to the enhancement of the very field's viability: (1) new governance and decision making models, e.g., cooperative forms of cultural organisations; and (2) new models for enhancing economic sufficiency of the field, e.g., alternative financing sources. Others related to the interface between arts and citizens or the consumers of arts: (3) digital media for social participation, e.g., crowdfunding, crowdsourcing or online communities for cultural initiatives; and (4) cultural co-production, e.g., 'artivism' or audience participation. A third area was concerned with the promotion of non standard outcomes through the application of arts based approaches: (5) arts for enhancing education, e.g., edutainment; (6) arts to promote better health outcomes, e.g., arts-based approaches in therapy and rehabilitation; and (7) arts as a means for enhancing social cohesion, e.g., place redesign and rejuvenation.

Across a screening of the fields in Italy, France, Spain and the Netherlands, digital media usage and place rejuvenation came out as the most pronounced. The relevance of digital media emerged mostly due to the increasing importance of crowdfunding for cultural activities, which in turn was seen by experts as a result of the budget cutting policies the field is subject to. Several experts were of the opinion that in this compensatory function, crowdfunding should not be seen as a viable innovation at this point. Place redesign and rejuvenation in turn were interpreted as important elements in fostering social cohesion in neglected spatial areas and as timely and effective responses to that challenge, which is why this was selected eventually.

Why New Governance Models for Reaching the Most Vulnerable in Social Services?

Social Services was inarguably the most diverse field in terms of emerging SI streams with a magnitude of different activities amounting to three broader trends: (1) reconceptualisation of social problems and shifts in agency, e.g., disabled people's right to live a 'normal life'; (2) citizen autonomy and integration of social services with other fields, e.g., personal citizen budgets to spend on services of their own choice; and (3) involvement of new actors and resources in service provision, e.g., telecare (as a technological approach) or the involvement of volunteers (as a human resource based approach). While areas (1) and (2) represent principles of action along which service provision is designed, area (3) directly addresses particular modes of service provision, which are more relevant given the aim of our investigation, namely, investigating the practical realisation of a social innovation. In addition, such new governance arrangements were interpreted by experts as effective tools to address the most vulnerable groups of the population. For these reasons, new actors and resources emerged as the object of study.

Since it was nearly impossible to distil one distinct social innovation within this area across Italy, Spain, Sweden and the UK, we chose to examine variations on the theme of new governance arrangements. While the empirical investigations in Spain and the UK focused on the provision of telecare and thus an advancement of social services' reach through technology, the involvement of volunteers in service provision and thus an increase in human capital was more relevant in Sweden. In Italy in turn we focussed on an enhancement of acting capacity through mobilising new financial resources and provider partnerships surrounding them based on social (impact) investment principles.

Why the Recovery Approach in Health Care?

In Health Care the previous specification of the field had led to a focus on the social model of disability as an important overarching trend that was not only of considerable relevance but also offered explanatory potential on the interplay of organisational actors, institutional factors and discourses in the field. Since physical health treatment is mostly still dominated by the clinical model, the field had also already been narrowed down to mental health. Within the latter, three distinct trends were identified in the expert consultation: (1) integration of service delivery between health care, social care and other services; (2) community capacity-building and patient involvement; and (3) active citizenship, that is user-directed and co-produced treatment.

In regards to other possible trends that could have been chosen, patient participation was a political priority for health services in all the national systems of the Czech Republic, Denmark, France, and the UK. However, activities under this heading (e.g., patient information, patient experience surveys, consultations about plans for service change) did not have the characteristics of a distinct social innovation. This means they did not necessarily suggest or lead to new ways of working and changes in practice, and it was not always clear which social welfare needs patient involvement met. Instead, it appeared to be characterised primarily by top-down government programmes, designed to support the implementation of government priorities and predominantly informed by the concept of patients as largely passive recipients of services. Similarly, whilst integration was a trend that was subject to major health reforms in Denmark, France and the UK, it did not appear to point at a specific social innovation stream. It had more features of a policy programme for solving problems associated with bureaucratic and professional boundaries in fragmented service structures (although policy makers might sell it as a mechanism for addressing social needs more effectively). User-directed and co-produced treatment in turn was a specific practice and found recognition cross-nationally under the label of 'recovery', which led us to choose the latter as the social innovation stream to be analysed.

Why the Promotion of Bike Use in Environmental Sustainability?

In the specification of the vast field of Environmental Sustainability, experts, both at national and regional level, had made clear that 'cities' and 'urban strategies toward sustainability' were very high on stakeholders' agendas. Departing from there, mobility emerged as a key priority. This is why we condensed the investigation in the Czech Republic, Denmark, Germany and Italy to major urban areas that had some track record of dealing with mobility issues, leading to a selection of Brno, Copenhagen, Frankfurt and Milan. Mobility had crystallised against a set of alternative sustainability areas, such as (1) real estate, e.g., energy efficiency or retrofitting and rebuilding; (2) food and greenery, e.g., urban gardening or expansion of green areas; and (3) neighbourhood scale and redesign, e.g., city planning, including the aims of revitalisation or modernisation.

Within mobility there was still a variety of social innovation streams, among which the 'sharing principle' was a joint characteristic. Examples of sharing in transport and urban mobility abound (e.g., new means of achieving mobility needs such as car sharing; new potential experiences and services in public transport; expansion of opportunities for walking and using other non-motorized modes of transporation, of which the most prominent is bicycle use). To some of the expert commentators this willingness and acceptance reflects a change of individual, governmental and business awareness that may be leading in sum to experimenting with new forms of sharing the urban space and to redefining the ways in which people collectively interact and move around in the city. While car sharing was considered as restricted in its transformational capacity, since it is supposed to lead to shifts within one means of transportation, the promotion of bike use as a social innovation stream was given priority since it aims to spur shifts between means of transport and simultaneously offers higher contributions to achieving sustainability goals.

Why Online Education for Financial Services in Consumer Protection?

Despite the comparatively narrow conception of the field of Consumer Protection as such and its further focus on alternative financial services provided outside the traditional banking system, the identification of SI streams across the Czech Republic, Denmark and Spain led to a comprehensive selection list which could be grouped into two key categories. The first category was concerned with fortifying the competencies of lenders through (1) online initiatives for raising awareness about the dangers of alternative financial services and (2) financial education, that is, initiatives promoting financial literacy, especially among disadvantaged groups. The second category was built around the idea of creating alternatives to the financial services industry and comprised (a) informal systems of peer-to-peer lending; (b) cooperative banking networks with a social mission aiming at promoting regional development; (c) crowdfunding platforms to support individuals or ventures; and (d) time banking, that is, the use of time as a currency that promotes mutual citizen support.

The second category, although serving that function, was more loosely coupled to the idea of Consumer Protection and it was also far less clearly embodied in the different countries. The first category in turn was not only more targeted, but enabled us to combine the two sub-aspects it comprised, yielding 'online financial education' as the SI stream to be investigated.

Why Cross-Sector Alliances in Work Integration?

Work Integration was probably the narrowest field of activity right from the beginning and consequently the social innovation streams identified were not as numerous as in the other fields. In addition to the general trends of increasing quality management in Work Integration initiatives and the ambition to bring them to bigger scale, three organisational phenomena could be identified as relevant social innovation streams across the Czech Republic, France, Germany and Spain: (1) work integration social enterprises (WISEs) as separate initiatives promoting new approaches of employing disadvantaged people; (2) formalised cross-sector partnerships promoting the integration of disadvantaged people into the first labour market in a joint effort; and (3) integrated approaches of Work Integration that complement training and employment by life counselling, health or therapeutic help, etc.

To our surprise, despite being considered as often performing innovative practices, WISEs as an approach were not seen as the cutting edge of innovation by the consulted experts. According to them the most prominent social innovation stream was the combination of sector resources through the formalisation of alliances between actors from all sectors to be able to offer complementary support to beneficiaries. Integrated approaches in turn were not found to be sufficiently distinct, and are potentially still too immature, to allow for a comparative screening of the SI stream. It remains to be remarked that cross-sector partnerships as a social innovation in Work Integration by definition demand substantial contributions from all actors. However, it is still possible to look for the initiating force and analyse which particular functions and roles the different actors had.

Why Self-Organised Integration of Refugees in Community Development?

The focus on refugees in the Community Development field had already been identified in the screening of the field. The focus had been developed to the particularly challenging task of building communities that involve those who are not only new to the local community but also to the country. It is also a pressing issue. It needs to be remarked, however, that our research focus was identified in late 2014; that is, before what became known as the 'refugee crisis'. Within this realm two SI streams were identified as relevant against the national background of the Czech Republic, Italy, the UK and the Netherlands: (1) social activation, capacity building and work integration with the aim of increasing the skills and capacities of refugees, which may range from job training to narrative-based life resumes, and from internship programs with local entrepreneurs to general entrepreneurship courses, and (2) self organisation and local community integration, with approaches ranging from 'human libraries' in which resettled refugees met locals in a public library to neighbourhoods supporting refused asylum seekers in squatted buildings, and from volunteer projects with refugee community organisations to housing refused asylum seekers in private residences.

To avoid overlaps with the Work Integration field and due to its more enabling and less passive character, the second SI stream, 'self-organised integration of refugees', was selected. For the local focus of this field we have performed a reduction of the geographic scope of our empirical work to one urban context per country, targeting cities with a supposedly vital scene in this area: Brno, Milan, Utrecht and Birmingham.

Process Tracing

The study of the selected social innovation streams is based on the method of process tracing. Following the tradition of this method applied to the analysis of policies or legislation in political science (Ford, Schmitt, Schechtman, Hults, & Doherty, 1989; Tansey, 2007), the establishment of social innovation was followed back to its origins. Thereby we could find out who the initiator of the innovation was, and what and who the driving forces in its subsequent process have been. Essentially, in the empirical chapters we go about it just the way political scientists do:

> The logical way to identify these elements [referring to elements essential to the passing of a legal act] is to "write history backwards" starting at point B, which would typically be an important and visible political decision-making process. If we find that some, otherwise plausible, alternatives were not chosen or even considered at that point, this would be an indication of where to find the previous point or points A. Comparing the situations at these two points should then give a clue to what type of actor-based mechanism has been at work between the two events.
>
> (Bengtsson & Ruonavaara, 2011, p. 405;
> see also Bengtsson & Ruonavaara, 2017)

Process tracing helps us establish causal connections between particular incidents and to uncover mechanisms at play. Thereby, the 'dependent variable' is the social innovation. We traced the respective SI stream to its origins, starting with its state today. For delineating historical cut-off points in order not to stretch our historical investigation too far into the past, we have used several guiding questions, including: What are the key characteristics of the state of the SI stream today? What differentiates it from potential alternatives? This approach enhances the dynamic perspective of the analysis, as temporal shifts in conditional factors can be detected. One example for changes in political influence could be the end of governmental support after elections, with potential consequences for a social innovation. Since we included field-country setups that included settings in which the social innovation was not or less successful, we met an important aspect for the method of process tracing: We also incorporate analysis of the counterfactual, that is the absence of a given phenomenon (Collier, 2011).

To illustrate the method as applied in our research more concretely, we draw again on the hypothetical crowdfunding example we gave in relation to the identification of the SI stream (see Box 3.1). After the case selection we dive into 'the case' by asking ourselves: What is the situation in 'crowdfunding' at present in the pre-selected countries A, B, C and D? More specifically, for each of the countries, we ask: how does crowdfunding work, who is involved, what are the involved actors' interests, who benefits and who does not, where exactly is the innovative element in our case, etc.? We study this by means of strategic action field theory as also applied to the wider actor environment outlined in the previous chapter. The more specific strategic action field here is the system or the scene of 'crowdfunding', which is located within our field of activity X. Naturally the description of 'crowdfunding' differs across countries, and that is where the comparative element comes in for the first time.

Once we have described commonalities and differences in and between the countries we can ask: How did this come about? And this is where the method of process tracing comes in. Given the state of 'crowdfunding' at present, we ask ourselves: How did this system emerge, how has it been transformed over time, who/what were the driving forces, and who/what was blocking its unfolding? This is where we start thinking about organisational actors more specifically, and the case of crowdfunding is split up into a deeper analysis of the involved actors—always under a procedural lens of analysis. Let's take the purely speculative situation where in country C a large 'crowdfunding' platform is being operated by the Ministry of Social Affairs to stimulate the realisation of local projects. Given this situation we would ask: Was it that ministry that also drafted the idea? Did it initiate the platform without the influence of other actors? Has the impulse emerged in country C or did the ministry draw inspiration from another country?

The formulated questions help us not only to systemise the analysis in the specific country, but also across countries and in fact across all our fields of activity. In the case of 'crowdfunding' in field X in country C, we would of course consider the ministry as part of the case work and try to investigate how the system is run, who is responsible and who (else) is involved. Going back from there we might learn that in fact the ministry was pushed to adopt and run this system by a number of independent civic crowdfunding initiatives that advocated a shift of the formerly informal and scattered system to a higher level of visibility and stricter administration. Then these civic groups would become part of the case work. Or it might be that firms in country C were running such platforms to raise money for risky technology projects and the ministry simply mimicked their successful attempts. Then we would of course want to study the practices in these firms. All of these avenues are traced with the goal of finding out: Who has shaped the idea? Who has advocated it? Who has developed it further? Who has brought it to a higher level? And thus eventually: Who has been most strongly involved in making the social innovation stream of crowdfunding emerge and thrive overall and what are the connections between involved actors?

In this process we are not only looking for organisational entities but also for more informal constellations. We are keeping the identification of actors and the tracing of their influence as iterative and reflective as possible. That is, we perform discussions among the partners working on field X in their respective country, but also across fields of activity and among all consortium partners on questions such as: Does it make sense to take a closer look at this particular actor or network of actors? Have we overlooked specific other actors? Have we missed a junction and thus a completely alternative road in the tracing of the origins of the social innovation? etc. Essentially we are establishing a system of continual peer review to make sure that not only the selection of the social innovation case, but also its tracing and the analysis of involved parties, is convincing.

To outline this from an additional angle and to effectively link the examples provided in this and the previous chapter, the sequence of how we move from one broad field of activity to one particular SI stream is outlined in Figure 3.1. It outlines the three-step approach of (1) the *scoping* with regards to field-country combination and field reduction by means of the vignettes; (2) the *selection* of the SI stream (recovery approach) among a variety of alternatives within a more specified field (social model of disability); and (3) the *analysis* of the SI stream by means of process tracing under a field theoretic lens, which, as should be re-stated, was also applied in the preceding steps.

The examples of crowdfunding and of the recovery approach in Health Care show how we defined our unit of analysis and subsequently generated in-depth, qualitative data on each stream. The results were specific actor traits and field conditions that enabled the social innovation to occur. The data that formed the basis of the analysis has been collected in a fashion following the data collection for the field description. Desktop research was used to gather structural data, policy documents and media articles that provided information about the social innovation stream. Due to the focus on one specific social innovation this data was far from comprehensive and mainly helped to identify those that played a role in the actor

> *Field of activity*: Health—general description with country-vignettes for all ITSSOIN-countries, enabling field-country selection and giving leads on significant *sub-fields*.
>
> > Reduction to *field 'social model of disability'*—focused description relating to this subject and related sub-themes and identifying *social innovations* in the field (could include patient participation empowerment and coproduction movements, health promotion and prevention initiatives).
> >
> > Selection of *social innovation stream* 'recovery approach in mental health'.
> >
> > > *Analysis of* social innovation stream (*the case*) by means of process tracing and in accordance with field theory.

Figure 3.1 Sequence of identifying and analysing 'the case' in Health Care

landscape. Departing from there, we approached the engaged actors and talked to them, spurring a process of snowball sampling and leading to more and more actor representatives. We also partly drew on the knowledge of the experts we had consulted in the identification of the social innovation streams to point us at the national and local actors involved. The actor representatives we talked to were from firms, public administration and non-profit organisations identified as relevant to the emergence of the social innovation stream.

Depending on the constellation of countries in which the SI stream was to be investigated, the project resources available and the degree to which the stream was absent or present in the countries, we performed 10 to 15 interviews per country. This resulted in more than 270 in-depth interviews overall and at least 35 interviews per each of our seven fields of activity/SI streams. Most interviews were conducted in person, but partly by telephone, and we also performed a number of focus groups if feasible and if found useful by the participants of the research. Interview guides were composed in the style of expert or elite interviews (Tansey, 2007). They were semi-structured and guided by the questions outlined earlier in relation to crowdfunding. They lasted between 30 and 90 minutes, were transcribed and analysed by use of coding software such as Atlas.ti, NVIVO and MaxQDA—the specific software varied across the national teams. Once we had arrived at a definite set of innovation actors we also performed a content analysis of relevant information on their websites, reports, official statements and press releases that referred explicitly to the SI stream. In the execution of the analysis we upheld the four criteria typically applied to judge the quality of a case study design (Yin, 2003): construct validity, internal validity, external validity and reliability.

Construct validity refers to the establishment of operational measures in accordance with the studied object. This can be ensured by using multiple data sources, the establishment of a chain of evidence and the review of results by stakeholders (Yin, 2003, 35f.). Altogether a broad range of data and data triangulation (Denzin, 1970; Flick, 2011) was applied to bring the case study to life, in which the focus lay on a thorough tracing of the SI stream and a description of the actor landscape as well as actors' roles and interplay informed by field theory. In addition to control exerted by researchers and participants of the research, intermediary results were discussed in stakeholders workshops addressing researchers, practitioners and policy makers not directly involved in the research in order to reflect it and make adaptions if necessary.

Internal validity is of special relevance for case studies that aim at causal explanations as ours do. It is established throughout the data analysis by matching patterns and building explanations. Furthermore, rival explanations need to be addressed and logic models should be used (Yin, 2003, p. 36). In the case study framework presented, a logic model is underlying all explanations to be developed. It is the theoretical concept of 'episodes of contention' (McAdam, Edelman, & Leachman, 2010). Following this, the implementation of the analysed social innovation is described as a process that starts with the mobilisation of actors. It continues with the skillful embedding of the new concept by these actors and through support of additional actor groups. The method of process tracing ensures internal validity by documenting the relevant steps and subsequently identifying all actors involved. Based on these factors a valid explanation can be built, describing those organisational traits especially supporting organisations in implementing social innovations.

External validity is needed to allow for a generalisation of the results of a case study. This is granted by a research design of multiple case studies that contains a replication logic (Yin, 2003, p. 37). The presented framework embeds the replication logic, since its purpose from the very beginning was to ensure comparability and synthesis across all 27 cases. The entire research project was performed as a coordinated effort, allowing for adaptions across fields of activity but maintaining a joint framework that not only allowed cross-country comparisons within one field but also a synthesis across fields. Work package leaders played a significant role in maintaining this balance and ensuring external validity.

Reliability of the analysis is mainly ensured by well-reflected procedures of data collection. With regard to case study work the aim is to ensure that the same study could be repeated and would produce the same result. Yin suggests conducting a case study protocol and a case study database for this goal (Yin, 2003, 37f.). In accordance with these considerations researchers were provided templates for the various stages of composing the case study by the project coordinator. These emerged in an iterative process of discussion in consortium meetings and more ad-hoc exchanges. They were adapted along the process if needed and ensured a structured and uniform execution of the research throughout. Researchers additionally documented the single steps of data collection in a case study protocol. This included not only rationales for the inclusion, but also for the exclusion of specific data sources.

This chapter has outlined the joint structure of the empirical work performed and thus also of the empirical chapters of this book to follow. All chapters contain the same elements. After a brief introduction of the SI stream, they go on to explain central concepts, such as, for example, 'self-organisation' in the Community Development chapter. Since they have been briefly summarised in this chapter, the empirical chapters of Part II do not go into detail as to alternative SI streams and the selection process involved. The methods section then outlines how specific settings have been selected, especially if a reduction to more restricted geographic settings (such as cities) has been performed and how the relevant innovation actors have been identified. Since the joint methodological approach has been outlined here, the empirical chapters do not go into detail regarding the performance and the modes of data analysis. The core of the chapters is composed of the tracing part, in which first general remarks across all analysed countries are made, and second the SI stream and the actor landscape surrounding it is portrayed in detail for each country. The synthesis section distils insights across countries but also reflects on general and potentially unexpected discoveries that have been made by the teams when performing the research. All chapters close with some conclusions on implications for the policy, practice and theory surrounding the studied social innovation.

Note

1. We would like to thank the work package leaders of the respective fields and their teams for valuable input on the sections dealing with the specific field settings, in particular Alex Turrini on Arts & Culture, Marta Rey-Garcia on Social Services, Annette Bauer on Health Care, Maria Figueroa on Environmental Sustainability, Vladimir Hyanek on Consumer Protection, Anne-Claire Pache on Work Integration and Wouter Mensink on Community Development.

References

Anheier, H. K. (2005). *Nonprofit organisations: Theory, management, policy.* New York, NY: Routledge.

Anheier, H. K. (2010). Social origins theory. In H. K. Anheier & S. Toepler (Eds.), *International encyclopaedia of civil society* (pp. 1445–1452). New York, NY: Springer.

Anheier, H. K., Krlev, G., Mildenberger, G., & Preuss, S. (2015). *Country selection: Country-field combinations evaluated in the empirical case studies in the ITSSOIN project.* A deliverable of the project: 'Impact of the Third Sector as Social Innovation' (ITSSOIN). Brussels.

Anheier, H. K., Krlev, G., Preuss, S., Mildenberger, G., & Einarsson, T. (2014). *Theory and empirical capturing of the third sector at the macro level.* A deliverable of the project: 'Impact of the Third Sector as Social Innovation' (ITSSOIN), European Commission—7th Framework Programme. Brussels.

Arts, W., & Gelissen, J. (2002). Three worlds of welfare capitalism or more? A state-of-the-art report. *Journal of European Social Policy, 12*(2), 137–158.

Bengtsson, B., & Ruonavaara, H. (2011). Comparative process tracing in housing studies. *International Journal of Housing Policy, 11*(4), 395–414. https://doi.org/10.1080/14616718.2011.626603

Bengtsson, B., & Ruonavaara, H. (2017). Comparative process tracing: Making historical comparison structured and focused. *Philosophy of the Social Sciences, 47*(1), 44–66. https://doi.org/10.1177/0048393116658549

Bertola, G., Disney, R., & Grant, C. (2006). *The economics of consumer credit.* Cambridge, MA: MIT Press.

Bourdieu, P. (1992). *Die verborgenen Mechanismen der Macht.* Hamburg: VSA.

Brink Lund, A., & Lilleor, A. (2015). *Media framing of third sector activities in Europe.* A deliverable of the project: 'Impact of the Third Sector as Social Innovation' (ITSSOIN). Brussels.

Clemens, E. S. (2006). The constitution of citizens: Political theories of nonprofit organizations. In W. W. Powell & R. Steinberg (Eds.), *The nonprofit sector: A research handbook* (pp. 207–220). New Haven, London: Yale University Press.

Coleman, J. S. (1988). Social capital in the creation of human capital. *The American Journal of Sociology*, 94(Supplement: Organizations and Institutions: Sociological and Economic Approaches to the Analysis of Social Structure), 95–120.

Collier, D. (2011). Understanding process tracing. *PS: Political Science & Politics*, 44(4), 823–830. https://doi.org/10.1017/S1049096511001429

Cooney, K. (2011). The business of job creation: An examination of the social enterprise approach to workforce development. *Journal of Poverty*, 15(1), 88–107.

Curl, J. R. I. (2012). *For all the people: Uncovering the hidden history of cooperation, cooperative movements, and communalism in America*. Oakland, CA: PM Press.

Davister, C., Defourny, J., & Gregoire, O. (2004). *Work integration social enterprises in the European Union: An overview of existing models*. Working Paper. EMES working paper 04/04.

Denzin, N. K. (1970). *The research act: A theoretical introduction to sociological methods. Methodological perspectives*. New Brunswick NJ: AldineTransaction.

DG Health and Consumers. (2013). *Webpage*.

Dubini, P., & Provera, B. (2008). Chart success and innovation in the music industry: Does organizational form matters? *Journal of Media Business Studies*, 5, 41.

Enjolras, B. (2009). Between market and civic governance regimes: Civicness in the governance of social services in Europe. *VOLUNTAS: International Journal of Voluntary and Nonprofit Organizations*, 20(3), 274–290. https://doi.org/10.1007/s11266-009-9091-2

Esping-Andersen, G. (1990). *The three worlds of welfare capitalism* (Pbk. ed.). Cambridge: Polity Press.

European Commission. (2005). *Commission white paper of 1 December 2005 on financial services policy 2005–2010*. Working Paper (No. 629). Brussels: European Commission.

European Commission. (2009). *Communication from the commission to the European parliament, the council, the European economic and social committee of the regions: Mainstraming sustainable development into Eu policies*. Review of the European Union Strategy for Sustainable Development. Brussels.

European Commission. (2011). *Commission staff working paper impact assessment: Accompanying the Communication from the Commission 'Horizon 2020'*. The Framework Programme for Research and Innovation. Brussels. Retrieved from http://ec.europa.eu/research/horizon2020/pdf/proposals/horizon_2020_impact_assessment_report.pdf#view=fit&pagemode=none

Fiorentini, G. (2006). *Impresa sociale e sussidiarietà: Dalle fondazioni alle spa; management e crisi. Management*. Milano: Franco Angeli.

Flick, U. (2011). *Triangulation*. Wiesbaden: Verlag für Sozialwissenschaften.

Fligstein, N., & McAdam, D. (2011). Toward a general theory of strategic action fields. *Sociological Theory*, 29(1), 1–26.

Ford, J. K., Schmitt, N., Schechtman, S. L., Hults, B. M., & Doherty, M. L. (1989). Process tracing methods: Contributions, problems, and neglected research questions. *Organizational Behavior and Human Decision Processes*, 43, 75–117.

Garrow, E., & Hasenfeld, Y. (2012). Managing conflicting institutional logics: Social service vs. market. In B. Gidron & Y. Hasenfeld (Eds.), *Social enterprises: An organizational perspective*. Basingstoke: Palgrave Macmillan.

George, S., & Irwin, A. (2002). Re-interpreting local-global partnerships. In T. de Bruijn & A. Tukker (Eds.), *Partnership and leadership: Building alliances for a sustainable future* (pp. 61–76). Dordrecht: Kluwer Academic Publishers.

Giner, S., & Pérez, M. (Eds.). (1988). *El corporatismo en España*. Barcelona: Ariel.

Hall, P. A., & Soskice, D. W. (Eds.). (2001). *Varieties of capitalism: The institutional foundations of comparative advantage*. Oxford, New York, NY: Oxford University Press.

Hall, P. D. (2006). A historical overview of philanthropy, voluntary associations, and nonprofit organisations in the United States, 1600–2000. In W. W. Powell & R. Steinberg (Eds.), *The nonprofit sector: A research handbook* (pp. 32–65). New Haven, London: Yale University Press.

Hansmann, H. (1980). The role of nonprofit enterprise. *The Yale Law Journal*, 89(8), 835–902.

Kelly, M. (2012). *Owning our future: The emerging ownership revolution: Journeys to the generative economy* (1st ed.). San Francisco, CA: Berrett-Koehler Publishers.

Kerlin, J. A. (2009). *Social enterprise: A global comparison. Civil society*. Medford, MA, Hanover: Tufts University Press and University Press of New England.

Krlev, G., Einarsson, T., Wijkström, F., Heyer, L., & Mildenberger, G. (forthcoming). The policies of social innovation—a cross-national analysis. *Nonprofit and Voluntary Sector Quarterly*.

McAdam, D., Edelman, L. B., & Leachman, G. (2010). On law, organizations, and social movements. *Annual Review of Law in Social Science*, 6, 653–685.

Merlo, A., & Turrini, A. (2002). 'L'impegno del nonprofit culturale': (The commitment of arts nonprofit organizations). In AA.VV. (Ed.), *La valorizzazione del Patrimonio Culturale per lo Sviluppo Locale: Primo Rapporto Annuale Federculture* (pp. 24–36). Milan: Touring University Press.

Newman, J. (2004). Modernizing the state: A new style of governance. In J. Lewis & R. Surender (Eds.), *Oxford scholarship online: Welfare state change: Towards a third way?* (pp. 69–88). Oxford: Polity Press.

OECD—Organisation for Economic Co-operation and Development. (2006). *Improving financial literacy: Analysis of issues and policies*. Financial Market Trends (No. 2005/2).

Putnam, R. D., Leonardi, R., & Nanetti, R. (1993). *Making democracy work: Civic traditions in modern Italy*. Princeton, NJ: Princeton University Press.

Ragin, C. C., & Becker, H. S. (1992). *What is a case? Exploring the foundations of social inquiry*. Cambridge: Cambridge University Press.

Restakis, J. (2010). *Humanizing the economy: Co-operatives in the age of capital*. Gabriola Island: New Society Publishers.

Rhodes, R. A. W. (2001). *Understanding governance*. Buckingham: Open University Press.

Roelants, B., & Sanchez Bajo, C. (2011). *Capital and the debt trap: Learning from cooperatives in the global crisis*. New York, NY: Palgrave Macmillan.

Salamon, L. M. (1995). *Partners in public service: Government-nonprofit relations in the modern welfare state*. Baltimore: Johns Hopkins University Press.

Salamon, L. M., & Anheier, H. K. (1996). *The emerging nonprofit sector: An overview*. Manchester: Manchester University Press.

Salamon, L. M., & Anheier, H. K. (1998). Social origins of civil society: Explaining the nonprofit sector cross-nationally. *VOLUNTAS: International Journal of Voluntary and Nonprofit Organizations*, 9(3), 213–248.

Schneider, M., & Paunescu, M. (2012). Changing varieties of capitalism and revealed comparative advantages from 1990 to 2005: A test of the Hall and Soskice claims. *Socio-Economic Review*, 10(4), 731–753.

Smith, A. (2011). The transition town network: A review of current evolutions and renaissance. *Social Movement Studies, 10*(1), 99–105.

Smith, S. R., & Grønbjerg, K. A. (2006). Scope and theory of government-nonprofit relations. In W. W. Powell & R. Steinberg (Eds.), *The nonprofit sector: A research handbook* (pp. 221–241). New Haven, London: Yale University Press.

Snow, D. A., & Trom, D. (2002). The case study and the study of social movements. In B. Klandermans & S. Staggenborg (Eds.), *Social movements, protest, and contention: Vol. 16. Methods of social movement research* (pp. 146–172). Minneapolis: University of Minnesota Press.

Spear, R., & Bidet, E. (2005). Social enterprise for work integration in 12 European countries: A descriptive analysis. *Annals of Public & Cooperative Economics, 76*(2), 195–231.

Steinberg, R. (2006). Economic theories of nonprofit organizations. In W. W. Powell & R. Steinberg (Eds.), *The nonprofit sector: A research handbook* (pp. 117–139). New Haven, London: Yale University Press.

Steward, F. (2012). Transformative innovation policy to meet the challenge of climate change: Sociotechnical networks aligned with consumption and end-use as new transition arenas for a low-carbon society or green economy. *Technology Analysis & Strategic Management, 24*(4), 331–343.

Tansey, O. (2007). Process tracing and elite interviewing: A case for non-probability sampling. *Political Science and Politics, 40*(4), 765–772.

Turrini, A. (2009). *Politiche e Management Pubblico per l'Arte e la Cultura. Biblioteca dell'economia d'azienda.* Milano: EGEA.

Turrini, A., & Irigoyen, J. M. (2010). From pioneers to partners? Arts and cultural policies and the third sector in Italy. In A. Evers & A. Zimmer (Eds.), *Third sector organisations facing turbulent environments: Sports, culture and social services in five European countries* (pp. 89–106). Berlin: Nomos.

United Nations. (1987). *Our common future: Report of the world commission on environment and development.* Transmitted to the General Assembly as an Annex to document (No. A/42/427).

The United Nations Conference on Environment and Development. (1992). *The Rio declaration on environment and development.* Rio de Janeiro: United Nations.

Vaughan, S. K. (2010). The importance of performance assessment in local government decisions to fund health and human services nonprofit organizations. *Journal of Health and Human Services Administration, 32*(4), 486–512.

Verschuere, B., Brandsen, T., & Pestoff, V. (2012). Co-production: The state of the art in research and the future agenda. *VOLUNTAS: International Journal of Voluntary and Nonprofit Organizations, 23*(4), 1083–1101. https://doi.org/10.1007/s11266-012-9307-8

Walker, J. L. (1991). Interests, political parties and policy formation in the American democracy. In D. T. Critchlow & E-W. Hawley (Eds.), *Federal social policy: The historical dimension.* Pennsylvania: Pennsylvania State University Press.

Weisbrod, B. A. (1977). *The voluntary nonprofit sector: An economic analysis.* Lexington, MA: Lexington Books.

Wyler, S. (2009). *A history of community asset ownership.* London: Development Trusts Association.

Yin, R. K. (2003). *Case study research: Design and method* (3rd ed.). Los Angeles, London, Neu Deli, Singapur: Sage Publications.

Young, D. R. (2000). Alternative models of government-nonprofit sector relations: Theoretical and international perspectives. *Nonprofit and Voluntary Sector Quarterly, 29*(1), 149–172.

Part II

The Evidence

Social Innovation and Actor
Involvement (Empirics)

4 Social Innovation in Arts & Culture

Place-Regeneration Initiatives Driven by Arts & Culture to Achieve Social Cohesion

Giulia Cancellieri, Alex Turrini, María José Sanzo Perez, Noelia Salido-Andres, Jeanet Kullberg, and Aurélie Sara Cognat[1]

Introduction

Arts & Culture emerge as a particularly fruitful field for the development of social innovation and civic engagement. First, the arts—by their own nature—are likely to establish meaningful forms of dialogue among different societal actors. Second, the remarkable changes experienced by such sector during the last decade have paved the way for cultivating innovative (social) experimentations—in light of the deeply renewed roles of the pivotal actors involved. Such new experiences include the implementation of institutionalized forms of enlarged corporate governance (e.g., participative foundations), the sharing of decisional power on production and funding through online platforms (e.g., crowdfunding and crowdsourcing) and new forms of participative governance and self-government mechanisms by socio-cultural movements.

This chapter focus on a particular type of trend characterizing the artistic and cultural field, presenting the evolution of the social innovation stream of "place-regeneration initiatives driven by arts and culture to achieve social cohesion".

Such initiatives occurred since the 1960s, but nowadays they are blossoming throughout Europe also because of their greater media and institutional attention. We label this phenomenon as an "innovation" as it has shifted the attention from the economic to the social impact of place rejuvenation in depressed urban setting. Culture-led regeneration projects are no longer intended only as vehicles of neighborhood urbanistic amelioration or local economic development of distressed urban areas, but also as a means to produce social cohesion (defined as the on-going process of developing a community of shared values, shared challenges and equal opportunities based on a sense of trust, hope and reciprocity; see Jeannotte, 2000).

We therefore explore the evolution of this social innovation stream in a comparative and dynamic way. More specifically we analyze which initiatives and which actors contributed to the development of the stream over time in different geographical settings located in Italy, Spain, the Netherlands and France. The study aims at assessing common trends or constraints in the spreading of this social innovation in the arts and cultural field.

Central Concepts

Urban Setting

Over the last decades, urban and cultural studies have put much emphasis on the use of culture as a means to regenerate declining urban areas (Ebert et al., 1994; Bianchini, 1993; Bailey, Miles, & Stark, 2004). Within this perspective, studies have largely focused the attention on the use of cultural initiatives as a driver for urban regeneration resulting in the enhancement of the image of areas that have suffered from structural declines. The economic resurgence of these neighborhoods have typically occurred through the attraction of investments from outside, economic diversification and employment (Booth & Boyle, 1993). Most of these studies have focused on place regeneration as the outcome of artistic initiatives and projects, mainly concentrating the attention on the economic impact and broad social benefits produced by these initiatives in terms of overall improvement in the quality of life of residents (Betterton, 2001, p. 11).

By contrast, the use of culture-led place regeneration as a means to achieve social outcomes in terms of social cohesion and integration has been still an under-examined and emerging phenomenon.

Place Regeneration

We label this phenomenon as a social innovation for two main reasons. First, it shifts the attention from the economic to the social impact that cultural and artistic initiatives may have on depressed urban settings, uncovering how culture-led regeneration can be understood not only in terms of a physical and economic improvement of distressed urban areas but also as a means to produce social cohesion. Second, it highlights a new, different role of culture-led urban regeneration considered as the means through which social cohesion and integration can be pursued. This new perspective on cultural-led urban regeneration departs significantly from previous ones (which, as mentioned, has extensively been analyzed by urban and social studies) (Florida, 2003; Landry, 2012). We define social cohesion as the ongoing process of developing a community of shared values, shared challenges and equal opportunities based on a sense of trust, hope and reciprocity (Jeannotte, 2000). Drawing on this definition of social cohesion theorized by Jeannotte (2000) and Jenson (1998) we describe the most relevant of dimensions of social cohesion driven by culture-led urban regeneration as follows:

- *Belonging* is what makes people feel they belong in a deep and permanent way to a specific group, community or even to a project, an ideal or an aspiration. Culture-led urban regeneration initiatives can enhance the feeling of belonging of people living in areas subject to regeneration by fostering their cooperation in shaping the identity (in terms of values, norms and social challenges) and the future of the local territory where they live.

- *Inclusion* refers to a reduced social exclusion of socially fragile targets (young, unemployed people, immigrants). Social exclusion is the process by which individuals or entire communities of people are systematically blocked from (or denied full access to) various opportunities and resources that are normally available to members of a different group, and which are fundamental to social integration within that particular group (e.g., employment). Culture-led urban regeneration initiatives can therefore reduce social exclusion by developing knowledge, competences and skills of disadvantaged targets in degraded districts of a city, enhancing their education, their professional training in the artistic field and opening new professional opportunities for them.
- *Participation* can be a way to stimulate civic engagement and active involvement of local residents in the life of their communities. This outcome can be achieved by culture-led urban regeneration initiatives through the active involvement of different targets of residents in creative processes, stimulating their willingness to be at the center of the life of their communities.
- A key part of social cohesion, as expressed by Jenson (1998), is nurturing those institutions that contribute to, rather than undermine, practices of recognition of differences. In this scenario, social cohesion stems from the promotion of *diversity* both in terms of different ways of life and in terms of different forms of artistic expressions. This outcome can be achieved through cultural and artistic initiatives that elicit the understanding and the appreciation of different forms of culture rooted in highly heterogeneous cultural milieu.

Given the lack of studies focused on the role of culture as a driver of social cohesion in deprived urban areas, we explore the evolution of this social innovation in a comparative and dynamic way. More specifically we analyze which policies and which actors contributed to the development of the stream over time in different geographical settings. The study aims at assessing common trends or constraints in the spreading of this social innovation in the arts and cultural field.

Methods

To analyze the social innovation stream, the research team in charge of conducting the analysis in different countries (Italy, Spain, France and the Netherlands) collected relevant data to monitor its evolution locally, following a two-step procedure. The first one was focused on the identification of the most relevant policies and events shaping the development of the stream in each country. In the second the analysis of the relevant institutional and organizational actors involved in the development of the social innovation stream was carried out.

The first step was critical to draw a meaningful picture of the normative pillar driving the social innovation in the geographical area selected by each research team. In this regard, each country selected a specific geographic area where to conduct the study. The selected areas of interests were Milan (Italy), Lugo (Spain), Paris (France) and Rotterdam (the Netherlands). The choice of the area was mainly driven by its prominence and relevance in terms of size and overall stage of development of the innovation stream within the countries. To identify the relevant policies (that the team conceives as initiatives and courses of action developed by different stakeholders together), each team was provided with consistent temporal and content criteria. First, policies should be related to place regeneration (e.g., laws regulating the (re)use of public spaces, setting up new bodies or establishing networks with actors involved in culture-led place regeneration). Second, policies had to be developed in the geographical area of interest in the last 10 years, i.e., within the timeframe 2005–2015. To retrieve information on the relevant policies, two main sources of data were used. First, interviews were conducted with key actors at the institutional level relevant for the geographical area selected by each team. Interview data were complemented with archival analysis performed on a selected number of key documents, including open calls, institutional documents, regulations, laws, etc.

Table 4.1 reports the structure of the interview guide to uncover the most relevant policies (step 1—questions 1–3, 5) and also includes a focus on actors further examined in the second step of the analysis described in the following (question 4). These actors facilitated the emergence and diffusion of cultural initiatives to improve social cohesion in places subject to urban regeneration.

Table 4.1 Structure of interview guide for process tracing

1.	What policies in (country) from 2005 to 2015 have contributed the most to the emergence and diffusion of cultural activities aimed at fostering social inclusion?
2.	What events (social, economic and political) have influenced the development of those policies?
3.	What policies—if any—adopted by other levels of government (e.g., regional and national) have affected (either positively or negatively) the policies defined in the questions above?
4.	What local actors have played the most central role in the definition and implementation of those policies? • Which among them come from the public sector? • Which ones are from the private sector? • Which ones are from the third sector?
5.	What are the critical issues that may arise in the implementation of those policies?

The second phase was devoted to the analysis of the relevant actors involved in the development of the social innovation stream for data collection. The research teams were interested not only in service providing agencies, but also in political actors, advocates, legislators and other actors that contributed to the formulation, adoption, implementation and diffusion of the policies identified. To retrieve information on the relevant actors, semi-structured interviews were conducted with stakeholders belonging to both the public, private and third sectors.

Each research team conducted a number of interviews with relevant actors who have been considered appropriate to the stage of the social innovation in the specific country. Each team was also provided with a common template for collecting information (name, position, competence, date of the interview) of the interviewed relevant actors.

Table 4.2 summarizes the list of relevant actors interviewed in each country.

Table 4.2 Relevant actors interviewed in selected countries

Country	Relevant actors
Spain	Pilar Gonzalo (Director at Good Practices and Culture Forum)
France	Éléonore de Lacharriere (Chief Executive, Fondation Culture et Diversité)
	Marie Beaupré (Head of Development and Local Action, DRAC Ile-de France)
	Chantal Bonneau (Head of Finance and Administration, Directorate CTSY, Greater Paris)
	Clément Lavault (Director, Youth Mission, Virofilay-Chatillon in the Greater Paris Region)
	Marie-Laure Cherel (Head of Public Involvement, Dir. of Cultural Affairs, City of Paris)
	Céline Pigier (Founder, Le Hazard Ludique)
	Sophie Le Coq (Maitre de Conferences at Universite de Rennes II)
The Netherlands	Sandra Trienekens (Lector at University of Amsterdam and the Academy of Holland)
	Eugene van Erven (Professor Arts and Society, Utrecht University)
	Joop Vaissier (artist and project leader of a community arts program in Delft)
	Karel Wintering (past project leader at the Kunstgebouw Zuid Holland)
Italy	Bertram Niessen (President and Scientific Director of Che Fare)
	Roberta Franceschinelli (Culture and Communication Web Director, Unipolis Foundation)
	Daniela Benelli (councilor for the development of the metropolitan area of the city of Milan)
	Cosimo Palazzo (coordinator councillorship for social policies)
	Andrea Rebaglio (Vice-director of Cariplo Foundatio)
	Silvia Tarassi (consultant at the arts and culture department of the city municipality)

Tracing the Social Innovation Stream

We might highlight common traits (but also some relevant differences) when tracing the steps leading to the emergence and development of the identified social innovation stream (*social cohesion in contexts of culture-led urban regeneration*) across the different countries involved in our study. For what concerns the Italian case, the evolution of the stream has predominantly revolved around the emergence of bottom-up cultural projects aimed at social cohesion in contexts of urban regeneration, initiated and carried out mainly by non-profit and for-profit organizations. The emergence of these initiatives was fostered by effective urban regeneration policies developed by the city municipality through the consultation of the Milanese citizens. Beside its role as policy-maker, the city municipality was also playing an important role in promoting cultural entrepreneurship initiatives by increasing its support to these organizations together with private grant-making organizations. Contrary to the Italian case, in the Spanish one, the social innovation stream emerged and developed as a cross-sector partnership between public and third sector organizations that cooperated in the co-creation and co-development of cultural initiatives with a strong social vocation. This occurred through the involvement of non-profit organizations that operate in the social field in the activities of a public network of museums. Indeed, private third sector organizations played a fundamental role in increasing the public organizations' understanding of the social issues recognized as in need of actions. The local public administration contributed to the stream with a role of institutional support to the network. As in the Spanish case, the evolution of the stream in France was characterized by both bottom-up and top down logics. However, instead of revolving around a partnership between public and non-profit organizations (as in the Spanish case), in this context the activities were focused on the emergence and development of culture-led place rejuvenation initiatives undertaken either by non-profit or public sector organizations. While in Italy and Spain, local public administrations played a relevant role in supporting the evolution of the stream, the French model of evolution of the stream has been characterized by the important contribution and interplay of different levels of government (both national and local) in creating stability and allowing organizations active within the stream to survive and grow. Also in the Netherlands, the evolution of the stream has predominantly focused on bottom-up initiatives initiated and managed by third sector organizations. However, unique to the Dutch case, we might highlight the role of housing associations, private organizations in charge of funding and providing buildings and spaces for art initiatives in neighborhoods.

On a more important note, the evolution of the stream presents different degree of disruptiveness with respect to previous place regeneration initiatives in the different countries involved in the study. In Spain, France and in the Netherlands the innovation stream has evolved slowly and incrementally while in Italy the social innovation brought a faster and radical departure compared with previous place rejuvenation activities. This transformation implies a radical change in the cultural activities or *genres* proposed to bring social cohesion in contexts of urban regeneration, in the social objectives pursued as well as in the process through which these activities are conducted. In most of the countries the social innovation stream is in the sustaining phase as newly formed organizations and projects need to become more economically sustainable over time and at the same time, successful mechanisms should be put in place to strengthen their diffusion and scalability.

SI Stream in Milan, Italy

Milestones

Since 2011, Milan has been able to experiment with social innovation initiatives in the form of culture-led urban regeneration initiatives aimed at social cohesion due to the development of a series of public policies put in action by the city municipality. The speed of diffusion of the innovation stream has been quite high and now these newly formed initiatives need to become more economically sustainable over time and at the same time, successful mechanisms should be put in place to strengthen their diffusion and scalability. The most important milestones that shaped the evolution of the stream in Italy are reported in Figure 4.1.

As mentioned before it was the new left-wing coalition governing the Municipality of Milan which directed a new attention to the necessity to rejuvenate degraded urban spaces. This started from the recognition of a social problem: the presence of a huge number of empty and abandoned public spaces (e.g., empty buildings and offices, abandoned railroads and disused farmsteads) in degraded urban areas that could have been used as places for the implementation of cultural initiatives aimed at fostering socialization among citizens and for community building initiatives. Although those spaces were sometimes occupied by associations and foundations which had their legal headquarters there, cultural and social activities targeting the local community were very rarely implemented and offered inside them. Indeed, before 2011 policies for the allocation of public spaces to non-profit and commercial organizations have mainly favored criteria such as the status, age and size of those organizations while the nature, quality and frequency of the projects that those organizations would have conducted inside the assigned spaces played a more marginal role. The rise of a new coalition governing the city of Milan marked a shift in the social policy which resulted in an increased attention to the social needs of economically and socially fragile and disadvantaged people. In particular, the increasing economic and social inequalities among citizens led to the emergence of new

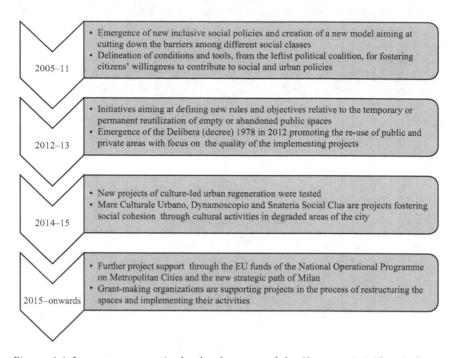

Figure 4.1 Important events in the development of the SI stream in Milan, Italy

inclusive social policies targeting all citizens and aiming at cutting down the barriers among different social classes. A new way for addressing citizens' need for social services emerged. This model put people and their needs at the center and recognized the necessity for citizens to be part of a network of social ties that could protect them from isolation. The model was particularly suitable to serve the needs of citizens located in the poorest or most degraded areas of the city where the necessity to activate mechanisms of solidarity and socialization by creating connections among people from different social, urban and cultural milieu was more urgent.

Civil society increasingly manifested the desire to participate with concrete ideas and projects to the processes of social and urban development of the city and to the redefinition of the criteria for the allocation of public spaces. The new left/social democratic political coalition started to delineate the conditions and the tools that could foster citizens' willingness to propose new ideas and to contribute to the definition and implementation of social and urban policies. In this regard, the local government started to think and act as a facilitator for the definition of new ideas and projects proposed by citizens who expressed the desire to participate in the development of their local community. New events and open public debates were organized in order to make politicians meet informal groups and non-profit organizations to discuss citizens' social needs and possible solutions to address them. If new ideas of services that could improve people's lives or foster cohesion came up, the government set up public procedures (through public announcement) to select organizations (and projects) able to transform those ideas into everyday practice.

The next phase of the evolution of the social innovation stream was related to the events that led to the emergence of new ideas about how to deal with the problem of social cohesion in contexts of urban regeneration. It included a series of events such as workshops, open debates, co-working activities where politicians asked citizens to help them in the design of new criteria to guide the allocation of abandoned or underused public spaces and to select cultural projects that could have a social impact on distressed urban areas. Those initiatives were aimed at defining new rules and objectives relative to the temporary or permanent reutilization of empty or abandoned public spaces. The ideas that arose during those events were systematized in the *Delibera (decree) 1978* in 2012. This decree marked a radical shift in the allocation of the spaces and a new attention to the implementation of projects aimed at promoting the re-use of public and private areas that have been left abandoned, underused. The new criteria were focused on the quality of the projects that should be implemented inside the spaces rather than on the prestige or status of the organization to which the space was assigned. Some spaces began to be temporarily assigned free of charge to organizations that had presented a high-quality project of social and public interests together with a detailed planning of the activities to be realized as part of those projects. The temporary re-use (free of charge) of the space could have been renewed after presentation of a new activity plan. In this regard, the decree opened the possibilities for different types of entities (organizations, informal groups, single citizens) to participate and to receive a space. At the same time, it rewarded the most interesting and creative projects (in terms of objectives, activities and impact on the local residents' quality of life). One of the innovative traits of the decree was also the possibility for creative start-ups or informal groups of citizens who had not started their own business or entrepreneurial activity yet to receive a space after having presented a project with a high social potential.

The previously defined events and conditions (summarized in stage 1 and 2) triggered the emergence of new ideas and projects to foster social cohesion through cultural activities in degraded areas of the city. From 2012 new projects on social cohesion in contexts of culture-led urban regeneration started to be tested. The most relevant projects in terms of size and impact on the respective local communities are presented next:

- **Mare Culturale Urbano.** In 2014, Mare Culturale Urbano, an innovative start up with a social vocation, received spaces by the Municipality of Milan for the development of pioneering projects aimed at the requalification of an urban area near an abandoned bus station (Area 7, Milan). Mare became soon a point of reference to bring the theme of social innovation from theory to practice through complementary competences and the capacity of experimentation on abandoned urban spaces. It operated in a district that included several heterogeneous but close local communities: San Siro, Quarto Cagnino, Cenni di Cambiamento (a co-housing initiative). These communities were characterized by the presence of low-income residents, immigrants (a huge presence of Arabic population) and other economically and socially fragile targets. Mare was attempting to break down the barriers between different targets and to foster community building processes through cultural initiatives that enhance the sense of belonging of local residents to their communities. Those cultural productions have encompassed theater, dance, concerts, cinema and often implied the active involvement and participation of the local communities (citizens, groups of associations) and a common reflection upon the identity of the places where these communities were located.

- **Dynamoscopio.** Still now Dynamoscopio is an interdisciplinary association involved in research and cultural production. It operates within the Giambellino-Lorenteggio district in the city of Milan, a district characterized by the presence of different ethnicities and foreign communities and strong cultural barriers between them. The association wants to work with all ethnicities to understand the expression of their needs and build bridges between them. At the same time, the organization tries to rebuild a system of interchange between the center and the periphery of the city of Milan which is one of the most critical issues of the Milanese reality. In 2014 Dynamoscopio launched a project to regenerate the Giambellino-Lorenteggio Market. The project's objective aimed at creating a space for cultural production hosted by the market of Lorenteggio-Giambellino. A series of cultural events and workshops were planned to take place inside the market together with its conventional commercial activities. It was a pioneeristic experience of cultural and communitarian welfare, based on accessibility, coproduction of culture, and distribution of economic resources to be invested in social and economic activities.

- **Santeria Social Club** is a private for-profit organization that received a space (an ex-car dealer) from the Municipality of Milan and transformed it into a cultural factory where a variety of shows, workshops, educational and other artistic initiatives are offered to a very broad audience ranging from 25 to 55 years old, coming from all areas of the city of Milan. Santeria's cultural offering mainly revolves around the production and distribution of high-quality events that are conceived as new and can help in attracting and educating people to artistic innovation while at the same time offering possibilities for aggregation and socialization.

Although high-quality projects have started to be prototyped and tested since 2014, economic difficulties have often posed constraints on their further expansion and development. In this respect, the most important problem has been connected with the high expenses that organizations had to bear to restructure the spaces where they operate. This in turn has obstructed their ability to realize the full cultural and social potential of their projects on a long term basis.

A further concern is related to the fact that young entrepreneurs who have taken the risk of initiating their own cultural and social activities to reactivate urban spaces often needed to receive a support by the city municipality beyond the allocation of the space free of charge. This support has also encompassed technical, administrative and promotional aspects that are essential to enhance the projects' success. Moreover, the organizations responsible for the development of the projects are often reported to have encountered troubled experiences with the bureaucracy that have obstructed their innovation efforts.

Over the last years, the municipality of Milan has started to address these issues. First, it used the European funds of the National Operational Programme on Metropolitan Cities (PON)—whose function is to make metropolitan cities more socially inclusive and connected to each another—to support some of the organizations to whom it assigned spaces in the process of restructuring the buildings.

Second, the municipality started a new strategic path built around its role as facilitator in providing organizations active within the stream with reinforced support in terms of visibility, legitimacy, technical resources and competences. This enhanced visibility and legitimacy may enable these organizations to attract the support of other actors and to attract further resources essential to the success of their activities.

Grant-making organizations (e.g., the banking foundation Fondazione Cariplo, Unipolis Foundation, the association Che Fare) are also playing an important role in supporting the success of culture-led urban regeneration initiatives aimed at social cohesion. Over years, and in particular from 2015, grant-making organizations have strengthened their support to projects that they deem valuable by helping young cultural entrepreneurs in the process of restructuring the spaces and, more broadly, in the implementation of their activities. Both Dynamoscopio and Mare's activities, for example, are supported by Cariplo Foundation, the major banking foundation in Italy. In addition, Dynamoscopio also received the support of "Culturability", the initiative through which Unipolis Foundation selects and finances projects aimed at promoting social inclusion, solidarity and new professions through the passion and concrete vision of young entrepreneurs.

Actors and Interplay

The following groups of stakeholders played the most important roles in the previously described evolution of the social innovation:

- **Public administration** is the main public actor that supported the development of the stream in Milan is the local government coalition that governed the city from 2011 to 2016. The municipality played a complex, multidimensional role in the evolution of the social innovation stream as it pursued different types of actions that lie in the areas of policy-making, facilitation and support to innovative organizations and projects. First, the municipality created the conditions for non-profit and for-profit private organizations and informal groups of citizens to develop culture-led urban regeneration projects aimed at social cohesion. In this respect, it played the role of facilitator of civic engagement by enabling the engagement and active participation of citizens in the definition of policies concerning the regeneration of distressed areas of the city. Second, the municipality actively supported the development of bottom-up initiatives undertaken by informal groups, new organizations and innovative start-ups with a social vocation by assigning spaces in need of regeneration free of charge and by monitoring the development of the projects to be implemented inside those spaces. Finally and more recently, the municipality has increased the provision of financial, technical, and promotional support for the previously described initiatives acting as a broker to foster information exchange, cooperation and knowledge sharing among the different actors (organizations and groups of citizens) active in the system. In doing so, it gives its contribution to overcome difficult operating conditions (technical, bureaucratic, legal) and the scarcity of financial resources that sometimes reduces the potential impact of social innovation initiatives within the stream.
- **Private, grant-making organizations** such as banking foundations, corporate foundations (e.g., Cariplo and Unipolis Foundations) engaged with grant-making activities to the arts and cultural field, and non-profit organizations with the mission of providing support to the development of culture-led urban regeneration initiatives aimed at social cohesion (e.g., Che Fare). These organizations played an important role by launching calls for innovative projects with a strong social impact that are financially and technically supported by them. Over years, those organizations have strengthened their commitment to sustain the stream which is testified by their reinforced financial and technical support (in terms of mentoring and training) to the organizations whose projects lie within the stream. The support offered by these organizations is not occasional. Evidence of their long term engagement can be found in the long term oriented nature of the initiatives launched by these organizations. For example, starting from 2013 the Unipolis Foundation

has begun to select high-quality projects that attained the objective of urban and social renewal through socially and culturally meaningful projects developed by entrepreneurs aged under 35. The initiative, called "Culturability", enabled the six most interesting projects (judged and evaluated by experts) to be supported by a contribution of almost 40,000 euros along with 20,000 euros to fund planned activities. The projects, selected from among almost 1,000 from across Italy, should have demonstrated their ability to foster creativity and know-how, helping citizens enjoy their territory and exploiting the many buildings that are often abandoned and run down. Over the last years, the foundation has increased its total financial contribution to these social innovation initiatives which have moved from 300,000 to almost 400,000 euros per each edition.

- **Citizens, informal groups and organizations** manifested an increased willingness to participate with concrete ideas and projects to the process of social and urban development of the city of Milan. This results in their active participation and contribution in the design of new criteria for the allocation of abandoned public spaces in the city and fosters their willingness to design and develop innovative cultural projects aimed at social cohesion in degraded areas of the city. In this respect, new organizations and projects have emerged with the experimental purpose to test and implement new ideas about how to produce cultural initiatives in places in need of urban regeneration to achieve social cohesion objectives in terms of belonging, inclusion, participation and diversity.

SI Stream in Lugo, Spain

Milestones

The case of Spain revolves specifically around place rejuvenation initiatives of old and peripheral cities driven by social museology focusing on disadvantaged publics to achieve social cohesion. This activity combines place rejuvenation issues (e.g., the new uses of public spaces or the creation of new local participatory networks) and social museology (which focus on important issues such as sustainable development of museums, social participation, awareness of social problems, urban and cultural regeneration). Within this scenario, the case under study is specifically related to the emergence and further development of a cross-sector partnership involving a provincial network of public museums and a constellation of third sector organizations. This paragraph sheds light on the most important milestones that shaped the evolution of the social innovation stream in Spain which can be summarized as follows.

The provincial museum network was created in 2006 in the province of Lugo. The central node of the network is a public sector organization, the

Museo Provincial de Lugo, which has been recently considered as one of the most socially valued museums in the country (beyond renowned national museums). The subsequent participation of third sector organizations and other civil society actors in all the public museum's network activities, from personnel management—hiring blind people as regular guides of the museum—to program design was aimed at involving different disadvantaged groups in the daily life of the museum so that art and culture become part of their lives.

Before the collaboration between the public sector organization (The Museo Provincial de Lugo) and the third sector organizations had begun, there barely existed cultural initiatives oriented to the real inclusion of vulnerable groups (i.e., in situation of or at risk of social exclusion). These segments of population have very specific needs, not only into the museum but also in relation to the access and use of other urban areas. Moreover, the emergence of this innovation is transformative with regard to previous initiatives of urban regeneration. The reason is that people with disabilities (physical, mental disability, mental disease, people suffering blindness and/ or deafness, autism, etc.) have started to be involved in the co-creation and coproduction of artistic and cultural activities.

From an organizational viewpoint, a key milestone related to the social innovation stream was the creation of the Department for Accessibility and Different Capabilities of the provincial museum network (see Figure 4.2). Regarding this issue, in October 2007 this cultural institution asked for the creation of a new department that provided a specific attention to diversity.

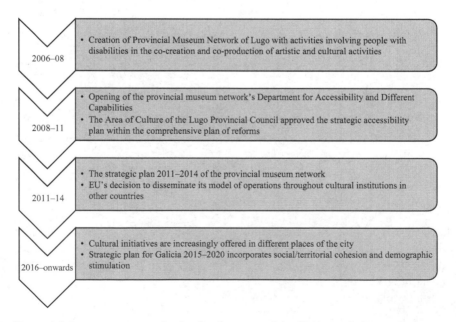

Figure 4.2 Important events in the development of the SI stream in Lugo, Spain

The Department for Accessibility and Different Capabilities was approved by the plenary of the Lugo Provincial Council on February 26, 2008. Also in the same year, the Area of Culture of the Lugo Provincial Council approved the comprehensive plan of reforms of the provincial museum in which the strategic accessibility plan was included. In this respect, people with disabilities have also started to become involved in the co-design of the accessibility of particular cultural heritage sites and buildings, together with another well-known cultural heritage area of the city of Lugo (i.e., Roman Walls of Lugo are currently accessible for people with disabilities thanks to the incorporation of an adapted lift).

The EU decided to disseminate its model of operations throughout cultural institutions in other countries such as Austria, Belgium, Italy and Sweden. Specifically, one of the purposes of the Directorate-General for Migration and Home Affairs of the European Commission is to disseminate the best practices of the provincial museum network since "it is at an advanced level in terms of managing diversity".

Further development of the museum network activities and strategic plan for Galicia 2015–2020. Besides the museum facilities, cultural initiatives have been increasingly offered in different places of the city such as open, central places with high circulation of people in Lugo (i.e., performances in high street, squares or pedestrian areas) in order to boost social cohesion in terms of diversity, belonging, participation and inclusion. An example of the latter is the collective painting on the wall of the Santa Maria Chapel during the International Day of the Forests in 2016 (artists and people with disabilities participating in a collective colorist and short-lived painting, within the inclusive campaign The Collective Forest). The strategic plan for Galicia 2015–2020 can contribute to further advance the social innovation stream as it incorporates the two objectives of social/territorial cohesion and demographic stimulation. One strategic focus is digital society, culture and reinforcement and the relevance of Galicia and its environment. The Strategic Plan of Galicia 2015–2020 intends to foster a model of economic growth based on innovation and human capital, which favors a modern, socially and territorially cohesive Galicia that allows reducing unemployment as well as increasing the productivity and welfare of the population by collaborating in the resumption of population growth and making it a territory more attractive to work, invest and coexist.

Actors and Interplay

There are basically four main categories of stakeholders involved in the aforementioned cross-sector collaborations between public sector and third sector organizations:

- The **provincial museum** as institutional node (epicenter).
- The **provincial museum network** as institutional gatekeeper. Although it started to operate informally since 2000, the provincial museum

network was formally created in 2006. It is the assigned cultural institution in charge of the main provincial cultural equipment of Lugo, having also the authority to formulate local arts and cultural policies and procedures.

• **Other public administrations.** Particularly, the Area of Culture of the Provincial Council. It acts as an institutional support for museums as social transformers, providing funding to the network, support to third sector organizations, and feedback and reports for cultural initiatives, programs, and activities.

• **Third sector organizations** (social communities and associations). Some of these have been even created as a result of meetings with the provincial museum network.

SI Stream in Paris, France

Milestones

The emergence of the stream in the French area under study, the Greater Paris Region, has its roots in the '80s when the "Friches Culturelles", cultural hubs in abandoned sites, appeared on the French cultural scene and started to be diffused. The Friches Culturelles valued the social and symbolic contributions of amateurs to the arts and created shared artistic projects between professionals and amateurs drawn from the local community. In doing so, they sought to create hybrid artworks, bridging different disciplines. The Friches were focused on the idea of imagining a more interactive and equal relationship between arts, populations and the territory. At the same time they wanted to be focused equally on artistic innovation and social inclusion. Yet, the Friches faced a constant tension between, on one hand, their desire to be a place for artistic experimentation and, on the other hand, their desire to take into account the identity and cultural concerns of the people living close to those projects. In general, for most Friches Culturelles, social cohesion came after artistic creation in a Friches hierarchy of goals. Furthermore, the engagement with the place was variable across projects. Last but not least, many of them grappled with economic difficulties which hampered their artistic and social contributions. In more recent times new public and non-profit cultural institutions with a strong orientation toward the achievement of social objectives have been founded in Paris. This was mostly due to the leadership of Mayor Bertrand Delanoë, a champion of the arts, who strongly supported the role of culture in social cohesion. Public and private actors are now working together in France to foster the development of the stream. But the overall picture is of a quiet, steady revolution, with the greater weight placed on the stream by Betrand Delanoë as Mayor of Paris between 2001 and 2012 being an exception. The social innovation in France does not seem to have been particularly disruptive, at least over the last ten years. The Friches Culturelles were presumably radical when they emerged. Today, the question is as to how the organizations active within the field can sustain their work, and to what extent they are involved in the local community. The most important milestones that shaped the evolution of the social innovation stream in France are summarized in Figure 4.3.

Under Mayor Delanoë's leadership (2001–2014), the creation of new cultural institutions to reach out to new audiences in deprived areas was strongly encouraged. In 2001, after many years of conservative rule, the socialist party took back Paris City Hall. Mayor Bertrand Delanoë opened two new cultural institutions (*établissement public culturel*) dedicated to community involvement and social cohesion, both in buildings that had fallen into disrepair. In 2007 it opened La Maison des Metallos which occupies a building that used to house the metalworkers' union before a community group bought it out with the aim of finding support to turn it into a cultural center. In 2008 it founded the Centre 104, in one of Paris' former state funeral homes. In addition to high-quality artistic programs, these organizations have dedicated outreach programs to involve people with no previous exposure to certain forms of arts and culture, and are situated in diverse, working-class districts of Paris. These organizations are largely financed by public subsidy. La Maison des Metallos, for example, receives 67% of its funding from the Paris City Hall and the Greater Paris Region. La Maison des Metallos is a particularly interesting case because it has a specific mandate to work with communities whose previous engagement in the arts has been limited, and because it is largely publicly funded. La Maison de Metallos gets two-thirds of its funding from public sources. Arguably, this makes it vulnerable to shifts in policy, but as a "Cultural Institution of the City of Paris" the city of Paris is effectively committed to fund it.

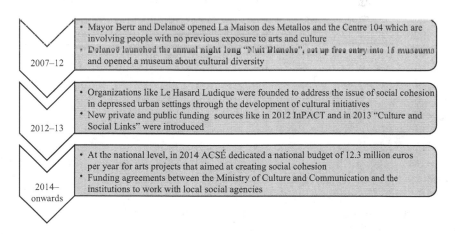

Figure 4.3 Important events in the development of the SI stream in Paris, France

Furthermore, Delanoë started to launch new cultural events, notably the annual night-long "Nuit Blanche" (which means the all-nighter), during which modern artworks and instillations were exhibited in buildings not usually used for that purpose, including churches, markets, office buildings and public buildings. Parisians can now visit those installations all night long, on a date that usually falls in October. He also made 15 museums' permanent collections free-entry and opened new museums on the themes of cultural diversity while putting in place new funding for cultural events at a local level.

At this stage of development of the social innovation, new organizations were founded to address the issue of social cohesion in depressed urban settings through the development of cultural initiatives. One of the projects that have been particularly relevant for the evolution of the stream is Le Hasard Ludique. Le Hasard Ludique is located in a former Saint-Ouen train station built in 1889 and renovated by three young Parisians. It offers artistic events with a collaborative and community building spirit. Beginning as a collaborative crowdfunding project, Le Hasard Ludique has seen 1,200 "builders" and volunteers helping with each stage of the construction and contributing with their know-how to the creation of a yearly festival. The result is a multi-functional building offering a wide range of commercial, artistic and social activities such as a restaurant, concerts and a practicing collective workshop. Le Hasard Ludique officially opened its doors to the public in 2017 after a five-year construction. It made extensive use of private funding compared with La Maison de Metallos and used digital methods to encourage participation in the construction of the project. Differently from La Maison de Metallos, Le Hasard Ludique is a société coopérative. Most of its funding sources comes from private actors even if it also receives a small contributions from the Paris City Hall. Both La Maison de Metallos and Le Hasard Ludique have a plausibly more stable and sustainable economic model than the Friches Culturelles and are more focused on achieving social cohesion outcomes.

In 2012 and 2013, new private and public funding sources were introduced to support the development of the social innovation stream and the economic sustainability of the organizations active within it. First, in 2012, the Ministry of Culture and Communication succeeded in bringing together a number of prominent corporate foundations to work with it on the arts and social cohesion. In doing so it launched InPACT endowment fund. This fund works to develop artistic creation with populations lacking access to local cultural events (regions, hospitals, prisons, etc.). InPACT is a collective that seeks to stimulate the emergence of a new form of philanthropy, working together to develop creative solutions, enabling dialogue, contributing its skills and knowledge to create an extensive network of solidarity and best practices, finding local financing sources, and boosting local and regional initiative. The companies and foundations involved include: Neufville SA, Credit Agricole, Compagnie de Phalsbourg, Groupe Dassault, Groupe Mazars, Caisse des Dépôts et Consignations, Fondation La Poste and Fondation Crédit Coopératif. Second, since 2013, the DRAC Ile-de-France—the Greater Paris Region's delegation of the Ministry of Culture and Communication— has put in place a funding stream called "Culture and Social Links" which spends about 750,000 euro each year on cultural projects looking to foster social cohesion. This funding is aimed at areas that have been identified by the Ministry of the City, Sport and Young People to be deprived and in need of additional public funding. At the national level, in 2014, ACSÉ the Agence Nationale pour la Cohésion Sociale et Égalité des Chances (The National Agency for Social Cohesion and Equal Life Chances) had a dedi- cated national budget of 12,3 million euros per year for arts projects that aimed at creating social cohesion. Since then, it has been abolished and replaced by the Comité Générale d'Égalité des Territoires (National Com- mittee for Reducing Local Inequalities), which works with the Ministry of Culture on issues of access to the arts. Their 2014–2016 joint plan contains a commitment to use the funding agreements between the Ministry of Cul- ture and Communication and the institution, including Museum and Gal- leries, to work with local social agencies as a way of reaching disadvantaged populations. Further, there is a commitment to using mediation between artists and the local community in areas undergoing urban regeneration.

Actors and Interplay

- **City/town government:** The Mayor of Paris has considerable poten- tial to affect the cultural and artistic development of the city, but also considerable latitude over the extent of his implication. It seems clear that the arrival of Bertrand Delanoë at Paris City Hall in 2001 brought about a considerable change in the cultural ecosystem, mimicking the effect of socialists elected after years of conservative rule in Nantes and Rennes.
- **Local governments:** Regional government DRAC Ile-de-France. The DRAC Ile-de-France is the Greater Paris Region's delegation of the Ministry of Culture and Communication. They are charged with imple- menting and tailoring to local circumstances the Ministry's Policy.
- **Ministry of Culture and Communication:** Founded in 1959 by General de Gaulle, the Ministry of Culture and Communication has a mandate not only to promote and conserve the arts and culture, but also to make sure that they are seen and visited. From its beginning the Ministry had a calling to democratize the arts. Today, the Ministry of Culture af- firms that interprets its mission by supporting a great variety of cultural offerings, their quality diversity and by undertaking actions to widen access to the arts. In cooperation with the Ministry for Cities, Young People and Sport, the Ministry of Culture and Communication encour- ages, under its "Culture and Urban Policy", its regional delegations, the DRACs, to take in consideration artistic projects that include a social

cohesion aspect. These projects have in common a desire to mobilize in priority people who, by virtue of their position in society, find it difficult to access cultural goods and services, reinforced by the negative image of their style of life, and also struggle to find their place in a shared vision of society.

- **Private funding:** This has come to have an important role in the development of programs which facilitate access to culture. It seems that some of them have become involved in the social innovation stream to secure their legitimacy, as much as to meet their social objectives.
- **Civil society:** This has a considerable role to play. Where cultural institutions reach out to vulnerable populations, they do not go out searching each individual themselves—they work with citizen's groups, social agencies and schools.

SI Stream in Rotterdam, the Netherlands

Milestones

The development of the stream in the Netherlands was marked by the creation of bottom-up cultural initiatives to face societal challenges, fostering the societal participation of particular target groups. Indeed, a major political ambition of the past couple of years has been to transform Dutch society into a 'participation society'. This political discourse aims to foster bottom-up solutions to major societal challenges (health care, environmental sustainability, etc.). The arts and culture sector also plays a particularly important role in this respect due to its strong potential to foster the participation and inclusion of different disadvantaged targets while improving community building actions in areas in need of urban regeneration efforts.

In 2007 it was noted that previous urban regeneration efforts in the Netherlands had not much focused on the satisfaction of social issues and challenges in many of the targeted neighborhoods (see Figure 4.4). For this reason the urban rejuvenation policy was intensified and focused on 40 neighborhoods throughout the entire country that were supposed to be ranking the lowest in terms of livability. Among these neighborhoods, no fewer than seven were located in Rotterdam, the geographical area under study. One of the characteristics of many of the chosen neighborhoods was a large representation of immigrants. The intensified 40-neighborhood program lasted for about five years. The largest financial contribution was to be made by the housing associations—private organizations in charge of funding and providing buildings and spaces for art initiatives in neighborhoods—with the central government and the municipalities contributing as well.

The Fund's policy plan for 2013–2016 included three 'renewal' programs, which involved the organization of the amateur arts and the cultural supply for the elderly and the community arts. These developments imply a shift from policies to increase the 'reach' of the cultural field to policies targeting

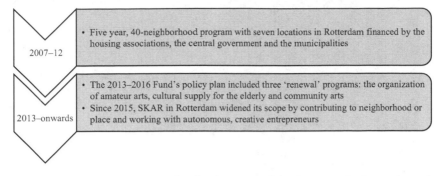

Figure 4.4 Important events in the development of the SI stream in Rotterdam, the Netherlands

'active' participation. At the same time, those policies position the cultural sector as a domain well-suited to foster the different dimensions of social cohesion including belonging, inclusion, diversity and participation. In particular culture and arts are seen as a means of fostering the general societal participation of particular target groups, and cultural policies in the Netherlands are more and more supposed to contribute to social cohesion and a sense of community.

Since 2015, SKAR, the Foundation for Art Accomodation in Rotterdam widened its scope by contributing to neighborhood or place development on the one hand and working with autonomous, creative entrepreneurs to enhance talents and opportunities of local residents on the other hand.

Actors and Interplay

- **SKAR**: Foundation for Art Accommodation in Rotterdam; the foundation used to provide studios for starting artists. It owns or manages real estate in Rotterdam and rents it out for cultural and creative use. New in its approach is that it regards what artists can do for the city rather than just the reverse. The real estate consists to a large degree of old school buildings. As this organization mediates in the use of vacant real estate, it can work towards more exclusive branding of town districts towards some creative kinds of activity. It also aims to connect the artistic performance with the local audience.
- **Dutch housing associations**: Their special position needs some explanation. They are private organizations with public tasks. These public tasks are to be performed with the assets that they built up during the many decades that they were state-led and financed. They can operate as funders for art initiatives in neighborhoods, as provider of buildings and space and as initiators in appointing artists for a contribution in the neighborhoods they manage. They own and manage substantial parts of the Dutch housing stock, especially in cities. In Rotterdam, as of

2006, over 50% of all housing stock was owned by the housing associations operating there. Since then, the number has decreased somewhat due to sales. In 2016, there were nine housing associations active in Rotterdam.

- **Municipal policy level:** Apart from the national attention for arts and culture, there is the municipal policy level for the larger cities, whereas for smaller cities the provinces act as policy agents on behalf of the municipalities. Larger cities like Rotterdam have their own four-year plans for local arts organizations. The collected municipal budgets are estimated at 1.7 billion euro yearly, which is 2.5 times the national budget. This is an estimate based on actual expenses, rather than a norm. From the lump sum that municipalities receive from national and local taxes, budgets for arts and culture are not earmarked. The municipal budgets also diminished starting 2010, which led to— among others—severe cuts in expenses in the arts, however, average expenditure on museums was exempt. This is because a fair number of larger museums had drastic and costly renovations. Despite the local budgets, local art organizations generally have to hunt for additional funds. In the Rotterdam cultural plans, subsidies are distributed among the museums, libraries, performing arts companies, film and festivals.

- **Funds:** There are a number of funds of different kinds that may be addressed to sponsor culture-led place rejuvenation initiatives. First there are the national arts funds: Fund Performing Arts, Mondiaan Fund (visual arts), Literature Fund, Architecture Fund and Fund for Cultural Participation (amateur art). Then there are national social funds which may want to grant initiatives that combine arts and culture with social goals like cohesion or enabling vulnerable groups, like the national Orange Fund (which was a present for the wedding of the current king). A variety of local private funds exists, which often have a restricted geographical range. In Rotterdam there are over 50 funds including Verre Bergen, Prins Bernhard cultural fund South Holland, Erasmusfund, Rabobank. A fair number of the 50 funds can be approached for initiatives that have to do with arts and culture or social cohesion, enabling or combinations of those.

- **Artists and residents:** In the Netherlands, artists and/or other residents are taking an active role in founding new cultural initiatives and organizations within the stream. Residents, either artists or not, can take the initiative to start a cultural facility in their neighborhood (see Box 4.1). It is then up to them to get organized and seek funding. The social capital needed to create such an initiative is unevenly spread over the city, so citizens' initiatives are less likely in the most deprived neighborhoods. Little is known so far about the sustainability of self-organizations. A condition is financial stability. Therefore initiatives are being challenged to create 'durable earning models', based on varied sources of income and self-organizations are encouraged to keep their independence and 'selfness'.

- **Volunteers:** The arts and culture sector is characterized by a high share of volunteers, which varies significantly over subsectors. Music festivals, for instance, rely on staff that consists of 84% volunteers, whereas 'only' 42% of museum employees are volunteers (OC & W, 2015). The number of volunteers in the cultural sector grew rather spectacularly between 2005 and 2011, with 75% (Van den Broek, 2014). This sector is exceptional compared to general trends in volunteering. For the volunteers the same can be said as for resident-initiators of cultural facilities. Volunteering is to some extent related to educational level and is thus less likely in deprived areas. As we will see in the cases, it is nevertheless possible.

Box 4.1   Examples of Citizen Initiatives in Rotterdam

One of the most recent self-organized cases within the stream is that of *Library-west*, a self-organization founded by residents of the neighborhood that opened in 2013 and in a few years gained a reputation as a lively, pleasant and interesting urban spot. Library-West is a public meeting place that revolves around language, literature, imagination, participation and the neighborhood. The Reading Room thereby acts as a place to find information or a good book, to work, to study or to meet friends, acquaintances and strangers. In addition, cultural activities, related to language, literature, imagination and participation are held. Each time a link is established with the neighborhood. In addition to a meeting and information function there is room for all kinds of cultural programs.

Another interesting case is the Rotterdam neighborhood theater (RNT). Its objective is to introduce theater among target groups that normally are not likely to visit the theater. RNT tries to accomplish this objective by approaching, usually through intermediary (welfare) organizations, disadvantaged groups throughout the city to let them experience culture in general and the theater in particular. This starts with talks and workshops. Those who are interested can participate as actors in a theater production about a topic that concerns them directly. Usually, this topic is related to a certain kind of problem that the target group experiences, for example discrimination, substance abuse, female circumcision, and other such personal problems that are often difficult to discuss, and the theater helps to make it a topic of discussion. By producing and experiencing this kind of community art, the target groups widen their horizons. Also, they improve their networks and relationships with other groups and individuals.

Participants are generally not familiar with this kind of art. Some will eventually start to visit regular cultural institutions like theaters on their own, for which they will get financial support in the form of a discount on the tickets.

Conclusions

Results of the examination of the development of the social innovation stream "social cohesion in contexts of culture-led place rejuvenation" in Italy, Spain, France and the Netherlands highlight two elements of concerns: the higher capacity of non-profit organizations to pursue social cohesion outcomes through cultural initiatives in contexts of place rejuvenation, and the fundamental role of public agencies in supporting or initiating the development of the stream. In Italy and in the Netherlands non-profit organizations gave the highest contribution to the stream, outperforming the commercial sector. Similarly, in Spain and in France the contribution of these organizations to the stream is relevant. Their capability of developing a huge and heterogeneous web of relationships with different kind of partners enables and accelerates the achievement of such outcome as inclusion and diversity. Their capacity to cultivate high-quality relationships with the local residents and informal groups living in the community enable them to acquire the right knowledge of the social and cultural characteristics of the territory where they operate. This in turn enables them to involve local residents in the coproduction and co-creation of projects with a strong social vocation. The local communities (citizens and associations) provide these organizations with relational competences and play the key role of connectors between these organizations and the local territory where they operate. In this regard, a network characterized by mutual trust, good interpersonal and inter-organizational relationships (at a formal and informal level) and cooperation in the development of activities with the different actors involved is fundamental in the success of the initiatives.

In most of the identified cases (Italy, Spain and France) public agencies play a relevant role in the facilitation and promotion of innovation activities undertaken by non-profit organizations. It seems that public agencies give an important contribution to the stream above all if we think at the policy method used to support cultural initiatives aimed at social cohesion in contexts of place rejuvenation. In exchange for this, third sector organizations contribute to the regeneration of spaces of the city that needed to be reopened, reactivated or restructured, while fostering community building in the local area.

Note

1. We would like to thank all who made important contributions to the ITSSOIN project deliverable that formed the basis for this chapter: Cappellaro, G.; Alvarez Gonzalez L.I.; Rey-Garcia, M.; Van den Broek, A.; Sandford, S.; and Pache, A.C.

References

Bailey, C., Steven, M., & Peter, S. (2004). Culture-led urban regeneration and the revitalisation of identities in Newcastle, Gateshead and the North East of England. *International Journal of Cultural Policy, 10*(1), 47–65.

Betterton, J. (2001). Culture and urban regeneration: The case of Sheffield. *Sub-Regional Commentary*, 11.

Bianchini, F. (1993). Culture, conflict and cities: Issues and prospects for the 1990s. *Cultural Policy and Urban Regeneration: The West European Experience*, 199–213.

Booth, P., & Boyle, R. (1993). See Glasgow, see Culture. *Cultural Policy and Urban Regeneration: The West European Experience*, 21–47.

Van den Broek, A. (2014). Nederlanders en cultuur anno 2012. The Hague: SCP.

Ebert, R., Friedrich, G., & Kunzmann, K.(1994). The creative city. *Comedia*, Stroud, UK.

Florida, R. (2003). Cities and the creative class. *City & Community, 2*(1), 3–19.

Jeannotte, S. (2000). Tango Romantica or liaisons dangereuses? Cultural policies and social cohesion: Perspectives from Canadian research. *International Journal of Cultural Policy, 7*(1), 97–113.

Jenson, J. (1998). *Mapping social cohesion: The state of Canadian research*. Canadian Policy Research Networks Study No. F-03.

Landry, C. (2012). *The creative city: A toolkit for urban innovators*. Earthscan, London.

OC & W. (2015). *Cultuur in Beeld 2015. De stad als Cultureel knooppunt*. Den Haag: Ministerie van Onderwijs, Cultuur en Wetenschappen.

5 Social Innovation for Filling the Resource–Needs Gap in Social Services

New Governance Arrangements

*Marta Rey-Garcia, Ana Felgueiras,
Annette Bauer, Torbjörn Einarsson,
and Giulia Cancellieri*[1]

Introduction

The innovation stream that is the focus of this chapter is the new governance of social services systems. By new governance of social services systems, we refer to the new ways of formulating and implementing policies and organising and controlling social services provision, which are becoming more decentralised and involve a network of interdependent, cooperative, and diverse actors from the different socioeconomic sectors (Hodges, 2005; Newman, 2004; Rhodes, 1997, 2007). These actors share goals and may, or may not, have formally prescribed responsibilities (Rosenau, 2000).

Innovative governance of social services has appeared in the context of a generalised perception that the existing models of provision are unsustainable in the long run, given the socioeconomic and demographic changes occurring across Europe for the few last decades. The ageing of the population, the integration of women in the labour market, new family models, immigration flows, new policy and regulatory frameworks and the generalised economic crisis starting in 2008 have affected both the demand and the supply of social services. In a context of escalating needs and shrinking public budgets, the gap between citizens' needs and expectations about the scope of social services and about the role of actors in the field, on the one hand; and the actual resources, capabilities and roles of funders, providers and beneficiaries, on the other hand, has broadened (Rey-Garcia & Felgueiras, 2015a).

This resource–needs gap is clearly patent in the case of social services needed by population segments that are the most vulnerable, because they depend on other people's care and/or on technical assistance to perform basic daily-life activities (mainly dependent elders, people with dementia, dependent people with chronic illnesses, and/or dependent people with disabilities).

Hence, changes are taking place in the ways the systems of social services are governed, so that such resource–needs gap may be bridged for the most vulnerable citizens, and new understandings about which services should be provided, how and by whom may be accommodated. The emergent governance of the social services system builds on: (1) a re-conceptualisation of social problems; (2) attraction of new actors, resources and capabilities to the field; (3) integration of social services with proximate fields (most notably health care and social inclusion); (4) personalised care; (5) market competition; (6) cross-sector collaboration and partnerships through informal and formal networks and (7) increased participation of the beneficiaries and co-responsibility of citizens in general in configuring demand and supply (Rey-Garcia & Felgueiras, 2015b). Since these building blocks are hardly separable in the field of social service provision, they are not treated as distinct social innovations but together form a social innovation stream with different embodiments across different contexts.

Whereas this new governance of the social services systems serves as the overarching theme for the social innovations occurring in the field of social services in the four countries included in this chapter—Spain, Italy, Sweden and the United Kingdom—we have decided to focus our investigation on new governance arrangements aiming to mobilise organisational resources and capabilities for the provision of social services to vulnerable segments of population. These may manifest in increasing reach by new technologies, the extension of human resources through the engagement of volunteers, or the attraction of financial resources through new financing tools. We analyse how these result from collaborations among organisations of different sectors, and specifically try to understand the extent to which citizens participate in the social innovation stream, and the roles they participate in. Two overarching research questions have guided this chapter:

1. What does the social innovation stream look like today and how has it evolved over the last decade across its country-specific manifestations or activities?
2. Which are the most important actors involved in the social innovation activities and which are their distinctive characteristics and contributions to the broader social innovation stream?

Central Concepts and Key Questions

Civic Participation and Empowerment in Social Care

New governance arrangements in the social services system combine intra- and cross-sector competition and collaboration with increased participation of citizens in the provision of social care. The Spectrum of Public Participation developed by the International Association for Public Participation specifies a continuum of five levels of participatory processes: inform, consult, involve, collaborate and empower (Iap2, online). Collaborations between participating actors allow for (re)distributing responsibilities and roles among them (funding, regulating, delivering services, supplying technology and other inputs, receiving services, etc.) and (re)combining their distinctive resources and capabilities in order to help extend social services reach to the most vulnerable citizens. Empowerment of actors may develop as a result of these collaborative participatory processes.

The goal of empowerment, as culminating stage of the participation continuum, is to place final decision-making in the hands of citizens. They may have the power to make a limited range of decisions (e.g., on a specified issue or for a limited time), or they may have extensive decision-making powers. The rewards of an empowerment approach are often more innovative results that incorporate the knowledge of all participants as well as reduced conflict, greater ownership of outcomes and commitment to ongoing action. Therefore, empowerment goes beyond simply participating in others' activities, processes and decisions. Empowered citizens share responsibility for making decisions and accountability for the outcomes of such decisions.

Therefore, by citizen empowerment in the field of social services we refer to the processes by which people create or are given opportunities to gain increased access to social services and care, increased autonomy and influence over decisions that affect the care and services they receive, as well as increased opportunities to socialise and participate in community life. As we will see when we come to different country perspectives on our social innovation stream, citizens can participate and eventually be empowered in different roles, including those of direct or indirect beneficiaries or users (the main perspective explored for Spain and the UK), social impact investors, venture philanthropists or social entrepreneurs (Italy and also the UK), or volunteers (Sweden).

Empowerment objectives and processes in adult social care—ideas such as 'active participation', 'co-production', 'independent living', 'living with dignity', 'co-responsibility', 'self-care', 'personalisation of care'—have only recently appeared in social services discourse and activity. In the case of direct beneficiaries, they reflect both their right to participate in daily-life activities and relationships as independently as possible, and the vision of users as active partners in their own care instead of passive recipients of care. "Empowered users are more likely to avoid falling into a dependency through institutional care, more likely to make proactive decisions about their own well-being and consequently fulfill the objectives of active and healthy ageing and life extension" (European Commission, 2014, p. 44). Therefore, the logic of user empowerment stems from both ideological (the beneficiary should be an active partner rather than a passive recipient of public care) and efficiency or cost savings (delaying or avoiding institutionalisation reduces costs) motivations; and to the latter one, the economic crisis was paramount.

Methods

Case Selection

The investigation focused on specific social innovation activities in each of the four countries in order to allow for reducing the scope of the analysis to country-specific manifestations of the social innovation stream and better identifying relevant actors and their contribution to social innovation. This was particularly useful as many of the actors are large organisations with diversified fields of activity. It needs to be mentioned that social services was clearly the most diverse field in terms of potential social innovations considered. Due to the breadth of the field, it was hard if not impossible to pin down a social innovation stream that was as clearly defined as in the other fields of activity. For this reason it was important to move to more specific innovation activities in each of the countries, which are diverse at face value but share the central thread that they exemplify modes for extending available resources and capabilities and access to them by embracing new governance constellations, extending reach through mobilising technology, human resources or new modes of financing.

The selection of the social innovation activities was based on a quantitative and qualitative analysis combining the degree of innovativeness with the explanatory potential of a set of 12 social innovations (three in each country) that had been previously identified by each country partner. Concretely, we looked for social innovation activities where the object of analysis can be clearly established while being representative enough of the new governance in the social services system of each country; that take place mainly at an organisational or meso level; and whose evolutionary stage is beyond the prototyping or pilot phase (Rey-Garcia & Felgueiras, 2015b).

As for the time frame for our selection, the breeding ground for new governance arrangements for social care can be found in the last decade of the 20th century when (often inspired by what the scientific debate has called New Public Management and Public Governance) the state started to massively outsource service delivery to private non-profit and for-profit actors (Greene, 2007). Social services, in particular, became increasingly delivered by third sector organisations (TSOs) and also private firms within market logics; encompassing both competitive and collaborative schemes, and mostly financed and regulated by the state. The idea that citizens should actively participate in solving the resource–needs gap in the provision of adult social care, not only in their user or beneficiary role, but also as investors, entrepreneurs or volunteers, is clearly a new development qualifying as an innovation as judged by the experts we consulted within the given context and dating back approximately one decade.

As a result of an iterative selection process, the following social innovation activities within the broader stream were identified:

- *Spain—extending reach for independent living through telecare.* The focus is on the promotion of independent living of beneficiaries or users with the support of telecare services, broadly defined as the provision of remote social care supported by ICTs. This encompasses from the most basic format—i.e., tele-alarms, including phone monitoring and pendant buttons—to extensive daily activity monitoring, data gathering and lifestyle analysis through sensors and the Internet of Things. The Spanish system of social services to persons in situations of dependency establishes independent living ("autonomía personal" or personal autonomy) as its key stated aim, defined as "the capacity to control, face and take personal decisions, by own-initiative, about how to live in accordance to personal norms and preferences, as well as to develop basic daily life activities" (Ley, 39/2006). Aligned with the goal of independent living, home-care related services, particularly telecare, have been prioritised in Spain as an alternative to institutionalisation through residential and day-care centres. The goal of telecare is to enhance the autonomy of beneficiaries within their usual environment (home, community) by providing an immediate response to situations of emergency, insecurity, solitude or isolation.

- *UK—personalising services for people with dementia and their carers through telecare.* In parallel to the case in Spain, if with a particular emphasis on person-centred telecare for people with dementia, the UK case is about matching needs of people with technology, usually as part of a care planning process and a care package that ensures the individual needs of the person (and their carers) are met. There are a range of telecare products and assistive technologies that are considered suitable to people with dementia and their carers and may provide real benefits. Examples given included traditional telecare products such as alarms; technologies for people with mobility issues; mobile applications (new technologies); technologies for self-medication (for early onset dementia); and GPS devices. Certain devices, such as those that help people use gas or electric cookers, take medication, communicate or track their movements (through satellite) will be more suitable for people with dementia than others (for example, those that operate passively and do not require the person to press buttons). However, simply offering technical devices on a market might not be considered a social innovation although it might be considered a technological innovation.

- *Italy—extending resources for service provision through social impact investment.* In Italy, over the last few years, new movements have been lobbying for social impact investments, social entrepreneurship, philantrocapitalism and social start-ups. Impact investment is proposed as a solution for supporting the scaling up of social enterprises and social entrepreneurship and in particular for filling the resource–needs gap in social services. The Italian case focuses on the new forms of social impact investing and how they have fostered (or not) the promotion of social services for supporting (mostly indirectly) independent living of beneficiaries. Our focus is placed on new forms of investment for developing social enterprises and hybrid organisations in social and health care services. Collaborations in this country-field—mostly between businesses and TSOs—are used for investing in social enterprises (e.g., new start-ups) and for increasing capabilities of the organisations for providing new services.

- *Sweden—The use of volunteers in public organisations and activities.* The Swedish case is focussed on the phenomenon of volunteer centres, which is a quite general and widespread, although not well-known, phenomenon, which often involves both TSOs and public actors. A volunteer centre is a physical contact point or hub for people that would like to volunteer and for people that need help. Volunteer centres often both mediate volunteers directly to needing people or to TSOs and organise activities in their own premises. One important outcome of these activities is that the resource of volunteer time is made available for public and semi-public social services. Most volunteer centres en tail collaboration between municipalities and TSOs, but there are also examples involving private companies. The latter, however, seem often to be of a temporary nature and through sponsorships (Socialstyrelsen, 2007). While standard in many other European countries, volunteer centres were seen as a very new development in Sweden against a welfare provision system almost exclusively governed by the state. Through the extension of human resources and by changing the character of the help, volunteer centres were seen as extending social services reach, in parallel to how new conceptualizations of care, technological applications and financing modes have transformed the governance arrangements in Spain, the UK and Italy.

Data Collection

A combination of primary and secondary sources and methods were used for data collection, including academic and practitioner literature review, internet search, documental analysis, and face-to-face and telephone interviews to representatives of a selection of key organisational actors from different socioeconomic sectors and to renowned experts in the field. A total of 28 interviews were conducted from February to June 2016: 11 in Spain (2 to public, 2 to business, 3 to third sector, 2 to hybrid third sector-business representatives, and 2 with experts); 4 in the UK (1 business and 3 public in a dual representative-expert role); 6 in Italy (1 business, 1 third sector, 2 hybrids and 2 experts); and 7 in Sweden (2 public, 3 third sector and 2 experts). Adapted versions of the semi-structured questionnaire elaborated by the authors (Spain, Italy, Sweden) or a set of guiding (open) questions (UK) were used. All interviews consisted of open questions to a large extent, and lasted from a minimum of 15 minutes to a maximum of over 2 hours. They were conducted under conditions of confidentiality. This has led us to anonymise most of the quotes included in this chapter, in order to avoid direct identification of interviewees and their organisations. Additionally, a half-day workshop with stakeholders was organised in Spain for presenting, discussing and validating the very early findings of the research at a local level (Rey-Garcia et al., 2016).

Tracing the Social Innovation Stream

SI Stream in Spain: Extending Reach for Independent Living Through Telecare

Milestones

The Spanish Red Cross was the initiator of the idea of telecare in Spain, importing and adapting what was then perceived mainly as a technological innovation to national context in 1990:

> The Red Cross looks outside and brings telecare as a way to incorporate technology to services of much utility.
>
> (SS.5.ES9a)

Telecare grew at a fast pace in the 1990s and early 2000s with the support of state, regional and local authorities, extending its user base beyond traditional target segments (i.e., elderly people, people with disabilities and people suffering acute or chronic illness) to include women victims of gender-based violence, and advancing in terms of service standardisation and quality. The 2006 Dependency Law (Ley, 39/2006) meant the key institutional turning point of telecare as a social innovation allowing for customised services towards independent living. The principles underlined by this regulation are independent living, personalised care, deinstitutionalisation of care by keeping the beneficiary in his/her surrounding social environment, avoidance or delay of unnecessary hospitalisation and admission in residential homes, participation of businesses and the third sector in social services, and inter-agency cooperation. Following its adoption, telecare became included in the catalogue of services of the public System for Autonomy and Attention to Dependency (SAAD), as one of the services for the promotion of independent living, attention and care. The Dependency Law establishes a minimum level of protection, which is defined and financed by the central government.

After the economic crisis hit Spain in 2008 the service experienced a slowdown. Public expenditures in social services decreased and the full implementation of the Dependency Law was postponed. Incompatibilities of telecare with other entitlements increased, the entrance into the System to persons with moderate dependency was delayed, and the state level co-funding reduced. The main institutional milestones directly affecting field dynamics and telecare development are summarised in Figure 5.1.

Actors and Interplay

Telecare is mostly financed by the public sector and delivered by private organisations—business and non-profit—within the limits and conditions regulated by each regional and/or local authority. In order to be entitled to telecare within the SAAD, a person must be recognised as in a situation of dependency. The regional autonomous communities are competent to make the assessment and recognition of the degree and level of dependency, to determine the corresponding service entitlements, and to provide, manage, monitor and control such entitlements. Within this process of assessment and recognition, the corresponding social services elaborate a personalised care plan (known as PIA, "Plan Individualizado de Atención") that determines the most adequate entitlements from among the services foreseen within each degree of dependency. This legal framework materialises in a complex funding structure that makes it difficult to identify which public agency is funding telecare in each individual situation. Furthermore, a person that has not been entitled to telecare within the public system (within the SAAD or not) may contract the service directly with a private (for profit or non-profit) provider. One of the organisational actors interviewed pointed to three roles of the public sector: policy and regulatory, clients (because they contract

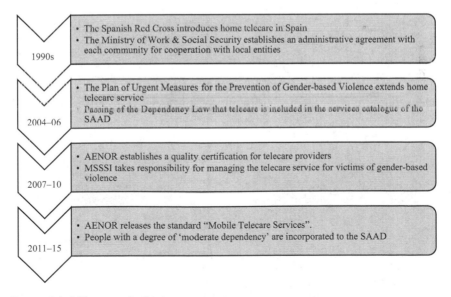

1990s
- The Spanish Red Cross introduces home telecare in Spain
- The Ministry of Work & Social Security establishes an administrative agreement with each community for cooperation with local entities

2004–06
- The Plan of Urgent Measures for the Prevention of Gender-based Violence extends home telecare service
- Passing of the Dependency Law that telecare is included in the services catalogue of the SAAD

2007–10
- AENOR establishes a quality certification for telecare providers
- MSSSI takes responsibility for managing the telecare service for victims of gender-based violence

2011–15
- AENOR releases the standard "Mobile Telecare Services".
- People with a degree of 'moderate dependency' are incorporated to the SAAD

Figure 5.1 Milestones in Spain

with private providers), and funders, commenting critically on a high public intervention in this arena as they set the criteria and decide what services correspond to each beneficiary (SS.5.ES9a).

Very few traditional non-profit organisations provide telecare services; the most relevant being the Spanish Red Cross. A few service providers adopt hybrid organisational forms, such as social enterprises. The Spanish Red Cross is not only a major service provider but also the only TSO co-developing and providing innovative telecare with social value added to a wide set of beneficiaries in a current context of business domination.

The majority of service providers are currently private companies that fiercely compete with TSOs—the major player being Tunstall, a sizeable British group supplying technology for social and health services, that recently acquired Televida, a large Spanish provider of telecare services. At the same time, businesses collaborate with TSOs in joint technological developments and also as hardware and software suppliers.

Although the social innovation was introduced and strongly influenced by a TSO—co-designing and co-developing it in collaboration with public, business and informal actors—and the service is fundamentally delivered on the basis of market competition, the overall assessment of interviewees is that the dynamics of implementation of telecare have been fundamentally top-down (SS.EXP1; SS.EXP2), being that it is currently "a hyper-regulated sector" (SS.5.ES10b). Main actors and their roles are further detailed in Table 5.1.

Table 5.1 Main actors involved in telecare in Spain

Public organisations	Public authorities at the State (e.g., MSSSI, Ministry for Health, Social Services and Equality), regional (Governments of the Autonomous Communities) and local (provincial and municipal authorities) levels and public organisms with an executing or intermediation/representation role (e.g., IMSERSO).
Third sector organisations	– Service providers: Spanish Red Cross, ASISPA. – TSOs promoting the application of technologies to social care: TECSOS Foundation (participated by the Spanish Red Cross and Spanish Vodafone).
Business organisations	– Service providers: Tunstall-Televida [a merge of the British group Tunstall (hardware and software) and the Spanish provider Televida (first private company to be granted a public contract for telecare provision in 1994)]; SARquavitae, EULEN, Atenzia. – Technology suppliers: Televés, Bosch, Vodafone.
Hybrid organisations	Service providers: Ilunion Sociosanitario belonging to ONCE (National Organization of the Spanish Blind) Corporation.
Informal actors	– Direct beneficiaries or users. – Families and other non-professional carers, grassroots organisations and informal groups.

SI Stream in UK: Personalising Services for People With Dementia and Their Carers Through Telecare

Milestones

The first use of assistive technology and care in the UK that specifically addressed the needs of people with dementia and their carers dates back to the 1990s. In 1999 the First National Carers Strategy stressed the role of telecare. The early 2000s witnessed the first telecare projects for people with dementia. During that decade the Department of Health set out guidelines to inform local authorities of the resources, systems and procedures necessary to implement telecare effectively, and provided grants to adult social services departments within local authorities to promote its widest possible use in collaboration with other agencies from the voluntary, health and housing sectors. In parallel, the Department of Health funded online information resources on assistive technologies for use by people with dementia, carers and professionals.

However, it was not until 2010 that the 'Living Well with Dementia' Strategy for England was formulated with a focus on independent living in peoples' own homes. In the early 2010s the Department of Health funded 21 pioneering research projects for people with dementia, including a study on telecare. This includes a large trial called Assistive Technology and Telecare to maintain Independent Living At home for people with dementia (ATTILA) that aims to understand whether telecare can help people with dementia living in their own homes longer and whether this is cost-effective. Main institutional milestones and regulatory milestones in the field affecting the social innovation in the UK are displayed in Figure 5.2.

Actors and Interplay

Early in this process, the provision of telecare was seen by local authority representatives as a potential way to address increasing needs of an ageing population under budget pressures. Some local authorities jumped on board quite early hoping for financial solutions for their organisation. It was considered a win-win situation. This is also how telecare has been marketed by private companies to local authorities. It is quite possible that this has stifled certain social innovations and the growth of telecare into certain markets such as the market for self-funders (as private companies saw their most immediate profits from government budgets).

However, the adoption of telecare by local authorities has been slow and incremental and it is seen as almost impossible to change things at a system level. Telecare has often been more fitted in with existing services rather than utilised as an opportunity to reconfigure services. Locally, practitioners in local authorities and social care departments sometimes resisted the change and implementation of telecare because of fears that telecare could substitute social care (and they could lose their jobs) (JW; SS.UK.EXP2).

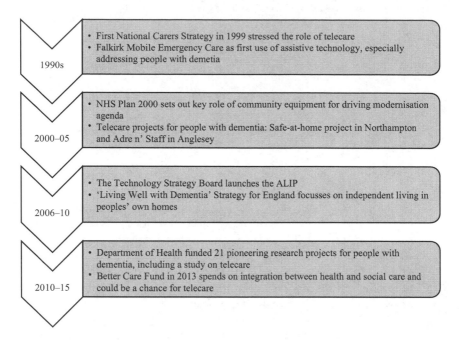

1990s
- First National Carers Strategy in 1999 stressed the role of telecare
- Falkirk Mobile Emergency Care as first use of assistive technology, especially addressing people with demetia

2000–05
- NHS Plan 2000 sets out key role of community equipment for driving modernisation agenda
- Telecare projects for people with dementia: Safe-at-home project in Northampton and Adre n' Staff in Anglesey

2006–10
- The Technology Strategy Board launches the ALIP
- 'Living Well with Dementia' Strategy for England focusses on independent living in peoples' own homes

2010–15
- Department of Health funded 21 pioneering research projects for people with dementia, including a study on telecare
- Better Care Fund in 2013 spends on integration between health and social care and could be a chance for telecare

Figure 5.2 Milestones in the UK

Private business providers were identified by all interviewees as major players and drivers of the social innovation, strongly influencing their development. Tunstall as the largest provider of telecare used to have a monopoly position and dominated the market: it was the first company providing telecare products and started with providing uniform, standardised tools (call centre alarms, falls detectors) and selling those to sheltered housing providers instead of approaching local authorities and social care departments. Although some of the dynamics on the market have changed (with smaller providers entering the market), there is a question whether in having one large provider (and lack of competition) has prevented certain types of social innovation. As one of the local authorities' representatives put it,

> the ways investments flow (from public to private sector) has stifled innovation and prevented scaling up.

Another interviewee (SS.UK.EXP2) thought that innovations in telecare sector need to be seen in the context of a dysfunctional system of care home provision (i.e., telecare products needed to allow people living in their home which was the only option for many people who could not afford quality care homes).

Research played an important role in driving and hindering this social innovation. For example, small evaluative studies from very early on demonstrated the usefulness of telecare for people with dementia and their carers. Findings from a large government funded cluster randomised controlled trial (the Whole System Demonstrator or WSD), which has looked at the (cost-)effectiveness of telecare, did not confirm health or cost benefits had a large impact on the market. Although the WDS did not specifically look at people with dementia (and in fact excluded them from the trial), it influenced the market of telecare generally across all groups. It had a "damaging effect on the business case" (SS.UK.EXP3), one local authority interviewee said. The same local authority representative thought that findings of the trial had a particularly negative impact on small providers that just had emerged and started to develop new range of products. On the other hand, the WSD also started new discussions about issues that had been raised by researchers and practitioners previously: that telecare might only be (cost-) effective if provided as part of a personalised care package that considers the individual environment of the person and family (such as their house, their lifestyle and the community they live in).

Collaborations between the private sector and the public sector were another influencing factor. One expert felt that these collaborations had sometimes a collusive nature and that boundaries were blurred (JW). For example, the Association of Directors of Adult Social Services (ADASS), the membership body of local authorities asked Tunstall Ltd. to develop the telecare strategy for local authorities. Telecare developments, as driven by those sectors, have not typically been person-centred (although some exceptions exist). Researchers had potentially an influence on driving person-centred approaches through developing and communicating evidence that suggested that telecare is only effective if it is implemented in a way that it takes account of the individuals' home environment, their needs, networks and preferences. The third sector had been traditionally largely absent from telecare developments and there is a question whether the absence of the role of the third sector could explain to some extent why person-centred telecare had fallen short.

SI Stream in Italy: Extending Resources for Service Provision Through Social Impact Investment

Milestones

Back in the 1990s, reform of the national health system included the adoption of New Public Management principles. Against this background, the Law 328/2000 officially integrated the third sector in the planning of social policies and in delivering public services. The field of social services is currently very much influenced by this legislation. The 2000s witnessed the creation of the impact investment movement in the country that participated in the G8 Task force on social impact investing, together with further innovative reforms of other related organisational forms and sectors that have accelerated in the last few years

> such as volunteering legislation, social enterprise legislation (even if it was a failure), crowdfunding and benefit corporation.
>
> (SS.IT.EXP1)

These legislative and institutional developments culminated with the 2015–2016 Law of Benefit Corporation and with third sector and social enterprise reform. They have resulted not only in strategic transformation at a field level—with the adoption of new governance arrangements, the entrance of new actors and the emergence of new shared understanding of the relationships—but also in operational changes. These comprise the import and adaptation of tools new to the field, including innovative funding instruments aimed at combining financial and social impact so that social services reach is enhanced:

> new mechanisms of social innovation based on synergies with sectors that before were not considered in the social field, such as technology, finance and new operative ways of doing enterprise.
>
> (SS.IT.EXP1)

Along these lines, the social innovation stream is trying to

> connect financial instruments with a system presenting low equity, promoting impact measurement as well.
>
> (SS.IT.EXP2)

The main regulatory and institutional milestones are summarised in Figure 5.3.

Actors and Interplay

Among the players working on promoting social service reach for vulnerable populations through social impact investment, there are traditional financial actors or for-profit organisations that are looking for new instruments to invest in fostering and developing social enterprises in the field of social services. The majority of investors are private for-profit companies that invest in equity in organisations. Furthermore, some interviewees saw in foundations and their philanthropic activities a fundamental player in the social innovation stream, given that "the traditional philanthropy that changed the way of financing" (SS.IT.EXP2) by investing not only money but also capabilities inside the organisations. Interviewees agree that business investors and philanthropic donors and grantmakers with a previous

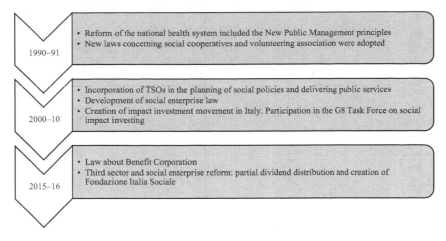

Figure 5.3 Milestones in Italy

track record in the field are the key actors driving the innovation. As high lighted by one expert

> the majority of players and partners are social service experts. There are only some new players, they are very few.
>
> (SS.IT.EXP2)

However, there is disagreement about who the other relevant actors driving the social innovation stream are, which could derive of its early stage of formation. One of the market organisations highlighted that the only other traditional actors involved are "for profit companies in microcredit, healthcare and social housing" (SS.3.IT2). Regarding new entrants in the offer side, there are

> 4–5 new impact investing funds which are willing to invest in equity. There are two funds more related to the social cooperative world. There are some social impact bonds experiences, but different from the UK ones, and there are as well some funds related only to innovative start-ups.
>
> (SS.IT.EXP1)

A key new actor is Oltre Venture, the first venture capital firm in Italy, which promotes and supports social enterprises in the fields of health care, social services and education. Regarding the demand side, almost all the organisations that receive social impact investing are business-non-profit hybrids, due to the possibilities of partially repaying equity investors—only a few

TSOs access social impact investing coming from philanthropy. The main beneficiaries of this innovation stream are thus social enterprises and social cooperatives. New investee profiles include innovative start-ups, benefit corporations or for-profit organisations with a social mission.

This very incipient social impact investment ecosystem is supported by cross-sector collaborations, including international ones. A case in point is U-Life, a start-up that won the Impact Hub fellowship programme for longer lives in partnership with AXA and Swiss Re Foundation with a project focused on the creation of a web and offline platform capable of customising holiday packages for elderly travels and fragile target categories. However, this stream is only making its first steps and "there is still a kind of mistrust among the key actors" (SS.IT.EXP1). In this context, some interviewees focussed on the important role of policy-makers or national and international institutions for governing the process of innovation and creating trust between social organisations and financial operators. Therefore, not only the role of policy-makers in supporting these instruments is very important, but also the demand side (recipient organisations and end beneficiaries) should be further taken into account if diffusion of these instruments is to be fostered. One of the experts highlighted the importance of

> opening a dialogue with the organisations that should receive financial investment. It should be an integrated system;
>
> (SS.IT.EXP1)

while another organisation highlighted the importance of involving final beneficiaries such as

> people that deal with disabilities, tourism, associations that work with people with disability because they were all important for exploring the needs and understand how to answer these needs.
>
> (SS.1.IT1)

We further detail in Table 5.2 the main types of actors involved in the social innovation.

SI Stream in Sweden: The Use of Volunteers in Public Organisations and Activities

Milestones

Under the traditional Swedish model of welfare, social services are operated by the public sector through professional, paid staff, and many citizens think that the involvement of volunteers in public welfare provision threatens such model (Frederiksen, 2015). However, in the 1990s liberal

Table 5.2 Main actors involved in social impact investing in Italy

Public organisations	Public authorities at national and international level that: – may foster the development of social impact investing in different countries in Europe – may "regulate" the agreements among beneficiaries (organisations such as social enterprises) and financial operators
Third sector organisations	– Investors: some foundations in their new philanthropic activities, e.g., those investing in U-Life – Investees: very few TSOs
Business organisations	The majority of investors are private for-profit companies that invest in equity in organisations, e.g., Oltre Venture
Hybrid third sector/market organisations	Social enterprises, innovative start-ups, benefit corporations or for-profit organisations with a social mission, e.g., Impact Hub (which functions as an innovation lab, business incubator and a social enterprise community centre) or Detto Fato

opinion-makers started to advocate for a deregulation of welfare services, and in the wake of a recent costs crisis, parts of the public debate on how to match greater demands with fewer resources have described voluntary and third sector contributions as a possible solution. This has led to more and more public organisations starting to use volunteers, often justifying it both by reducing costs and by that volunteers can bring different qualities to the work. One way of introducing volunteers into public or semi-public services is through volunteer centres providing services to third sector organisations, as well as to public sector organisations.

Volunteer centres are not a new phenomenon in Sweden, but they were largely unknown until the early 1990s, when the Centre for societal work and mobilisation (Cesam) situated in Örebro, developed a Swedish model of volunteer centres inspired in Norway and started the first (new) volunteer centre. It acted as a model for volunteer centres all over Sweden—and got State grants and contract with municipalities to develop more volunteer centres. The support and grants from State and municipal authorities was important for the idea of volunteer centres to be acknowledged and legitimised. When this new wave of volunteer centres became publicly known, more and more people and municipalities became interested (SS.1.SE6). In 2005 there are about 70 volunteer centres, most of them started and/or supported by municipalities in collaboration with the third sector (Socialstyrelsen, 2007).

In the mid-2000s there were high hopes that volunteer centres would grow into a big movement and public actors as SKL—an interest organisation for municipalities—and The National Board of Health and Welfare (Socialstyrelsen) got involved in various ways, mainly through public-non-profit partnering. However, these great expectations would never be fulfilled. First, volunteer centres became a source for controversy:

> It was a very big issue, and there were many who wondered how volunteers could be used as a resource in the welfare system. There were also discussions whether this was a way of exploiting people or if it actually could be about empowerment also for the volunteers.
>
> (SS.2.SE3)

Secondly, during the 2010s, public welfare sector deregulations have resulted in mainly commercial corporations taking over operations, while TSOs have only to small degrees been able to get contracts. Third and last, although the number of volunteer centres grew rapidly during periods when state grants were readily available, the movement does not seem to be strong enough to expand further on its own. The problem is framed by one interviewee as follows:

> The government is working in silos and we do not fit into any one of these silos. There are so many departments involved in our activities. . . . There would not be any problem if we had selected a niche. But we do not want to select a niche. We should be there for all people. We do not fit into the Swedish system.
>
> (SS.1.SE6)

Currently, the opinion that welfare services should not be left in the hands of TSOs and volunteers is still a prevailing opinion, in several respects even growing among citizens (cf. Frederiksen 2015; von Essen, Hegermalm, & Svedberg, 2015). The main regulatory and institutional milestones directly affecting field are summarised in Figure 5.4.

Actors and Interplay

The State with various authorities has probably been most important for the development of volunteer centres in Sweden, playing an important role in legitimising, raising awareness and funding some initial methods and knowledge development.

> That volunteer centres came to Sweden, I would like to say that it has to do with the serving government. That they gave money to various projects about volunteer centres and resource banks.
>
> (SS.1.SE6)

Without State support the idea would have had less chances of spreading. All interviewees agreed that municipalities have played a central

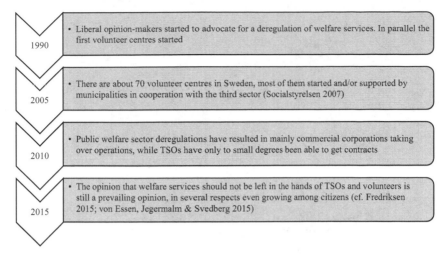

Figure 5.4 Milestones in Sweden

role by financing and operating a large share of the volunteer centres, sometimes in cooperation with one or more TSOs. General third sector umbrella organisations have impacted on the development by following it, spreading information, and arranging educational activities and seminars about third sector and volunteer management. However, the two specialised umbrella organisations for the field, Volunteer Coordinators' Federation and Volunteer Centres of Sweden, have not yet had any large visible impact on the development of the field. Networking between volunteer centres is weak.

The majority of the persons receiving help through volunteer centres have different kinds of physical or mental disabilities and many of them are older persons. Most volunteers are also older persons, people on long-term sick leave or unemployed (Socialstyrelsen, 2007). Consequently, there is a large overlap between the groups of volunteers and beneficiaries. Several of the interviewees talked about volunteering making people feel needed and useful (which suggests a contribution to empowerment of citizens, in this particular case those who volunteer). They also mention that it is quite usual that people that have visited the volunteer centres' activities turn, with time, into volunteers themselves organising activities for others (again, suggesting empowerment). One of the experts interviewed reflected over the obvious lack of private companies in the field:

> I am surprised that no one has started a company that makes money on this. Creating a business model to [convey volunteers].
>
> (SS.SE.EXP1)

Synthesis

Comparative Analysis

Levels and Dynamics of the Social Innovation

The economic crisis has intensified the understanding that new, untapped resources and capabilities had to be mobilised and alternative forms of governance (including delivery and/or funding) had to be tried out in order to maintain the level and coverage of social services. This background has largely influenced the development of the social innovation stream across the four countries. We have abstained from engaging with the exact level of the innovation taking place in the introductory chapters of this book and in the other empirical field investigations. However, given the breadth of the SI stream in social services and the exemplary activities therein, it can be useful to think about those levels and the dynamics of change across our four countries.

The telecare service, as it has been implemented in Spain, represents a combination of product/service, process and marketing innovations (following the Oslo Manual, OECD/European Communities, 2005). The evolution of that social innovation took (and is taking) place in an incremental, progressive way since the service was introduced. When it first appeared, telecare represented a new form of delivering social care to people in situations of dependency by linking beneficiaries and care providers electronically. Since then new developments have spurred social innovations, in particular the formation of actor coalitions to co-design and co-deliver social care service based on telecare technology, broadening target user groups, enlarging complementary services, or developing improved or new functionalities. As new collectives (e.g., women victims of gender-based violence, deaf people) and new needs (e.g., protection, companionship, health issues) emerge, innovations happen in the service. Technologically speaking however, it has not evolved much and remains based on standard approaches and applications. Thus, it really is the social not the technological elements that mark this development as innovative.

It is interesting to note that in the UK instead the novelty has been more on telecare as a product/service innovation and technological advancement. However, and in line with the Spanish case, innovation in telecare was more about adapting existing technologies rather than inventing new ones and the analysis will show that stakeholders thought there was generally not enough focus on process changes and on changes in reaching out to new target groups, communication, relationships and personalisation; making those elements less pronounced than in Spain. The social component seems indeed much less developed in the UK and, in general, the service seems less developed (although it was one of the countries that served as an inspiration for Spain when the technology was first imported).

In Italy, different opinions are presented concerning what kind of innovation is represented by the stream and activity. Financial organisations highlight that they work on product, process, market and organisational innovations. However, process innovation was most likely the main one. This might be due to the fact that the social innovation is still in the initial stages of development and only a few players are involved in it at the moment.

In Sweden the augmentation of personal resources through the mobilisation of volunteers has been embraced by many stakeholders concurrent with a relatively strong growth in the number of volunteer centres. It seems however, that as of today volunteer centres are now lacking in the public debate of social problems and their solutions. The interest seems to have disappeared after the government's financial support ended, which had a particular impact on the visibility of the centres with no one closing this void as of yet. In Norway and Denmark for example the idea and practices of volunteer centres seem to have been more accepted and normalised than in Sweden. One reason behind this is probably that the governments in Norway and Denmark continued to support the volunteer centre movement while the Swedish government soon seemed to lose interest followed by a reduction of available financial resources.

The Role of Socioeconomic Sectors in the Social Innovation

Generally, social services are no longer exclusively in the hands of the public sector (in cases supplemented by social action TSOs). Other socioeconomic sectors are broadening their traditional role or acquiring new ones, and citizens in general (and beneficiaries in particular) are allocated more responsibility in managing their own care, although processes towards their true empowerment seem to be at very early stages, if at all relevant.

In Italy the attention is put on alternative ways of financing social services (impact investing) and promoting the establishment of new organisational forms: social enterprises and, more recently, benefit corporations that are required to report their social, environmental and community impacts in a rigorous and transparent way. These new investment tools and organisational forms are seen as more transparent, efficient and effective, of social service provision as far as funders want to see their investments paying off.

In Sweden, given the comprehensive provision of social services funded by the State, the third sector has traditionally had an advocacy role providing social services in particular niche areas. The novelty is the introduction of volunteers as a new resource for public social services (reducing costs and enhancing citizens contribution), not without controversy.

In Spain and the UK, telecare has been introduced as a new form of delivering social services to people in situations of dependency, serving the purposes of both costs savings and beneficiary independent living. However—and surprisingly we could say, given the devastating effects of the economic crisis in Spain—it seems that the economic aspect is more dominant in the UK than in Spain. In UK, we can find a systematic concern about demonstrating cost-effectiveness of the service, which we cannot find in Spain, with an extremely complex and changing funding system.

As to actor interplay, in the case of Spain and Sweden, the dynamics of implementation are mostly top-down, politically induced or promptly appropriated and implementation sponsored and paced by public sector intervention. This very much contrasts with the UK, where the social innovation is overall perceived as a bottom-up dynamic, its advancement mostly relying on local champions. In the case of Italy, perceptions are mixed yet; the most common view is that of the social innovation following more horizontal dynamics.

The public sector has a large role as the overall legislator and regulator of the innovation in the four countries, but in Sweden this is complemented with an important role also in direct service provision. This function is pretty much absent in the other countries where public authorities do fund the services but usually contract them out to third sector, business or social economy entities. In Spain, public authorities jumped in very quickly in adopting and moving forward the innovation, while in the UK this was a very slow and incremental process. In all country cases, it is interesting to note that the social innovation seems to move forward where there is state support; that is, where the state provides a favourable regulatory and financing framework for the social innovation stream. At the same time, when state intervention moves beyond supporting or facilitating, and towards taking over the social innovation, it risks hindering it within the public sector. See, for example, the case of Spain where a very strong regulation prevents trying new things within the public social services system; however, the market is open for those who want to try new things outside the state sponsored system. On the contrary, state support seems a necessary but not sufficient condition, as societal values and norms may hinder the strength of the innovation.

Cross-sector collaboration has been key in Spain for the social innovation activity to flourish, first between the public sector and TSOs, and then also with businesses. Continuous steps are being taken in regards to enhanced cross-sector collaboration, but as a conclusion we can say that in general, the existing partnerships can be typified mostly as transactional with some tendency to becoming integrative. At the current stage, though, businesses are not only partners in the development of the service and suppliers of technological inputs for the public sector and TSOs, but also fierce competitors of TSOs in service delivery. The private, for-profit sector has become a key service provider in Spain and the UK (adding up to its role as technology supplier). In Italy financial operators have entered the field as investors promoting the creation of social enterprises for social services delivery. This contrasts with Sweden where the presence of business organisations in the social innovation seems to be meaningless (yet a very incipient opening up to business organisations in social service delivery could be appreciated, again not without controversy). It is worth noting, that although business organisations are not present in the particular social innovation activity we have looked at in this report in Sweden, businesses do operate in social services on a contractual basis but they do not use volunteers (to any relevant degree that we know of).

In regards to the third sector, there are significant variations across the four countries. In Spain, it has traditionally played a major role in social service provision and as partners for public authorities. However, and although it was a TSO that introduced telecare in Spain, its role as the predominant service provider is currently being superseded by competing for-profit organisations (and, it seems, gladly received by public authorities as they are cheaper than TSOs, as interviewees have remarked). Nonetheless, when it comes to participation in social policy formulation, advocacy for social needs, and direct contact with beneficiaries and citizens in general, TSOs are still the preferred channels. Also in the UK, the third sector has a role in service delivery, which is complemented with a relevant advocacy role. In Sweden, we can appreciate that the two umbrella organisations are getting more legitimacy in the field. However, this cannot be generalised as the opinion of citizens is not in favour of using volunteers for tasks citizens think should belong to the public sector. In the particular case of the introduction of volunteers in public social services and activities, they currently run many of the volunteer centres. In Italy, the third sector is still the key partner for policy formulation and delivery of social services. Yet, social enterprises are to be ever more promoted considering the latest developments in the field. However, common to all countries is that the third sector plays a unique role when it comes to advocating for the needs of the most vulnerable citizens and educating the population about the relevance of the social innovation stream, particularly at a local level.

Learnings

Social innovation literature is mostly about clearly positive novelties, successful products and processes, planned change, and scaling up of promising solutions. Our focus has been on the new collaborative governance arrangements that make them possible. However, this research suggests that conceptual ambiguity, internal tensions, competition, unexpected consequences within the collaborations, failure, and social controversy seem to be at least as relevant components of all the social innovation activities, particularly when it comes to influencing their diffusion.

First, conceptual ambiguity is illustrated by the UK case, as telecare can be conceptualised as a social innovation that allows for personalised adult care, or as a mere technological innovation that allows for massive cost savings. The argument that if telecare works for people with dementia it will work for everyone, makes it attractive to look at this particularly vulnerable population segment that might be at high risk of being left out of the technological debate. However, though older people might buy their telecare with personal budgets, large national evaluation of personal budgets has shown that some older people find it difficult to use (Glendinning et al., 2008). Thus, an important issue was whether the way telecare was implemented was person-centred. The individualisation process is particularly important to ensure that technology is used in a way that makes a difference to peoples' lives. For example, personalised processes might require a lengthy and time-consuming assessment of the person's situation and environment—the like of the Spanish SAAD. Furthermore, it is particularly interesting to look at telecare development with reference to the economic crisis as this was likely to have an important influence on dynamics in the sector. For example, economic pressures might have reduced the spending on telecare (if it were perceived as an add-on or luxury consumption); on the other hand spending on telecare might have increased because commissioners try to realise cost savings from telecare.

Second, the case of Spain exemplifies the intensity of internal tensions and competition within innovative cross-sector collaborations, leading to unexpected and even paradoxical results for certain types of actors, however successful the overall diffusion of innovation may be. Though telecare was pioneered by the third sector, strong business competition and reduced public budgets have made the telecare market a hard terrain for TSOs, arguably because private companies offer lower prices and are in a better position to win public procurement contracts, mostly granted based on economic criteria. In a scenario where competition is very high, the third sector loses market share. On the one hand, it's because TSOs (and also social enterprises) cannot compete in terms of prices; on the other, because the format of public procurement contracts does not fit their model of intervention, often more social, customised and integrative. Therefore, the social value added by TSOs to the telecare service is paid by their own budgets. However, it can also be seen as a window of opportunity to innovate within the third sector, as it places TSOs where the beneficiaries want them to be, and can eventually result in empowerment of both direct and indirect beneficiaries.

Third and last, the cases of the UK and Sweden are illustrative for the presence of failure and controversy in the social innovation stream. In the case of the UK, some public funding schemes to build infrastructure for local service delivery have been criticised for being focussed on numbers (outputs, how many products sold) rather on outcomes; or for not being specifically targeted at certain populations and lacking clear aims which led to some kind of diversion (ultimately not being used for those most in need such as people with dementia and their carers). Experts stated that the Dementia Strategy initiated discussions among senior administrative staff in local authorities and other parties about the use of telecare for this group (although less clear if it led to actual changes in provision). In the case of Sweden, and after the raise and stagnation of the volunteer centre movement in the country, there is a critical backlash against volunteers taking care of public welfare.

Conclusions

Across the countries, the evolution of the social innovation can be considered to be struggling to meet the sustaining stage (Murray, Caulier-Grice, & Mulgan, 2010). What we can actually appreciate is that there are feedbacks and loops between different evolutionary stages and also a certain degree of overlapping between prototyping and pilots where (new, additional) solutions are being tested and refined, and sustaining the social innovation with steady funding and supporting legislation and regulations. There are differences and specificities of the evolution with regard to countries, organisational actors and even the different particular aspects of the social innovation stream. Let's look at the social innovation activity in Spain as the one with the longest record among the cases analysed here.

Telecare was introduced as a technological innovation some 25 years ago. Nowadays a true social innovation has developed, new governance arrangements have emerged to further evolve it, there is supporting legislation, public funding is largely secured (despite some criticisms on budgetary cuts), quality standards and certification processes have been established, telecare is well-known by the population and demand exists, there are many providers, and the service has been largely mainstreamed. Looking at this, we could even say that the innovation has reached the stage of scaling and diffusion. However, incremental innovations are constantly being tried on (new profiles of end-users, new services, new products, etc.) and not all of these have reached broad acceptance or have been implemented beyond local or specific contexts. Furthermore, when we look at the extent to which new ways of corporate governance have been implemented within the actors involved, inquire whether cross-sector partnerships have reached a transformational stage, or wonder about the extent of beneficiary or user participation, we can see that the picture looks different. It is true that beneficiaries have needs that are attended to by the collaborative action of actors in different sectors, but they are far from being empowered as citizens who participate in decision-making regarding telecare services designed to improve their own independency.

Overall, the point has not yet been reached where we see a definite embeddedness of the social innovation stream across the four country settings. But shortcomings and tensions just described could only be spotted in the comparative research design applied here and rest on the fact that different embodiments of the same social innovation stream have been chosen, including such that were in rather early stages of formation, lost traction or turned out to be contested depending on the context they appeared in. While increasing the difficulty of drawing neat conclusions, the design has also increased the explanatory potential of the analysis.

Note

1. We would like to thank Francesca Calo, who made important contributions to the ITSSOIN project deliverable that formed the basis for this chapter.

References

European Commission. (2014). *Development of interoperable and independent living solutions*. A Compilation of Good Practices—First Edition: European Innovation Partnership on Active and Healthy Ageing.

Frederiksen, M. (2015). "Dangerous, commendable or compliant: How Nordic people think about volunteers as providers of public welfare services. *Voluntas: International Journal of Voluntary and Nonprofit Organizations, 26*, 1739–1758.

Glendinning, C., Challis, D., Fernández, J.L., Jacobs, S., Jones, K., Knapp, M., Manthorpe, J., Moran, N., Netten, A., Stevens, M., & Wilberforce, M. (2008). Evaluation of the individual budgets pilot programme. Final report. York: Social Policy Research Unit University of York.

Greene, I. (2007). The potential for government privatization to the nonprofit sector. *The Innovation Journal: The Public Sector Innovation Journal, 12*(3), 1–11.

Hodges, R. (Ed.). (2005). *Governance and the public sector*. Cheltenham, UK: Edward Elgar Publishing.

International Association for Public Participation (IAP2). (n.d.). *Spectrum of public participation*. Retrieved from www.iap2.org.au/Tenant/C0000004/00000001/files/IAP2_Public_Participation_Spectrum.pdf

Ley 39/2006, de 14 de diciembre, de Promoción de la Autonomía Personal y Atención a las personas en situación de dependencia (LAPAD). Retrieved from www.boe.es/buscar/act.php?id=BOE-A-2006-21990

Murray, R., Caulier-Grice, J., & Mulgan, G. (2010). *The open book of social innovation*. The Social Innovator Series. London: NESTA.

Newman, J. (2004). Modernizing the state: A new style of governance? In J. L. R. Surender (Ed.), *Welfare state change: Towards a third way?* (pp. 69–88). Oxford: Polity Press.

OECD/European Communities. (2005). *Oslo manual: Guidelines for collecting and interpreting innovation data* (3rd ed.). Paris: OECD Publishing / Eurostat.

Rey-Garcia, M., & Felgueiras, A. (2015a). *Field description in social services*. Part 1 of deliverable 5.1 of the project: "Impact of the third sector as Social Innovation" (ITSSOIN), European Commission—7th Framework Programme, Brussels: European Commission, DG Research.

Rey-Garcia, M., & Felgueiras, A. (2015b). *Report on the selection of case studies for the field of social services*. A deliverable of the project: "Impact of the Third Sector as Social Innovation" (ITSSOIN), European Commission—7th Framework Programme. Brussels: European Commission, DG Research.

Rey-Garcia, M., Felgueiras, A., Bauer, A., Einarsson, T., Calo, F., & Cancellieri, G. (2016). *Social innovation in social services: Filling the resource-needs gap for the most vulnerable through cross-sector partnerships and civic engagement*. Deliverable 5.4 of the project: "Impact of the Third Sector as Social Innovation" (ITSSOIN), European Commission—7th Framework Programme, Brussels: European Commission, DG Research.

Rhodes, R. A. W. (1997). *Understanding governance: Policy networks, governance, reflexivity and accountability*. Buckingham: Open University Press.

Rhodes, R. A. W. (2007). Understanding governance: Ten years on. *Organization Studies, 28,* 1243–1264.

Rosenau, J. N. (2000). Change, complexity, and governance in globalizing space. In J. Pierre (Ed.), *Debating governance: Authority, steering and democracy* (pp. 167–200). Oxford: Oxford University Press.

Socialstyrelsen. (2007). *Frivilligcentraler i Sverige—en kartlaggning*. Stockholm: Socialstyrelsen.

Von Essen, J., Hegermalm, M., & Svedberg, L. (2015). *Folk i rorelse—medborgerligt engagemang 1992–2014*. Stockholm: Ersta Skondal Hogskola.

6 Social Innovation in Health Care

The Recovery Approach in Mental Health

*Annette Bauer, Gerald Wistow,
Vladimír Hyánek, Maria Figueroa,
and Sarah Sandford*[1]

Introduction

We investigated the recovery approach in mental health across four European countries. Mental health care is an area that is increasingly prioritised by governments, and in some countries—like the UK and US—it has been given equal status to physical health care ('parity of esteem for mental health'). Those attempts respond to the substantial burden caused by mental ill health: When including substance misuse disorder mental ill health is the leading cause of years lived with disability worldwide (Whiteford et al., 2015). Different from most physical diseases it is an area which is substantially influenced by stigma and discrimination, which explains the need for wider societal responses. Despite an increasing realisation by governments of the importance of investing in mental health care, it is still an area of substantial unmet needs (WHO, 2013). We thus argue that it is an area in which innovations are important and likely to have a high social impact. Our decision to look at innovations in the mental health field was also supported by a number of factors and considerations:

- Mental health care has been found to undergo many innovations in the past decades and it has been argued that other parts of the health system could learn from those (Wise, 2014);
- Innovations in mental health care often incorporate or overlap with innovations in other parts of health care systems such as those in areas of: integration, patient or citizen involvement and public health (health promotion);
- In line with the notions of the social model of disability (e.g., Beresford, 2002), some innovations in mental health care have played an important role in shedding light on those dimensions of health that go beyond physical aspects and that are more closely linked to social care and public health.

The recovery approach is a popular and widely recognised social movement that influenced and transformed mental health policy and practice in many high-income countries (Jacobson, 2003, p. 4; Jacobson & Curtis, 2000; Slade, 2012). In many high-income countries (such as the UK, New Zealand and the US) the recovery approach presents possibly one of the largest social innovation streams in the mental health field, which evolved over many decades.

In our research we sought to examine the events, actors, conditions and factors that facilitated or hindered the development of the recovery approach in different European countries, with a particular focus on the role of third and public sector organisations (which were known to dominate movements in this area). We included the perspective of four different countries: the Czech Republic, Denmark, France and the UK.

Central Concepts and Key Questions

Social Model of Disability

In order to conceptualise the recovery approach we first introduce the social model of disability as an important underlying political driver of the recovery approach. The social model of disability is based on a realisation by most governments and non-government organisations over the past decade(s) that good health is not simply an outcome of good health care and that wider physical, mental and wellbeing aspects and social and environmental factors play an important role (Wilkinson & Marmot, 2003; WHO, 2006). It is supported by evidence, which suggests that only a small proportion of poor health stems from shortfalls in medical care and that other domains are far more important in impacting on individuals' health and wellbeing such as: Individual behaviour; genetic predispositions; and social and economic circumstances. This wider understanding of health and its determinants has substantial implications for roles and responsibilities of government, including a greater focus on areas such as health promotion, prevention, personalisation and self-management. More fundamentally, it directs government responsibilities towards addressing the 'causes of the causes' of poor health (Dahlgren & Whitehead, 1991). A changing role and responsibility of individuals towards their own health is also implied by the social model as they are conceptualised as potential co-producers of health rather than passive recipients of health care (subject of course to a recognition that opportunities and capacities for such co-production are also socially structured). Within the last decades, participation approaches have become prominent paradigms in public health and, like the social model of care, they often aim to reduce social inequalities in health outcomes. They potentially share a focus on principles of personalisation and empowerment (Wallerstein, 2006). It can be argued that a point of potential difference is that most public health approaches retain some kind of emphasis on the individual as a patient whereas the social model of disability might demand a stronger emphasis on the empowerment of individuals as active citizens.

In the UK the social model of disability stemmed from disability movements which took place decades ago, and which aimed for an understanding of disability that—by deviating from a focus on personal limitations—helped to reduce the barriers that prevent disabled people from fully participating in society or experiencing disadvantage compared to non-disabled people (Oliver & Sapey, 2006; Goodley, 2001). Barriers included environmental ones (e.g., inaccessible buildings and services), people's attitudes (e.g., stereotyping, discrimination and prejudice) and organisational barriers (e.g., inflexible policies, practices and procedures). The social model is the one supported by the vast majority of disabled people and their organisations, and encourages society to become more inclusive. In addition and possibly related to this, there has been a political drive for a cultural change of the relationship between patients and professionals and how 'services' have been defined.

The Recovery Approach

The recovery approach is based on an ideology as well as on evidence that people with mental ill health are not automatically ill or disabled for their whole life but that there is a recovery pathway. Recovery is defined as a "deeply personal, unique process" (Anthony, 1993) rather than something that can be imposed. The concept does not assume immediate or full recovery for everyone but that there is a path which enables the individual to lead as full a life as possible. The recovery approach is thought to be based on principles of individuals' capability and strengths rather than their deficits. It is focused on restoring a person's identity and self-esteem rather than on the remission of symptoms (Davidson et al., 2006). Whilst there is no single definition, the recovery approach is anchored in principles of life satisfaction, hope and optimism, empowerment, knowledge about mental ill health, co-production and community capacity (Deegan, 1997; Resnick et al., 2004; Farone, 2006). The recovery approach is supported by evidence that people can get better and that the principles it promotes (e.g., life satisfaction) are strong predictors of self-reported poor health and depression (e.g., Al-Windi, 2005; Chovil, 2005). The recovery approach focuses on helping people with mental ill health to live as part of and participate in their local community and is thus closely linked to concepts of social inclusion and citizenship (Repper & Perkins, 2003) and therefore located within the realm of the social model of disability.

Methods

We examined the role of individuals and organisations (actors) over time and identified important milestones (legislation, policies, events, publications); this also covered an analysis of the interactions between actors from different sectors. We gathered information by asking experts in the field and by carrying out our own web-based searches.

Case Selection

We spent some time and effort in selecting the recovery approach as the case study we wanted to focus our investigation on (for details see Bauer & Wistow, 2015). In addition to the importance of the topic as described previously, the rationale for our choice was as follows: Focusing on the recovery approach allowed us to investigate characteristics and determinants that were likely to be applicable to other social innovations in the field of health; the recovery approach reflects the social model of disability applied to the mental health field, which has been a driving force for change in the traditionally highly medicalised world of health care (Degener, 2016). The social model of disability places the responsibility for how illness and disability is defined as well as its causes within the context of society rather than the individual and has been included in the UN Convention on the Rights of Persons with Disabilities (United Nations, 2008). In addition, the recovery approach is likely to address a number of important aspects of other areas of innovation in health care, which were candidates for our case studies such as: integrated care (because the recovery approach takes place at the interface with different government departments, professional disciplines and service user groups); personalisation (because the recovery approach is based on principles of empowerment, choice and control); patient and public involvement (because the recovery approach is driven by user movements).

Data Collection

Innovative practices and activities embodying the recovery approach and driving it have been collected in a snowball sampling effort and resulted from consulting experts in the field knowledgeable about such activities. This process shall be outlined here in an exemplary fashion in relation to our case work in the UK. We applied an equivalent strategy in all other countries. With the help of the "external experts" we identified the organisations described in Table 6.1, most of which were examples of so called recovery colleges or similar co-produced activities. Recovery colleges (also called Recovery Education Centres) were seen as an important activity under the recovery approach, which might be traced back to a South London-based one which started in 2009. Since then projects emerged across England and the UK. A recovery college is run by both peer trainers and mental health practitioners. Courses are typically co-produced, co-delivered and co-received by staff, people with mental health problems and those close to them. They can be public or third sector provided and dynamics between public and third sector vary strongly depending on the organisation that is chosen.

Table 6.1 Exemplified overview of organisations participating in the research, UK

Organisation	Purpose
Creative Minds is a Charitable Trust hosted by South West Yorkshire Partnerships NHS Foundation Trust (SWYPFT).	Development of community partnerships. Co-funding of creative projects across Creative Minds' localities and the Trust's forensic services. Support of voluntary organisations that work with Trust. Partnerships and co-production are core to the conception and development of Creative Minds.
Dorset Mental Health Forum (DMHF) is a peer-led charity founded in 1992. The establishment of WaRP allows DMHF to maintain independence from statutory provision.	Promotion of peer-led services. 1-to-1 advocacy service for the whole region and advocacy as organisational identity. Employment service, collaboration with schools, production of evidence.
WaRP (partnership with local NHS Trust) was established as partnership in 2009 of DMHF and NHS Community Health Services.	Purpose and objectives lie within the structure of publicly funded health care, seeking to bring together in partnership people's lived experience expertise and professional expertise to promote personal recovery and unlock people's potential. The overall aim is to change the culture of mental health services and people's attitudes to mental health and wellbeing in Dorset.
Recovery College, South London and Maudsley (SLaM), NHS Foundation Trust.	Workshops and courses aiming to provide the tools to make recovery happen, to help people become an expert in their own recovery or that of someone they care for or work with. Offer of a learning approach that complements the existing services provided by the Trust. Every course and workshop is co-designed and co-run by trainers with lived experience working alongside trainers from the mental health professions.
Nottingham **'Real Lives'** is a third sector non-profit (community interest) company.	Support of people 18 and older in their home or community with mental health challenges and/or learning disabilities. Employment of people with lived experience and help for them to gain and retain employment. Provision of self-directed social support packages to people in the Nottingham community via personal budgets. Support of local community via a café, and volunteers and people on placement in the company seeking experience.
Mental Fight Club (MFC) is a registered charity and constitutional objective is to promote social inclusion. Currently the main service delivered is the **Dragon Café.**	Emerging of new strands of work including ReCreate. Provision of creative training and facilitation for health and social care professionals. The Dragon Café is the first mental health café in the UK. Non-medical model of provision. A space both safe and inspiring which helps service users take the journey through mental ill health, onwards into recovery and new-found sustainable modes of mental wellbeing.

Organisation	Purpose
Scottish Recovery Network collaborates with other local organisations and individuals with experiences of mental health. They cover the whole of Scotland.	Promotion of paid supportive role in recovery. Support of other recovery organisations and individuals with experiences of mental ill health. Work with local organisations to develop knowledge and services such as peer support projects and community-based projects on recovery. Advice to other organisations, guiding and sharing best practice on recovery.

All identified activities were strongly reflective of user-led recovery streams and enabled us to study the interplay of actors in driving the approach. After the identification of the relevant actors we performed interviews, mostly with one interviewee from each of the listed organisations. These were considered "internal experts". Both viewpoints were brought together in the analysis.

Tracing the Social Innovation Stream

The recovery approach has been rooted and contextualised in a number of developments that occurred (although in different chronological order and in different strengths) in many high income countries (Starnino, 2009): The evolution of the psychiatric social work discipline (Schaefer Vourlekis, Edinburg, & Knee, 1998); a focus on deinstitutionalisation and independent living programmes in the community (Schnapp, 2006); psychiatric rehabilitation and the introduction of new forms of therapy such as cognitive rehabilitation strategies and art therapy (Corrigan, 2003); the survivor or ex-patient movement, which challenged the concept of mental ill health as a disease and instead defines it as a societal problem (Jacobson, 2004; Thornicroft et al., 2008); the user-centred (consumer) movement, which puts the consumers' interests at the centre of improvements to quality and outcomes (Mead & Copeland, 2000).

Across the four countries that we investigated, experts agreed that the development of the recovery approach was importantly contextualised in the deinstitutionalisation of mental health services; our experts thought that the deinstitutionalisation had led to the conditions, in which the recovery approach could happen. This included: The provision of services through community mental health teams; the softening of professional boundaries (in particular through the influences of the social work, community development and occupational therapy disciplines on the psychiatric discipline); and a strengthened voice of people with lived experience of mental ill health and of treatment. Because of these overarching trends we outline milestones across countries, with a particular emphasis on the UK as the exemplary case, and go into national specific in terms of actors and their interplay further in the following.

Milestones Across Countries

Perhaps most evidently in the UK (following international examples from the US and New Zealand) the recovery approach started off (during the 70s) as a 'movement' that was initiated by pioneers. Individuals with lived experiences of mental ill health and of treatment (including psychologists or psychiatrists) shared their stories about what helped them in moving beyond the role as a patient. In addition, there were professionally led movements in each of the countries starting also during the 70s. The influence of professional-led movements on driving some of the principles of the recovery approach that led to new branches of traditional psychiatry was particularly evident in Denmark ('social psychiatry'), France ('citizen psychiatry') and the UK ('critical psychiatry').

In each of the four countries, experts reported how professional or user advocates of the recovery approach faced major challenges in scaling up the approach and in achieving changes in the system of mental health services. Some of the challenges were similar between countries: government departments working in silos; a command and control culture within the mainstream public sector; and a strong resistance from large parts of the mental health profession, which were often protective of traditional structures and practices.

Despite those challenges, there were noticeable policy, practice and research changes over time. In the UK and Denmark, the recovery approach was finally incorporated into national mental health policies and strategies (2006 to now), suggesting a more systematic change (although to a lesser extent in Denmark). A key milestone in England that signalled an important shift in policy attention and thinking was the creation of a national flagship programme called ImROC (Implementing Recovery through Organisational Change) in 2006. ImROC consisted of and was led by individuals who had been campaigning for the recovery approach at a national level and involved organisations (and representatives of those) which had implemented the recovery approach locally (some of them had driven the recovery approaches locally for decades). They successfully influenced the policy and practice landscape. Over the past decade, national mental health policies and strategies have incorporated a focus on recovery and governments have made recovery-oriented practice a key priority and requirement for mental health services; this included the introduction of performance indicators to measure how well services were doing on the recovery dimension.

In Denmark, a key milestone was the introduction of a government-initiated Knowledge (and Research) Centre for Social Psychiatry in the late 90s, which consisted of people who acted as pioneers in the field of social psychiatry and included the concept of recovery. In 2012, the Danish government set out a national framework which included a section for how mental health services should become more recovery oriented. There were a number of developments that promoted and disseminated evidence on recovery, and advocated for the rights of people with lived experience of mental ill health and treatment.

In France, the recovery approach was much more difficult to 'trace', which was by some experts explained by a resistance of many to what was perceived to be an 'Anglo-Saxon' concept that did not fit to the national context.

> The French have difficulty tolerating the idea that Anglo-saxons are ahead of them on this subject—in their worldview, it must be the French who are ahead. They absolutely do not want to hear about recovery.
>
> (Interview 1)

However, a strong role of central government had allowed a wide dissemination of models that incorporated some of the principles of the recovery approach such as Housing First and peer support. Experts had strong and diverse opinions about whether or not the recovery approach had been implemented through those programmes. In addition, an innovative bottom-up project, which incorporated many of the principles of the recovery approach (led by a mental health professional and her husband) had been rolled out to thirteen sites.

In the Czech Republic, movements and practice developments around peer support and user involvement also evidenced an increasing role of the recovery approach (although this had not yet made their way into national policies). Different from France, international influences in particular from countries like the UK were viewed as important drivers of the recovery approach, and international evidence was utilised to support the development of the recovery approach. A range of organisations nationally as well as locally promoted and taught principles of recovery. There was also evidence that those organisations were working together in networks, and that this had facilitated some important developments such as the organisation of a conference on this topic.

Overall, we identified some factors that appeared to act as drivers of the recovery approach (and their absence appeared to hinder its development): a policy focus on prevention and on evidence-based practice; a clear stand on human rights legislation for people with mental ill health (including stigma reduction work); an openness towards international influences; an openness towards collaborative working across disciplines and sectors; and economic pressures on the system that demanded new solutions. However, experts in countries where there had been a wider dissemination (namely in the UK and Denmark) also noted that this had happened by fitting it with existing political agendas and practice developments and had ultimately led to some deviation from its original concept.

The important role of bottom-up movements by third sector organisations (starting from the early 90s) was evident in all four countries: They had often—although perhaps more indirectly—influenced governmental decision-making by demonstrating that the recovery approach was feasible and could be implemented successfully. Sometimes, individuals who founded such organisations and advocated for the recovery approach locally had also strongly influenced national developments. Third sector organisations in form of national user-led organisations, research centres and think tanks had an important role in driving the recovery approach (or some of its principles) in each of the four countries at the national level. Most of them were supported and—at least partially—funded by the government. Whilst some of them had a specific remit to drive recovery-oriented practice, others had a broader remit to inform mental health reforms. It is important to note that experts in all four countries referred to individuals (rather than organisations) who had been driving the recovery approach, and who had acted as recovery pioneers. The engaged actors and their influence on the social innovation stream will be discussed in the following within their national contexts.

Actors and Interplay in the UK

In England, experts agreed that ImROC (Implementing Recovery through Organisational Change) was the most important actor driving the recovery approach. It was led by individuals, who had advocated for the recovery approach for decades and created as a partnership between the third and public sector. It was also closely linked to the academic sector as well as to professional associations, which was likely to reinforce its large influence. At a national level, it promoted key messages of recovery through its guidance materials and at a local level, it supported local recovery initiatives by promoting and informing their good practice. In Scotland, the Scottish Recovery Network had taken on a similar role.

Before the time of ImROC and the Scottish Recovery Network, it was mainly user- and professional-led networks, which promoted the recovery approach (although sometimes with different perspectives); some of those had their origins in international networks and movements. This included the Hearing Voices Network which started as a political psychology and anti-psychiatry movement in 1987 and the Critical Psychiatry Network, which was created by group of British psychiatrists in 1999. Their role is still influential. In addition, there have been more recent movements such as Open Dialogue, which started originally in Finland in the 1980s and made (and continues to make) its way to the UK and other parts of Europe over the last decade.

Some experts emphasised broader changes in societal thinking through complementary policies and societal reflectivity in which the UK's recovery approach gained popularity. For example, one expert thought that whilst historically health and social care service provision had focused on treating illnesses, "Nowadays services are all about wellbeing". One expert described the increasing dissemination and diffusion of the recovery concept's terminology. Commissioners and people from other professional disciplines started to use it for example in publications in nursing journals:

> Every profession now has recovery paper . . . even OTs (occupational therapists) . . . bizarrely, even security settings had recovery plans and recovery leads.
>
> (Interview 2)

Professional associations and membership bodies for psychiatrists and psychologists were important drivers for the recovery approach. Some of the recovery pioneers had also established positions in the Royal Colleges and advocated the recovery approach to their profession 'from within'. However, some experts were critical of some of the involvement by the psychiatric profession, which they thought had sometimes redefined the term recovery to serve their purpose and reconstructed its meaning.

The key role of the third sector in initiating and driving the recovery approach was highlighted by experts and evident from the literature: Organisations such as the Centre for Mental Health were leading campaigns for the recovery approach in collaboration with and on behalf of people with lived experience. More recent initiatives that support recovery principles included the Time to Change anti-stigma campaign (led by two large third sector organisations in the mental health field: MIND and Rethink). Many other third sector organisations had an influence in driving the recovery approach at a national and local level (although sometimes from different angles) including Making Space, Turning Point and St Mungo's (to name but a few). In addition, there were numerous local third sector organisations, which partnered up with commissioners and providers of publicly funded mental health services to implement the recovery approach locally. They had an important role in informing the evidence base for such approaches by sharing their knowledge nationally and internationally. Those included Dorset Mental Health Forum, Recovery Devon, and the South London and Maudsley (SLaM) NHS Trust Foundation Recovery College (to name but a few).

Actors and Interplay in Denmark

In Denmark, the Knowledge Centre for Social Psychiatry (Videnscenter for socialpsykiatri) had been established in 1997 by the Ministry of Social Affairs and was an important forerunner in the field. The Centre collected existing international knowledge and evidence on recovery and published it in Danish in order to make the literature available to a wider national audience. Furthermore, the Centre initiated an association that became the

Danish Society for Psycho-social Rehabilitation (Dansk selskab for psyko-social rehabilitering). Whilst the Centre was closed in 2011, the Danish Association for Psycho-social Rehabilitation still exists. It is an association of professionals who promote the recovery approach; its members are regularly invited by the Danish Government to participate in policy making.

Experts thought that municipalities (councils) had an important influence on driving and implementing the recovery approach locally: Most Danish councils ran recovery projects or had a recovery strategy for the field of social psychiatry. Aarhus was the first council to implement the recovery approach and was identified by experts as the most progressive council in regard to the recovery approach. Even though municipalities showed a great ambition in implementing the recovery approach, an expert noticed that this did not necessarily led to the best services in practice. The expert thought they could not pave the way for a structural setting that supports large-scale recovery initiatives before they fully grasp the meaning of recovery. (S)he concluded that today: "Large-scale recovery initiatives are often started by individual enthusiasts".

However, some experts thought that most councils had not yet grasped the meaning of recovery and instead used it only as a tool that could be implemented as part of their political agenda, which was concerned with getting people (back) into the labour market or into education. This is outlined in the following quote from a study scrutinising the approach in Denmark:

> When Recovery is used as a tool and is thereby integrated in the existing system the system itself is not changed. In this process there has been a development towards more humanity and equality in the system, but the difference between citizen and system is preserved and hence the power relations in the healthcare system are not dismantled.
>
> (Neidel, 2011)

In addition, there was national support and funding from the National Board of Social Services Fund to develop and pilot local prevention programs for people with lived experience of mental ill health. Those projects were organised as partnerships between government, private sector and civil society and their goals included the social inclusion of this population.

Similar to the UK, there have been national and international service user movements, including the Hearing Voices Network, which exists in Denmark since 2005 and had influences on the professional discipline of psychiatry. The national service user organisation (LAP) was established in 1999 and was identified as a key actor with national and international influence in the mental health field. Other important third sector organisations, which were driving the recovery approach in Denmark at a national level included Outsider, a Copenhagen-based journal and association of people with lived and treatment experience, which received government funding (from the Ministry of Social Affairs and the local councils); and The Social Network, a prevention oriented organisation founded by the Prime Minister, and which promoted and influenced recovery-oriented practice as well as the integration between mental health and social care. In addition, experts referred to a private company (PsykoVision) as an important actor, which promoted evidence-based recovery practice—it was seen as an exception, however, and the only private sector provider of recovery-oriented treatment and support.

At a regional level, some professional associations (such as the Joint Council of the Psychiatric Associations—Psykiatriforeningernes Fællesråd) had become active in the recovery field and provided guidance on hospital discharge that followed principles of recovery.

Actors and Interplay in France

In France, whilst there was less of an identifiable movement towards the recovery approach, there had been some important bottom-up and top-down developments led by third sector organisations and partnerships that supported similar principles. Most of them were still recent developments.

Les Invités au Festin (The Guests at the Feast) started off as a bottom-up movement in one region led by two recovery pioneers and was subsequently rolled out across France promoting and offering social inclusion for people with lived experience by creating environments, in which they work and spend time together with volunteers (without lived experience).

'Un Chez Soi D'Abord' (Housing First) is a model that is based on the American model of Housing First, and has been implemented by third sector organisations in four cities in France. The implementation was led and supported by the WHO Collaborating Centre for Research and Training in Mental Health (CCOMS), which was named by experts as the most important public (health) sector actor; the priorities of the Centre are the empowerment of people with lived experience of treatment and the promotion of citizenship psychiatry.

Groupe d'Entraide Mutuelle (GEM) is an association of 80 self-help groups; it was originally established in the context of the national Disability Law in 2005. Three third sector organisations had actively promoted and supported its establishment. Fédération Croix-Marine pour la Santé Mentale (a movement of psychiatrists, which grew out of Institutional Psychotherapy movement), UNAFAM (an organisation representing the families of people with mental ill health) and FNA-PSY (a movement of service users).

Whilst some experts thought that those self-help groups were primarily about self-management and did not engage in wider policy and practice issues, others felt that they had created an environment and infrastructure for the recovery approach.

> These mutual-help clubs, governed by users themselves, have emerged very quickly as special places where users can engage in their recovery journey and discover the importance of peer support away from the gaze of professionals.
>
> (Interview 3)

An expert emphasised the intra-organisational challenges of programmes introducing and evaluating the integration of peer mentors into health care teams. Professionals' resistance was at least partly explained by their concerns that peer mentors could take over their role with less training and for lower pay.

Another expert described the consequences when professionals did not incorporate the wider social determinants of mental ill health in their practice (e.g., through peer mentoring) as follows:

> If a patient is denied recognition as a person, if his or her fundamental rights are not respected, if his opinion is not taken into account, on the ground that he is 'mad' then it is impossible to imagine a fulfilled life, a recovery journey or path as a recognized citizen.

> (Interview 4)

In addition, there were some public sector organisations identified as key actors. This included a mental health service provider (Hôpital Maison Blanche), which had a research unit attached to it that was headed by an Australian psychologist, which most experts viewed as the most prominent advocate of the recovery approach in France.

Actors and Interplay in the Czech Republic

In the Czech Republic, experts thought it was not only important to name key players in the recovery field but also in the mental health field more broadly: The health system was still very medically and physical health focused, and recent mental health reforms had been important in also driving the recovery approach (by providing an infrastructure for change). Experts thought that international bodies such as the European Union and the World Health Organisation had been driving national reforms and policies in mental health, and that without their involvement the recovery approach would not have had any foundation. In addition, they mentioned the following key actors in recent mental health reforms: The Ministry of Health; the National Institute for Mental Health; the Centre for Mental Health Care Development (CMHCD); the largest national health insurance company (VZP); mental health providers such as Česká psychiatrická společnost; and the Bohnice psychiatric hospital.

At a national level, the National Institute of Mental Health (NIMH) and the Centre for Mental Health Care Development (CMHCD) were third sector organisations that had importantly contributed to the mental health reform by providing knowledge about evidence-based practice and about ensuring that user's voices were incorporated. Another third sector organisation that had played an important role in driving the recovery approach and makes the voices of people with experience of treatment heard was Kolumbus, the largest user-led organisation in the country. At a local level, a number of third sector initiatives had been driving the recovery approach: FOKUS, Práh (Treshold), Ledovec (Iceberg) and Kolumbus (which also worked at the local level). They were described by experts as 'role models' in the field of community mental health services and had an important role in demonstrating good practice and that the recovery approach was feasible. They also had started offering accredited courses on recovery-oriented practice.

In terms of public sector organisations (and individuals representing those), the Director of the Bohnice Psychiatric Hospital was viewed as the most important person behind the mental health care reform and driver of movements in support of the recovery approach; this included the implementation of peer-led models at his hospital. At the same time, experts described a more or less open opposition to the recovery approach by the managements of some psychiatric hospitals. This included elite psychiatrists, who continued speaking 'very medically' about the remission of symptoms. Public sector providers of community mental health services appeared more open towards the principles of the recovery approach than institutional providers: Nearly all of the big providers employed some experts by experience (users) which experts saw as an important step towards the implementation of the recovery approach.

Nonetheless, experts saw variations in the implementation of the recovery approach. The type of institution (e.g., providers of community services, mental hospitals, researchers, patients' and family organisations) seemed decisive with regard to differences in comprehensions of the term 'recovery'. According to one expert non-profit actors showed a particular openness towards the approach:

> There has been no problem with the involvement of peer consultants across the country. However, generally it is much easier to introduce recovery orientation in non-profit organizations, which is true for innovations more broadly.
>
> (Interview 5)

Synthesis

Comparative Analysis

Most evidently in UK the recovery approach started off as a 'movement' that was initiated by pioneers including individuals from the US and New Zealand. However, the movement existed for a long time under the radar of policy makers. So whereas pioneers (through third sector organisations) had advocated for the recovery approach for several decades, it required it at an opportune time when the government was faced with real demand and finance pressures. In England and the UK, the recovery approach has in some regards affected large parts of the mental health system; this relates to the awareness among professionals and support from governments; however, the resistance from large parts of the medical discipline meant that the medical model still predominates mainstream clinical practice. Experts also thought that the wide dissemination of the recovery approach had partly led to a deviation from some of the original principles by focusing on a narrow understanding of recovery that could be included in performance monitoring.

In Denmark, the beginnings of the recovery approach were marked by the introduction of a government initiated Centre and of a new professional discipline that supported the principles of the recovery approach by combining social, rehabilitative and psychiatric approaches. Since then the implementation of the recovery approach had been driven and implemented by some municipalities (although geographical variation remains strong). Third sector (user-led) organisations had an important influence on those changes. Similar to the UK, some experts thought that the dissemination had happened at the expense of the original, user-focused principles of the recovery approach. The resistance from the traditional mental health profession was described as strong and so was the culture of the medical model within mainstream public services that needed to change. Experts thought that the impact of the recovery approach on the system of social psychiatry had been at least moderate to strong (dependent on geographical location) but its impact on mental health and the broader health system had been limited.

In France, the recovery approach as a movement was more difficult to identify and trace compared to the other three countries because the terminology had not been used and was sometimes actively rejected as an Anglo-Saxon concept. However, there had been some important national developments that supported initiatives that followed principles of the recovery approach and which were led by and given to the hands of third sector organisations. Those changes were initiated and organised centrally, which meant they have the potential to be implemented more systematically than in the other three countries. However, so far some initiatives have only been piloted and it thus remains to be seen whether this will lead to a more systemic change at a national level. Overall, there was evidence suggesting that—similar to the other countries—the recovery approach experienced a powerful resistance from the traditional mental health profession that prevented its scaling up.

In the Czech Republic, the recovery approach started much later than in the other three countries. Until now it has not become part of the political agenda as such but there are a range of actors—mainly from the third sector—who continue advocating for the recovery approach and there was also evidence of some government funding and support. A range of practice developments have happened over time; however, they had not scaled up and were often limited to the third sector. Not all developments were directly supporting the recovery approach but they supported some of its principles and were seen as providing an infrastructure. Overall, the recovery approach had not led to systematic changes but it was likely that it contributed importantly by creating capacities for change in the mental health field. The resistance from the medical discipline and from (large) parts of society was particularly strong thus putting a question mark on whether there can be a wider diffusion any time soon.

Learnings

The recovery approach, as probably many other social movements and innovations, is a complex process that consists of multiple perspectives. Our research involved some particular challenges. For example, ensuring consistency in data collection between countries was difficult. Perhaps unsurprisingly, it was easier to gain information in countries in which the recovery approach had developed stronger and under this name. There were differences in the ways in which research participants could be approached for the purpose of the research and sometimes it was difficult to involve participants in the research. Another challenge was that the recovery approach was a particularly 'controversial' topic as it is critical of mainstream mental health provision. Experts felt often quite strongly about developments in this field, which made it more difficult to establish robust information. In order to address some of these limitations we carried out additional data searches to validate the information provided by experts. We also sought to make the uncertainty of the information transparent. Whilst some caution needs to be applied to the findings, we believe that we summarised some important trends and highlighted common drivers and barriers of this particular social movement, that might also apply to other areas of social innovations and movements.

Conclusions

In this study, we investigated the recovery approach by using process-tracing methods. Specifically we examined the milestones that signalled important changes in the landscape of the recovery approach and investigated the role of actors (individuals and organisations) in driving it. By doing so we identified some common trends, drivers and barriers as well as some important differences in those between countries.

Across countries, there were some commonalities in the way individuals or organisations were driving the recovery approach. In all four countries there was some evidence that the recovery approach (or at least some of the principles of the recovery approach) was initiated and driven by pioneers at a national as well as at a local level. National user-led organisations had an important role in driving the recovery approach by influencing central government. Other types of national third sector organisations played a role in influencing government including think tanks and research centres. There was evidence of some bottom-up developments in all countries, which were often third sector led. Overall, psychiatric institutions did not play a major role in driving the recovery approach although there were exceptions: some leading psychiatrists had shown interest in the recovery approach and had started promoting it. Overall, the culture within psychiatric institutions (and other mental health services) did not support recovery and the professional discipline of psychiatry was seen by most experts as one of the biggest challenges for a wider dissemination of the recovery approach.

The important role of collaboration and networks in driving the recovery approach was evident in all four countries and most evident in the UK. Government departments working in silos appeared to be a main barrier in all countries (although possibly to a lesser extent in the Czech Republic). Across countries, and perhaps most evidently in Denmark, there were strong attempts to break down barriers of disintegration (in particular between health and social care). In the UK, where the recovery approach had been implemented most widely (followed by Denmark), the multitude of different policy priorities, complexity of relationships between a wide range of stakeholders as well as quickly changing environments and structures presented barriers towards a systematic dissemination of bottom-up movements. The important role of networks between individuals with the same values and beliefs across organisations and sector boundaries was evident in the UK and the Czech Republic but less so in Denmark and in France.

Note

1. We would like to thank all who made important contributions to the ITSSOIN project deliverable that formed the basis for this chapter: Spalkova, D.; Bardi, J.; and Greiffenberg, C.

Interviews

Interview 1	France	09/2015
Interview 2	England (United Kingdom)	02/2016
Interview 3	France	09/2015
Interview 4	France	09/2015
Interview 5	Czech Republic	10/2016

References

Al-Windi, A. (2005). The relations between symptoms, somatic and psychiatric conditions, life satisfaction and perceived health: A primary care based study. *Health and Quality of Life Outcomes*, 3, 28–37.

Anthony, W. A. (1993). Recovery from mental ill health: The guiding vision of the mental health service system in the 1990s. *Psychosocial Rehabilitation Journal*, 16, 11–23.

Bauer, A., & Wistow, G. (2015). *Case study selection report—social model of disability: The mental health recovery approach.* Deliverable 5.3 of the project: "Impact of the Third Sector as Social Innovation" (ITSSOIN), European Commission—7th Framework Programme, Brussels: European Commission, DG Research.

Beresford, P. (2002). Thinking about mental health: Towards a social model. *Journal of Mental Health*, Editorial, *11*(6), 581–584.

Chovil, I. (2005). First psychosis prodrome: Rehabilitation and recovery. *Psychiatric Rehabilitation Journal*, *28*, 407–408.

Corrigan, P. W. (2003). Towards an integrated, structural model of psychiatric reha bilitation. *Psychiatric Rehabilitation Journal*, 26(4), 346–358.

Davidson, L., Lawless, M. S., & Leary, F. (2006). Concepts of recovery: Competing or complementary. *Current Opinion in Psychiatry*, *19*(suppl. 6), 619–624.

Dahlgren, G., & Whitehead, M. (1991). *Policies and strategies to promote social equity in health*. Stockholm: Institute for Future Studies.

Deegan, P. (1997). Recovery and empowerment for people with psychiatric disabilities. *Social Work in Health Care*, *25*(3), 11–24.

Degener, T. (2016). Disability in a human rights context. *Laws*, *5*, 35. doi:10.3390/laws5030035

Farone, D. (2006). Schizophrenia, community integration and recovery. *Social Work in Mental Health*, 4(4), 21–36.

Goodley, D. (2001). 'Learning Difficulties', the social model of disability and impairment: Challenging epistemologies. *Disability & Society*, 16(2), 207–231.

Jacobson, N. (2003). Defining recovery: An interactionist analysis of mental health policy development, Wisconsin 1996–1999. *Qualitative Health Research*, *13*(3), 378–393.

Jacobson, N. (2004). *In recovery: The making of mental health policy*. Nashville: Vanderbilt University Press.

Jacobson, N., & Curtis, L. (2000). Recovery as policy in mental health services: Strategies emerging from the states. *Psychosocial Rehabilitation Journal*, 23(4), 333–341.

Mead, S., & Copeland, M. E. (2000). What recovery means to us: Consumers' perspectives. *Community Mental Health Journal*, *36*(3), 315–328.

Neidel, A. (2011). *På vej? Kritiske analyser af recovery-orienteringen af det socialpsykiatriske arbejde* (PhD Afhandlinger). Roskilde Universitetog Forskerskolen i Livslang Læring. ISBN: 978-87-91387-48-7

Oliver, M., & Sapey, B. (2006). *Social work with disabled people*. (4th ed.). Basingstoke: Palgrave Macmillan.

Repper, J. & Perkins, R. (2003). *Social inclusion and recovery. A model for mental health practice*. Oxford: Baillicre Tindall.

Resnick, S. G., Rosenheck, R. A., & Lehman, A. F. (2004). An exploratory analysis of correlates of recovery. *Psychiatric Services*, *55*, 540–547.

Schaefer Vourlekis, B., Edinburg, G., & Knee, R. (1998). The rise of social work in public mental health through aftercare of people with serious mental ill health. *Social Work*, 43(6), 567–575.

Schnapp, W. B. (2006). The C's in community mental health. *Administration and Policy in Mental Health and Mental Health Services Research*, 33(6), 737–739.

Slade, M., Adams, N., & O'Hagan, M. (2012). Recovery: Past progress and future challenges. *International Review of Psychiatry*, 24(1), 1–4.

Starnino, V. R. (2009). An integral approach to mental health recovery: Implications for social work. *Journal of Human Behavior in the Social Environment*, *19*, 820–842.

Thornicroft, G., Brohan, E., Kassam, A., & Lewis-Holmes, E. (2008). Reducing stigma and discrimination: Candidate interventions. *International Journal of Mental Health Systems*, 2(3), 1–7.

United Nations. (2008). *Convention on the rights of persons with disabilities.* United Nations Treaties Series, 2515. Retrieved May 21, 2018, from https://treaties.un.org/doc/publication/unts/volume%202515/v2515.pdf

Wallerstein, N. (2006). *What is the evidence on effectiveness of empowerment to improve health?* Copenhagen: WHO Regional Office for Europe.

Whiteford, H. A., Ferrari, A. J., Degenhardt, L., Feigin, V., & Vos, T. (2015). The global burden of mental, neurological and substance use disorders: An analysis from the global burden of disease study 2010. *PLoS One*, *10*, 2. doi:10.1371/journal.pone.0116820

Wilkinson, R., & Marmot, M. (Eds.). (2003). *Social determinants of health: The solid facts* (2nd ed.). Copenhagen: WHO Regional Office for Europe.

Wise, J. (2014). NHS should learn lessons from mental health services, says report. *BMJ*, *348*, g1386. doi:10.1136/bmj.g1386

WHO. (2006). *Health evidence network report.* Retrieved June 5, 2015, from www.euro.who.int/Document/E88086.pdf

WHO. (2013). *Mental health action plan 2013–2020.* Retrieved May 21, 2018, from http://apps.who.int/iris/bitstream/handle/10665/89966/9789241506021_eng.pdf%3bsequence=1

7 Social Innovation in Environmental Sustainability

Promoting Sharing Public Spaces for Bicycle Use

*Maria Figueroa, Jiří Navrátil,
Alex Turrini, and Gorgi Krlev*[1]

Introduction

This chapter studies civil society's engagement in social innovations that facilitate, promote or challenge the sharing of public spaces for bicycle use in cities. The chapter illustrates civil society organisation's expanding role with innovative practices aimed at changing local environmental, social, cultural or economic unsustainable patterns and, impacting the field of environmental sustainability (van der Have & Rubalcaba, 2016; Howaldt et al., 2015; Jessop et al., 2013).

Civil society organisations encompass a wide range, including community-based organisations, grassroots organisations, coalitions or advocacy groups and other associations operating between the state, individuals and the market (Androff, 2012; Belloni, 2001). Across Europe, there has been a proliferation of civil society organisation's engagement in social innovation practices seeking to affect complex environmental challenges. Adding motivation to these organisations's innovative work for sustainability is the strong mobilisation of the international community that in 2015 adopted two high-level agreements targeting seventeen sustainable development goals and limits to climate change. European nations and local authorities have been supporting these two high-level agendas for many years and a number of European cities have been leading and supporting innovative solutions that contribute to achieving sustainability goals (Københavns Kommune, 2012). The stream of social innovation explored in this chapter focuses on the practices of engaged actors regarding the promotion of sustainable living patterns and sharing soft-modes of transportation in cities, specifically bicycle use.

Bicycles provide a soft and flexible mode of transportation in urban areas. Their use is associated with numerous positive environmental, social and economic impacts ranging from improved human health to cleaner air and lower carbon emissions, from reduced noise to an overall improvement in a city's quality of social life (Rabl & de Nazelle, 2012; World Health Organization, 2010; Oja et al., 2011; Woodcock et al., 2014).

Many European cities have invested in building new and improving existing bicycle infrastructure to facilitate increasing and safe bicycle use (Pucher & Buehler, 2008). European public actors, in general, seem to understand well and increasingly promote the benefits and opportunities of supporting cycling and walking (European Cycling Federation, 2016; Pucher & Buehler, 2008). The number of research and advocacy reports and projects offering recommendations to all levels of public and private city decision-makers has multiplied over the last decade (Colville-Andersen, 2018). Additionally, new forms of multi-stakeholder agreements are proliferating in many cities (Handy et al., 2014; Pucher et al., 2010).

Urban studies and direct observations confirm that improvements made in bicycle infrastructure's quality and level of provision results in additional cycling in cities, whereas a lack of safe infrastructure can severely limit the scope of sharing space for bicycle use (Pucher & Buehler, 2006; Andrade et al., 2011). Beyond this knowledge, however, there is still a lack of understanding of the role that social engagement and civil society organisations can play to deter, mobilise and sustain bike traffic in a city.

This chapter contributes to increasing our understanding of the role of civil society's organisations in the field of environmental sustainability through an analysis of social innovative practices and the impact they produce concerning the promotion of bicycle use in cities. We compare the role of social innovation in four cities: Copenhagen, Frankfurt, Milan and Brno. The questions guiding this analysis are the following:

- How is social innovation shaping, accelerating or decelerating change trajectories in promoting bicycle use in these four European cities?
- How have these particular forms of social innovation emerged and evolved over time within their local contexts?

Central Concepts

Environmental Sustainability in Cities

The environment is where we all live and cities are home to more than half of the world population. These two aspects are inseparable, as stated in 1987 by the Brundtland report (United Nations, 1993). Achieving sustainability in cities requires attending to all the dimensions: economic, environmental and social, and considering present and future generations' needs. Although grounded in the field of *environmental* sustainability, our study considers all these dimensions. From its inception, the concept of sustainability created the framework and narrative that prompted nations' and cities' actors to act. The year 1993 is used here as the base year to initiate observations in the four cities under investigation. The assumption is that the year 1993 created an initial moment of contention (Fligstein & McAdam, 2014), which affected all four cities with a seminal understanding of sustainability in a similar way (Figueroa et al., 2015).

Social Innovation for Environmental Sustainability

Beyond an understanding of social innovation as 'the development and implementation of new ideas (products, services and models) to meet social needs and create new social relationships or collaborations' (European Commission, 2013, p. 6); we emphasise new ways of resolving environmental problems by civil society groups. We seek to understand the impact and forms of engagement in collective efforts and practices and in their interactions with state, business and other non-state actors. We distinguish some components to refine our understanding of social innovation within environmental sustainability drawn from the literature (van der Have & Rubalcaba, 2016). We select and compare social innovation cases that promote: (a) a move from individual to community approaches; (b) help create a sense of empowerment toward solving common urban environmental problems or meeting common needs; (c) deal with issues of sharing urban space to scale up a sustainable solution; (d) promote creative participatory processes that are oriented to social/environmental goals.

Thus, we try to understand how social innovation actions can contribute to and be directed by the achievement of mutual understanding among individuals and communities, and how the resulting understanding can facilitate advancing coordinated actions (van der Have & Rubalcaba, 2016; Moulaert et al., 2013). We will argue that civil society's social innovative practices can facilitate achieving a level of social coordination that is based on a collective interpretation of the social context (Habermas, 1984; Cajaiba-Santana, 2014) and supported by innovative practices. With support from Habermas and Cajaiba-Santana's concepts we will seek to develop an understanding of how social innovative actions are part of a process of communicative action that confers legitimacy to the practices of sharing space for bicycling and how this process can potentially spark a virtual cycle. An example of this occurs in at least one of our cities. Key in this understanding is that social innovation can help create a practice that people accept as worth imitating, supporting and sustaining (Cajaiba-Santana, 2014).

Methods

Case Selection

This study focuses on four European cities: Brno (Czech Republic, pop. 378,000 in 2017), Copenhagen (Denmark, pop. 1,304,000 in 2017), Frankfurt (Germany, pop. 749,000 in 2017) and Milan (Italy, pop. 1,700,000 in 2017) (United Nations, Population Division, 2018). These four cities share some traits that are important for our investigation, including population, overall density and each city's economic vitality with respect to the nation state. Moreover, these four cities provided an exemplary variety of environmental initiatives and a level of experimentation important for social innovativeness in the promotion of sharing space for bicycle use. Despite the commonalities, we will observe major differences in how the social innovation materialises. We found the most advanced cases of social innovation in sharing space for bicycle use in Copenhagen, whereas Frankfurt, where most of the infrastructure for cycling is in place, is a city where the promotion and use of bicycles and the degree of social innovation are less significant. Milan is a case where high social innovativeness promoting sharing is meeting a sparse provision of safe cycling infrastructure. Brno, in turn, is starting to develop its cycling infrastructure but social innovation processes are not concurrent with an emergent meaning that creates a supportive push for sharing space for bicycle use in this city.

Data Collection

Our central tool for organising data collection was mapping of key events based on desktop research, literature review and expert interviews for each city. We selected a period of 20 years to follow with this approach, highlighting key observations between 1993 and 2015. For each city, the initial and current conditions serve as guiding milestones to trace the evolution of the stream of innovation. The mapping of activities and milestones developed for each city served as a tool to refine the interview questions prepared for those actors actively engaged in the social innovation process. The interview questions targeted the evolution of the particular social innovation around key milestones and allowed us to trace events and actors back in time to the origins of the stream and within the past two decades. The mapping helped us identify key actors within organisations. We targeted them for a follow-up interview process. This step helped us further refine our reflexive process. We completed thirty-nine expert and practitioner interviews in the four cities as shown in Table 7.1.

Table 7.1 Number of organisations and persons interviewed

	Third sector	*Government*	*External expert*	*Total*
Germany	8 (11)*	1 (4)	4 (6)	13 (21)
Denmark	6 (6)	5 (5)	2 (2)	13 (13)
Italy	6 (8)	2 (2)	2 (2)	10 (12)
Czech Republic	2 (4)	1 (2)	–	3 (6)
TOTAL	22 (29)	9 (13)	8 (10)	39 (52)

* Number of organisations/initiatives interviewed, number of people included in brackets.

Tracing the Social Innovation Stream

Tracing the evolution of the stream of social innovation included selecting intermediate milestones during the period and mapping the contributions of key actors in advancing the innovation toward that milestone as reached within each respective city. The resulting analysis produced a thick story for each city. We discuss the results in the next sections covering them in three parts: the city background, the dimensions of innovativeness and the evolution of social innovation. As mentioned earlier, local developments happened against a joint agenda and against global developments that drive this agenda. Table 7.2 illustrates the main milestones considered in observing the city evolution from 1993 to 2005. The global insight driving events is the knowledge that biking might serve as one potent means of sustainability in cities. After 1993 many academic debates and international advocacy groups strongly promoted a shift away from car culture, promotion of safe bike lanes and other bike facilities in the urban planning process. We find some of these ideas reflected in the evolution of our four cities. However, it will become clear that implementation of these principles differ remarkably across cities.

Social Innovation (SI) Stream in Copenhagen: Creating Social Value and Legitimacy for Sharing Space for Bikes

Copenhagen is one of the world cities that has achieved the greatest dynamism in sharing urban space for bicycle promotion and use. By 2016, 62% of all inhabitants biked to their workplaces or education places, and 45% of all those who travel for work or study used their bike. The number of people who bike to work or education in Copenhagen has continued to grow from 36% in 2004 to 45% in 2014 (Københavns Kommune, 2002, 2006, 2007, 2011, 2014a, 2014b).

Table 7.2 Milestones delimiting the period of observation and coding in process tracing for all cities

1993 (UN Conference on Environment Rio/Local Agenda 21)	2015
No approach for sharing public spaces and no link between bike culture and sustainability	Higher acceptance of sharing of public space and biking as one key aspect in promoting sustainability in cities
Car culture more promoted	Alternative traffic culture promoted
Transport infrastructure does not include bike lanes by default and design	All roads typically include safe lanes for bicycle use
No existence of widespread off-road facilities for parking or storage	Extensive bike facilities (safe parking/ near public transport)

An increasing number of civil society organisations and from all sectors whose work contributes to support the biking agenda shows the dynamism of this field of social innovation. Engaged actors range from direct interest organisations like the Danish Cyclists' Federation to other non-biking non-profits such as the Danish Cancer Society, the Danish Heart Association and the Danish Diabetes Society, to many municipalities (Copenhagen, Odense, Aarhus), to private firms like Gehl Architects, to national institutions like the Ministry of Foreign Affairs and ambassadors around the world. New civil society organisations such as Cycling Without Age and Copenhage-nize are important actors in this field that are promoting the bicycle culture of Copenhagen to other countries and localities (Colville-Andersen, 2011). Milestones pertaining to infrastructure, policy implementation and cultural lifestyle factors have co-evolved and over time, helped create an intense dynamism as discussed in the following.

Milestones

NATIONAL HISTORY

The history of bicycle use in Denmark dates back a long time (Colville-Andersen, 2018), but in contrast to Copenhagen bike use nationally has slightly decreased of late (Britz Nicolaisen, 2016). After a law passed in 2012 lowered fees and taxation of motorised traffic (Government et al., 2012), the share of people who bike nationwide has started to stagnate and then even dropped. Recent numbers show that young people overall are biking less, perhaps due to a good offer of public transport service including access to Wi-Fi on board, whereas it is illegal to use a phone when riding a bike. Bicycling has become a political priority in Copenhagen, but according to interviewed experts, this is not the case at the national or regional level where existing power structures, wealthy constituencies and powerful political actors support maintaining car traffic and oil imports. The bicycle traffic indicators show that outside Copenhagen, bicycle use levels drop and do so significantly in rural areas.

LOCAL HISTORY

Bicycles have been present in Copenhagen for many more decades than those covered in the present analysis. During the last decades, by means of a pub-lic Bike Fund, the city has channelled investments into the planning, build-ing and maintenance of more than 250 km of biking lanes, keeping account of the number of bike users and using this information to plan for better and safe biking (Københavns Kommune 2012). As a stream of social inno-vation, bicycle promotion grew stronger between the years 2006 and 2009 when cycling became a more prominent topic supported in the local politi-cal agenda, (e.g., two prominent bike-oriented figures became Lord Mayor and Mayor of Technical and Environment Department within the city in that period). This led to systemic changes and more resources devoted to bike-targeted projects around the city. Leadership from the activist turned political leader and help from the technical side (activist turned city planner) and the municipal level, as well as the pressure and advocacy work of many years (even back in the 1980s) from interest organisations such as the Danish Cyclist Federation, helped to move the city bicycle agenda forward (Cycling Embassy of Denmark, n.d). Advocacy work from very active groups like the Danish Cyclists' Federation and more recently the Bicycle Innovation Lab have contributed to bringing many wishes and proposals into formal policy development pushing the agenda of cyclists. New projects have literally changed the mobility network and improved the possibilities for biking in the city. In addition, market actors have contributed with innovative designs, playing a significant role for the dynamism of the social innovation stream in this city. Some of the major steps are outlined in Figure 7.1 and picked up in the discussion of actors and their interplay.

Actors and Interplay

Sharing space for bicycles in Copenhagen has co-evolved gradually and complementary to the improvement of other forms of mobility in the city, including walking and pedestrian-only central areas. As the biking infrastructure improved, safety has also been enhanced. The work of new civil society organisations such as the Bicycle Innovation Lab and Cycling Without Age is more radical and transformative than previous developments.

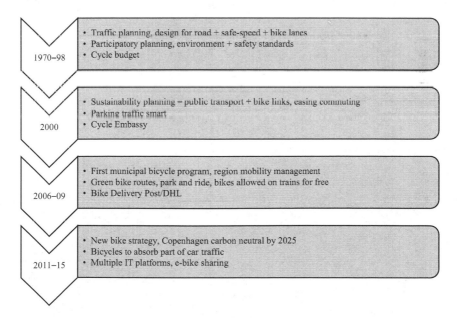

Figure 7.1 Copenhagen, Denmark: milestones

The two organisations are rethinking bike use, shifting perceptions of biking as a mere instrument of mobility to a tool to deliver a green, inclusive, healthy, quality of life as well as effective mobility. One interviewee goes even further saying:

> Bike use is not just a means of green and healthy transportation but also a socially innovative force.
>
> (Interviewee from Cycling Without Age)

Cycling Without Age is running a project concerned as much with mobility as with enhancing social life by promoting the improvement of the quality of life for the elderly through biking. Similarly, the Bicycle Innovation Lab promotes bike use in the business world through their mobile Bicycle Library. Here, they promote work-related bike use instead of the use of cars at the Danish Broadcast Corporation. Disruptive changes, innovation and new approaches to bike use seem to come from civil society organisations, rather than from the state actors, though the latter are simply paramount in creating, maintaining and extending bike use with safe conditions for the universal purpose of mobility. People who bike in Copenhagen come from all cultural, social and age backgrounds. The Copenhagen Bike Accounts' efforts to increase safety has also enhanced shared use of space with pedestrians, facilitating the use of bikes by children and people of all ages (Dansk Arkitektur Center, 2014). With high ridership, the arrival of new brands of luxury bicycles creates a counter tendency in the direction of high-end commodification. As the purposes for using bicycles in the city multiply, the market has expanded to offer new models, new services and possibilities from foldable bicycles to family bicycles. Despite being more prohibitive in terms of costs, the rise of luxury bikes does not have a crowding out effect on established bicycle use.

Many years of learning experience in Copenhagen led to a point at which the social value created by the social innovation stream has consolidated the status of the city as a bicycling hub. In other words, the social innovation stream in and around bicycle use in the city has become institutionalised. There is a Cycling Embassy in Copenhagen, and bicycle consultants are constantly developing new business models around bicycle culture and life (Colville-Andersen, 2018). Some ideas occur in the commercialisation of bicycle services. Others are finding opportunities to bring about greater social inclusion. The number of bikes in Copenhagen has grown to a point where congestion is the result at some of the busiest intersections. Increases in bike traffic in Copenhagen may require the achievement of new compromises to limit car traffic and difficult political decisions. Curiously, within Denmark, the innovativeness of the Copenhagen system, instead of serving as a blueprint for other cities, makes it a magnet for innovators, bicycle lovers and even bicycle leaders in the country. This produces what one of the Danish experts called a seesaw effect, where further innovative gains in terms of the resources that organisations invest in Copenhagen, including time, energy and ideas, come at the cost of deploying these same resources of innovation in other cities.

SI Stream in Frankfurt: Improvements in Infrastructure but Deficits in Bicycle Culture

The number of people that use bikes has significantly increased within the last 20 years: starting at 6% of the whole traffic in Frankfurt in 1998, bike use increased to about 11–13% by 2013.

Milestones

NATIONAL HISTORY

Biking has a long tradition in Germany, but local developments in recent years are more important for understanding the SI stream than lines of national history. At the national level, a recent report called the 'Sinus Study' commissioned by the Ministry of Transport in 2015 has shown deficiencies in relation to the aims in the 'national bicycle traffic plan' issued a year before by the same Ministry (Bundesministerium für Verkehr und digitale Infrastruktur, 2014; Sinus Markt- und Sozialforschung GmbH, 2015). The first report proposed the aspiration of increasing the share of bike travel further from the level of 10%. The Sinus Study instead points out that the popularity of bike travel has decreased in the population as compared to previous years. A study in 2014 has furthermore shown that the concept of e-mobility, mainly concerning cars but also bikes, is less accepted in Germany than in other European countries, for example the Netherlands or Norway (Breitinger, 2014). This provides evidence that in Frankfurt, as in the rest of Germany, a strong pro-auto narrative is present.

LOCAL HISTORY

Frankfurt is labelled the 'city of commuters' and this branding resonates with the automobile narrative referred to previously. Despite this, the ambition in Frankfurt has been to increase the share of biking relative to other forms of transport. As a social innovation stream, promoting bike use has picked up in terms of trajectories and dynamism in recent years and much effort is devoted to expanding public spaces for bicycles in the city. The opening of one-way streets to counter-directed bike traffic, which had peaked around 2006–2009, for instance, has been of great influence for improving the bicycling conditions in the city (Allgemeiner Studierendenausschuss Goethe Universität Frankfurt am Main, 2016). The use of bikes is essentially not a pay-for-service system and comparatively the cheapest form of transport available. This might have changed slightly by the initiation of bike renting systems, which comes still at low costs, or the increase of e-mobility, which makes bikes significantly more expensive.

Similar factors, but also demographic characteristics may have an influence on the stratification of bicycle use across society. In Frankfurt, but also across Germany, local government officials expressed the view in the interview that the use of bicycles is becoming trendy, mainly by young urban people. The fact that e-bikes are currently still expensive makes them more attractive to wealthier target groups than to others. Among immigrant groups, the observation is for a tendency to use fewer bicycles than among people without a migration background (interviewee from Frankfurt). Yet, this may be changing. Another interviewee indicated the share of bikes is on the rise, partly because public transport is comparatively expensive. Altogether, biking does not have a special target group and, if anything, the heterogeneity of bicycle users has steadily increased as compared to previous years, adding:

> It is becoming more diverse. There are significant shares of bike users in all groups of society.
>
> (Interviewee 9 from Frankfurt)

Cycling users span all types of people and all ages and is available to everybody. However, the number of users has currently stagnated and political actors interviewed, while having the ambition to increase shares further, think that there is not much room for further improvement. This was despite initiatives promoted by ADFC Frankfurt (the local branch of the national cyclists' association Allgemeiner Deutscher Fahrrad Club) such as 'bike + business' or 'Frankfurt bike night' that are meant to increase bike use among employees and bike culture generally. These and further milestones discussed in the following are illustrated in Figure 7.2.

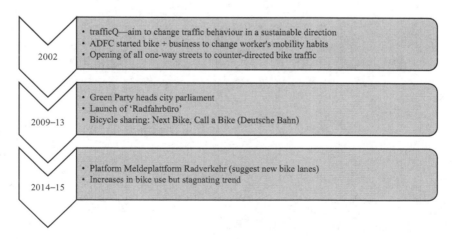

Figure 7.2 Frankfurt, Germany: milestones

Actors and Interplay

In Frankfurt, all identified actors have a great interest in promoting bicycle use and the responsible actors are mostly seeking forms of pro-active cooperation. The interviewees pointed at the importance of personal relationships as a key to initiating and maintaining such collaboration: '[E]verything fits together, and we are a small family, and all of us know each other'. Another person reiterated the network aspects and called it a form of 'give and take' between the involved organisations:

> There is a network of people, who know each other well and who, and this is the prerequisite for this to work, each give and take, people who can work pragmatically and who try to build a good working atmosphere.
>
> (Interviewee 4 from Frankfurt)

As a result, for example, ADFC Frankfurt and the City of Frankfurt, along with other (quasi)public actors such as IVM (a mobility management agency) or traffiQ (the regional public transport provider), are working in a cooperative way and not against each other. This is what, according to the interviewees, differentiates Frankfurt from other German cities even within the same federal state and at close proximity.

The election into the city parliament of the Green Party in 2011 resulted in a very big influence and produced a major leap in the city's priority given to biking. One result was the foundation of the 'Radfahrbüro' in 2009, which has since become a new central player if not *the* central player in Frankfurt's actor landscape. It is not only important in terms of its coordinative function between actors but also and in particular as a link between these actors and cyclists. In the words of one interviewee:

> The Radfahrbüro has a central function not only with regard to coordinating processes within the public administration, but also since it provides a link to cyclists into the community.
>
> (Interviewee 9 from Frankfurt)

On the municipal level, despite the efforts referred to before, a report in 2014 showed that bike routes in Frankfurt needed further improvement and expansion (Stadt Frankfurt am Main, 2016). The media also frequently reports that bike-parking facilities at Frankfurt main station are few and not well organised. Better examples at close proximity could be found in Bad Homburg or Darmstadt (Rippegather, 2014). Big companies like Deutsche Bahn or Next Bike currently dominate the issue of bike sharing or bike renting, and there is no established private bike sharing culture in Frankfurt. Most interviewees, however, saw these systems as limited in their capacity to substantially leverage bike use further. Overall innovativeness in the field in Frankfurt is advanced via state intervention in cooperation with the third sector. Market actors are less relevant. Frankfurt demonstrates a solid record of development of facilities, services and integration with public transport but the challenge for Frankfurt to stimulate increasing bike ridership in the city will still require further innovation.

SI in Brno: Social Innovation Stream Challenging Sharing

In Brno, there is a demand for bike sharing particularly from cyclist movements and students who are looking for alternative means of mobility. One of the first successful projects is Mezikavárenská půjčovna kol (Inter-cafeteria bike rental). According to interviewees, bike sharing programmes in Brno were also developing without civil society but they would probably have taken longer and might have focused more on creating a for-profit business than on the promotion of cycling for environmental or other reasons. Promotion of bike use through various cultural contests and campaigns from organised civic associations, and by a change in the attitude of, for instance employers, said one interviewee, explained the current rise of interest in bicycle use (Brněnský cyklo-koordinátor, 2010). In spite of this favourable attention, the topic of bicycle traffic can be highly unpopular within another group of people. This group of people are less welcoming to changes in road traffic to favour cyclists. They are organising to represent their mostly adversarial position to the development of bicycle transportation in the city. As explained by one interviewee, this civil society organisation work reflects:

> The association favours development of a comfortable individual transportation system "exclusive" for private cars, not to accommodate a wide range of the citizens that are considered [by the association] as "transport promiscuous" [wanting to use roads for several means of transport].
>
> (Interview with Brněnský cyklo-koordinátor)

Milestones

Three major factors supported the development of cycling and brought new people into the field. The first one is local tradition: a large share of Brno's inhabitants comes from the neighbouring towns and villages of South Moravia which is a geographically flat region. A biking culture has always been part of these areas and therefore has also become part of the mainstream way of living in Brno. The second factor is the embracement of bike riding as part of leading a healthier life that includes physical exercise. Finally, according to one interviewee, biking in the city has become a part of youth subcultures, especially hipster culture. This together with its economic advantages and the fact that several universities are located in Brno and thousands of young people live and study in the city, make biking a preferred mobility vehicle of youngsters in the city.

NATIONAL HISTORY

There are some national or regional factors other than culture that have had an influence on biking in Brno. The role of civil society organisations and associations aiming at popularising bicycle use and advocating for the development of particular infrastructure was important. Many of these advocates, but also service providers have not originated in Brno. Prague serves as a source of inspiration and of financial resources: some of the non-governmental organisations (NGOs) working in the field in Brno are local branches of Prague NGOs. Brno has also benefitted from the influence of countries abroad—most notably Austria and Sweden (at least in the field of bike sharing).

LOCAL HISTORY

Bike sharing and bike use in general are seen in Brno partially as a disruptive form of innovation. The most important reason for this categorisation relates to the perception of using public spaces jointly and the aspect of sharing, which have not been pronounced in Czech culture until recent years. A dramatic social, political and economic shift toward privatisation and commercialisation took place after 1989, as a result of which the return of 'sharing' is regarded as something suspicious. This might explain the comparatively strong commercial drive of the bike-sharing initiatives in Brno with some organisations prepared to become fully commercial services once they have enough 'customers'. A dichotomy exists between biking as a social practice and biking as a new form of commercial service.

We discuss three major countertrends regarding bicycle sharing in Brno beyond those mentioned previously. First, there is a strong perception that biking is part of a personal lifestyle that makes the bicycle a symbol of the particular social status of its owner. This combined with the 'civic privatism' just referred to, may lead to the development of biking subcultures but not necessarily to substantial increases in the use of bikes. Second, there are initiatives driven partially by the right-wing parties and civil society actors supported especially by the elderly citizens who object to the creation of spaces for biking at the expense of individual car transportation, particularly during the reconstruction of the streets and squares. This represents the continuation of a trend that favours development of a comfortable individual transportation system exclusive for private cars anywhere in the country as a sort of 'citizens' right' for which they are 'paying their taxes' (Bárta, 2010). Third, and paradoxically, the existence of a very dense and well-operated network of public transportation which fully supplements individual car transportation may discourage citizens from using bikes.

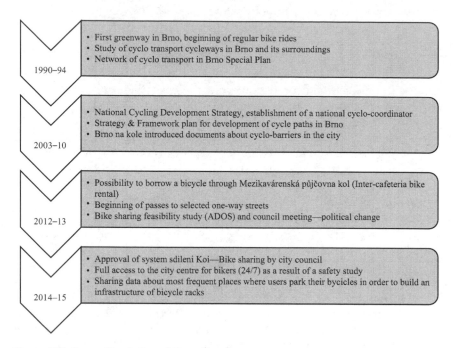

Figure 7.3 Brno, Czech Republic: milestones

Furthermore, bicycle infrastructure lacks connectivity to the public transportation network of trams and buses and other necessary infrastructure (e.g., there is lack of bicycle parking, not enough space for bicycle transportation on board trams across the city, low number of bicycle friendly buses, etc.).

Thus, we find two trends clashing in Brno. First, we witness a quantitative increase in users and beyond that a gradual rehabilitation (if not invention) of bike transportation as part of the city's transportation strategies. This trend is accompanied by a rise in investment in infrastructure and by a relatively low and declining levels of resistance of significant political forces (see Figure 7.3 for the major milestones). The availability of public resources for the construction of biking infrastructure and Brno's geography are two important restrictive factors. In contrast to the region, Brno's topography is quite mountainous, a circumstance which likely decreases the attractiveness of cycling.

Actors and Interplay

There is a mix of motives and reasons of actors active in the field. On the one hand, most of the activities which aim to support cycling are driven by civil society organisations. These are usually motivated by environmental and cultural values—dealing with environmental pollution, gentrification of some part of the city, transportation problems etc. At the same time, bike sharing is promoted by organisations between the profit and non-profit motives who aim at some form of ethical business rather than strictly non-profit activities. Many of these organisations consider themselves 'start-ups' rather than NGOs and have business ambitions for the future. At the same time and for the reasons mentioned previously, the cycling culture has become commercialised and many cycling events or projects are sponsored by businesses which aim at targeting certain parts of the population with their products (sports equipment, alcohol, media etc.). While cycling is available for most of the citizens and no stigmatisation of users for old or cheap bikes is visible, bicycling is also seen as an attribute of a certain type of leisure activity, related to fitness and a healthy lifestyle and thus, associated with the habitus of the educated middle class. In this sense, the field can be seen as stratified and excluding of certain social groups.

SI Stream in Milan: Creative Innovation Confronting Paucity of Safe Bike Infrastructure

In recent years, more bike paths have been built in the city of Milan and by 2011 there were 130 kilometres of cycle paths. Additionally, the restriction of car entry into the city centre has encouraged citizens to use their bicycles more. An important factor according to one of the interviewees had also been the economic crisis:

> people can't afford anymore all the expenses related to car maintenance, namely: insurance, taxes, petrol, etc. they are therefore opting for the cheaper alternative the bicycle.
>
> (Interviewee Municipality of Milan)

The cyclist image has changed deeply within Milan with businesspersons riding the yellow bicycles that are part of the municipal bike sharing initiative. The bicycles in Milan are often considered a fashion item, and some of them are expensive because of the peculiar design or layout.

In Milan, the state has recently adopted strategies and deployed resources in direct interaction with market actors. Market actors are coming forward with innovative ideas that might gain attraction in other cities, since they are making biking fashionable in Italy and potentially beyond. Conditions for safe bike riding, however, are not yet present in Milan, which might be another factor contributing to the fact that biking is currently most relevant among the young, healthy and those interested in fashion.

Milestones

NATIONAL HISTORY

Bicycles have been present in Italy as in several other European nations since the end of the nineteenth century. Bicycles are a part of many aspects of Italian life (work, sports, leisure) and for many decades the interactions of bicycles in public space and even the bicycle's social meaning has changed (Mari, 2015). The space available for bicycling in Italian cities is characterised by frequent discontinuities. Usually bicyclists are in need to share off-street facilities or to share space with either motorised vehicles or pedestrians. Nationally, guidelines such as the Codice della Strada, along with the Decreto Ministeriale number 557 of 1999 set the structural and functional features regulating cycling facilities. These guidelines regulate bike path planning and design and state the objective of achieving a proper level of safety and functionality to help promote bicycle use to reduce congestion and meet environmental sustainability goals (Bernardi & Rupi, 2015). However, these guidelines are not always followed since local administrators may see some of these indications as limitations; frequently, provisions of cycling facilities standards are waived and the separation from pedestrians is assessed merely by means of a painted stripe. Thus, with the design of some sub-standard facilities and no sufficient space for both cyclists and pedestrians a decrease in number of cyclists and in safety of the users follows (Bernardi & Rupi, 2015).

LOCAL HISTORY

In Milan, recent data highlight an increasing number of bikes and bike-sharing users. This number has increased by 26% over the last eight years and by 56% compared with 2003. The highest number of passengers use the bike-sharing service to move from home to work. More recently, after a slight reduction in 2013, the data have risen again and are now close to their value in 2012, with the total number of bike riders at 34,100 (FIAB Milano, Ciclobby, 2013).

The inspiration for change comes from the programmes run by the municipality in partnership with the private sector. In this partnership, the private sector offers financial support with projects such as the one called 'Bicittadini', an educational project aiming at increasing awareness in the use of bikes in the city (AMAT, FIAB, 2015). Another factor driving the inspiration are grassroots organisations, e.g., 'Massamarmocchi' consisting of parents who are educating their children to be responsible for the environment by picking a less polluting means of transport. The bike-sharing service is more and more successful as evidenced by the fact that more than 13% of the bicycles counted in the town centre belong to the public bike-sharing service with a peak in the Largo Augusto area.

All the groups mentioned, along with others to be discussed in more depth later, have been lobbying for better policies and safer biking lanes. The municipality, from 2007 onwards, has made a great effort to promote a biking culture in Milan. There are more people using bicycles because of improved infrastructure, but according to one interviewee:

> Milan's main problems are cars that occupy public spaces impeding the development of alternative means of mobility.
>
> (Interviewee Municipality of Milan)

Figure 7.4 displays the milestones referred to in the preceding; they will be guiding the expanded discussion in the following section on engaged actors and their interplay.

Actors and Interplay

The strength of the SI stream started picking up toward 2005, when various institutions were involved in the Mobility Management Project. In 2011, a new mayor was elected. Letizia Moratti began to implement some

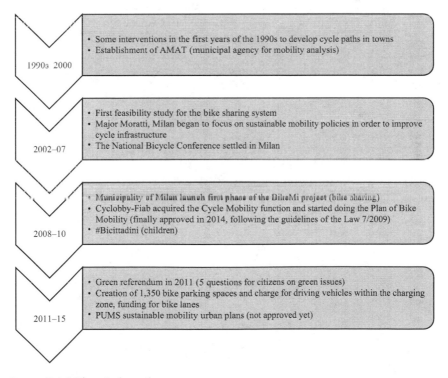

Figure 7.4 Milan, Italy: milestones

interventions, building new infrastructures and promoting cycling events. First, she proposed the 'Green Rays Project' that defined and promoted a new 'slow mobility', designing green corridors in Milan's urban fabric. There have been countertrends to a broadening spread of bike use in Milan; one of the more prominent ones is the fashion movement that bike sharing has created. The more expensive and uniquely designed the bike is, the more status it gives to the cyclist. Most of the bike sharing activities and campaigns are done in collaboration with the municipality and are mainly driven by the private sector. It is the private sector players that act as lobbyists and often engage as co-financiers to municipality-run projects (e.g., #Bicittadini). Civil society in the form of self-organised parent groups also play an important role in trying to create awareness in the general population of the environmental benefits of biking. There have however been instances where the city of Milan has not worked in partnership with third sector organisations specifically the project 'Cyclobby-Fiab' with the result of undesirable outcomes, according to one interviewee:

> In Milan it has always been preferred to build expensive and, sometimes, useless infrastructure rather than listening to the cyclists' voice and save money!
>
> (Interviewee from Cyclobby-Fiab)

Milan has the state and market as the primary innovating actors in the field. The state in Milan, to a certain extent is ahead of Frankfurt and Copenhagen in engaging on two fronts: first, by directly strategising and entering partnerships with business, and second, by waging the first confrontational battles to limit access to car owners (taxes and imposing access restrictions). These may be unpopular policies but they also create the demand markets require to thrive. Whether or not that will help drive the use of bikes as much as the civic system that Copenhagen has been capable of, remains an open question. Milan seems to be tapping into the high-end forms of idea creation and innovativeness observed in Copenhagen, however, the physical supporting infrastructure for safe riding is simply not there. Therefore, a large and all-encompassing increase in ridership seems unlikely.

Synthesis

Comparative Analysis

Historical and geographical conditions are different between these four cities and therefore, each city context produces specific conditions affecting the resulting stream of innovation. Common to the four cities is timely key intervention from state actors highlighted in the milestones throughout the period considered. We have seen how state intervention sets the ground for sharing space and with it social innovation begins to take root and, in some places, starts flourishing. A clear progression takes place in all four locations toward greater sharing of space for bicycles. However, counternarratives or deviations (biking as a fashion), as well as barriers (motorised traffic) have been observed. In Copenhagen, the social innovation stream has reached maturity in comparison with the other three cities. However, the strength of state presence and support to the stream of innovation further promotes creativity from civil society and fruitful opportunities for market actors. In Frankfurt, there is a strong lead from state actors, while organisations from civil society are fewer but also important. Despite joint efforts, the use of bicycles has stagnated at a comparatively low level in recent years. Systemic foundations for a strong value promotion are there but the creativity of civil society and the market is tempered by a strong car culture prevailing in the city spaces. In Brno, the innovativeness of the stream is still in the ideation phase. Some civil society actors engage in the promotion of bicycle use wanting to become business actors and they are taking sharing initiatives to the test. However, Brno is also an example of a place where organised civil society efforts may be capable of producing a profound move against sharing. In Brno, appreciation of the value of sharing space for bicycling is challenged by historical narratives questioning this new meaning for 'sharing' in a post socialist era.

The cases demonstrate how civil society organisations can contribute to producing a concrete form of social value, in particular the value exercising acceptance and giving legitimacy to adopting norms, good aspects but also inconveniences associated with sharing public space for bicycles beyond pure mobility purposes. A common observation in the four cities is that the narratives that generate more traction and innovativeness in sharing space for bicycling are less related to awareness and political prioritisation of environmentally friendly practices per se, and more linked to improving health (all), enjoying life (Milan/Copenhagen) or recovering local traditions (Brno) in the urban context.

Where the collective value of sharing space for bicycle use is stronger, scalability to levels of significance for environmental sustainability are possible. This is the case only in the city with the most vibrant stream of innovation of the four cities, Copenhagen. Civil society is also demonstrating strong creativity in Milan but there needs to be a match with provision of safe infrastructure that permits further increases in bike use there. Social innovation in environmental sustainability for sharing urban space can contribute to a re-embedding of social meanings and values of public space use. Social innovation enhances volunteer practices and contributes to innovating services but its possible values and meanings will be contextual. More generally, in the four cities, sharing space relies upon the networks and interactions supported by social innovation from organised civil actors, in interplay with actions from state and market actors. We have sought to document this interplay between stakeholders but further analysis such as network analysis could prove this further.

Learnings

We have answered the question of how social innovation is shaping change trajectories in the case of promotion of sharing space for bicycle use in Brno, Milan, Frankfurt and Copenhagen. Our qualitative analysis of these four cities highlights a systemic and dynamic interplay between organisations and actors, where practices, narratives, stakeholder claims, new and old struggles, are simultaneously and continuously in interplay resulting in opportunities but also challenging the sharing of space for biking in these cities. The analysis highlights the dynamic interplay of civil society actors in practices of social innovation. Over time, we argue that SI contributes to consolidation particularly supporting social narratives, aiming at re-embedding social claims of how and why the right to mobility in a city can be distributed. The longitudinal evolution of social narratives and claims related to bicycle use in each city reflects a process of societal practical learning. As this practical learning accumulates over time, we observed the emergence of a form of legitimation of sharing space as a form of collective interpretation. We observed a form of communicative value system around bicycle use that citizens learn to recognise and (partly) embrace. In the most successful of our four cities, this legitimation works in facilitating and supporting the scaling up of bicycle use. In the other three cities, other forces are preventing consolidation of a similar collective value gain that legitimates sharing of space for bicycle use. These other forces (e.g., lack of bike infrastructure, a car-oriented culture) remain at work and social innovation alone may not have the same impact there. Further studies are necessary to understand why and how social innovation promoting bicycle use can become part of a virtuous cycle in some cities but remain in an embryonic stage in others. The most important realisation is that social innovation has a potential for unlocking seemingly locked-in conditions. Our results illustrate how experimentation in social innovation can produce forms of social coping mechanisms that can help advancing new imaginaries for long-term desired social and environmental change.

Conclusions

We answered how the SI stream and the local variations thereof have emerged and evolved over time within their local context.

Social innovation is contextual, therefore, social innovation for environmental aims is difficult to replicate from city to city. A key role in the evolution of social innovation for environmental sustainability in all the cities is played by the state. Concerning bicycle use, the state creates a safe playing field with clear rules and appropriate infrastructure that supports the emergence of creative innovative efforts from civil society. Remarkably, where there was a lack of provided infrastructure (Brno and Milan), market actors engaged more profoundly, but also with (more) limited capabilities of promoting bike use effectively. Copenhagen shows that a supportive culture is indispensable for reaching dimensions that have a lasting environmental impact, but it is less clear how the other cities could engage in creating a similar larger impact. The study confronted a number of limitations as to the insights produced in this regard. A more rigorous implementation of the process tracing would have been needed, which would have required delving more concretely into tracing events at the organisational level, potentially linking actors' roles to specific outcomes in a more detailed fashion than we have been capable of. We have added different steps to gain further traction in our analysis but not sufficient to claim that we have established causal relations. The process has been fruitful nonetheless, to identify systemic and relational dimensions, plausible links and elements. Further research in analysing specific individualised segments of influence and interaction concerning the SI stream can build on these insights.

Note

1. We would like to thank all who made important contributions to the ITSSOIN project deliverable that formed the basis for this chapter: Greiffenberg, C.; Akinyi, E.; Brink, A.; Behrendt, C.; Placier, K.; Pejcal, J.; Cavola, F.; and Cancellieri, G.

References

Andrade, V., Jensen, O. B., Harder, H., & Madsen, J. C. O. (2011). Bike infrastructures and design qualities: Enhancing cycling. *Tidsskrift for Kortlægning og Arealforvaltning*, 46(1).

Androff, D. K. (2012). Can civil society reclaim truth? Results from a community-based truth and reconciliation commission. *International Journal of Transitional Justice*, 6, 296–317. https://doi.org/10.1093/ijtj/ijs012

Allgemeiner Studierendenausschuss Goethe Universität Frankfurt am Main. (2016). *Kostenlose Registrierung bei Call-A-Bike*. Retrieved from http://asta-frankfurt.de/angebote/teil-1-neue-infos-zum-asta-campusrad-call-bike-anmeldung-jetzt-moeglich

AMAT, FIAB. (2015). *#Bicittadini. Interventi a Favore della Mobilità Ciclistica*. Milano Bicocca: Università degli Studi.

Bárta, D. (2010, December 1). *Brněnský cyklo-koordinátor. Brno Na Kole*. Retrieved from www.brnonakole.cz/brnensky-cyklo-koordinator/

Belloni, R. (2001). Civil society and peacebuilding in Bosnia and Herzegovina. *Journal of Peace Research*, 38, 163–180. https://doi.org/10.1177/0022343301038002003

Bernardi, S., & Rupi, F. (2015). An analysis of bicycle travel speed and disturbances on off-street and on-street facilities. *Transportation Research Procedia*, 5, 82–94. https://doi.org/10.1016/j.trpro.2015.01.004

Breitinger, M. (2014, September 24). Elektromobilität. Aktionismus ohne Wert. *Die Zeit*. Retrieved from www.zeit.de/mobilitaet/2014-09/elektroauto-subventionen-kommentar

Britz Nicolaisen, C. (2016). *Danskerne cykler mindre*. Retrieved from www.cyklistforbundet.dk/Aktuelt/Nyt/Nyheder/Vi-cykler-mindre

Brněnský cyklo-koordinátor. (2010, December 1). *Brno Na Kole*. Retrieved from www.brnonakole.cz/brnensky-cyklo-koordinator/

Bundesministerium für Verkehr und digitale Infrastruktur. (2014). *Fahrradverkehr*. Retrieved from www.bmvi.de/SharedDocs/DE/Artikel/G/fahrradverkehr.html

Cajaiba-Santana, G. (2014). Social innovation: Moving the field forward. A conceptual framework. *Technological Forecast and Social Change, 82*, 42–51. https://doi.org/10.1016/j.techfore.2013.05.008

Colville-Andersen, M. (2011). *Copenhagenize origins*. Retrieved from www.copenhagenize.com/2011/01/copenhagenize-origins.html

Colville-Andersen, M. (2018). *Copenhagenize: The definitive guide to global bicycle urbanism*. London: Island Press.

Cycling Embassy of Denmark. (n.d). *Our services*. Retrieved from www.cycling-embassy.dk/our-services/

Dansk Arkitektur Center. (2014). *København: Verdens bedste cykelby*. Retrieved from www.dac.dk/da/dac-cities/baeredygtige-byer/alle-cases/transport/koebenhavn-verdens-bedste-cykelby/

European Commission. (2013). Social innovation research in the European Union. Approaches, findings and future directions: edited by Jenson, Jane and Harrisson, Denis. *Policy Review*, doi:10.2777/12639.

European Cycling Federation. (2016). *Cycling delivers on the global goals*. Brussels: European Union.

FIAB Milano, Ciclobby. (2013). *13° Censimento dei Ciclisti*. ACTL (Associazione per la Cultura e il Tempo Libero). (2009). *Ciclo Milano, Il Dossier*.

Figueroa, M., Tygstrup, C., Hyánek, V., Navrátil, J., Preuss, S., Ferlisi, M., & Turrini, A. (2015). *Field description in environmental sustainability: Sustainability in cities*. Part 1 of deliverable 6.1 of the project: "Impact of the Third Sector as Social Innovation" (ITSSOIN), European Commission—7th Framework Programme. Brussels: European Commission, DG Research.

Fligstein, N. & McAdam, D. (2014). The field of theory. *Contemporary Sociology, 43*, 315–318. https://doi:10.1177/0094306114531283a

Government et al. (2012). *Aftale mellem regeringen (Socialdemokraterne, Socialistisk Folkeparti og Radikale Venstre), Dansk Folkeparti og Enhedslisten om: Takstnedsættelser og investeringer til forbedring af den kollektive trafik*. Retrieved from www.trafikstyrelsen.dk/~/media/Dokumenter/04%20Kollektiv%20trafik/01%20 Koordinering%20af%20kollektiv%20trafik/Takstnedsaettelser/Aftaletekst%20 11%20juni%202012%20bedre%20og%20billiger%20kollektiv%20trafik.pdf

Habermas, J. (1984). *The theory of communicative action: Reason and the rationalization of society*. Boston: Beacon Press.

Handy, S., van Wee, B., & Kroesen, M. (2014). Promoting cycling for transport: Research needs and challenges. *Transportaion Review, 34*, 4–24. https://doi.org/1 0.1080/01441647.2013.860204

Howaldt, J., Kopp, R., & Schwarz, M. (2015). Social innovations as drivers of social change – exploring Tarde's contribution to social innovation theory building. In *New frontiers in social innovation research* (pp. 29–52). London, UK: Palgrave Macmillan. https://doi.org/10.1057/9781137506801

Jessop, B., Moulaert, F., Hulgård, L., & Hamdouch, A. (2013). Social innovation research: A new stage in innovation analysis? In F. Moulaert, D. MacCallum, A. Mehmood, & A. Hamdouch (Eds.), *The international handbook on* social innovation collective action, social learning and transdisciplinary research (pp. 110–130). Cheltenham, UK: Edward Elgar Publishing.

Københavns Kommune. (2002). *Cykelpolitik 2002–2012*. Retrieved from http://arkiv.cykelviden.dk/filer/313_2002_2012_cykelpolitik.pdf

Københavns Kommune. (2006). *Oversigt over cykelprojekter besluttet I 2006 og foråret 2007 (Cykelpakke I og II)*. Retrieved from www.kk.dk/sites/default/files/edoc_old_format/Teknik-%20og%20Miljoeudvalget/06-02-2008%2015.00.00/Dagsorden/04-02-2008%2011.31.27/Doknr%202008-20470%20-%20Bilag%203.%20Cykelfremkommelighed.PDF

Københavns Kommune. (2007). *Eco Metropolis: Our vision for Copenhagen 2015*. Retrieved from http://kk.sites.itera.dk/apps/kk_pub2/pdf/674_CFbnhMePZr.pdf

Københavns Kommune. (2011). *Fra god til verdens bedste. Københavns cykelstrategi 2011–2025*. Retrieved from http://kk.sites.itera.dk/apps/kk_pub2/pdf/818_YF8zF5k7Cr.pdf

Københavns Kommune. (2012). *KBH 2025 Klimaplanen*. Retrieved from http://kk.sites.itera.dk/apps/kk_pub2/pdf/930_QP7u8mn5bb.pdf

Københavns Kommune. (2014a). *København Cyklernes By Cykelregnskabet 2014*. Retrieved from http://kk.sites.itera.dk/apps/kk_pub2/pdf/1362_cFTGCXHzmE.pdf

Københavns Kommune. (2014b). *København cyklernes by. Cykelregnskabet 2014*. Retrieved from http://kk.sites.itera.dk/apps/kk_pub2/pdf/1362_cFTGCXHzmE.pdf

Mari, C. (2015). Putting the Italians on bicycles: Marketing at Bianchi, 1885–1955. *Journal of Historical Research in Marketing, 7*, 133–158. https://doi.org/10.1108/JHRM-07-2013-0049

Moulaert, F., MacCallum, D., Mehmood, A. & Hamdouch, A. (2013). *The international handbook on social innovation*. Cheltenham, UK: Edward Elgar Publishing.

Oja, P., Titze, S., Bauman, A., de Geus, B., Krenn, P., Reger-Nash, B., & Kohlberger, T. (2011). Health benefits of cycling: A systematic review: Cycling and health. *Scandinavian Journal of Medicine & Science in Sports, 21*, 496–509. https://doi.org/10.1111/j.1600-0838.2011.01299.x

Pucher, J., & Buehler, R. (2006). Why Canadians cycle more than Americans: A comparative analysis of bicycling trends and policies. *Transport Policy, 13*, 265–279. https://doi.org/10.1016/j.tranpol.2005.11.001

Pucher, J., & Buehler, R. (2008). Making cycling irresistible: Lessons from The Netherlands, Denmark and Germany. *Transportaion Review, 28*, 495–528. https://doi.org/10.1080/01441640701806612

Pucher, J., Dill, J., & Handy, S. (2010). Infrastructure, programs, and policies to increase bicycling: An international review. *Preventive Medicine, 50*, S106–S125. https://doi.org/10.1016/j.ypmed.2009.07.028

Rabl, A., & de Nazelle, A. (2012). Benefits of shift from car to active transport. *Transport Policy, 19*, 121–131. https://doi.org/10.1016/j.tranpol.2011.09.008

Rippegather, J. (2014, April 12). *Parkende Autos sollen weichen. Frankfurter Rundschau*. Retrieved from www.fr-online.de/stadt-rad/abstellflaechen-fahrraeder-parkende-autos-sollen-weichen,26706880,26826924.html

Sinus Markt- und Sozialforschung GmbH. (2015). *Fahrrad-Monitor Deutschland 2015: Ergebnisse einer digitalen Online-Befragung. Heidelberg.* Retrieved from www.bmvi.de/SharedDocs/DE/Anlage/VerkehrUndMobilitaet/Fahrrad/fahrrad-monitor-deutschland-2015.pdf?__blob=publicationFile

Stadt Frankfurt am Main. (2016). *Gibt es Krokodile im GrünGürtel? Familien-Radtour auf der Safari-Route zum Zoo.* Retrieved from www.frankfurt.de/sixcms/detail.php?id=2855&_ffmpar[_id_inhalt]=30953446

United Nations. (1993). *Report of the United Nations conference on environment and development, volume I, resolutions adopted by the conference.* New York, NY: United Nations.

United Nations, Department of Economic and Social Affairs, Population Division. (2018). *World urbanization prospects: The 2018 revision,* custom data acquired via website. Retrieved from https://esa.un.org/unpd/wup/DataQuery/

van der Have, R. P., & Rubalcaba, L. (2016). Social innovation research: An emerging area of innovation studies? *Research Policy, 45,* 1923–1935. https://doi.org/10.1016/j.respol.2016.06.010

Woodcock, J., Tainio, M., Cheshire, J., O'Brien, O., & Goodman, A. (2014). Health effects of the London bicycle sharing system: Health impact modelling study. *BMJ, 348,* g425–g425. https://doi.org/10.1136/bmj.g425

World Health Organization. (2010). *Environmentally Sustainable & Healthy Urban Transportation (ESHUT)—towards public bike rental system.* Malaysia: World Health Organization.

8 Social Innovation in Consumer Protection

Online Education in Alternative Financial Services

Vladimír Hyánek, Jiří Navrátil, Klára Placier, Maria Figueroa, Begoña Alvarez García, and Luis Ignacio Álvarez-González[1]

Introduction

Financial consumer protection has become an important political issue in economically advanced countries. Following the socioeconomic impact of the Great Recession of 2007–2013 and subsequent rise in both new types of financial services and broad social demand for these services, new initiatives have been launched by governments, civil society, and also the private sector in this area in order to protect citizens from negative side effects. The World Bank, G20 initiatives, OECD Task Force, and other international bodies have also started to focus on enforcement of the consumer protection regime to enable consumers to make well-informed decisions when using financial services—especially outside the realm of established financial institutions. In addition to the general population, special attention has also been dedicated to the needs of vulnerable groups (notably the elderly, young people, and more specifically over-indebted individuals and families).

In this chapter, we focus on a specific innovation stream in the area of alternative financial services (AFSs), namely online financial education and awareness-raising targeting vulnerable social groups. The innovation of internet education consists of online and therefore widely available means enabling direct contact with target groups as well as sharing information needed for consumers' competent decision-making.

The AFS industry—including banks—usually offers access to cash and/or credit and is growing as increasing numbers of consumers are unable to access the traditional banking system, which requires a reasonable level of financial health. This was exactly the situation exacerbated by the financial crisis when indebted people could not meet traditional banks' requirements (Fields & Jackson-Randall, 2012). Sometimes, AFSs are substantially more expensive than traditional banking services and may involve unfair and deceptive practices (Caplan, 2014). The primary goal of public policy should be to assure equal consumer protection for customers of both traditional services and AFSs. Consumers who use AFSs should have access to fairly priced alternatives and be provided with information to make informed choices because their financial education and knowledge is usually lower (Birkenmaier & Fu, 2016). In addition, when consumers use AFSs they should be protected from unfair and predatory practices that can lead to a long-term "financial treadmill" (Hermanson & Gaberlavage, 2001). This is where space has opened for social innovations (SIs)—be it the provision of financial resources via alternative means (e.g., crowdfunding, peer-to-peer lending, time-banking) or the protection of consumers against AFS providers.

The nature of the SI stream "online financial education for AFSs" is clearly dependent on, and arguably more so than the other SIs under study in this book, the economic and social conditions of the particular country. Different economic impacts from the Great Recession, diverse constellations of collective actors in the field, various political and cultural patterns—all of these have had an impact on the demand for AFSs, determined the type of actors who get engaged in the field, and affected the speed and outcome of the SIs under study.

We conducted our study on three European countries—the Czech Republic, Denmark and Spain. These cases represent different European socio-political regimes as well as countries with different impacts from the financial crisis. The aim of this chapter is to explore how the key actors and properties of the selected SI differ in various national contexts.

Central Concepts

Alternative Financial Services

AFSs can be defined as financial services provided outside the established realm of the traditional banking/insurance system and used by consumers who need to conduct financial transactions without a bank account or credit card (i.e., transaction AFSs) or who need flexible—often short-term—credit (i.e., credit-related AFSs) (Hermanson & Gaberlavage, 2001; Bradley et al., 2009; Despard et al., 2015). The AFS industry aims to provide ready access to cash or credit for people who would not usually get these from standard financial institutions. The scale of AFSs is incredibly large and includes crowdfunding, peer-to-peer lending, rent-to-own stores, and pawnbrokers (Bradley et al., 2009). The industry itself is quickly developing both because of the digital revolution and arrival of mobile devices, internet tools, and platforms which increase its accessibility and because of the rising demand for AFSs related to the Great Recession (Gross et al., 2012; Lusardi & Scheresberg, 2013; Wardrop et al., 2015; Navrátil & Placier, 2016).

In such a specific and dynamic framework, we can expect a wide array of SIs aimed at protecting consumers from abusive practices, excessive borrowing, or just limitations in their capacity to process and incorporate all relevant information which prevent them from making well-informed decisions (cf. Sunstein, 2006; Lusardi & Scheresberg, 2013; Robb et al., 2015). To analyse the role of actors in the innovation dynamics in online education in AFSs, we specified the type of SIs in the field for the analysis. We opted for online applications/initiatives and financial education as the innovation stream with the greatest potential insight into understanding of the role of various actors in the process of SI. This type of SI is of high social and political importance as it helps consumers to fight information asymmetry and a lack of transparency and fairness in an area traditionally connected to lack of financial knowledge, inexperienced consumer behaviour, and social and economic exclusion. Moreover, this stream is related to the rise of digital technologies which are closely interrelated with contemporary AFSs.

Contextual Determinants of SIs in AFSs

All aspects of the AFS field are closely related to the economic conditions of particular countries. Clearly, pressure from a worsening economic situation and rising unemployment gives rise to demand for AFSs as these often serve low-income and working-poor consumers, people from various minority neighbourhoods, and other disadvantaged groups (Hermanson & Gaberlavage, 2001). The Czech case represents a country moderately hit by the recession of 2007–2008, the Danish case represents low impact from the recession, and the Spanish case represents a country with massive effects from the financial crisis.

While the immediate economic situation affects the strength of demand for AFSs, there are also other important structural conditions which affect the pace, participants, and composition of SI processes taking place in the field. One of them has been described by the concept of welfare regimes (Esping-Andersen, 1990; but see also Anheier, 2010). It emphasizes that countries are marked by varying levels of market pressures (decommodification) and social pressures (stratification) which inevitably affect the legitimization and social desirability of various SIs in AFSs. This results in differentiation among liberal, conservative, social-democratic, and later on also post-socialist regimes (Esping-Andersen, 1990, Salamon & Anheier, 1998; Arts & Gelissen, 2002; Anheier et al., 2014).

When considering online education initiatives in AFSs, we might assume that different types of actors will be engaged in this particular innovation. One might expect that the involvement of civil society actors in promoting this SI will be higher in conservative regimes, as these combine a low level of stratification (and high solidarity influence) with low decommodification and low state regulation, which combines with the delegitimization and blaming of market forces after an economic downturn. Furthermore, we might expect that the involvement of civil society actors in promoting this SI will be lower in post-socialist regimes, as these combine a low level of stratification with medium (but quickly rising) decommodification, weak civil society, and continuing delegitimization and blaming of state activities after the socialist period. Thus, the role of civil society is expected to be supplemented by the market or state actors. Finally, we might expect that the most important role in the SI under study in social-democratic settings will be played by the state and its agencies.

Despite the fact that all the three national contexts represent different settings, there is also an international environment with international political institutions and organizations which exert some influence on the national fields, and there are also some aspects of the SI stream which remain mostly constant across all countries. We control for these commonalities when listing joint (international) milestones.

Methods

Case Selection

Online education in AFSs serves as the strategic action field in our investigation—a particular unit of collective action in society, a socially constructed arena within which actors with varying resources compete for advantage. Membership in these arenas is based on subjective perception rather than objective criteria (Fligstein & McAdam, 2011). In other words, we analysed the interactive environment for the innovation of providing online education to protect consumers from abusive practices in AFSs and its implementation, including the main collective actors such as state actors, market actors, and third-sector organizations and their relations, regulations, funding schemes, and so on.

We broke down the SI stream with the aim of identifying specific SI projects (websites) in the countries. These websites were selected in the following way: in the first step, the 10–20 most important websites providing financial education in the field of AFSs were identified in each country by means of desk research, expert interviews, and media analysis. In the next step, an online social network analysis (SNA) was conducted in order to generate further online education projects via the snowball method. This technique enabled us to map and enlarge the population of our cases and served as a tool within the process of sampling cases for subsequent process tracing. In the second step, all online projects generated via the snowball method were coded for their organizer, target group, method of education, main sponsor, and age, and hierarchical cluster analysis was applied in order to select two projects representative of the most distinct groups of projects in each country.[2]

Afterwards, the two most dissimilar groups in the set of all SI projects were identified. In the next step, a representative was selected for each group. For the Czech case, these representatives were Read Before You Sign! (*Podepsat můžeš, přečíst musíš!*) and Financial Education (*Finanční vzdělávání*). For Denmark, these were Back on Your Feet (*På Fode Igen*) and Debt Counselling in the Lolland, Falster and Guldborgsund Municipalities

(*Gældsrådgivning i Lolland og Guldborgsund*). Finally, for Spain, the selected representatives were Solidarity Economy (*Economía Solidaria*) and the Spanish Network of Financial Education (*Red Española de Educación Financiera*). Even if selection of only two core projects per country might not comprehensively cover the stream in its complexity and diversity, this reduction in the number of cases (which was necessary because of available resources) was offset by a deep focus on each project during the process tracing phase of the research and by the selection the two most dissimilar cases in order to capture the variability of cases in each country. What is more, the websites typically provided links to a network of engaged actors, which helped to identify involved organizations.

Data Collection

After the selection of online projects, we identified the organizations involved and approached their representatives for interviews. In the Czech Republic, four interviews lasting between 45 minutes and 1.5 hours were conducted. In Denmark, we consulted four representatives within a time range of 30–40 minutes. In Spain, three interviews lasting between 1 hour and 2.5 hours were conducted.

In order to embed the selected websites into their context, another SNA technique was applied. Here, we applied co-link analysis. The list of all SI projects generated before the final selection was made was crawled for hyperlinks and those pages that received at least two links from the sites were retained for further analysis. We mapped the online context of all selected SI projects, often interconnected with others that had been dropped during the reduction phase, by listing all co-references to other websites and by classifying these websites as civil society (the websites of NGOs, foundations, etc.), for profit (the websites of business companies), regulator (the websites of public or semi-public agencies imposing administrative control in the field) or media (websites oriented predominantly towards mass communication of news or entertainment). This enabled us to describe the prevailing types of context for SI projects in particular countries, which turned out to be very dissimilar.

Tracing the SI Stream

Before diving into our country cases, it is necessary to mention that all three countries in the study are member states of the OECD and the EU and therefore take into account recommendations arising from the OECD as well as directives and legislation coming from the EU in the field of consumer protection and subsequently financial education. Milestones that had international overlap and influence were associated mostly with the OECD and the EU and their regulatory and advisory activities, such as the OECD's Improving Financial Literacy (2005), the first major study of financial education at the international level which identified and analysed financial literacy surveys in member countries and evaluated the effectiveness of financial education programmes; the establishment of the European Expert Group on Financial Education (2008); and the High-level Principles on Financial Consumer Protection endorsed at a G20 meeting in 2011. Moreover, a gradual common trend from offline to online projects has become visible within our SI stream.

The SI Stream in the Czech Republic

The development of the SI stream in the Czech Republic was influenced by several focal points, in particular changes in socioeconomic conditions that have shaped consumer protection. It is also evident that the breakthroughs occurred as a result of legislative changes (and the influence of the EU) as well as business activities (both beneficial and harmful ones).

Milestones

Generally, the socioeconomic phenomena of relevance, namely indebtedness, over-indebtedness, and poverty, are considered important factors standing behind the urgent need for stronger consumer protection in finance and the effort to increase financial literacy among the Czech population through financial education projects. This cannot be seen as an effect exclusively from the Great Recession, however, as the indebtedness of Czech households has been steadily increasing since 2001.

Figure 8.1 indicates the main milestones of the field. In 2005, the number of non-banking financial institutions rose and loan providers (those considered as fair), banks, and financial intermediaries together with other financial institutions started to feel the need to increase the financial literacy levels of their clients and to educate them.

> At the beginning, there was goodwill that they [banks and non-banking institutions] wanted to have informed clients. That they wanted clients to repay them, . . . that they wanted it [the money] back and did not want clients who were extremely indebted, who didn't have it [the money], or who lied. They wanted informed clients.
>
> (Interview 1, 2016)

The aim of financial institutions and associations was mainly to achieve a state where their clients would not get tricked or forced into getting something that did not meet their needs (Interview 5, 2016).

> The illiteracy of clients is rather painful; [they] don't grasp many things and then claim that these things weren't explained.
>
> (Interview 5, 2016)

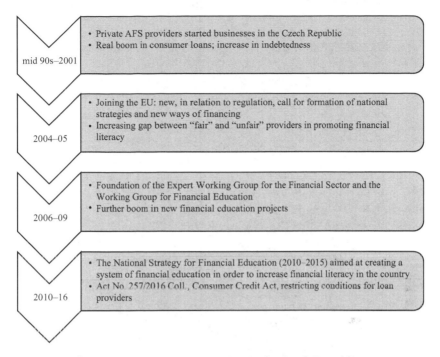

Figure 8.1 Milestones in consumer protection in the Czech Republic

Financial institutions therefore started to get involved in consumer protection through financial education projects as well as cooperation with the relevant ministries and supervisory authorities and commenting on regulation of the field.

> [It started to be evident] how important it was that people read documents [contracts] . . . in order to be capable of responsible borrowing and, on the other side, that those individuals who were lending follow some rules.
>
> (Interview 4, 2016)

The dynamism in the field on the market level has also been very strongly affected by concentration in the industry. The need for well-educated clients able to distinguish between "fair" and "unfair" loan providers proved to be important especially in times when competition in the non-banking sector started to get fierce.

Moreover, the dynamism in the field has been influenced by foreign forces on the levels of the market and the international community. In particular, joining the EU in 2004 brought new dynamics into the field of consumer protection in finance in relation to its regulation, calls for the formation of national strategies, and new ways of funding (the number of new financial education projects is strongly determined by calls for grant proposals). Nevertheless, many successful projects switched from private to European funds during their existence.

The state's activities represent forces that affect the field of consumer protection in finance but the influence has been rather indirect. The legislation on consumer protection is, for instance, a source of actions and reactions in the field on many levels. It imposes new conditions on financial institutions, empowers consumers, and also creates an almost constant need for updating current financial education projects. Moreover, the funding of these projects provided by the state is considered to be a significant tool influencing financial education in the country. Many project providers from the market as well as civil society hold off on launching their projects until they get funds from the state.

Actors and Interplay

In the Czech Republic, the major actors contributing to the development of the SI stream of online education in AFSs are recruited from the private and public sectors and civil society. We can also observe frequent inter-sectoral cooperation that has been a driving force behind innovation.

On the national level, the central actor representing the public sector is indisputably the Ministry of Finance, a policymaker and the main public institution responsible for consumer protection and financial education in the Czech Republic. It is the co-creator of the National Strategy for Financial Education together with the Ministry of Education, Youth and Sports. There are also other institutional members of the Working Group for Financial Education, chaired by the Ministry of Finance. Another important actor is the Czech National Bank, which is responsible for supervision over the entire financial market.

The Financial Arbitrator, a government agency, has been contributing to online education in AFSs on many levels. For example, it helps citizens to resolve various disputes with financial institutions in out-of-court proceedings in which people do not require a representative (e.g., an attorney). These services are provided free of charge. Moreover, the arbitrator has supported several financial educational projects.

In the Czech Republic, the private sector has been heavily engaged in the SI stream since the beginning of its development. This mostly concerns actors from the financial market, who are involved in consumer protection in finance directly, as providers and/or sponsors of financial educational programmes, or indirectly, through professional associations. The most important actor within the private sector is the Czech Banking Association, which has been actively engaged in the development of the stream through close cooperation with the Ministry of Finance while establishing the basis for a financial education system in the country.

Civil society organizations participate in the SI stream significantly as watchdogs and organizers of many online financial education projects, on which they usually cooperate with partners from other sectors. One of the key actors is the Czech Consumer Association, which has been active in the Working Group for Financial Education. It is also a co-partner in the selected platform Read Before You Sign! Other organizations which contribute to online education in AFSs include the SPES Association, a service provider and a member of the working group, and People in Need, an advocate and service provider in the field.

To identify the field structure, we looked at the hyperlinks on the websites that had been chosen as exemplary for the SI stream. We identified four groups of actors: regulators, media, civil society, and business. Regulators—in addition to imposing administrative control—often sponsored or co-sponsored financial education projects. In the Czech Republic, this group had the highest number of referential links. The second highest number was links to market actors who (often via civil society or in collaboration with it) organized and sponsored online activities. Figure 8.2 provides an illustration of how the SI exemplars (websites) are linked to (or torn between) regulators on the one hand and civil society actors and private/business entities on the other. This image might be representative of a post-socialist realm, where the marketization of public services and non-profit activity meet weakened but still effective state regulation.

A graphical representation of the SI environment confirms the significant contribution of market actors to the development of the SI stream.

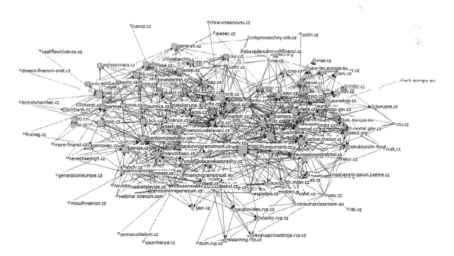

Figure 8.2 Structure of the strategic action field—co-link analysis (Czech Republic)

The extensive presence of the market in the field suggests a considerable level of commodification, where the participants cannot be seen as market-independent. The analysis reveals how the websites were linked with: regulators (42%), business (28%), civil society (24%) and media (6%).

The SI activities analysed within the Czech case represent two projects with substantially different characteristics in relation to their organizers, level of interactive tools used, and development over time.

SI Context

The Czech Republic as a post-socialist country faces a rather low degree of stratification, where status differentiation and class divisions are considered relatively small. What is more relevant to the reach of the services provided through the websites is the digital divide in the population as regards the use of information and communication technologies.

In terms of regular internet users, according to Negreiro (2015) the Czech Republic stands slightly above the EU average, with approximately 88% of the population regularly using the internet in 2014 and another 7% being occasional users. As of 2014, 39% of Czech citizens 55–74 years of age had never used the internet. Moreover, 71% of households from rural areas were able to access basic broadband in 2014 (Negreiro, 2015). These data show again very close or equal results to the EU average and suggest rather low stratification in the field.

These data support our statement of low stratification in the field and suggest that the illiteracy of target groups in this area did not materialize as a barrier to benefiting from the activities performed, in contrast to the potential threat suggested by one of the interviewees (Interview 7, 2016). In the Czech case, we may speak of a rather new phenomenon. There were virtually no pre-existing initiatives for protecting consumers in AFSs via education. Generally, consumer protection in general, which had previously been in the hands of the state, started to disintegrate soon after 1989, and new needs arising from the transition to the capitalist economy, the logic of the market, and the broadening of commercial providers of financial services remained largely non-reflected. Therefore, the appearance of online financial education was new, did not follow previous patterns, and was partially brought in from abroad. In that sense, online education in particular, driven by multiple stakeholders, can be considered a radical transformation.

The projects identified in the Czech Republic were most often 4 or 5 years old (in 2016). The Czech case is characterized by the close relationship between financial education in finance and online tools, as the former basically started to exist via the latter.

As far as the originality of the SI is concerned, the Czech case represents a mixed type. On the one hand, the non-profit sector initiated financial education via online tools. On the other hand, the private sector, which was far more important to the spread of this innovation, seems to have transferred education practices from other countries where their headquarters are situated. Their engagement in the innovation was motivated by commercial interests.

Two Case Studies: Read Before You Sign! and Financial Education

The project Read Before You Sign! was an educational awareness campaign which aimed to raise legal awareness among citizens and responsibility within lending and consumer loans. It was the first financial education project with online dimensions in the Czech Republic, launched in 2005. The project was created as a joint campaign of actors from the private sector and civil society, bringing in different perspectives. First, Provident Financial, Ltd. (a provider of non-banking short-term loans founded in 1997) followed the corporate social responsibility (CSR) strategy of its British parent company, recommending involvement in financial education projects. Second, the Czech Consumer Association (a civic association focusing on protection of consumer interests established in 1990) was seeking ways to deal with the increasing indebtedness of the population and related problems. As a result of the cooperation between the two partners, the campaign focused especially on the terms and conditions of contracts. The campaign was also supported by important official institutions; for example, support was expressed by the Ministry of Interior, the Financial Arbitrator, the British Chamber of Commerce, the Czech Bar Association and the Debt Advisory Centre.

This project helped to implement a set of actions based on media visibility and promotion of the importance of contracts, their particularities, and the possibilities (especially out of court) to resolve any disputes. The partial outputs of the project have been widely publicized, in the professional press as well as lifestyle magazines and websites of a very diverse nature. It therefore appears that the impact of the project was indeed relatively broad.

According to the project outputs (Dupal et al., 2006), the project was based on the experiences of the project partners with consumers' problems arising from their status as the weaker party to contracts. The problems mostly stemmed from imperfect contracts or even the absence of contracts and groundless customer confidence in the honesty of the contractor.

Financial Education is a project that aims to raise awareness of financial matters through an education website that was launched in 2008 and is therefore one of the oldest projects in the Czech environment. It was created by financial institutions and their associations as a response to insufficient regulation of the market accompanied by the number of complicated and non-transparent financial products and the increasing indebtedness of the population. The project was created as a joint activity of the Czech Banking Association (founded in 1990 as a voluntary association of legal entities from the banking sector and closely connected areas) and other professional associations (the Association of Financial Intermediaries and Financial

Advisers of the Czech Republic, the Czech Insurance Association, the Czech Leasing and Financial Association, and others).

This project was a response to the situation where information on finance and financial services was a matter only for experts. Therefore, the project objective was to offer the public a comprehensive and understandable view of banking and the functioning of the financial market. The idea was to provide cleverly explained reliable information that would serve the general public to better understand financial issues. This main mission persists even today.

All information on the project website is purely educational and informative and does not contain any offers, advertisements, or other commercial activities. The website also contains simple tutorials which help to resolve everyday financial issues. These include the selection of a suitable financial product or banking institution, recommended credit procedures, and the choice of appropriate pension insurance.

Crisis or potentially threatening situations represent another field of interest. These refer to situations where a person feels a sudden need for additional funds and is therefore willing to turn to, for example, unreliable financial services providers. Such situations include unexpected loss of employment, the temporary bankruptcy of an employer, divorce, a death in the family, a car crash, and the malfunction of household appliances (washing machines, fridges, etc.). A person in one of the aforementioned situations can find simple guidelines on this website and/or links and contacts to institutions that can help.

The SI Stream in Denmark

In Denmark, the field is strongly regulated and its dynamics are determined mostly by the state. The existence of projects that arise due to cooperation between the state, civil society organizations, and municipalities is dependent on the availability of funding from government institutions as well as meeting the demands of the state to decrease citizen indebtedness. At the beginning of the millennium, however, it was mainly the media that spread information on debt issues and promoted information about counselling possibilities.

Milestones

As the milestones briefly reflected in Figure 8.3 show, the role of the state in the dynamics of the field proved to be significant mainly during and after the Great Recession. The financial crisis was not necessarily felt directly by individuals as banks were bailed out by the state, but because the government has been making major cutbacks in various sectors, these cutbacks have contributed to debt problems through decreases in support for students, university funding, and the length of unemployment benefits (Interview 11, 2016).

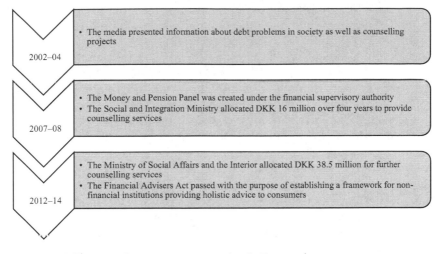

Figure 8.3 Milestones in consumer protection in Denmark

According to the Ministry of Business and Growth (2013), however, in order to maintain financial stability it became necessary for the government to get involved in the sector. As a consequence of the crisis and the increasing indebtedness of the population, the state started to fund several debt counselling projects organized by civil society organizations through various government ministries. The online provision of the projects in Denmark is therefore still not seen as an important tool of financial education and consumer protection. For the case of Denmark, we therefore also focused on offline activities.

In 2014, the Financial Advisers Act came into force. The purpose of the act was to establish a framework for non-financial institutions providing comprehensive counselling on financial products to consumers in order to conduct their activities out of the reach of financial companies.

Actors and Interplay

The central actors contributing to consumer protection in AFSs in Denmark traditionally come from national government, local government (in form of municipalities), and civil society, with substantial involvement from volunteers.

One of the major actors is the Danish Financial Supervisory Authority (Finanstilsynet), a regulator of financial markets in Denmark. It is part of the Ministry of Economic and Business Affairs and also acts as a secretariat for the Financial Business Council, the Danish Securities Council, and the Money and Pension Panel. The Money and Pension Panel is another key entity, appointed by the Danish Parliament in order to provide public information aimed towards helping consumers with their personal finances. In addition to information provision, the panel has been instrumental in creating successful campaigns focused on avoiding debt.

The Ministry of Social Affairs and the Interior and the Danish Agency for Labour Market and Recruitment have been key actors in terms of funding. An important role within the SI stream is also played by municipalities, who have partnered with civil society organizations to refer citizens registered with a debt problem to financial education and debt advice projects.

In Denmark, the involvement of the private sector in the SI stream is in general very low. Regarding the selected websites, only the Danish Bankers Association contributed to the protection of consumers by appealing to their employees to voluntarily engage in providing debt advice. In addition, local and national newspapers/media can be credited for raising awareness about existing projects dealing with financial counselling.

An important role in the SI stream is played by the Young Men's Christian Association Denmark (Kristelig Forening for Unge Mænd, KFUM), which has been working for many years with socially vulnerable people and recognized, through its volunteers, the need to deal with an increasing debt problem.

KFUM is currently organizing and providing the selected SI project Back on Your Feet, focused on financial counselling for disadvantaged groups. Another actor taking part in providing debt advice is Danish People's Aid, which works with young and vulnerable citizens from several municipalities.

The hyperlink analysis we performed revealed the important role of media, since this group had the highest number of links with the selected websites (see Figure 8.4). Quite surprisingly, the role of public agencies/regulators was not captured. This may indicate either the self-evident role of the public agencies in the field (which need not be demonstrated via hyperlinks) or the specialization and decentralization of public agencies involved in the field, which complicates the sharing of hyperlinks among websites. The composition of the strategic action field in Denmark is as follows: regulators (1%), business (7%), civil society (7%) and media (85%).

SI Context

Denmark as a social-democratic regime could be described as a country with a low degree of class divisions as well as a low degree of socioeconomic status differentiation. A strong welfare state is paired with well-coordinated integration of the volunteer sector into policy strategies: volunteering is quite popular in Denmark, with volunteer rates according to various data even higher than those in other Continental European countries, taking place most prominently in such areas as sports, arts, culture, and leisure activities, where around half of all volunteering takes place, and less prominently in other social issue areas (Jensen & Rathlev, 2009; Boje, 2010). Since a

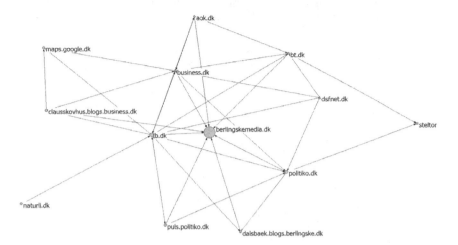

Figure 8.4 Structure of the strategic action field—co-link analysis (Denmark)

Note: Diamond-shaped nodes = public regulators; circles = media; triangles pointing down = civil society actors; squares = businesses; and triangles pointing up = individual examples of the SI (online education websites). The size of each node is relative to the number of incoming links (normalized in degree).

high level of social solidarity (accompanied by a high level of volunteering and participation) can be detected in Denmark, we can say that the level of stratification in the society is low (see also Denmark's GINI index according to OECD, 2016).

This level of "equality" is surprisingly mirrored in the use of online education in AFSs. We can detect an increase in citizens with different social statuses taking part in offered debt counselling and financial education services over the years. As the coordinator of the project Back on Your Feet noted, it is not only socially disadvantaged Danes who request counselling. It is more and more often working-class citizens who are seeking help, those who still have a job but who have lost control over their finances (KFUM development consultant, 2016), making the field and innovations in it more relevant for a larger part of the population against a rather well-off background. In addition, according to a report prepared by the Danish consumer council, 13.4% of Danish youngsters 18–30 years already experience debt problems (Jakobsen et al., 2015). As a consequence, the stratification in the field is decreasing since consumer protection, and particularly financial education, is reaching vulnerable groups but also the working middle class.

Correspondingly to the trend in many European countries, there is also a demand to give advice to young people in an effort to educate them financially given that most adults who have used counselling had started accumulating debt when they were younger. This does not, however, represent a possible change in stratification in the field.

In terms of the digital divide, Denmark has the most widespread internet access within the entire EU. In 2014, approximately 92% of Danes were regularly using the internet while another 6% of citizens were occasional users (Negreiro, 2015), showing no barrier to use of online services. In addition, disadvantaged groups had great access to the internet in 2014, with only 8% of the population 55–74 years of age having never used the internet before and 83% of households in rural areas with internet coverage. In terms of the quality or scope of innovation, we see that in the Danish case (which is additionally characterized by a much more important role played by public sector initiatives) the symbiosis of financial education and online tools is rather underdeveloped. The Danish case is also marked by a hesitant attitude among the public administration towards this model.

Two Case Studies: Debt Counselling in the Lolland and Guldborgsund Municipalities and Back on Your Feet

Lolland and Guldborgsund have been two of the municipalities in Denmark hardest hit by the debt problem in the past few years as listed on Experian. dk, a website mapping debt patterns across age groups, regions, and municipalities in Denmark. The inception of this project was therefore a response to this statistic, as noted by the project manager of the Debt Counselling project (Interview 8, 2016). The Ministry of Social Affairs and the Interior with funding from the Satspuljien (the Social Reserve Fund in which the government and political parties negotiate together and vote on the social causes to which money will be distributed each year) has partnered with the humanitarian organization Danish People's Aid to work on solving the debt problem. Danish People's Aid was established in 1907 as the Workers' Samaritan Association and provides aid and assistance to vulnerable people in Denmark and abroad.

Indebtedness affects not only a particular person but also entire families. These include families experiencing financial difficulties, social isolation, psychological problems, unstable school attendance, and a lack of healthy leisure time. Therefore, this project has broad overlaps implemented through cooperation between municipalities and civil society and aiming to improve the situation of vulnerable families. Together with other projects, it seeks to improve the position of vulnerable families, strengthen their social network, and give them the opportunity to return to "normal life".

In 2009, KFUM (founded in 1974) started the project Back on Your Feet to help Danes in debt get advice from volunteers with financial and legal expertise on how to manage their finances. According to the current project manager, there was a volunteer in a social café (a self-sustaining or non-profit business such as a second-hand shop) who thought that debt was becoming a problem within Danish society. Based on previous projects such as "Direct to work", the volunteers did some research which revealed that there was indeed a debt problem among the socially vulnerable and thus the project became operational in early 2009. This project was also a response to the Danish financial crisis (Interview 9, 2016). The project was first introduced in five major cities: Aarhus, Copenhagen, Odense, Esbjerg, and Vejle.

As part of this project, citizens can get independent advice from competent volunteer advisors, such as bank counsellors, social workers, and lawyers. They provide advice on such topics as budgeting, repayment, and debt restructuring. The counselling takes place in a relaxed form and an informal environment. This financial education project also has a (minor) online component, an information website serving mainly as a signpost that directs candidates to support provided offline.

The SI Stream in Spain

The analysis of how financial education initiatives have developed in Spain revealed two different alternative paths. The dynamics of implementation has been both "top-down" and "bottom-up", illustrating broader patterns in the Spanish context.

The "top-down" approach is represented by the Financial Education Plan (2008–2012) that was initially launched by supervisor bodies (the Bank of Spain and the National Securities Market Commission) and was only later joined by corporate actors and promoted by civil society organizations.

> These initiatives arise from the conviction of the public authorities of the need to encourage citizens' financial education. It is the responsibility of the authorities to detect these needs and encourage such practices. In most cases, citizens are not aware of the information gaps that exist about financial practices. If we expect this to come from the bottom up, it will never come.
>
> (Interview 13, 2016)

On the other hand, there are "bottom-up" dynamics where the field is built up through financial education projects.

Activities and services related to financial education (including online projects) are therefore provided either by the different types of financial organizations under the framework of the "top-down" model represented by the Financial Education Plan, especially as a result of the financial crisis, or they have been promoted by civil society and social economy-based organizations.

Milestones

As noted by Hyánek, Navrátil, and Placier (2015), the extent of initiatives in AFSs usually correlates negatively with citizens' economic and financial opportunities (the satisfaction of their basic needs, the availability of financial resources, their access to mortgages or consumer loans, etc.) and with dissatisfaction with the functioning of the institutionalized financial system. In the case of Spain, many SI initiatives within online education in AFSs have arisen from a crisis of legitimacy and trust in standard banking institutions and from the country's worsening economic situation. For example, the anti-austerity 15-M Movement or the Movement of Outraged People began with demonstrations on 15 May 2011. It led to several peaceful protests and gave rise to the birth of new political parties. Between 2011 and 2012, 492 new parties were created. Some of the parties, such as We Can (*Podemos*) and Party X (*Partido X*), emerged from the "street" or the assemblies and occupations that characterized the mobilization. Others, such as the Pirate Party (*Partido Pirata*), emerged from the movement against internet censorship (Tormey & Feenstra, 2015).

During the aforementioned protests, citizens made such various demands as a halt to evictions and improvements to democratic life without reliance on banks or corporations.

Act 2/2009 of 31 March, regulating contracting with consumers of mortgage loans or mortgage-backed facilities and brokering services for loan or credit facility agreements, can be interpreted as another important reaction to the recession.

Some of those milestones are briefly ilustrated in Figure 8.5.

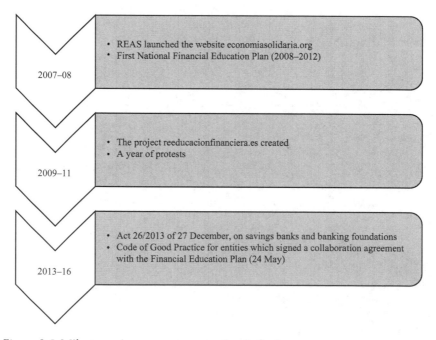

Figure 8.5 Milestones in consumer protection in Spain

Actors and Interplay

The structure of relevant actors is rather specific and complex in Spain. There are a variety of major actors involved in the SI stream. The most important actors within the public sector are the Bank of Spain and the National Securities Market Commission. These financial regulators elaborated the first National Financial Education Plan and created the online financial education project finanzasparatodos.es. There are also other partners participating in the aforementioned plan, such as the General Insurance and Pension Funds Directorate, which is also a financial regulator, and the government, the treasury, and the Ministry of Education, Culture and Sports, which play the role of policymakers and policy regulators.

The Spanish Confederation of Savings Banks (*Confederación Española de Cajas de Ahorros*, CECA), which is partly affiliated with civil society, is the private partner of the National Financial Education Plan. It is also the main actor in the analysed SI initiative Spanish Network of Financial Education (*Red Española de Educación Financiera*), which is sponsored, promoted, designed, developed, and provided by the CECA. In addition, CECA member entities (banks, savings banks, and banking foundations) which acceded to an agreement with the National Financial Education Plan play an active role in the SI stream as providers of financial education. There are also several media organizations which collaborate with the solidarity-based economy and therefore could be considered promoters and providers of financial education. Universities and secondary schools from both the public and private sectors also provide financial education in collaboration with civil society and businesses.

Civil society also engages in the SI stream in Spain. There is significant involvement, for example, from the Network of Alternative and Solidarity Economy Networks (*Red de Redes de Economía Alternativa y Solidaria*, REAS), which focuses on the solidarity-based alternative economy and is also the main actor behind the website Solidarity Economy (*Economía Solidaria*), which provides cultural, relational, and structural resources to its member networks. REAS represents more than 500 entities grouped into territorial and sectoral networks and is a response to the dehumanization of the economy, degradation of the environment, and loss of social values.

There is also SETEM, a federation of several civil society organizations developing, promoting, providing and funding a number of financial education initiatives. The National Union of Credit Cooperatives (*La Unión Nacional de Cooperativas de Crédito*) and the Junior Achievement Foundation are other providers of the financial education in Spain, together with several non-profits and foundations such as the Altekio Cooperative and the Enclau Association. Financial education in the country also receives contributions from consumer organizations, such as the General Association of Consumers (*Asociación General De Consumidores*), the Confederation of

Consumers & Users (*Confederación de Consumidores y Usuarios*) and the National Institute of Consumer Affairs.

The role of volunteers within the SI stream is significant since they participate actively in organizations providing online financial education. They largely come from civil society but also the private and public sectors. Many of them are users of Spanish financial education websites who wish to cooperate in improving the offered services.

As the structure of hyperlinks in SI projects shows, there are important ties between civil society actors, business, and regulators in the field. Figure 8.6 suggests that it is civil society that dominates (or populates) the field, while business and regulatory actors are incorporated to a certain extent. The state and business actors occupy the periphery of the field and contribute only to a smaller extent. The composition of strategic action field reveals that SI projects are linked with regulators (2%), business (9%), civil society (89%) and media (0%).

SI Context

Spanish society shows signs of moderate to high class divisions, with noticeable differences in citizens' social statuses. For illustration, the OECD (2016) estimated Spain's GINI index in 2013 as 34.5%. This situation worsened with the Great Recession through which the unemployment rate rose from 8.4% in 2007 to 26.3% in 2013 (World Bank Open Data, 2016).

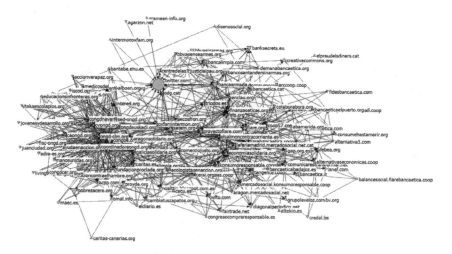

Figure 8.6 Structure of the strategic action field—co-link analysis (Spain)

Note: Diamond-shaped nodes = public regulators; circles = media; triangles pointing down = civil society actors; squares = businesses; and triangles pointing up = individual examples of the SI (online education websites). The size of each node is relative to the number of incoming links (normalized in degree).

The stratification in the field of online education in AFSs is even higher in comparison with the stratification on the national level.

> Undoubtedly, the first stage of empowering people is gaining access to the minimum content that allows you to analyse your personal or collective situation to connect with others who are in the same situation.
>
> (Interview 14, 2016)

Acknowledging the need for citizens' improved and guaranteed access to financial education, the basics were included in primary education through Royal Decree 126/2014 of 28 February. Similarly, financial education was included in the basic curriculum for compulsory secondary education through Royal Decree 1105/2014 of 26 December. The recent state intervention in the field, particularly in the regulation of financial education, is not expected to change the availability of materials, formal training, and instructions emanating from public institutions to citizens, no matter their social status.

As financial education projects in Spain are significantly oriented to online implementation, the digital divide plays an important role in the stratification in the field. According to Negreiro (2015), approximately 70% of citizens regularly used the internet in 2014 with little difference across urban and rural areas, with another 8% being occasional users. This is below the EU average. In terms of decommodification in the field, we can see noticeable influence from market actors, suggesting a lower level of decommodification, accompanied by activities by civil society organizations. Even though there is a strong presence from market actors, however, the decommodification in the field is not very low: consumer protection and financial education is not only part of the concept of corporate responsibility but is also seen as a service to society. Regarding the state, in contrast, financial education has not been perceived as a service explicitly recognized as a right of citizens, especially adults and vulnerable groups. According to an analysis developed by Romero et al. (2014), financial education has not had a broad presence in the Spanish legal system, which is consistent with the strategy focused on considering these activities as the responsibility of financial institutions.

In terms of the quality and scope of innovation in Spain, this innovation is produced largely by civil society organizations, which brings higher flexibility and broader scope for the use of financial education via new media and tools. Many actors have become engaged in the field, including citizens, solidarity organizations, civil society organizations, financial system supervisors, banks and banking foundations, the Ministry of Education, the government, and consumer protection bodies. A high level of impact has been achieved and many projects have been implemented.

Two Case Studies: Spanish Network of Financial Education and Solidarity Economy

The project Spanish Network of Financial Education promoted from the corporate website rededucacionfinanciera.es, launched in 2009, is included within the institutional model of the National Financial Education Plan provided by two of the most relevant financial supervision authorities in the country (the Bank of Spain and the National Securities Market Commission). This "top down" model is designed as a network formed by approximately 25 members, including public institutions (promoters), associations, foundations, several think tanks related to the economic and financial world, banks, savings banks, insurance companies, and consumer associations. Despite being initially promoted by financial supervisors, the plan works as a common link among all partners in such a way that the educational challenge could not achieve its intended impact without the cooperation of each and every partner. They share common purposes and codes of conduct and are also able to operate with freedom in order to develop their own educational projects. There is a working group led by the national financial supervisors and regularly attended by partner representatives which meets periodically in order to set objectives and study the actions taken. This network is directly related to the promotion of financial education in schools: many students between 14 and 16 are trained in financial education with instructional materials provided by the collaborators in the Financial Education Plan.

The aim of the REAS non-profit organization (founded in 1995), which is behind the development and management of the project Solidarity Economy (economiasolidaria.org), is to inspire a different way of understanding the economy and relationships based on a collaborative and social paradigm, one that moves away from profit. Therefore, financial education is part of a more global and comprehensive project with an important political and symbolic dimension: the main objective of economiasolidaria.org is not focused only on "traditional" financial education but on anything that might lead to a change towards a social and solidarity economy, including fair trade, responsible consumption, ethical finance, social markets, and a solidarity economy in general. It also reports on and denounces the factors that are generating the situation of social inequality and injustice. The portal, which was launched in 2007, is a space that provides mutual support and information for all participating organizations and society in general, as well as a space for exchanging ideas and experiences. All of the networks that are part of the civil society promoter are involved in updating the portal with news and content, which has also enabled extension of the network to other collaborative initiatives around the world.

Synthesis

The selected SI is clearly interconnected with general technological innovation and its social reception (development of digital media, the internet, digital literacy, electronic infrastructure, etc.), and some of its features and dynamics thus also depend on the techno-structural specificities of particular countries (Katz & Koutroumpis, 2013). At the same time, the significance of the differences we found among the countries under study clearly reinforces the importance of studying this SI with special regards to its social, cultural, and political aspects (cf. Büchi et al., 2015).

Comparative Analysis

Innovation Properties

The character of the innovation we focused on depends largely on the history of the field of consumer protection as such and on the character of the political framework. In Spain (where the innovation was implemented the earliest) as well as in Denmark, consumer protection was not disconnected from the past. That is why the new online initiatives often followed previous activities oriented at protection of AFS consumers and did not lead to dramatic transformation of the field. It is the Czech case where the financial education and internet tools were most closely intertwined as the former basically started to exist via the latter (i.e., later than in the other two countries). This also helped to make this symbiosis quite widespread and intensive. In this country, the innovation was largely produced by civil society organizations, which brings higher flexibility and broader scope for the use of financial education via new media and tools. In contrast, the Danish case was characterized by a much more important role for and initiative from public administration, and the symbiosis of financial education and online tools is rather underdeveloped.

Given that it was the very emergence of this innovation that transformed the field of consumer protection in AFSs in the Czech case, we may rate its substantiality in this case as very high. Somewhat lesser substantiality in this innovation may be identified in the Spanish case as it definitely helped to spread the financial education provided especially by grass-root civil society initiatives, but it might be argued that the large capacity of this sector to spread ideas and education in society would enable civil society to promote financial education in a substantive way also without online tools. Finally, it seems that in the Danish case the SI has not entirely transformed the existing field and some of the dominant actors were rather hesitant to promote it as something that could make a difference and dramatically improve the status quo.

Similarly, the radicality of the innovation was rather high in the Czech case (a quick and sudden increase in the innovation in a previously unregulated area), more incremental (or less radical) in the case of Spain, and rather incremental in the case of Denmark. The projects identified in the Czech Republic were most often 4 or 5 years old, and something similar applied also in Spain—but with the tendency to have both much more recent projects and much older ones. The case of Denmark was different, with a tendency towards the more recent emergence of projects. Curiously, the online provision of financial education in Denmark was more insignificant than it was in the other countries we analysed. The level of transformation of the field of financial education was less fundamental in Denmark than it was in the Czech Republic and Spain—the process of establishing the SI here was a process of digitalizing existing financial education initiatives rather than developing new ones. The transformation of 67 offline activities to online and interactive ones, however, is still in progress.

Actor Contributions

The role of various collective actors during the co-production of the SI also differed significantly across the three countries. The Czech Republic was characterized by a substantial role played by business in the organization, financing, and implementation of educational projects in the field with civil society acting in a more passive role. This seems to be a function of the neo-liberal policies launched in the aftermath of the regime change in 1989. The passivity of the government in the past two decades combined with the worsening reputation of the financial services market spurred efforts by business actors to improve their own image and reputation. The role of public institutions has been rather supportive and much less pronounced. Civil society actors may occupy more important positions as organizers of (or advisers to) business-led projects. In the projects under study, we identified only minor involvement of regulators. Most importantly, we seldom traced a leading role played by civil society.

Denmark fits into "traditional" social-democratic settings with a predominant role played by public institutions. However, it included a "modern" institutional framework admitting initiative from civil society with the government controlling the resources. The private sector (business) is employed in a "non-profit" manner, which is remarkable and in contrast with the almost strictly for-profit motives of the Czech private actors (or at least some of them). One Danish project was initiated by the regulator and civil society organizations and funded by the state and local municipalities, with a minor role played by businesses. The second project was initiated by civil society organizations, funded by the state, and had the private sector engaged purely in a non-profit manner (i.e., through individual engagement of its employees and without utilizing this engagement for public relations strategies).

Southern "conservative" settings characterize the Spanish case where a social economic environment enabled a surprisingly significant and active role to be played by civil society actors. Spanish projects are embedded within a framework designed by a network of public institutions, associations and foundations, think tanks, consumer organizations, and private partners, initiated and funded by the private sector (the CECA) with broad

experience in conducting social and solidarity-based activities and traditionally providing resources to social work. A similar environment was
characteristic also for the second Spanish project, which was rooted in the
non-profit and fair-trade environment, initiated and coordinated by a network of civil society organizations and local or territorial associations, companies, and the public administration sector. However, even though market
actors have a strong presence in the field, decommodification is not as low
as in the Czech case, where financial institutions provide financial education
mostly as a part of their CSR and public relations strategies. The reason is
that the Spanish actors orient themselves in a different societal framework
marked by the values of social responsibility and solidarity.

Learnings

Our analysis has revealed several aspects of the processes through which
SIs come into being and spread. First and foremost, the role of the socio-
political context proved to be a very strong determinant of the shape of
coalitions around SIs in online finance education and their dynamics. The
overall settings of social values and norms, political culture, and institutions
strongly affected the strategies of various classes of actors in the particular
field and their capacity to contribute to innovation in this field. Second,
it turned out to be very important to differentiate not only among vari
ous structural types of collective actors (business, public, civil society) but
also among various modes of action these actors perform (business actors
implementing genuine non-profit strategies, civil society actors engaged in
business CSR/PR activities, etc.). Finally, we found it hard to establish particular links between the given country's economic situation and the shape
of online education in AFSs (besides the fact that this situation generally sets
the stage for the appearance of this innovation).

Conclusions

The aim of this chapter was to explore how the key actors and properties of
the selected SI differ in various national contexts. Our analysis focused on
the relationship between the particular SI—online education in AFSs—and
its broader context in order to assess the types and roles of actors involved
and the attributes of innovation as such. The differences among the roles
played by these actors were probably less substantial than expected, and the
importance of civil society organizations was, in some cases, also lower than
expected. It was usually the interplay among all types of actors rather than
the sheer dominance of some of them which led to the rise of the SI (and the
role of collective actors' economic resources and social capital turned out
to be highly important during these interactions). In this case, digital infrastructure and internet literacy were quite important conditions, but they
seemed to play a much less important role than the general socio-political

framework (regime), which determined the position and influence of key collective actors (particularly businesses) and their comparative advantage in terms of knowledge and expertise. For instance, the previous public policies in general consumer protection affected the intensity and strength of the establishment of online education in AFSs. This led to key country differences with some rather unexpected coalitions around innovation which would be less probable in such fields as environmental protection or social services and to more radical and fast-evolving innovation processes when some of the "inside" partners were largely involved.

Notes

1. We would like to thank all who made important contributions to the ITSSOIN project deliverable that formed the basis for this chapter: Akinyi, E. A.; Salido-Andres, N.; Sanzo Perez, M.J.; and Rey-Garcia, M.
2. Cluster analysis is a tool aiming at establishing a group in which objects are bundled that have many traits in common, while these very traits also serve to delineate and differentiate a given group from other groups. Hierarchical clustering starts with every case being one cluster in itself, and similar clusters are merged during successive steps (Bartholomew et al., 2008). The analysis was conducted in IBM SPSS (Norušis, 2011).

References

Anheier, H. K. (2010). *Social origins theory.* In H. K. Anheier & S. Toepler (Eds.), *International encyclopaedia of civil society* (pp. 1445–1452). New York, NY: Springer.

Anheier, H. K., Krlev, G., Preuss, S., Mildenberger, G., Bekkers, R., & Lund, A. B. (2014). *ITSSOIN hypotheses.* Deliverable 1.4 of the project: "Impact of the Third Sector as Social Innovation" (ITSSOIN), European Commission—7th Framework Programme, Brussels: European Commission, DG Research.

Arts, W., & Gelissen, J. (2002). Three worlds of welfare capitalism or more? A state-of-the-art report. *Journal of European Social Policy, 12*(2), 137–158.

Bartholomew, D. J., Steele, F., Galbraith, J., & Moustaki, I. (2008). *Analysis of multivariate social science data* (2nd ed). Boca Raton: Chapman & Hall/CRC.

Birkenmaier, J., & Fu, Q. (2016). The association of alternative financial services usage and financial access: Evidence from the national financial capability study. *Journal of Family & Economic Issues, 37*, 450–460.

Boje, T. P. (2010). Civil society and social capital in the European tradition. In H. K. Anheier & S. Toepler (Eds.), *International encyclopedia of civil society* (pp. 300–306). New York, NY: Springer.

Bradley, C., Burhouse, S., Gratton, H., & Miller, R-A. (2009). Alternative financial services: A primer. *FDIC Quarterly, 3*(1), 39–47.

Büchi, M., Just, N., & Latzer, M. (2015). Modeling the second-level digital divide: A five-country study of social differences in internet use. *New Media and Society, 18*, 1–20.

Caplan, M. A. (2014). Communities respond to predatory lending. *Social Work, 59*(2), 149–156.

Despard, M. R., Perantie, D. C., Luo, L., Oliphant, J., & Grinstein-Weiss, M. (2015). *Use of alternative financial services in low-and moderate-income households: Evidence from refund to savings.* Center for Social Development Research Brief 15–57. Retrieved from https://csd.wustl.edu/Publications/Documents/RB15-57.pdf

Dupal, L., Schlossberger, O., & Toman, P. (2006). *Umíme si půjčovat? (podepsat můžeš, přečíst musíš!).* Praha: Sdružení českých spotřebitelů.

Esping-Andersen, G. (1990). *The three worlds of welfare capitalism.* Cambridge: Polity Press.Fields, G., & Jackson-Randall, M. (2012, December 9). Footnote to financial crisis: More people Shun the bank. *Wall Street Journal—Eastern Edition, 259*(60), A1–A12.

Financial Education Plan 2008–2012. (2012). Retrieved from https://www.cnmv.es/DocPortal/Publicaciones/PlanEducacion/PlanEducacion_een.pdf.

Fligstein, N., & McAdam, D. (2011). Toward a general theory of strategic action fields. *Sociological Theory, 29*, 1–26.

Gross, M. B., Hogarth, J. M., Manohar, A., & Gallegos, S. (2012). Who uses alternative financial services, and why? *Consumer Interests Annual, 58.* Retrieved from www.consumerinterests.org/assets/docs/CIA/CIA2012/2012-57 who uses alternative financial services and why.pdf

Hermanson, S., & Gaberlavage, G. (2001, August). *The alternative financial services industry.* AARP Public Policy Institute. Retrieved from www.aarp.org/research/credit-debt/credit/a research-import-198-IB51. html. The San Francisco Municipal Code also uses the term "fringe financial services" to refer to these types of establishments. San Francisco Muni. Code, 790.

Hyánek, V., Navrátil, J., & Placier, K. (2015). *Case selection in consumer protection in finance.* "Impact of the Third Sector as Social Innovation" (ITSSOIN), European Commission—7th Framework Programme, Brussels: European Commission, DG Research.

Jakobsen, T., Nielsen, N. R., Hansen, M. B. & Holm, J. S. (2015). *Ungdomsliv På Kredit: Gældsproblemer I Forbrugersamfundet.* Trygfonden: Forbrugerrådet Tænk.

Jensen, P. H. F., & Rathlev, J. (2009). Formal and informal work in the Danish social democratic welfare state. In B. Pfau-Effinger & L. Flaquer (Eds.), *Formal and informal work: The hidden work regime in Europe* (pp. 39–61). New York, NY, London: Routledge.

Katz, R. L., & Koutroumpis, P. (2013). Measuring digitization: A growth and welfare multiplier. *Technovation, 33*(10,11), 314–319.

Lusardi, A., & Scheresberg, C. B. (2013). *Financial literacy and high-cost borrowing in the United States.* NBER Working Paper (No. 18969). Retrieved from www.nber.org/papers/w18969

Ministry of Business and Growth. (2013). *The financial crisis in Denmark—causes, consequences and lessons.* Copenhagen: Danish Government.

Navrátil, J., & Placier, K. (2016). Social innovation types in consumer protection in alternative financial services after the great recession. In D. Spalková & L. Matějová (eds.), *Proceedings of the 20th international conference current trends in public sector research.* Brno: Masarykova univerzita.

Negreiro, M. (2015, December). *Bridging the digital divide in the EU.* [PDF]. European Parliamentary Research Service.

Norušis, M. J. (2011). *IBM SPSS statistics 19 statistical procedures companion.* Reading, MA: Addison-Wesley.

OECD Publishing. (2005). *Improving financial literacy: Analysis of issues and policies.* Paris: OECD Publications.

OECD Statistics. (2016). Retrieved August 24, 2016, from http://stats.oecd.org/

Robb, C. A., Babiarz, P., Woodyard, A., & Seay, M. C. (2015). Bounded rationality and use of alternative financial services. *The Journal of Consumer Affairs, 49*(2), 407–435.

Romero, A., García-Pintos, I., & Vázquez, N. (2014). La educación financiera y el sector financier. In A. Placencia Porrero (Ed.), *Nuevos desafíos del sector financiero: Recuperando la confianza y mejorando la cultura financier* (pp. 145–163). Papeles de la Fundación Estudios Financieros. Retrieved from https://www.fef.es/publicaciones/papeles-de-la-fundacion/item/291-52-nuevos-desaf%C3%ADos-del-sector-financiero-recuperando-la-confianza-y-mejorando-la-cultura-financiera.html

Salamon, L. M., & Anheier, H. K. (1998). Social origins of civil society: Explaining the nonprofit sector cross-nationally. *VOLUNTAS: International Journal of Voluntary & Nonprofit Organizations, 9*(3), 213–248.

Sunstein, C. R. (2006). Boundedly rational borrowing. *The University of Chicago Law Review, 73*(1), 249–270.

Tormey, S., & Feenstra, R. A. (2015). Reinventing the political party in Spain: The case of 15M and the Spanish mobilisations. *Policy Studies, 36*(6), 590–606.

World Bank Open Data. (2016). Retrieved August 12, 2016, from http://data.worldbank.org/

Wardrop, R., Zhang, B., Rau, R., & Gray, M. (2015). *Moving mainstream the European alternative finance benchmarking report.* London: University of Cambridge and Ernst & Young.

Interviews

Interview 1 with the chairwoman of the Association SPES, Olomouc 14/04/2016.

Interview 2 with the general secretary of the Association of Financial Intermediaries and Financial Advisers of the Czech Republic, Prague 20/04/2016.

Interview 3 with the executive director of Provident Financial, s.r.o., Prague 20/04/2016.

Interview 4 with deputy of financial arbitrator, the Office of Financial Arbitrator, Prague 12/05/2016.

Interview 5 with associate professor at Copenhagen Business School, Copenhagen 23/05/2016.

Interview 6 with the project leader of debt counselling project for single parents on Lolland, Falster and Guldborgsund municipalities, the Danish People's Aid, Copenhagen 06/04/2016.

Interview 7 with the project coordinator of Back on Your Feet, the Young Men's Christian Association—Denmark, Copenhagen 07/04/2016.

Interview 8 with expert from financial supervisory body, La Coruña 11/04/2016.

Interview 9 with expert from the project Economia Solidaria, Euskadi 17/05/2016.

[E-mail to Development Consultant KFUM]. (2016, March 31).

9 Cross-Sector Partnerships

A Social Innovation in the European Work Integration Sector

Bernard Leca, Sarah Sandford,
Aurélie Sara Cognat, Anne-Claire Pache,
Vanessa Mato-Santiso, Vladimír Hyánek,
and Gorgi Krlev[1]

Introduction

As the European Commission (2014) notes, many socially marginalized people have difficulty entering the labor market because they do not have the requisite skills, education or experience. For these individuals, taking a straight-forward training course may not be enough to help them into work. Using this issue as a starting point, this study intends to examine how cross-sector partnerships have developed in different European countries as a social innovation aimed at addressing the problem of work integration for disadvantaged people.

An initial exploration of the field of work integration in European countries (Lallemand Stempak et al., 2015) led us to select four countries in order to cover the diversity of the field at the European level: France, Spain, Germany and the Czech Republic. As outlined in the methods chapter of this book, we conducted a cross-country comparative characterization of social innovation in the work integration sector and identified three interesting innovations, present in each of the four selected countries: work integration social enterprises, integrative approaches to work integration and cross sector partnerships. As we compared how these three innovations emerged and unfolded in the four selected countries, guided by expert advice, we chose to focus our enquiry on cross-sector partnerships (hereafter CSPs) as an innovation with interesting variance across countries and as well as a strong potential for social impact.

We found instances of CSPs, where public actors, companies and third sector organizations join forces to contribute to work integration, in the four countries of interest, yet they took different forms. In the Czech Republic and in France, we identified narrow but deep partnerships, involving two partners collaborating around a localized project, with a specific profile of beneficiaries, in a specific industry. In Spain, we encountered a much broader partnership federating more than 1,000 organizations. More broadly, we observed vast differences between countries as to the degree of advancement in developing CSPs, the actors involved, the type of partnerships (who is involved and how?), the beneficiaries targeted and factors enabling the development of partnerships. In this chapter, we present these specificities and reflect upon what they may teach us about social innovation in Europe.

Central Concepts

Work Integration Programs for Disadvantaged People

We detail here the central concepts and key questions of our enquiry. Given our focus on the work integration of disadvantaged people, we started with defining *disadvantaged people* as

> people with low or no qualification at all (sometimes to the point of illiteracy), family issues (such as having to provide for several children as a single mother or having been abused by a partner etc.), lack of cultural and social capital (which might include immigrants who don't know the local language), poverty and housing issues. To these structural causes of disadvantage must be added the long-term effects of events that are in part driven by choices, missteps and job accidents, such as spending some time in jail or, more commonly, becoming long-term unemployed. Of course these issues are not exclusive of each other. Most of the time, they cumulate.
>
> (André et al., 2015)

Given the richness and diversity of the work integration sector, we narrowed down our focus by looking at *work integration programs* that are transitional initiatives rather than long-term programs providing an alternative work universe (such as adapted work conditions and programs for the long-term disabled). The aim of a transitional occupation is to provide work experience to these disadvantaged people with the purpose of achieving their full integration in the open labor market after a set period. We focused on organizations or programs which target disadvantaged people, meaning long-term unemployed people (i.e., people whose time unemployed exceeds one year) with low qualification.

Cross-Sector Partnerships

As mentioned, three possible developments in social innovation streams were initially considered in the field of work integration: *work integration social enterprises* (WISEs) that are organizations (associations or enterprises) which hire disadvantaged people for a limited period to produce goods and services sold on the commercial market. As such, they offer a pathway to full integration in the labor market. They typically combine a professional activity with personalized professional and social support. *Integrated approaches to work integration* emerged in recent years as holistic approaches aiming at addressing the issue of work integration by taking into account the multiple problems disadvantaged people face (including health, housing, literacy or administrative issues). Recently, some work integration initiatives have started to offer integrated, customized support to the unemployed people targeted by the initiative. *Cross-sector Partnerships* (CSP) is the less well-documented area of governments, associations and enterprises working together on work integration schemes but has been considered particularly innovative by the field experts we consulted across the countries involved in the research. WISEs were identified by the experts as a promising social innovation to study too, but it was considered as not really innovative in France, where WISEs have been widespread entities since the late 1970s.

Having reviewed the literature on the definition of *cross-sector partnerships*, which started to develop in the late 1990s, we found that no widely accepted definition exists, and that the diverse definitions available often lack clear criteria that allow partnerships to be classified in practice (e.g., Dahan et al., 2010; Rondinelli & London, 2003; Milne et al., 1996). This led us to put forward a definition that is both precise and workable. This definition was informed by the input that each academic partner provided on the partnerships they proposed to investigate. It was further discussed with, and tested by, an expert in cross-sector partnerships in France.

As a result, we defined a *cross-sector partnership* along five dimensions that we used as criteria to select our case studies.

- Involving partners from *more than one sector*. Partnerships involving three or more partners can be included, but the presence of three sectors is not required.
- *Being formalized* to some degree. It is not necessary that the partnership be an organization in its own right. It suffices that the project has a name, a website, a legal status or a physical location, or that there is a contract defining the partnership.
- Benefiting from the *investment of resources from each partner*. These resources could include time, money, skills or reputation.
- *Relying on reciprocity*. Each party must contribute towards the objectives of other parties, or towards shared objectives.
- Ensuring the *representation of partners from each sector in the governance* of the partnership.

In our attempt to define our focus of enquiry, we narrowed our definition to rule out less innovative forms of collaborations. In consultation with our academic partners in the four selected countries, and building upon previous work on CSPs (Le Rameau, 2015), we focused more specifically on two types of partnerships, namely CSPs promoting:

- Economic cooperation (i.e., cross-sector partnership involving the co-creation of a new joint product, service or unit).
- New approaches to social needs (i.e., cross-sector partnerships creating innovative practices to respond jointly to a social need encountered in the course of work integration initiatives).

Methods

Within the broader framework of the ITSSOIN project and methodology, we followed the following methodological steps.

Case Selection

Following this choice of CSPs as our focus of enquiry, we studied specific CSPs in the four selected countries (France, Germany, Spain and the Czech Republic), with the goal to unpack the specificities of this type of innovation in each country. Our academic partners identified and researched cases in their respective countries. This was a broad effort, screening initiatives across the country and guided by desktop research as well as expert advice. The resulting repertoire of partnerships was very wide, comprising for instance over 100 examples of cross-sector collaboration in Germany, of which around 30 were particularly promising and fitting our research focus. On the basis of this research, we however also found that, except in the case of France, there was only a small number of cross-sector partnerships that met the five dimensions defined as criteria in the previous chapter. In particular the governance aspect and the initial ambition to find collaboration from all three sectors were hard to fulfill. The further aspect of the cases having reached some scale was impossible to fulfill in the Czech Republic, where we had to choose an individual, rather small scale initiative of a call center in a prison that came closest to our conception of CSPs. In the French case instead, a short-list of partnerships had to be drawn up to choose between exemplary cases in a pool of CSPs.

Data Collection

In each country, we collected both archival and interview data. Researchers collected archival data on the field of work integration and on CSPs more specifically. It consisted of reports, websites, studies, and articles published on work integration. In addition, researchers conducted two types of interviews. Interviews with experts used to understand the specificities and dynamic of the work integration sector in that country. Four experts were interviewed in France, two in Germany, three in Spain and four in the Czech

Republic. Interviews with case protagonists were conducted to understand in depth the content and evolution of selected CSPs as exemplary for the broader social innovation stream.

Six case protagonists were interviewed in France, ten in Germany, nine in Spain and eight in the Czech Republic. All interviews were recorded and transcribed in the local language. All countries used a locally translated version of the interview guide provided by the University of Heidelberg. In each country academics coded the interviews that they had undertaken in line with the associated coding guide.

Tracing the Social Innovation Stream

The time horizon over which cross-sector partnerships in the field of work integration developed is quite different across countries: specifically, they began to emerge in France in the early to mid-1990s but in other countries, it was not until 2010 or later that cross-sector partnerships emerged. Thus we have adopted a flexible timeframe that allows for differences in development stages across countries. For France, we start in the early 1990s. For the other countries, we start around 2010.

The study was conducted at a time where European Countries had to face two major events likely to impact CSPs. First the economic crisis that has struck the European countries since 2008 has had different impacts on the economy and the employment rate across the continent. Another important external jolt is the impact of the rising number of refugees and migrants who came to the European Union since 2010 to seek asylum and better living conditions. Migrants and refugees are far from being the only persons concerned by work integration programs. But their growing numbers constitutes a great challenge in terms of work integration. EU member states received over 1.2 million asylum applications in 2015, a number that more than doubled in a year. Yet, all the European countries are not impacted in the same way. Germany, Hungary, Sweden and Austria received around two-thirds of the EU's asylum applications in 2015 (Eurostat, 2015). Their integration in the work market is important to ensure their social integration, yet it represents a challenge due to the differences in culture, language and diplomas.

We now present a cross-country perspective on cross-sector partnerships (CSP) in the work integration field. Particularly interesting are the differences that we observed across the countries that we studied (France, Germany, Spain and the Czech Republic), both in terms of the number of partnerships identified, as well as in terms of the content and scale of partnerships. We found striking differences between France, where CSPs have been developed and partly institutionalized, and the other countries, where CSPs remain exceptional occurrences. This translates into the way that we present our findings: we describe the evolution of the concept and practice of CSPs in France before we go into analyzing the engaged actors and their interplay within this broader development, whereas we focus mainly on describing specific CSPs in the other countries.

SI Stream in France

The French case stands out because it has a long history of cross-sector partnerships in the field of work integration, in contrast to some other countries in our sample. Yet, as our expert consultation highlights, this does not mean that collaboration has become widespread in France. Indeed, some argue that the development of links between WISEs, often the entity the CSPs have evolved from, and the world of business fall short of what is needed.

The first WISEs emerged in France at the end of the 1970s as entrepreneurial not-for-profit organizations founded by social workers who recognized, in the context of rising unemployment, the need to create "intermediary enterprises" (as WISEs were initially called) to help at-risk youths and long-term unemployed people learn—or relearn—the skills needed to get and hold down a job. The founders of WISEs developed a simple model: they created companies that hired the long-term unemployed for a maximum of two years to produce goods and services in low skilled industries (such as construction, catering, gardening, temp work or recycling), which are then sold at market price. Through caring supervision, tailored training programs and individual social counseling, they helped long-term unemployed people readapt to the world of work, regain self-confidence, and find jobs in mainstream companies at the end of their two-year contract.

Over the years, the French State identified the ability of these organizations to tackle structural long-term unemployment. Various laws (in 1979, 1985, 1991, 1998 and 2006) progressively provided structure for this emerging field. The State developed an accreditation process that granted systematic financial support to accredited WISEs to offset the opportunity cost of employing less productive people who require extra supervision and training. In recent years, on average, these subsidies have accounted for about 20% of WISEs' revenues, while sales represent the remaining 80%. Accreditation is conditional on WISEs hiring those most deserving long-term unemployed (as identified by criteria set out by the National Agency for Employment) and report on their ability to successfully place them in real jobs (as measured by the rate of positive graduation). Other than these two constraints, WISEs are free to organize and operate as they see fit.

CSPs in work integration are today characterized by a few important partnerships, mainly between large WISEs and private commercial firms. Whereas public actors did not play an operational role in the CSPs that we studied in France, they played the important role of creating the framework in which CSPs between WISEs and commercial firms operate. They played the important role of accrediting and financially compensating WISEs for the lower productivity of the long-term unemployed that they hired. They further introduced specific regulations, such as "social clauses", that created important incentives for the development of CSPs.

Existing CSPs have enhanced the capacity of the WISEs to offer credible pathways into stable, long-term jobs in the private sector. The WISEs that participate in these partnerships are, to our knowledge, among the largest WISEs in France, including Ares, Vitamine T, Groupe Id'ees and Reseau Cocagne. Indeed, these larger WISEs have sometimes multiple partnerships with the private sector actors, or, in the case of Reseau Cocagne, succeeded in federating a large number of private actors to conceive, develop and fund the scaling up of their activities. The literature and expert interviews paint a different picture for small WISEs—who may be too small to stand out as credible partners for private firms seeking collaboration in this sector.

Several factors seem to drive firms to enter into partnerships with WISEs. One is to conquer new markets or generate a new client base. For example, Belgian group Van Gansewinkel was able to create its first factory on French soil through its partnership with WISE Vitamine T in the north of France. Another motivation is to access a larger pool of potential employees. Indeed, that was one of the motivations of Norbert Dentressangle in entering into a partnership with the WISE Ares, that would help train unemployed disabled people in logistics. Further, corporate foundations such as Fondation Veolia and Fondation Chanel often seek to engage the employees of their parent companies in meaningful social projects; they do so by funding and participating in projects which speak to employees' values and concerns. Work integration is often a cause that ranks high on employees' priorities because it is palpable and speaks to employees who are, by definition, familiar with work environments.

Despite this collective commitment to address long-term unemployment by actors from all three sectors as well as the development of model partnerships, more is needed to address the issue of unemployment, especially for the most disadvantaged groups. Indeed, a report showed that the obligation that WISEs must fulfill in order to be eligible for state subsidies to report on their rate of reintegration to the mainstream labor market gave WISEs the incentives to work with the least disadvantaged people in long-term unemployment, in order to keep their re-integration statistics competitive (Baculard & Barthelemy, 2012). Whereas CSPs appear as a promising avenue to enhance the scale and effectiveness of work integration initiatives, they remain unevenly distributed, and limited to a few large pioneering organizations. An expert we interviewed summarizes it:

> We have a hard time replicating CSPs. It's pioneering, though it's getting better and better known.

Work integration CSPs developed in France around two important milestones (Figure 9.1): 1) the introduction of "social clauses" in French public

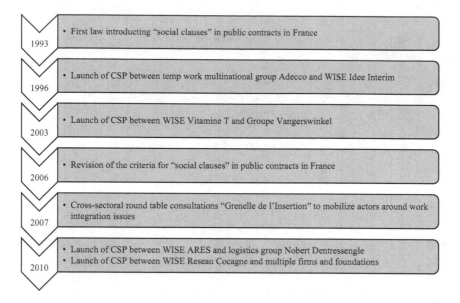

Figure 9.1 Milestones for the development work integration CSP in France

law and 2) the roundtable consultations "Grenelle de l'Insertion" convened by the French government to mobilize all three sectors (public, private and third) to enhance the impact of work integration policies.

The introduction of "social clauses" in French public law in the mid-1990s created incentives for companies to collaborate with WISEs to win competitive government-issued call for tenders. Social clauses are a stipulation in a local or national government contract that the winner of a tender should work towards a social or environmental objective: in this case, work integration. The clause might require that bidders who have a work integration objective are favored in the tender process, or it could go so far as to state that WISEs are the only sort of organization that can win the contract. The first social clauses for work integration were explicitly encouraged by a ministerial memo in 1993. Whilst private sector companies can put social clauses in their call for tenders, the original impetus (and their widest use) came from the public sector. Although during our interviews with Id'ees Interim and Adecco's, neither party mentioned social clauses as a motivation for their partnership, which started in 1996, not long after the introduction of social clauses.

Regulation defining the purpose and usage of "social clauses" has evolved over time, with the possibilities ranging from a mere "declaration of intention" to a legally binding requirement, with support from the European Union. From 2006 on, French public authorities have been given the possibility of either: 1) attributing the market based on price and quality of product criteria, but stipulating that an insertion objective must be attained by the firm that wins the market, or 2) making insertion objectives one of the criteria under which the contract is attributed. It is important to highlight that while providing important incentives for private companies to engage in CSP with WISEs, social clauses do not guarantee a robust approach to work integration. "Quite a few social clauses are badly managed, or simply consist in box ticking", cautions an expert that we interviewed. Their positive impact on work integration must thus be assessed on a case-by-case basis.

To further encourage the wide mobilization of actors around work integration, and under the pressure from major non-profit networks involved in poverty reduction, the French government launched, in 2007, the "Grenelle de l'Insertion", a government-sponsored year-long consultation on work integration. In that context, every aspect of the work integration ecosystem was examined and debated, with a view to reform. The crucial role of private enterprise was highlighted in the final report.

> Without [companies], without taking into account their constraints, we will not be able to change the scale of access to work. We cannot successfully fight social exclusion without an increase and a clarification of actions and policies using and mobilizing private enterprises. The investments of private enterprises in this area must rest not only on their goodwill but also on their interests and needs. Work integration efforts [on the part of companies] should not only be short-term actions motivated by social engagement but rather strategic engagement based on a pragmatic recognition of their interests.
>
> (Grenelle de l'Insertion, 2008)

The "Grenelle de l'Insertion" brought about several notable developments, including the mobilization of employers' unions (MEDEF, UPA and CGPME) to promote exemplary CSPs and encourage more of them. As a result of a recommendation of this consultation, employers' unions and the WISE federation produced a model legal agreement that could be used by a private firm and a WISE who wanted to conclude a partnership agreement. This was important, because from a legal perspective in France, concluding a partnership agreement is not simple.

Despite these positive evolutions encouraging the development CSPs in France, obstacles remain in the way of their generalization and positive impact. A first obstacle is the fragmentation of the sector. Historically, the sector developed around various work integration models (*associations d'insertion, entreprises d'insertion, régies de quartier*) promoting different visions for work integration, leading to the structuration of different—and at times competing—professional organizations. As a result, the sector is not easy to comprehend for outsiders, and remains largely fragmented, composed of small organizations operating with different legal forms, making it challenging for larger corporations to find adequate work integration partners. It is likely no coincidence that cross-sector partnerships that we have identified in the course of this research project have involved larger WISEs, notably Groupe Id'ees (4,000 "social" employees), Vitamine T (1,800 "social" employees) and Ares (650 "social" employees). An additional obstacle includes the perception, by SMEs, that WISEs are unfair competitors, because they operate on the same markets as they do, while receiving public subsidies. Although the employers' unions recognized, during the "Grenelle de l'Insertion" that these subsidies only fairly compensate for the lower productivity of the people that WISEs employ, this perception remains, at times, an impediment to closer collaborations between for-profit companies and work integration actors.

SI Stream in Germany

The field of work integration in Germany has historically been very state-centered. Bureaucratic restrictions and training requirements for job candidates, and the dominant position of the German employment agency as well as economic disincentives for enterprises to take on under-qualified employees have resulted in a lack of innovation in the field over the last few decades (Bode, 2011; Preuss, 2015a, 2015b). However, with the liberalization of regulations in 1997 (Employment Promotion Law by the Code of Social Law III (SGB III)), work integration providers from private companies and the third sector have gradually made their way into the field (Bäcker, Naegele, Bispinck, Hofemann, & Neubauer, 2010; Oschimansky, 2010). In the light of an ongoing skills shortage, private enterprises have changed their outlook, leading to an increasing openness to engage in work integration initiatives. Actors from different sectors have become more willing to cooperate to achieve their varied economic, political and social interests.

While work integration partnerships in Germany were traditionally limited to collaborations between the public and private for-profit sectors (PPPs), excluding the third sector, in our screening we have witnessed a recent and gradual evolution from PPPs to CSPs involving the third sector. This, according to one expert, is due to the growing recognition that the competencies brought in by civil society actors, as well as academic actors, are valuable in achieving better work integration outcomes, in particular when addressing vulnerable target groups such as disadvantaged youths, or, more recently, refugees. Co-occurring context factors can further explain this growing interest for CSP, including skills shortages in industrial markets as well as the recent significant influx of refugees as a result of war and humanitarian crises.

Thus, initiatives involving partners from all three sectors in a formalized fashion are a novel phenomenon in the field of work integration in Germany. One of our interviewees referred to this as "triple" or "quadruple" helix arrangements, the latter referring to the additional involvement of universities. In the work integration sector, these initiatives are perceived as "best practice examples" that could be promoted and extended to a bigger scale, inspiring state programs. Yet, we haven't found any of these initiatives run on a large-scale basis as of now. Following the methodology described previously, we studied two exemplary cases in Germany.

"Arrivo": Milestones and Key Actors

Arrivo—Flüchtling ist kein Beruf ("Refugee" is not a profession) has been initiated by the Chamber of Crafts Berlin (private sector), Schlesische27 (third sector) and the Senate of Berlin (public sector), with the goal to integrate refugees into the labor market. The CSP was launched in Berlin in December 2014 and draws on experiences from previous projects and networks, including the "Bridge", a loose partner network on the issue of forced migration. The three main partners draw on the complementary strengths of many regional and national stakeholders (including multinational firms; around 50+ regional businesses (low, medium and large businesses)). The Chamber of Crafts Berlin serves as the umbrella organization for 30,000 local businesses in Berlin. It has been active for more than 20 years, encouraging networking among member companies or promoting quality standards in craftsmanship. Schlesische27 is an educational institution, organized as a registered society (*eingetragener Verein*), promoting intercultural learning. It has been in existence for 36 years. The Senate of Berlin is the governmental institution of the federal state of Berlin. It is headed by the city's mayor (*Senatsverwaltung für Arbeit, Integration und Frauen*) and consists of eight chambers. One of them, the Chamber of Labour, Integration and Women, is involved with Arrivo.

The development of the partnership began with an informal contact between the Chamber of Crafts, the Senate of Berlin and Schlesische 27, who spurred and were integrated in this partnership, since they owned expertise in working with migrants for many years. The campaign Arrivo-*Flüchtling ist kein Beruf* was launched with a large poster and radio campaign, to sensitize the public and firms for this topic. The "Bridge" network served as a blueprint for Arrivo. But because the former is focused on refugee self-determination rather than work integration, a new approach proved necessary. Some earlier forays into the field were made by the project "*Bildungsmanufaktur*", which had a more pronounced work integration emphasis to it and was meant to build a connection and intensify contacts to the guilds.

After the CSP was initiated, a learning center was built at the location of Schlesische27, where refugees could experiment with and demonstrate their work skills at different activities. This enabled Schlesische27 to learn about their competences in different fields. Three months after the CSP started operating, the first refugee found a placement in a local firm via Schlesische27 and started his on-the-job training (Figure 9.2). Given the increasing number of people seeking asylum from the middle of 2015 onwards, the partners collectively decided to expand the partnership and started seeking

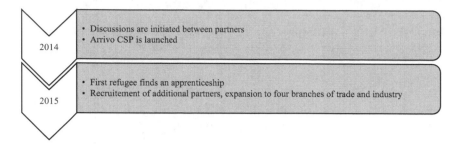

Figure 9.2 Milestones for the Arrivo CSP in Germany

the participation of more firms located in or around Berlin. Step by step the project was expanded: it covered, in 2016, four different branches of trade or industry.

The pilot phase resulted in 15 placements. This number rose to 400 placements as of early 2017. The complementary program "Arrived" focuses on supporting those refugees who have taken up a formalized training through "Arrivo" and is run by Chamber of Crafts.

"Rock Your Company!": Milestones and Key Actors

"Rock Your Company!" (RYC) was initiated by the Rock Your Life! gGmbH, a non-profit private limited company, and is run as a project under its roof. While Rock Your Life! focuses on external mentoring relationships between university students and educationally unprivileged pupils, RYC offers in-house mentoring for disadvantaged young trainees within companies. The project was launched in 2015 and draws on existing experience and contacts established by Rock Your Life!, including partner companies and foundations as well as staff and volunteer members. The two project coordinators of RYC formerly worked as volunteers for Rock Your Life!. The supervision and consultation of in-house mentors within RYC is also organized and carried out by trainers from Rock Your Life!. Staff of the participating companies is trained to be able to offer effective support to the trainees.

RYC supports undereducated youth to successfully complete their apprenticeship by developing trainees' soft skills through a one-year mentoring program. When soliciting companies, RYC insists on the opportunity to invest in initiatives related to CSR and position themselves as attractive employers on the market for apprentices. Stakeholders of RYC mainly involve actors from the private sector such as banks (Credit Suisse, German National Bank) or firms in the hotel industry (Ibis Hotels, Novotel). Additional partners include private non-profit actors, such as Caritas, or Kiron Higher Education, a social entrepreneurial start-up that aims at providing access to university education for refugees through massive open online courses in the first phase of studies as well as through support to join established universities. The training of mentors provided by RYC is funded in half by the participating firms and in half by the German Chamber of Industry and Commerce (IHK). Overall the CSP is based on mutual agreements between RYC and HR managers at the participating firms. While RYC initially focused on growing the number of firms involved beyond the initial circle of Rock Your Life! partners, it recently decided to focus on investing in the quality of cooperation by means of conceptual development of the program.

RYC has so far received funding from various foundations, including the Aqtivator gGmbH, PHINEO Stiftung, Karl Schlecht Stiftung, and Wübben Stiftung. It is intended to gradually set the project free from these investors to gain more financial independence. To reach this aim, "Rock Your Company!" introduced member fees for participating companies and is currently planning to increase the share of those in their overall budget.

"Rock Your Company!", the donating foundations and other partners could not have set up a similar project alone as the central stage for success or failure of the work relations with young trainees is set within the enterprises. As some companies do already follow similar projects without involving external partners, it can be supposed that setting up a mentoring program such as "Rock Your Company!" could have been achieved by the private actors themselves. However, what appears crucial for the success of "Rock Your Company!" is the idea of setting up a community spirit among participating companies and clients which motivates mentors and trainees to participate. These resources and motivation would be lacking if one of the partners was left out. The expansion of the partnership with Kiron and IHK offers opportunities to extend the general CSP model to new target groups.

SI Stream in Spain

The field of work integration emerged in Spain around WISEs, which appeared at the beginning of the 1980s with the goal of fighting social exclusion caused by long-term unemployment amongst those with low levels of employability. The first WISEs were created by leaders of local neighborhood and church associations, without formal support and on a voluntary basis, with the aim of creating jobs for people with low levels of employability. The approach used was based on personalized work paths, combining theoretical with practical training within a real working environment, in addition to offering the support services that such people usually need (Vidal & Claver, 2005). In this sense, WISEs emerged in Spain as spontaneous initiatives of civil society to solve problems of work integration. The public sector plays a role in regulating, funding and supplying work integration initiatives. In particular, Autonomous Communities run their own employment services, and local authorities often provide complementary employment services. Yet according to the experts interviewed, a public strategy to truly developing a work integration ecosystem in the country is missing.

The severe economic crisis that hit Spain from 2009 on and destroyed a third of the jobs of the middle class made the need for work integration more prevalent and urgent. The increasing need for work integration services has put pressure on the public service providers of work integration and encouraged third sector organizations as well as some private companies in the context of their CSR policies to play an increasing role in the provision of work integration services for the most disadvantaged.

In 2012, due to the unsustainable situation of unemployment in Spain as a consequence of the economic crisis, "Together for the employment of the most vulnerable people" (*"Juntos por el empleo de los más vulnerables"*) emerged. It is a social innovation based on the partnership of the private sector, third sector and public sector to search for alternative ways of promoting employment and self-employment of the disadvantaged. This initiative is led by Accenture through its corporate foundation. Its innovativeness stems from the fact that it is the first CSP for work integration in Spain. It currently gathers the collective efforts of over 1000 organizations from the three sectors. While *"Juntos por el empleo de los más vulnerables"* is not the only partnership in the work integration field in Spain, it is the only CSP that meets the criteria described in the preceding definition section. The occurrence of one paired with the large number of organizations involved makes it hard to say whether the SI stream is limited or widespread in the Spanish context.

"Juntos for el empleo de los mas vulnerables": Milestones and Key Actors

The main goal of the *"Juntos por el empleo de los más vulnerables"* initiative is to improve the employability of the most vulnerable actors of society by fostering collaboration between the business sector, the public sector and third sector organizations. Currently it gathers in this collective effort over 1,083 organizations from the three sectors: 1,000 third sector organizations, 70 businesses (either directly or through their corporate foundations) and 13 public administrations. The partnership allows for the combination of resources and capabilities from the different organizations involved, creating a model of work integration combining training, learning, self-employment, evaluation of results, and funding.

"Juntos por el empleo de los más vulnerables" (Figure 9.3) was launched in 2012, as a collective initiative led by Accenture through its corporate foundation, with the support of the Seres and Compromiso y Transparencia Foundations, both non-profit private foundations focusing on the engagement of companies with social issues. This partnership does not exist as an independent legal entity. It is hosted at Accenture headquarters and it is

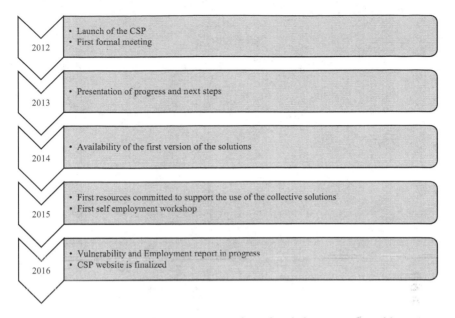

Figure 9.3 Milestones for the *"Juntos por el empleo de los más vulnerables"* CSP

governed by a rotating coordinating committee, where the private and third sector actors are represented and, to a lesser extent, the public sector as well (at the local and national level).

The partnership relies on the contributions from partners. Most contributions come in the form of human contributions (know-how, expertise, volunteers) and relational resources (networks). The largest contributor in the CSP is the Accenture Foundation, both through financial and volunteering contributions. Other partners occasionally contributed with in-kind or financial gifts.

The main activities of the partnership include knowledge generation, soft-skills training for vulnerable groups in employment and self-employment, labor market assessments in Spain, employability assessments of vulnerable groups, reporting, promoting sustainable microcredit for disadvantaged people not served by traditional banking, among others. Partners in the CSP formalized 21 "solutions" that support work integration, targeting both employment and self-employment (see Table 9.1).

These solutions are jointly developed by organizations from the three sectors involved in the partnership and are managed by the Accenture Foundation as CSP promoter and coordinator, using the support (advice, organizational requirements, and network capacities) of other partners from the public, private and third sector. The CSP benefits from the mobilization of seven employees as well as a wealth of volunteers from all three

Table 9.1 Solutions developed in the context of the *"Juntos for el empleo de los mas vulnerables"* CSP

Solution name	Target	Content
Observatory	Employment	Assessment of current labor market and identification of new opportunities for vulnerable groups
Diagnosis	Employment	Assessment of employability of vulnerable people within the employment framework
Competences	Employment	Training material for the evaluation and development of transversal skills in employment
Reporting	Employment	Structured management information in the employment context
Training guide	Employment	Best practices in training for employment
Practices guide	Employment	Definition of training practices in private sector
Diagnosis	Self-employment	Assessment of employability of vulnerable people and their business ideas within the self-employment framework
Competences	Self-employment	Training material for the evaluation and development of transversal skills in self-employment
Training	Self-employment	Training materials about technical knowledge in the self-employment context
Reporting	Self-employment	Structured management information in the self-employment context
Training guide	Self-employment	Training methodology for entrepreneurs
Microcredits	Self-employment	Sustainable Microcredit Program aimed at profiles not served by traditional banking
Online	Self-employment	Relationship Model of the YBS (Youth Business Spain) network

sectors involved. By May 2016, this CSP was estimated to have contributed to the creation of 5,639 jobs, to have worked with 233,730 beneficiaries, to have trained 194,451 people and to have offered more than 18 million of hours of training. This was archived through the collective investment of 240,000 hours of work and 75,000 euros.

SI Stream in the Czech Republic

Work integration activities focused on disadvantaged citizens take various forms in the Czech Republic. Most work integration initiatives take the form of WISEs. They cooperate with the private sector and with governments in a rather limited way. WISEs have standard commercial contracts with private firms, and they receive public funding and subsidies, but these relationships are not sufficiently interdependent to qualify as CSPs.

For many years, in the Czech Republic, the topic of social innovation has been pushed forward by the EU. The influence of the EU has led to the increased interest in social innovations and the development operational programs such as "Social Innovation (ESF)". These programs have helped to support many socially innovative projects and a wide range of WISEs. Many projects probably would not be viable without public support from EU Operational Programs. There is thus a concern about their future sustainability should access to those financial sources diminish. High dependency of notable (and internationally recognized and awarded) SI projects is a reality of the Czech Republic and their long-term sustainability without public support remains questionable.

While a variety of partnerships were identified involving a combination of work integration, private and public actors (such as, for instance, HUB Praha, Agency for Social Inclusion, Pacts of Employment and Local Action Groups), they were not specifically focusing on work integration of disadvantaged groups and thus did not qualify as work integration CSPs either. One project, called "Change is Possible", conducted by a private commercial company in partnership with the public sector, was identified as the most promising example of a work integration CSP. Such deep collaborations are still rare in the Czech context. The project has been widely recognized and awarded, but at the same time, it is currently undergoing substantial changes and transformation.

"Change is Possible": Milestones and Key Actors

The impulse for the launch of this CSP came from the needs of two institutional partners. Vinařice prison, a public entity, was looking for jobs that prisoners could perform while inside the prison. The other partner, A-GIGA, a private commercial company, was looking for a suitable space to develop a new call center with staff members who could work in it. One of first shoots of the initiative, which emerged inside of Vinařice prison, was the prisoners' vocal desire for employment opportunities. In 2008, in response to this expressed need, the prison therapist, Mr. Hruby began efforts to find jobs for prisoners. Yet these were not easy to find. At the same period, the company A-GIGA made the decision to open new call center. Because Mr. Hruby's wife worked for A-GIGA, she initiated discussions about a possible collaboration between A-GIGA and the prison. The response from both A-GIGA's and the prison's top management turned out to be positive. In 2009, Mr. Hruby was entrusted with the coordination of the project (Figure 9.4). He immediately started negotiations within the Prison Service and the Ministry of Justice. The call center in the Vinařice prison opened in 2010, under the banner of the "Change is Possible" project. One year later the project was accredited by the Ministry of Education.

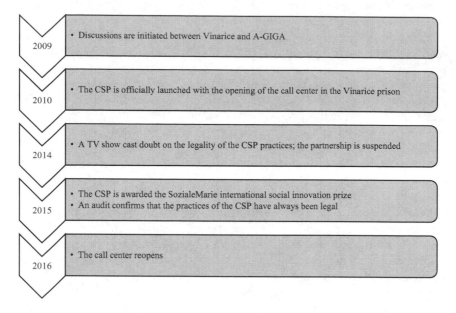

2009   • Discussions are initiated between Vinarice and A-GIGA

2010   • The CSP is officially launched with the opening of the call center in the Vinarice prison

2014   • A TV show cast doubt on the legality of the CSP practices; the partnership is suspended

2015   • The CSP is awarded the SozialeMarie international social innovation prize
       • An audit confirms that the practices of the CSP have always been legal

2016   • The call center reopens

Figure 9.4 Milestones for the "Change is Possible" CSP

An important and devastating milestone came about in the year 2014. TV NOVA, the most popular commercial Czech TV, broadcasted a false report about the "Change is Possible" project. This television report misrepresented the reality and clearly had a negative slant. This report strongly affected the public opinion about the project and finally led to the temporary suspension of the project. In May 2015, the project was awarded an international prize for socially innovative projects—SozialMarie. Finally, after investigation of the audit office, it became clear that the call center in Vinařice prison had never broken the law. The "Change is Possible" call center thus reopened in August 2016. Importantly, since 2015, in addition to its role of employer in the prison, A-GIGA also committed to employ only released prisoners (ex-offenders) in the nearby call centers located outside the prison.

The public sector (the prison system under the authority of Ministry of Justice, Ministry of Labour and Social Affairs, Ministry of Education and Sports) played the role of institutional enabler of the initiative. In terms of the respective contributions of the partners, Vinařice provided the space, while A-GIGA provided the initial investment (€14,570) required to fit the call center, as well as the operational costs (wages, training, etc.) (€5,000 monthly). Additional funding was provided by the European Social Fund (€65,000). Both partners contributed human resources to the project, in the form of project managers on A-GIGA side and coordinators and workers on Vinařice side. Whereas both partners suffered from a relatively negative reputation (as a prison and a call center company), this project provided them with rather positive publicity. These roles have not changed substantially over the course of the project and are not projected to change in the near future.

During the period 2010–2012, 164 prisoners were selected and trained to work in the call center, and received a salary. From 2013 to 2014, 247 were selected for retraining, and from them, 157 prisoners finished retraining, worked in prison, and were paid salaries which they could use for their expenses or to pay off their debts. Of these, 51 have been released so far, most of whom have started working on various positions, some in call centers of other companies. So far, 11 of the released prisoners have signed a contract with A-GIGA in a call center outside of the prison, as standard employees (A-GIGA employs both ex-offenders and other workers in the same teams). However, two of these 11 were later laid off because of addiction issues.

Synthesis

Our objective was to use work integration as a window to shed light on the nature and form of cross-sector partnerships as a social innovation stream in Europe. Our study design was deliberately narrow along three dimensions:

- It focused on work-integration CSPs rather than CSPs more generally.
- It defined a narrow focus group within work integration: that is to say, a focus on disadvantaged people taking part in transitional initiatives (as distinct from initiatives that set up a long-term supportive work environment distinct from the normal labor market).
- Rather than drawing upon the wide and diverse definitions of cross-sector partnerships available in the literature, we set out five tightly defined, testable criteria that circumscribe CSPs for our purposes.

Comparative Analysis

In spite of this, as we compared work integration CSPs in France, Germany, Spain and the Czech Republic, we uncovered considerable variation in the pattern of cross-sector partnerships in our sample. In France, CSPs for work integration go back to the 1990s and tend to involve a configuration of a single WISE having partnerships with one or more private companies. In Spain, WISEs founded back in the 1980s have broadly speaking failed to enter into partnerships with private companies, but more recently, an ambitious initiative catalyzed by the Accenture foundation has federated more than 1,000 NGOs with 70 private companies and three government entities to provide common pathways to work integration. In Germany, the state has traditionally assumed a dominant role in work integration, meaning that deep partnerships involving more than one sector have not been easy to constitute. For the last 20 years, however, a lessening of regulation on low-qualified candidates and changing economic incentives have propelled private companies to get involved in work integration initiatives—and a more recent recognition of the role of the third sector in assisting vulnerable groups—has meant that cross-sector partnerships are ever more viable. In the Czech Republic, social innovation as a concept is becoming engrained through the influence of the European Union, but partnerships for work integration are in their infancy.

If a pattern can be discerned from this diverse data, it is that endogenous and exogenous factors come together to breed distinct patterns of partnership in work integration. In Spain, exogenous factors dominated: the economic crisis seemed to create a sense of urgency for the partners in *"Juntos por el empleo de los más vulnerables"*, who, pre-2008, had already entered into dialogue but had not yet taken the first step toward action. In Germany, the impact of the refugee crisis coupled with the historical and evolving role of the state give context to the development of *Arrivo* and *Rock Your Life!* In France, government's earlier recognition of the role of private companies in work integration, through the creation and development of social clauses, seems to have acted as a catalyst for the creation of some CSPs. More recently, the roundtable on work integration organized in 2008 by the French government focused attention on the value of CSPs in this field, and launched the creation of tools such as a model partnership contract, intended to assist the emergence of new collaborations. Finally, the data from France and the Czech Republic underline the importance of personal relationships in creating conditions necessary to construct a cross-sector bridge.

Learnings

Interestingly, it appeared that work integration was the field of the ITSSOIN project where it was hardest to define conditions that could explain variance in the way that social innovation unfolded in different countries. This might be due to methodological issues. Yet, what emerges from case studies is that other factors might actually drive local differences. Cultural aspects, religious considerations, long-lasting relations as well as personal relations between individuals based in different organizations might also explain why different forms of cross-sector partnerships were created in different contexts. Although we made attempts to capture those factors, some seemed too "soft" to spot and dig into them within the comparative and standardized framework of the research. The case studies also pointed to the importance of "hubs"—either individuals or organizations—that would connect partners within those partnerships.

Focusing on the role of government underlines the complexity of the picture. The ITSSOIN project hypothesized potential explanations for the diversity of national situations due to the "varieties of capitalism" (see

Anheier et al., 2014)—that is, the specific institutional structure of each country (for instance whether a country is seen more as a liberal market economy, such as Spain, or a coordinated economy, such as France and Germany). Yet our research suggests that despite the similarities of France and Germany as coordinated economies, the influence of governments in these countries has been quite different: in Germany, the state has created a place for CSPs by reducing regulation, whereas in France, the state has stimulated partnerships by incentives and creating space for contact between WISEs, NGOs and private companies.

Eventually, what emerged from the insights gained from the case studies, the discussions in the workshops organized during the project and the ongoing dialogue between the teams, are more complex explanations to understand diversity, eventually pointing at multi-level explanations that would include historical, institutional, cultural and interpersonal aspects. Something that current research on the variety of capitalism model, which tends to adopt a more macro and institutional approach, do not necessarily embrace.

In order to serve the needs of disadvantaged people who have spent a long time out of the labor market, cross-sector partnerships provide a striking opportunity to pool the strengths of companies, NGOs, social enterprises and government in order to lift them out of unemployment. Many of the WISEs interviewed for this project particularly emphasized the necessity of private-sector involvement for the relevance of their work. Cross-sectoral partnerships do not develop uniquely out of recognition of their potential impact. They are nurtured by the development of personal relationships, mediated by the influence of exogenous factors such as the European economic crisis and refugee crisis, and stimulated by the stance and policy of national governments.

Conclusions

Our research does not give rise to directive recommendations for practitioners and policy-makers. Whilst it seems likely that creating the conditions conducive to the development of cross-sector relationships would stimulate partnerships in any country—such as by creating forums for cross-sector exchanges (as in the French "Grenelle de l'Insertion")—the diverse role of the state across the four countries studied suggests that what works in one country might not work elsewhere. For example, the state's disengagement was a factor in leaving space for the development of CSPs in Spain, whilst its engagement through incentives and creating encounters was a factor in France, and also partly in Germany.

Whilst the lack of conclusions may seem disappointing in the short run, it leaves the field open to scholars. The present study provides an unparalleled overview of innovative initiatives to favor integration through work in four European countries. It also provides a unique basis from which to draw to conduct further research which is arguably necessary to identify all the drivers of such highly contrasted situations in these four countries, each one a member of the European Union. One aspect might be that innovation in the domain of work integration might be more local and national than international. As such this diversity might be related to different national settings but also histories and cultures as well as the existence of well-established actors in the field. Eventually, this points to the need for further studies that would develop in depth multi-levels of analysis considering both distance reasons for the development of initiatives (e.g., historical, cultural, institutional) and proximate ones such as personal relations. External shocks and crisis might have to be considered separately as the present study suggests that they rarely motivate cross-sector partnership but rather that such partnerships adapt to respond to them. The massive influx of migrant populations across European countries may, however, may change this dynamic. As the need to provide migrant workers with work integration opportunities will increase, the dynamics around CSP may well be impacted in the coming years.

Note

1. We would like to thank all who made important contributions to the ITSSOIN project deliverable that formed the basis for this chapter: Behrendt, C.; Mildenberger, G.; Calvo Babio, N.; Rey-Garcia, M.; and Müllner, V.

References

André, K., Cognat, A. S., Lallemand-Stempak, N., & Pache, A-C. (2015). *Hypothesis testing in work integration and community development*. A deliverable of the project: "Impact of the Third Sector as Social Innovation" (ITSSOIN), European Commission—7th Framework Programme, Brussels: European Commission, DG Research.

Anheier, H. K., Krlev, G., Preuss, S., Mildenberger, G., & Einarsson, T. (2014). *Theory and empirical capturing of the third sector at the macro level*. A deliverable of the project: 'Impact of the Third Sector as Social Innovation' (ITSSOIN), European Commission—7th Framework Programme. Brussels.

Bäcker, G., Naegele, G., Bispinck, R., Hofemann, K., & Neubauer, J. (2010). *Sozialpolitik und soziale Lage in Deutschland*. Band 1+2, 5. Wiesbaden: Auflage.

Baculard, O., & Barthelemy, A. (2012). *Act together for work integration: An ambition we should share: The state of play and perspectives on work integration*. Paris: Secours Catholique and Volonteer.

Bode, I. (2011). Soziale dienstleistungen am arbeitsmarkt. In A. Evers, R. G. Heinze, & T. Olk (Eds.), *Handbuch soziale dienste* (pp. 317–332). Wiesbaden: Verlag für Sozialwissenschaften.

Dahan, N. M., Doh, J. P., Oetzel, J., & Yaziji, M. (2010). Corporate NGO collaboration: Co-creating new business models for developing markets. *Long Range Planning*, 43(2–3), 326–342.

European Commission. (2014). *Employment and social developments in Europe 2014*. Luxembourg: Publications Office of the European Union.

Eurostat, Statistical Office of the European Communities. (2015, April 30). *EUROSTAT: New release*. Euroindicators. 76/. Eurostat. Retrieved from http://ec.europa.eu/eurostat/documents/2995521/6807651/3-30042015-AP-EN.pdf/c619bed7-7d9d-4992-95c3-f84e91bfcc1d

Grenelle de l'Insertion. (2008). *Rapport général*. Retrieved from www.ladocumentationfrancaise.fr/var/storage/rapports-publics/084000308.pdf

Lallemand-Stempak, N., Cognat, A. S., André, K., Pache, A-C., Preuss, S., Navrátil, J., . . . Felgueiras, A. (2015). *Field description in work integration*. Part 1 of deliverable 7.1 of the project: "Impact of the Third Sector as Social Innovation" (ITSSOIN), European Commission—7th Framework Programme, Brussels: European Commission, DG Research.

Le Rameau. (2015). *Le Référentiel: Model d'Investisseur Sociétal*.

Milne, G. R., Iyer, E. S., & Gooding-Williams, S. (1996). Environmental organization alliance relationships within and across nonprofit, business, and government sectors. *Journal of Public Policy and Marketing, 15*(2), 203–215.

Oschimansky, F. (2010). *Öffentliche und private Arbeitsvermittlung: Historische Entwicklung*. Retrieved from www.bpb.de/politik/innenpolitik/arbeitsmarkt politik/55129/geschichte-der-arbeitsvermittlung

Preuss, S. (2015a). WoI-DE_20150519 (2015, May 19). Interview by S. Preuss.

Preuss, S. (2015b). WoI-DE_20150527 (2015, May 12). Interview by S. Preuss.

Rondinelli, D. A., & London, T. (2003). How corporations and environmental groups cooperate: Assessing cross sector alliances and collaborations. *Academy of Management Executive, 17*(1), 61–76.

Vidal, I., & Claver, N. (2005). *Work integration social enterprises in Spain*. Working Paper 04/05. Social Economy Initiatives Centre (CIES). Spain: University of Barcelona.

10 Social Innovation in Community Development

Self-organisation and Refugees

Wouter Mensink, Lucia Čemová,
Elisa Ricciuti, and Annette Bauer[1]

Introduction

The innovation stream that is at the centre of this chapter is self-organised community development with refugees. Self-organisation and bottom-up collective action is not a new development as such. The novelty lies in the increasing recognition of the importance of such activities by established players and governments. As in other studies, we define community development as an *activity* for the benefit of a *particular social group* (Bhattacharyya, 1995). In this chapter, we focus on heterogeneous groups of refugees—including those who have obtained the refugee status, those awaiting their procedures and those whose status applications have been denied—in particular localities.

The focus on refugees was set before the so-called "refugee crisis" but was accelerated by the sudden increase in the number of refugees coming to Europe over the course of the project. The vast numbers crossing the Mediterranean was certainly one of the most pressing issues of the year 2015. Never before had over 60 million people been displaced, worldwide. It seemed likely that new questions would come up soon enough: questions regarding cultural differences, fear of community disintegration, and how to gain and maintain public support for receiving refugees in the wake of the rise of populist politics. Headlines of European newspapers reflected widely differing sentiments, ranging from the *Willkommenskultur of* German Chancellor Angela Merkel's statement *Wir Schaffen Das* ['we will manage'], to Hungarian Prime Minister Viktor Orbán's plan to 'protect' his national community by fencing off the Southern borders. Every day we found articles about voluntary efforts to welcome refugees or to house them in private residencies, next to articles about worries regarding the 2015 New Year's Eve incidents in Cologne or protests of far-right groups like German Pegida. Looking beyond the immediately pertinent questions, such as shelter and other emergency support, a focus on community development seemed relevant with an eye to the future.

Despite the acuteness of the refugee situation, we decided to not only focus on new arrivals. Nor did we want to focus on asylum seekers, still in procedure, only. Community development is also highly—or perhaps even more—relevant for those who have already obtained their refugee status, and for refused asylum seekers.

The study was carried out in four countries: the Netherlands, the United Kingdom, Italy and the Czech Republic. Within each country, we decided to focus on one specific city, given the definition of community development as a *local* activity. The empirical work was carried out in four cities: Utrecht (the Netherlands), Milan (Italy), Birmingham (UK) and Brno (Czech Republic). We return to the motivation for these cities when describing the overall methodology of the chapter.

In this chapter, we aim to answer the following questions:

1. How did 'self-organised community development with refugees' emerge over time?
2. What actors, or interplay of actors, contributed to the emergence of this innovation stream?

Central Concepts

Community Development

Research about community development with refugees is often not based on an explicit definition of community development.[2] When explicit definitions *are* provided in articles dealing with refugees (Lenette & Ingamells, 2015; Mitchell & Correa-Velez, 2010; Stewart, 2012), they vary strongly. They have only one element in common: a focus on *enhancing relationships* (also referred to as connections, social capital, and external partnerships). Another often-found feature is a focus on *participation in decision-making*. These two points have informed the empirical work of this section. At the same time, we felt a more inductive approach was called for, asking: what does community development with refugees entail?

A question that these definitions do not address is: *what is to be understood as a community?* Bhattacharyya (1995) warns us for assuming that people sharing an ethnicity or living in the same area form a community. Communities may also be formed along lines of religion, political affiliation, or class, to name a few, or intersections thereof. Similarly, we may not assume that people sharing a refugee background will automatically form a community.

Self-organisation

We selected self-organisation as the 'innovation stream' on which we would focus, based on earlier desk research, expert consultation in three out of four countries, review of academic articles in which community-related projects and activities for refugees were labelled as socially innovative, interviews with representatives of international umbrella organisations and validation workshops with members from inside and outside the ITSSOIN consortium (for a more extensive presentation, see Mensink et al., 2015).

We take self-organisation to refer both to 'refugee self-organisations' (Zetter & Pearl, 2000, p. 676) and to 'grassroots initiatives of members of the host society for or with refugees' (Bakker, Denters, Oude Vrielink, & Klok, 2012, p. 397). The former were introduced mainly on the basis of interviews with experts, while the latter was introduced on the basis of validation within the project consortium. Both describe bottom-up forms of collective action: a group of people pursuing a collective goal, ideally with a high degree of self-organisation and self-determination, in the sense of being independent from government or market pressures (Bakker et al., 2012). Considering the definition of community development as activities establishing relations between refugees and members of the host societies, it was felt that the initiative for such activities ought to be regarded 'from both sides'.

We speak of organisations or initiatives 'with a degree of self-organisation'. Next to 'ideal typical examples', we were also interested in independent refugee groups operating in the context of a professional organisation, in initiatives that refugees and members of the host society take together, in citizen initiatives that partly fulfil a task for which they receive governmental subsidy, etc. Our objective is to provide a broad and open exploration of the notion of 'self-organised community development with refugees'. To sum up, the working definition of 'self-organized community development with refugees' that we apply here is: *local activities to establish and strengthen durable relations between refugees and members of the host society, allowing for processes of shared decision-making.*

Refugee self-organisation and grassroots initiatives are not new as such. More than a decade ago, Craig and Lovel wrote:

> Despite the generally hostile political environment to refugees worldwide, there is at grass-roots levels a new momentum to share community development expertise with groups struggling to tackle social exclusion resulting from armed conflict across the world.
>
> (2005, p. 133)

Similarly, refugee self-organisations have existed for a long time (Zetter, Griffiths, & Sigona, 2005; Zetter & Pearl, 2000). What is new, according to our preliminary investigation, and the subsequent case work that we present here, is the notion that these bottom-up initiatives are increasingly recognised as legitimate stakeholders in community development processes. This is the actual innovation stream we present in this report. For practical purposes, however, we refer to it as 'self-organised community development with refugees'.

Methods

Case Selection

We focused on residential areas with organisations or other civil society groups (e.g., refugee community organisations, local citizens groups, or vested civil society organisations) that meet the following criteria:

- They develop new initiatives that meet the need to foster community integration ('social innovation'), in a way that goes beyond offering basic services to refugees.
- These new initiatives should foster solidarity and agency ('community development'). This implies a two-way process, focusing on social inclusion, rather than 'assimilation'.
- These initiatives may include or target integration with various refugee groups, including asylum seekers, refugees with a status or undocumented migrants.

Partners in the Netherlands and the Czech Republic opted for a middle-sized city (Utrecht and Brno respectively), the UK and Italy for a large city (Birmingham and Milan). This makes for an illustrative diversity in the sample, within a generally urban frame. Argumentation for the choices in each country is fairly different. In the Netherlands, Utrecht is less over-researched than, e.g., Amsterdam, and The Hague provided fewer examples of innovative initiatives. Moreover, the municipality is known for its open and principled position towards providing shelter and additional services for undocumented migrants. The choice to focus on Brno in the Czech Republic is inspired by similar considerations: the researchers preferred not to focus on a more cosmopolitan city like Prague in order to find more locally embedded practices of community integration. The probable abundance of socially innovative initiatives in cities like Amsterdam and Prague might also be a downside in terms of a lack of overview. For the UK, the proportional presence of large refugee communities has played a role in selecting the geographical area (Birmingham). Moreover, it has its own refugee innovation strategy, being one of the important cities in the 'Cities of Sanctuary' movement. What the choice for Birmingham has in common with the choice for Utrecht, is that both are 'no gateway' for new arrivals into the country. Brno is located in the southeast of the Czech Republic, where many recent groups of refugees crossed the border. Interestingly, for Italy, Milan is mentioned as a potential focal area for nearly opposite reasons: it is a gateway for migrants to leave to the rest of Europe.

Data Collection

Interviews were held with (a) representatives of organisations, initiatives or projects that could be labelled as socially innovative (either a manager, staff member or a volunteer), (b) external experts that could report on these social innovations in a broader context (at the local, regional or national level) and (c) refugees involved (either as beneficiaries or as representatives of the organisations) with these innovations. Given the objective of shedding light on the role of different sectors (public, private and third sector), and on the way social innovations are embedded in a broader field of relations, we attempted to conduct interviews with a broad range of stakeholders. Generally, this involved interviews with third sector entities—ranging from established organisations to informal civic groups, both at the local and national level—and with public officials of the respective local or regional governments. Involvement of the private sector was less frequent and less intensive, with the exception of the Milan case. In Brno, the number of organisations working in this field was limited. The country sections provide an overview of the organisations and innovations covered. Table 10.1 gives an overview of the number of organisations and persons interviewed per country.

Table 10.2 provides an overview of the organisations that participated, also listing those that declined participation, or that did not respond to our requests to participate. Reasons for declining participation were generally due to time restraints due to insufficient funds. This was particularly apparent in the British situation.

Table 10.1 Number of organisations and persons interviewed

	Third sector	*Government*	*External expert*	*Total*
The Netherlands	8 (11)*	1 (4)	4 (6)	13 (21)
United Kingdom	7 (7)	–	–	7 (7)
Italy	6 (8)	2 (2)	2 (2)	10 (12)
Czech Republic	2 (4)	1 (2)	–	3 (6)
Total	22 (30)	4 (8)	6 (8)	32 (46)

* Number of organisations/initiatives interviewed, number of people included in brackets.

Table 10.2 Overview of organisations participating in the research

Organisation	Purpose
	The Netherlands
African Sky	Organisation of East-African women fighting for equality; focus on undocumented migrants, asylum seekers, status holders
New Dutch Connections	Using theatre, art and training to empower refugees to take charge of their own future; focus on undocumented migrants, asylum seekers, status holders
Ubuntu House	Community centre for people in poverty, homeless or social isolation; focus on undocumented migrants
Villa Vrede ('Peace Villa')	Community centre for undocumented migrants; focus on undocumented migrants

Organisation	Purpose
'Get down to work' (Project of Pharos, Dutch Centre of Expertise on Health Disparities)	Project to engage asylum seekers in volunteer work; focus on asylum seekers (residents of emergency shelters not allowed so far), status holders as volunteers
Welcome to Utrecht	Platform to co-ordinate grassroots support initiatives; focus on residents of emergency shelters, status holders as volunteers
Plan Einstein (Refugee Launch Pad) (Utrecht Municipality)	Neighbourhood-integrated housing facility foster 'integration from day one', focus on asylum seekers
Mexaena Foundation	Support activities for Eritreans, focus on status holders
Doenja Language coaching	Language coaching, additional to existing offering; focus on residents of emergency shelters, asylum seekers
Italy	
Comune di Milano (Social Policies Department)	Social services, minors and families, immigration, integration, elderly
ATS (Local Health Authority)	Public health
Fondazione Progetto Arca	Homeless, families in need, migrants, addiction
Cooperativa Farsi Prossimo	Migrants, marginalisation, minors and families, social housing
Save the Children (Italy)	Children's rights, education, health and nutrition
ISF (Informatics Without Borders)	Fighting digital divide
GMI (Young Muslims of Italy)	Active citizenship, culture, sport
Cambio Passo	Primary assistance of Eritrean migrants
United Kingdom	
Lifeline Options	Marketing and promotion of refugees
Humanitarian and Business Development Consultancy—Consortium	Help local refugee organisations to bridge the gap that was left by the increasing closure of projects and reduction of services provided by larger organisations
St. Chad's Sanctuary	Support refugees and asylum seekers
STAR-NETWORK	Welcome fellow refugee students as well as refugees in their local communities
Piers Road New Communities Association	Relieve suffering, loneliness, distress, educational disadvantage and other life challenging issues; focus on refugees, asylum seekers
City of Sanctuary	Welcome refugees and provide signposting to available services and support
British Red Cross	Services for refugees
Czech Republic	
Nesehnutí	Protect human and women's rights, organise debates about migration and refugees, encourage public participation; focus on refugees
Islamic Foundation	Foundation in connection to the Brno Mosque; focus on refugees, asylum seekers, refused asylum seekers

Tracing the Social Innovation Stream

The selection of countries—and cities therein—provides a relevant mix of 'destination countries' (Netherlands, UK) and 'transit countries' (Italy, Czech Republic), as seen from a refugee's point of view. At the start of the project we underestimated the implications of this mix. Countries that are considered 'transit countries' are no less active in dealing with refugees than 'destination countries', but community development is not the prime objective: a substantial part of all refugees does not intend to stay.

Particularly in the Italian case, finding projects relating to community development and refugees turned out to be difficult, if not impossible. For the Czech Republic, this was somewhat different, considering that it is developing into a destination country. It turned out to be possible to find a number of relevant innovative activities there. We decided to look for a 'counter case' in Italy: an innovation in refugee transit management. The 'Migrants Hub' in the central train station of Milan offers basic support to refugees in their transit to other destination. The Hub was closed in 2017, for reasons which will be explained in the relevant section. Even though it does not result in durable relations *between refugees and the citizens of Milan*, we can take learning from the way in which a *wide array of organisations formed relations* to provide this service. This locally networked form of service delivery will also turn out to be an important element in the other city-cases.

SI Stream in Utrecht, the Netherlands

Milestones

NATIONAL HISTORY

The history of civic engagement for refugees goes back quite a while, at least to World War I (Böcker & Havinga, 2011). Figure 10.1 presents a number of relevant historical events.

The 1980s were a decade of institutionalisation of bottom-up refugee support. Within six years, both the Refugee Council (VVN) and Refugee Organisations the Netherlands (VON) were founded as, respectively, a 'bundling of initiatives of citizens' (Weiler & Wijnkoop, 2011, p. 106) and an umbrella of seven existing refugee self-organisations (Altchouler, Baba Ali, Goudappel, Medema, & Sangin, 2008). The situation of support for irregular migrants was different: a number of NGOs were founded from the 1980s onward to counter policy developments which excluded undocumented migrants from essential basic services (Van der Leun & Bouter, 2015). Besides the involvement of NGO-vested formalisation of bottom-up activities, public support for refugees expanded as well. The introduction of the Regulation for Sheltering Asylum Seekers (ROA) implied a relatively

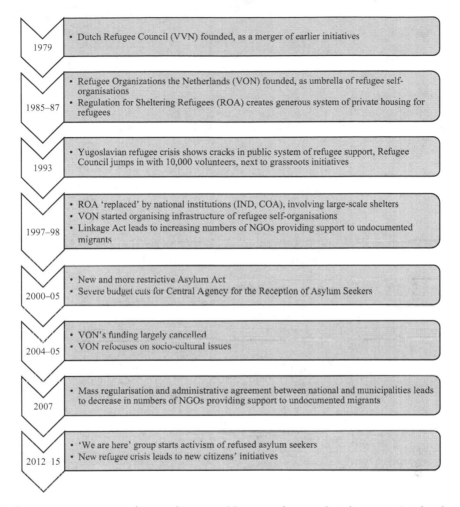

Figure 10.1 Events in the Dutch national history of co-produced community development with refugees

generous system of locally organised private housing. Some interview partners remembered that many of the activities fostering the integration of refugees were financed by public means, and organised within the framework of public refugee shelters, not depending on civic initiative. One of them argued:

> At that time, there was no emergency support yet, which makes a large difference, as this is a group for which nothing is organized [nowadays]. People simply assumed that asylum seeker centers would take care of

that part as well: the activities, sheltering, and that there was simply enough personnel to do all that [. . .] There were all sorts of holiday houses, tent camps, such things, but not the long-term emergency sheltering that we have these days.

(NL6, 2016)

A second phase started with the arrival of large groups of Yugoslavian refugees, for which this system was no longer tenable. This led to the introduction of a new 'professional', albeit less generous national infrastructure, both in the public and third sector, leaving less room for voluntary initiative (Korac, 2005).

A third phase started with new regulations around the turn of the century which implied a much stricter treatment of both new asylum requests and of irregular migrants. This led to new bottom-up initiatives again, but with limited means. There were many fewer asylum requests in this period and irregular migrants were legally excluded from using all sorts of public services. For the latter group, civic initiative was on the rise again, with the number of NGOs offering support expanding from 30 in 2000 to about 100 in 2006 (Van der Leun & Bouter, 2015).

A fourth phase started with the mass regularisation of 28,000 undocumented migrants in 2007 (Kos, Maussen, & Doomernik, 2015; Van der Leun & Bouter, 2015; Versteegt & Maussen, 2012). The number of NGOs offering support to these groups dropped significantly (Van der Leun & Bouter, 2015). For a while, it seemed that the deplorable situation of many refused asylum seekers improved significantly. The so-called 'We are here' group in Amsterdam signalled that this was not the case (Kalir & Wissink, 2016; Kos et al., 2015; Pitkänen, 2014). This group of refused asylum seekers received a good deal of media attention for their collaboration with the Amsterdam squat movement and the deaconate of a local church. The notion that refused asylum seekers 'came out', exclaiming that 'they are here', was quite a change compared to their previous subaltern lives. Such an outspoken form of self-advocacy was relatively new.

The fifth and final phase started with the sudden increase in new arrivals from 2014 to 2015 onward. Like with the arrival of Yugoslavian refugees, this sudden rise showed the limits of the system that was in place. New citizens' initiatives were founded in many cities. A number of informants pointed at recent developments, coinciding with this phase, which may have promoted or facilitated self-organisation. First, social media make it a lot easier to self-organise, as it allows for hosting crowdfunding campaigns, gaining community support, promoting events, spreading the word to local journalists and attracting volunteers. Second, the political debate on the so-called 'participation society' (TK, 2013/2014) is considered to be a push-factor. It became an umbrella term, similar to the British notion of Big Society, symbolising a view of society in which all citizens participate actively, and the government retreats. A third factor is the idea of 'integration from day one'. Several informants mentioned research that shows that such an attitude is very helpful for refugee integration at a later stage (e.g., Engbersen et al., 2015). This awareness, which is now spreading, has been very helpful in starting initiatives for and with asylum seekers who are still in emergency shelters.

LOCAL HISTORY

The local government of Utrecht has a considerable history of supporting undocumented migrants. This made the city an attractive breeding ground for new civil society initiatives focusing on this group. In 2002, the city council adopted a proposal of the municipal board to offer shelter to homeless migrants without papers, going against policy directions at the national level. This proposal also involved offering financial support to civic groups. One year after, the national LOS foundation, supporting local groups that work with undocumented people, was also founded in Utrecht.

In subsequent years, the municipality used international human rights standards and legal statements of both local courts in the Netherlands and the European Committee of Social Rights of the Council of Europe to back its 'rebel policy'. As of 2011, the municipality aspired to become a 'Human Rights City', aiming to live up to human rights principles, and jointly with local third sector organisations organised events and discussions in the city that would advance human rights consciousness and a culture of human rights (Van den Berg, 2016; Van den Berg & Oomen, 2014). The ambitions of the municipality regarding shelter and services for refugees fitted these aspirations.[3]

The municipality of Utrecht was the first municipality—in April 2016—that stressed that they will try to 'bind' refugees to the city (Huisman, 2016). This implies that those refugees for whom Utrecht was their first base of arrival will be able to stay in the city when they receive their refugee status. This, again, may be a context factor that spurred self-organisation.

When looking into the organisations we interviewed for this study, a first thing to note is that they were mostly founded in the last two phases that we distinguished earlier. Most of the ones that were formed between 2007 and 2015 focused on undocumented migrants, at least at the beginning. This is somehow at odds with the 'national history' we presented before, given that research suggests that the number of organisations supporting undocumented people dropped after 2007 (Van der Leun & Bouter, 2015). This is probably coincidental. The initiatives that started in 2015 or 2016 are more diverse in terms of target audience.

Actors and Interplay

The social innovation in Utrecht is embodied by the initiatives that operate as self-organisations, or that at least have a degree of self-organisation. They do not necessarily push for this innovation; they are the innovation. Then, what does their work entail? A number of people we talked to stressed that the innovativeness of their work does not lie in their activities. Even though some adopt creative approaches many argue that their activities are fairly basic. The novelty was rather that many initiatives were not set up for refugees, but with refugees. A representative of a project to promote volunteering by asylum seekers stressed:

> At the job itself, social organizations [including civic groups] are strongly involved. They are simply Dutch people, so the idea is not to have a group of asylum seekers come over to do a job. No, they do these jobs together with Dutch people.
>
> (NL5, 2016)

Similarly, a representative of the municipality said:

> The refugee council [Utrecht branch of the Dutch Council for Refugees] will co-ordinate voluntary activities together with 'Welcome to Utrecht' [a civic group]. We want to make a transition from volunteering for refugees to volunteering by refugees.
>
> (NL7, 2016)

'External' experts at Amnesty International and at Church in Action corroborated this as a more general trend. This is a new dimension of the social innovation, which had not come up in the preliminary investigations.

As specified earlier, the innovation was reported to not lie in self-organisation as such, but in the legitimacy of self-organisations as players in the field. Because of this, interplay with other actors is important. We found that a form of local network governance (Hall, Kettunen, Löfgren, & Ringholm, 2009; Nah, 2016; Nair & Campbell, 2008; Sheaff et al., 2014; Skovdal, Magutshwa-Zitha, Campbell, Nyamukapa, & Gregson, 2013) developed in Utrecht, in which bottom-up groups are recognised. Representatives of third sector organisations and civic initiatives recognised the progressive stance of the municipality of Utrecht. They reported about local meetings and events initiated by the municipality which brought together third sector organisations, municipal officials and professional organisations in the city. Our informants are positive about the relations with the local government. Officials are supportive and accessible. More than half of the initiatives and projects we included in our fieldwork received municipal funds. They also feel recognised by the local government in other ways, e.g., after a visit from the mayor.

Also collaboration with other initiatives and third sector organisations (Galaskiewicz, Bielefeld, & Dowell, 2006; Kneebone, 2014; McGehee & Santos, 2005; McLennan, 2014) is likely to contribute to recognition of the importance of self-organisations. Initiatives that share the same target group, such as Villa Vrede and Ubuntu Huis, show visitors the way to each other's services and fine-tune their activities. Also welfare professionals are reported to show people the way to these activities. Organisations and initiatives also meet each other in local meetings and events, outside the ones organised by the municipality. Our informants also mentioned contacts and cooperation with churches and diaconal offices, sports groups or organisations that offer language coaching. In addition, the initiatives participate in national and international networks, which might be helpful in terms of growing their visibility and legitimacy.

Collaboration can also foster new initiatives: one of the groups we studied was the 'offspring' of an earlier established organisation. The initiators of Mexaena had met each other while volunteering and being coached in a project of New Dutch Connections. After the establishment of Mexaena, New Dutch Connections contributed to training sessions of the new organisation.

SI Stream in Milan, Italy

Milestones

NATIONAL HISTORY

As in other cases, the issue of innovation in integration policies is not on the national political and policy agenda, neither at the strategic level (*which vision do we have on immigration as a country?*) nor at the level of implementation or service delivery (*how to guarantee better integration of migrants' groups?*). In the last few years the political level has been involved: at the national level, debating whether to provide welcoming to migrants or not (the Northern League, far-right and rising political party, has made anti-immigration policies its major issue in political campaigns); and at the international level, negotiating new conditions with other EU Member States for the integration of migrants within the EU, asking for a strong commitment from other countries to take responsibility of the increasing flows of migrants arriving to Europe, thus considering to change, at least in part, the agreement reached with the Dublin Regulation. While this was the national situation, some innovations emerged locally—all with strong input from activists, civil society organisations and the Church.

Specifically concerning legislation, it is worth mentioning that Italy does not have a long tradition in immigration and integration policies. In 2006, the United Nations pointed out that Italy was the only country in Europe without an organic legislation about the right of asylum protection yet (UNHCR, 2006). Also, Italy ranks quantitatively less significant regarding the applications for international protection with respect to other countries. It is only at the end of the 1990s, with the Dublin Regulation entering into force, that Italy became a country of forced settlement for many migrants and the need to create a coordinated system of provision of welcome and assistance became a public priority. In 2002, the SPRAR (Sistema di Protezione per Richiedenti Asilo e Rifugiati—System of Protection for Asylum Seekers and Refugees) was set up, which represents the first fully institutionalised system of centralised, standardised and coordinated management of services to migrants (Calloni, Marras, & Serughetti, 2012). It was established by Law n. 189/2002 and consists of a structural network of local authorities, which have access, in the limit of the available resources, to the National Fund for the policies and the services of asylum (FNPSA) to organise and deliver services to migrants. Several steps have been made in the last ten years, but still the discipline on immigration is one of the most recent and contested in any electoral cycle.

LOCAL HISTORY

The so-called "migrants' emergency" in Milan started in 2013: in October, the Municipality launched the Emergenza Siria programme: a network of volunteers and NGOs began to operate in the Central Station area. Unexpectedly, the arrivals continued during the winter too. By the end of January 2015 the presence of refugees was much more than the shelters of the City could absorb.

In this situation, the idea of the Hub started to arise. In particular, by observing that more than 90% of migrants did not in fact request asylum, there was the need for a system that would ensure assistance for a maximum of 3 days before their leaving, in order to avoid, on the one hand, that they slept in the station or on the streets and, on the other hand, that they became a target for smugglers who were concentrated around the Central Station. Together with Fondazione Progetto Arca, many organisations were active in welcoming migrants.

The Hub was chosen as a case study primarily for two reasons. First, it is considered highly innovative in the field of migrants' transit management, and second its potential to be replicated in other urban contexts is considered extremely high confirmed by all informants of both rounds of interviews.

> for how it was built and the number of organizations involved, but even more than this, it is an innovative model of action to the issue of departing migrants . . . that is something you can agree with or not, you know . . . with the Dublin regulation you may have some troubles.

> (IT4, 2016)

In 2 years, since the beginning of the emergency, Milan offered assistance and shelter to 84,500 refugees (62.2% Syrians, 27.7% Eritreans; among them, 16,700 children) through a network of organisations formed spontaneously right after the observance of the emergency situation around the

Central Station, and able to cope with the high peaks of arrivals. Civil society was also extremely active: calls for donation of food, clothes and other goods found an impressive response of a large part of citizens. The support received in distributing goods and communicating with migrants was also impressive. Also companies made contributions, donating goods for more than 520,000 euros.

At the time of writing, the Hub has been closed and dismantled. Reasons for this choice from the municipality can be found in a turbulent political scenario in the country, as well as in the difficult dialogue between Italy and the European Union concerning immigration policies. As an 'informal' gateway for migrants, the risk for the Hub to promote actions and behaviours not in conformity with the Dublin Regulation was too high. Nonetheless, its short but intense history is deemed relevant from the municipality and the civil society organisations involved in providing welcome and assistance to migrants. Learning from this experience has led to strengthening the city shelters and reconsider the whole system of migrants' welcoming in Milan. All information reported in the following sections comes from the accounts of interviewees at the time of major peak of activity of the Hub.

Actors and Interplay

Many organisations from different sectors worked in the Hub: Save the Children and Albero della Vita (literally Life's Tree, an Italian voluntary association working with minors) set up a space for children; IKEA furnished the space; Terres des Hommes (an association born with the aim to protect and improve children's rights) distributed kits for personal hygiene and water (donated also by Amazon, the world's largest online retailer, with the Milan headquarters close by the station); the ATS guaranteed medical assistance; Informatics Without Borders (an association of computer technicians with the mission of narrowing the digital divide; hereafter, ISF) donated computers and Wi Fi cables in order to ensure the possibility for refugees to communicate with their families. Paediatricians from both the Cultural Association of Paediatricians (hereafter, ACP) and the Italian Society of Paediatricians (hereafter, SIP) volunteered to cover health assistance in morning hours and an immense quantity of linguistic and cultural mediators and translators, but also volunteers and citizens speaking African and Arab languages and dialects ensured the communication with refugees.

The involvement of the community and the high number of partners of very different sectors, with different values, competences and target areas of need has contributed, in the accounts of many informants, to foster solidarity and reciprocal trust between the organisations involved and the local community. To say it in the words of an informant

> the Hub is innovative because it is a project realized by people in a context of emergency, they did not know each other, they did not have any kind of collaboration before, but they shared the same value, the need

to help these people, and only on this basis they were able to do a very good team work.

(IT7, 2016)

As the informant from the Municipality reported,

the first aspect of innovation I see is that it was a way to make the third sector responsible: they entered the project completely, supporting also all costs [. . .] This is completely new, we have always had some national funds supporting these kinds of initiatives.

(IT1, 2016)

SI Stream in Birmingham, UK

Milestones

NATIONAL HISTORY

Figure 10.2 presents the most important events with respect to understand the history of this stream.

The notion of community development entered refugee policy discussions in the early 21st century. In 2000, the Home Office, through the National Asylum Support Service started operating the newly introduced dispersal

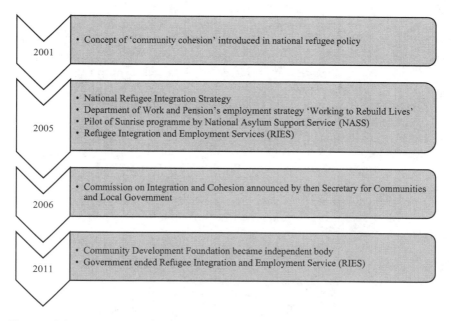

Figure 10.2 Key events in the UK

policy. The National Refugee Integration Strategy was introduced in the same year (Home Office, 2000), and was updated in 2005. This Strategy promotes community development as a useful approach for achieving integration. The National Refugee Integration Forum (NRIF) was established by the Home Office in 2001 to implement, monitor and develop the government's National Refugee Integration Strategy. Following a number of riots and disturbances in England in 2001 and the subsequent *Report of the Independent Review Team* (Cantle, 2001), the concept of 'community cohesion' was also introduced in national policy. This period is also characterised by more restrictive legislation and increased government control. This sometimes led to tension between the national governments and local authorities.

A next phase started with the introduction of the Nationality, Immigration and Asylum Act in 2006. This provided the Home Office with new rights to refuse any person from protection if there was a suspicion of terrorist involvement. The NRIF was removed by the Home Office in 2006. That same year, a Commission on Integration and Cohesion was announced by the then Secretary for Communities and Local Government. The Commission produced the report "Our Shared Future" in 2007, in which community cohesion was presented as something that needs to happen so that different groups get on well together. More specifically, the aim was to tackle tensions in communities between different ethnic groups. The Community Development Foundation, a government funded body set out the role of community development in relation to refugee integration and community cohesion. However, the focus of this body (which was in 2011 transformed to a social enterprise and closed business in 2015) was on development approaches applicable across different communities.Indicators to measure community cohesion and inclusion were introduced in performance monitoring. The Public Service Agreement (PSA) 21 covered community cohesion and included "the percentage of people who believe people from different backgrounds get on well together in their local area".The past couple of years were mainly characterised by severe austerity measures. In 2011, the national government ended the Refugee Integration and Employment Service (RIES). This led to major cuts for the Refugee Council's one stop, bilingual support service, totalling 62%, or an amount of £2 million. This severe reduction in public funding available for refugee integration left the sector with very little public support. At the same time, there had been funding cuts from the community development side. At these times of austerity, the role of self-organisation and abilities to secure additional funding from the private or third sector seems particularly important.

LOCAL HISTORY

Some respondents felt that there had been a patchy infrastructure for refugee community support in Birmingham and that this had gotten worse over the past years in light of cuts in public funding; some thought that changing this was an almost impossible task. Even organisations such as the British Refugee Council and Refugee Action, which traditionally had more funding than bottom-up projects that supported refugees, were (severely) overburdened.

Unsurprisingly, financial pressures formed the context in which our Birmingham-based respondents defined social innovation. For Lifeline Options, established in 2005, innovation was seen in the context of operating with small funds and the desire of coming together with other organisations to address refugees' and asylum seekers' needs. The interviewee stated that the refugee sector has drastically changed over the past decade and that the community needed to adapt and address these changes through linking themselves with other organisations (building networks) and through self-organisation. For the Piers Roads Association, formed in 2007, innovation in times of austerity implied to think creatively and focus on what was needed most urgently. For St. Chad's Sanctuary, the primary concern was that asylum seekers whose asylum claims had been rejected, had 'vanished' from those communities and it was difficult to continue engaging with and supporting them. They saw their own innovation capacity primarily in the context of providing basic welcoming and a 'face of hospitality' for asylum seekers and refugees following Christian values.

An important effort toward more networking was reflected in attempts to found a new local consortium, consisting of six organisations. At the time of our interviews, this was still in its very early stages. The respondent we interviewed described the vision for this consortium as "a new desire" of small refugee organisations to reach out to local communities, for example represented by their community leaders. This new desire might suggest that historically some refugee organisations have focussed more inwards. The respondents thought that in some ways the cuts in public funding could also present new opportunities for small refugee organisations to take charge and organise themselves through collaborations such as the consortium.

Next to new forms of local networking, also nationwide networks help to establish a new local infrastructure with limited means. The Regional Asylum Activism Project (RAA) was founded in June 2012 out of a partnership between the Still Human Still Here coalition, Student Action for Refugees (STAR) and the Network for Social Change. It coordinates activities/campaigns across the three largest dispersal areas outside London i.e., Birmingham, Manchester and Leeds; the aim of RAA is to connect these with political decision-making which is still often centred in London. Also the effort of establishing Birmingham as a City of Sanctuary (BCS) in 2015 can be seen as step toward developing intercity networks. However, the interviewee expressed the difficulty of establishing a strategic agenda that might facilitate attracting funding for their activities.

Actors and Interplay

One could argue that in Birmingham (and perhaps in England more broadly although we did not investigate this) 'self-organisation community development with refugees' was necessitated by major budget cuts that national and local governments (and refuge projects as a result of this) were facing. We managed to interview representatives of a number of local refuge projects, who had been severely affected by those changes, some of whom reported major plans in restructuring themselves to collaborate more closely in order to survive as organisations but more importantly to secure some kind of support for refugees and asylum seekers.

For individual organisations, 'loose networking' was seen as crucial to their functioning. Some examples: Lifeline Options describes itself as an 'un-unified' organisation, which operates to a large extent through networks. St. Chad's Sanctuary works through a loosely defined network with other organisations, in particular Christian ones, but also including public and private sector organisations. The organisation is funded by the Catholic Archdiocese and the Salvation Army, which allows them to operate independently from public sector funding. Student Action for Refugees (STAR) is a national student-led charity that engages students to welcome fellow refugee students as well as refugees in their local communities in the UK. STAR societies exist at 35 universities with 15,000 to 20,000 students being involved; student volunteer groups participating in 53 refugee projects provided different activities across the country. Locally, they have built strong connections with communities, for example through their student volunteers but also through collaboration with local organisations.

The British Red Cross has good relationships with other charities and grassroots organisations in the area, like the Hope Projects or St Chad's Sanctuary, as well as the large private sector company, G4S. The BRC described the relationships with those smaller third sector projects or organisations as reciprocal. Besides that, the organisation's refugee service team in Birmingham is active in regional networks and attends multi-agency forums like the West-Midlands Strategic Migration Partnership. They are facilitator of the West Midlands Asylum and Destitution Group, which hold monthly meetings bringing together different organisations that support asylum seekers and refugees, including social services and health organisations. The BRC interviewee described the connections and links established through those networks as formal in an informal way:

> By being able to have those organisations there, you are presenting it almost in an informal way to see what is the best way forward; before getting to the stage where you have to write formal letters.
>
> (UK7, 2016)

Other than that, support from the local council is important for both advocacy and (although to a lesser extent and more indirectly) service provision, as an informant from the Piers Roads Association explained. They are not funded by the council directly, but the fact that their work is recognised and well regarded by counsellors helps them in getting funding elsewhere—at the point we carried out the study this was mainly from a large charity (Trust), which belonged to an international private sector company.

Overall the role of community development bodies in the refugee sector appeared to be limited: Community development approaches in this area (and bodies adopting those) have been focused on building links between migrants and host communities more broadly. Their work has been focused on supporting different sections of the community to work together and to increase access of vulnerable individuals (assuming they are entitled) to service provision. It appeared that in practice most community development work in relation to refugees was left to organisations that specifically worked with refugees.

Local, regional and national media had a substantial influence in shaping and influencing public perceptions of refugee issues. Media players were also influenced by political parties and by local councils; for example, nationalistic political parties such as the British National Party used the media to present refugees as scapegoats in their campaign for votes in North East England towns. Some council have made agreements with the local newspapers that would get in contact/check accuracy of the refugee news with them first before publishing them.

SI Stream in Brno, Czech Republic

Milestones

NATIONAL HISTORY

The Czech Republic is clearly in a different position than the Netherlands, UK and Italy when it comes to refugees. Communism turned the Czech Republic into a country that produced, rather than received refugees (with the exception of receiving refugees from the Greek civil war in 1948–1949). Figure 10.3 provides an overview of key events.

The era of refugee-reception started after the fall of the Iron Curtain in 1989. The first large refugee group was from war-torn Yugoslavia, which led to an initial system of governmental integration support—the so-called State integration programme. Becoming part of the European Union, Czechia became a party to European treaties. New funding schemes for refugees and migrant-integration started to be available.

Even afterwards, like in other Central European countries, Czechia has not received large numbers of refugees. During the refugee crisis, the Czech Statistical Office (ČSÚ, 2016, 2017) counted 470 individuals who were granted international protection in 2015 and 450 in 2016. The political as well as the public discourse has revolved around securitisation, rather than around solidarity. The state integration programme, which was innovated

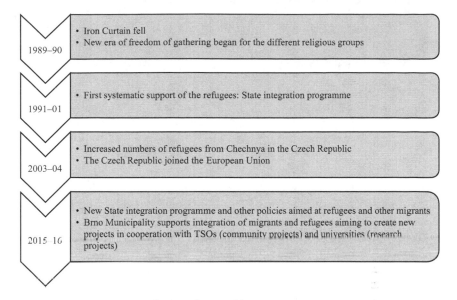

Figure 10.3 Key events in the Czech Republic

in 2015, aims at basic needs such as housing, work, education, health and social (financial) support. The so-called Conception of Integration of Foreigners in the Czech Republic (2005, 2011, 2016) states the goal of supporting the relationship between "the majority and the migrants". Nevertheless, the Ministry of the Interior states that this concerns third country nationals, but not refugees. The document does not mention community or self-organising activities as an integration tool.

Given the lack of explicit governmental commitment, the innovation in integration policies in the Czech Republic was most explicitly raised in a community of NGOs, social workers and academia after the European migration crisis. Generally, these attempts to modify the formulation and implementation of integration policies took place in the atmosphere of polarisation over immigration. In terms of social policies, the social innovation in connection with refugees is rather at its beginning, despite experiences with community work for the integration of the Roma population.[4] Despite that, the European migration crisis changed the public and political visibility of the migration issue in the country and since 2015 we may further observe the changes in this area.

> A new phase started after the crisis broke out, during this time the things started to professionalize. But it is still in the beginnings.
>
> (CZ3, 2016)

> The refugee wave was important. Before that, there were some people in the field who were dealing with this [integration of immigrants] in some ways. Nobody from outside cared about it and maybe also the environment was blocked. There were no innovations and even if there were some, they usually failed. There was no potential for any systemic pressure. As people started to be interested because of the migration crisis, they started to perceive it as urgent. They started to perceive it as an issue . . . which is good.
>
> (CZ3, 2016)

In the Czech context, community development as a tool for refugee integration is conducted mostly by activists and NGOs. It is tolerated, rather than supported by national government. Initiatives that aim at community integration arise spontaneously in non-profit organisations, including the selected cases. As funding schemes and calls for projects or political will to support similar initiatives are largely absent, such activities arise on a voluntary basis.

LOCAL HISTORY

Compared to Utrecht and Birmingham, local integration strategies are significantly underdeveloped in Czechia. Nevertheless, Brno can be considered a one-eyed king in the land of the blind, as local integration has at least some history here. The South-Moravian region, to which Brno belongs, was the only region to establish its own integration centre in 2009. Moreover, Brno also has a number of organisations supporting migrants and refugees. In 2015, the municipality created a position for a foreigners and refugees-advisor in the social care department. This helped to create a more favourable environment. The municipality started to be open towards social innovations after 2016.

> If I shall speak for the local level, at least certain part of the representatives is very inclined to the cause
>
> (CZ3, 2016)

However, the data collection took place in a too-early stage of this change and the municipality did not cooperate with the self-organised communities at that time (which changed later on). It is important to point out that the number of refugees is so low, there are essentially no community activities exclusively aimed at refugees. The activities studied apply to all migrants.

In Brno, and the Czech Republic in a broader sense, community self-organisation builds on ethnicity, nationality or faith. We did not encounter self-organising based on a refugee background (Gestnerová, 2014). This is also the case for the Islamic foundation in Brno. The evolution of activities within the Mosque stemmed from the political situation in the Czech

Republic since the early 1990s. The Muslim community began to be formed after the fall of the socialist regime, since similar grouping was forbidden before. The Mosque grew steadily, going through a reorientation after the attacks on the World Trade Centre in 2001. The recent European migration crisis led to a dramatic deterioration of public opinion about Islam. Since then the Mosque has faced attacks (through social media etc.). Representatives have attempted to change the situation and the public perception about Islam.

The other two studied cases originated in the grass-root organisation Nesehnutí ("Independent social and ecological movement"). The idea of the Multicultural Tea Parties project arose in 2011 with funding from the EU programme Youth in Action. At that time the initiative was part of a project called Aid to Refugees. The project was established in a period of massive migration of Chechen refugees to the Czech Republic. Aid to Refugees involved leisure activities in the Zastávka Reception Centre and remedial classes in the Czech language for kids of refugees at the elementary school for foreigners ZŠ Staňkova in Brno. The women's group Multicultural Tea Parties project was one of these activities. It was the only project that has survived.

It was modified into the Community Building Initiative in 2016, the second case we studied within Nesehnutí. The Community Building Initiative, besides building on the Multicultural Tea Parties, was created in response to the European migration crisis as well as to the current level of integration policies that lack emphasis on social and community integration of refugees.

Actors and Interplay

Due to the major rise of xenophobia in the Czech society, the Brno Mosque backed away from the public space but kept providing services for the community—religious services, community activities and support for the newcomers, who were naturally becoming part of the religious community. Next to other reasons, this may have prevented the Mosque from joining other initiatives and networks. Later on, some of those involved in the Mosque started to cooperate with the organisation BeInternational on organising events for Syrians and Czechs called Syreczech, which was later even supported by the municipality.

As community development and self-organisation was not the most pressing issue at the time of data collection, there was virtually no network gathered around this social innovation. People tended to be connecting extensively around more emergent issues such as a need to calm down the public discourse of xenophobia based on misinformation (e.g., the demystification campaign "Form your own opinion" or the network of students teaching facts about migration at schools). Nesehnutí took an active role, next to organisations such as Amnesty International, the Brno Expat centre, and certain informal collectives and even individuals from the municipality.

Another issue that massively mobilised civil society and created networks was the humanitarian crisis with refugees on the Balkans trying to reach the European Union border. This activated thousands of Czech volunteers marked as the "Czech team". Later the initiative was formalised and named "Helping fleeing people". The support networks involved large numbers of students and their universities, aid workers, officers, activists and politicians but also a large number of people, who had not had anything to do with foreigners or refugees before, but wanted to help and fight the mainstream discourse around immigration.

These networks were of use in the later stages when the crisis was not so exigent any more and more initiatives developed that needed to recruit engaged people (e.g., international "Refugees welcome" initiative). Furthermore, relations of engaged professionals from the NGOs supporting foreigners in Brno were definitely strengthened by the cooperation in the support networks. It might have also been one of the factors for creating the platform of the actors of integration in Brno, which strives for coordinated integration activities.

Synthesis

As we already highlighted in the introductory section, we incorrectly assumed that 'community development and refugees' is a relevant issue in all countries. Particularly given the increasing numbers of new arrivals of the past years, refugee-related projects often focused on basic needs first. There are deeper reasons than this though. Take Italy, where initial interviews with experts quickly brought forward that refugees generally regard Italy as a transit country, as a result of which community development is not a strong need. As said, we decided to use Italy as a counter case for this reason. The central station Migrants Hub, when it existed, was rather an innovation in transit management, than in community development. Similarly, with the Czech Republic making the transition from being a transit to a destination country, community development with refugees still seems to be in its early stages. 'I cannot tell how it works here as we are still in the beginning and I cannot evaluate it', says one respondent. This makes it hard to pinpoint innovation *within* this domain, even though there are signals that the communities themselves are involved more in the work. Innovation is thought to stem from activists and civil society, rather than from government.

Comparative Analysis

Tracing the Process of Social Innovation

Our first research question was: How did *'self-organised community development with refugees'* emerge over time? We have attempted to answer this question at both the local level, tracing the history of a set of local organisations, and at the national level, taking a broader perspective of relevant policies and trends influencing the emergence of the stream.

It is very hard to draw a general conclusion about the stage of the innovation stream 'self-organised community development with refugees' as a whole. Considering the varying meanings of 'community development' and 'degrees of self-organisation' at the local level, any generalised statement would probably fall short. The value of this chapter has rather been to show the variance and experiences in all these contexts. Generally, we can say that the stream is developed further in the Netherlands and the UK than in Italy and the Czech Republic. This is largely due to the notion that the former two countries have a longer history of being 'destination countries' than the latter two.

Another major milestone that all cases share is the sudden peak of new arrivals of the past couple of years. In Italy, this was already very noticeable in 2013, while the other countries mainly experienced a peak in 2015. That is not to say that this refugee crisis is the prime driver for the innovation that we studied, again, with the possible exception of the Milan case. There are many examples of self-organised community development that arose before this period already. However, the crisis as an "episode of contestation" in the language of field theory increased the urge of action in the field. In other words, the rise in numbers led to a greater pressure on the system on the one hand and increased awareness that 'something needed to be done', creating opportunities on the other. Many new projects and initiatives started around 2015.

Actor Contributions

Our second research question was: *What actors, or interplay of actors, contributed to the emergence of this innovation stream?*

Taking a step back from self-organisation, we can argue that communities were formed and maintained in all four cities, no matter whether this happened in an innovative manner or not. Formal community organising entities often do not play a central role; initiatives rather stem from the (informal) third sector. Both in Birmingham and Brno, there are efforts to arrange meetings between refugees and other residents. One organisation in Birmingham makes an effort to not let refugees 'disappear' from the community. In Milan, we might argue that an active community of organisations and individuals formed around the Central Station Hub.

Especially in Utrecht and Birmingham, the initiatives and organisations work in an extensive field of third sector organisations, consisting of both vested organisations and self-organised, sometimes informal groups made up of citizens and refugees. The practice of referring people to services of colleague-organisations holds for both Utrecht and Birmingham. The situation is not that all relevant organisations cooperate with everyone in the refugee sector, but organisations are acquainted with each other and are often part of loose local networks and platforms both aimed at service delivery and advocacy. Brno respondents also pointed at the barriers of cooperation by redirecting people to services of others: competitiveness and the fear of losing funds through losing a client.

In the four cities, the local governments generally stand out as pragmatic, as they aim at solving urgent humanitarian problems that occur around the influx of refugees in the city, and they seek to do that in interaction with the third sector. The local governments are supportive of the innovative initiatives, projects or organisations represented in the country-studies, although the level of support and the amount of energy and resources put into the field varies across cities and countries. In Utrecht and Milan, some of the initiatives receive funds from the local government. Whereas initiatives and organisations in Utrecht have easy access to the local government, and the government facilitates coordination of third sector and governmental activities for refugees, respondents also see that more could be done to facilitate participation of refugees. In Milan, the local government funded a local third sector organisation to coordinate the Central Station Hub (which was seen as a novelty in itself), but respondents also criticised the local government for a lack of vision for sustainable long-term solutions. In Birmingham, the mayor and city council supported the idea of making Birmingham a 'City of Sanctuary', but this support was merely symbolic.[5] The municipality of Brno is underway in developing a more active role in community integration of refugees. Brno relatively recently employed staff in its organisation to work on community planning and the integration of national minorities, and the municipality organises platform meetings and round tables with the third sector.

In Utrecht, Milan and Birmingham, stringent immigration policies of regional and national governments conflicted with pragmatic approaches and choices of local governments. Utrecht called its local policy on housing and supporting various groups of refugees and undocumented migrants 'rebellious' as compared to the national policy. Also, the City of Sanctuary Movement in the UK aims to distance municipalities adhering to humanitarian principles from the more stringent national principles.

Learnings

A first learning relates to the 'reach' of the social innovations studied. Models tracing the development of social innovation over time often take 'systemic impact' to be the stage that is finally strived after (e.g., Murray, Caulier-Grice, & Mulgan, 2010). Other authors stress, by contrast, that social innovations are particularly relevant in a local context (e.g., Moulaert, Swyngedouw, Martinelli, & Gonzalez, 2010). While this chapter has shown examples of local organisations and of organisations with a national reach, the point to stress here seems to be that local impact is a very relevant and viable aim in an innovation process.

Organisations in the stage of 'emergence' have typically only recently developed a proposal describing their future activities. They are likely to develop further, perhaps even at a rapid pace. Organisations sustaining their ideas are either one step further, attempting to formalise their initiative (Nesehnutí, Brno), or are struggling to keep the operation afloat due to funding constraints (Lifeline Options, UK). Organisations reaching local impact are generally well-established at the local level, and often do not intend to expand their scope. Organisations 'scaling' their work obviously do expand, but are not established to such a degree that they have achieved systemic impact yet. Organisations that have an impact at the national level are often well-established organisations, but they may also be local organisations that serve as an example for developments at the national level.

Conclusions

In the previous synthesis, we have only touched upon what the innovation we studied actually meant in the context of the cases we studied. We return to it in this conclusion, with a view to practitioners and policy-makers that may take benefit from the experiences we gathered. When considering 'self-organized community development with refugees' locally, it makes sense to adopt a broad view of strategies that might befit the local context.

Community development may, first of all, involve building a community 'from scratch', notwithstanding the idea that its members may also belong to other, existing communities. This may refer to refugee self-organisations, but also to fixed venues in which a more or less consistent mix of refugees and members of the host society convenes on a regular basis (sometimes on a daily basis, sometimes less frequent). A second strategy is to form networks around individual refugees. They often lack a good perspective towards the future in the country to which they migrated. Strong networks can help. Third, community development may apply to establishing interfaces between different groups, organisations or communities. Some projects establish connections between grassroots initiatives, link refugees to other relevant organisations, or create an interface between local organisations that do not primarily work with refugees. Even though the Italian case did not focus on 'establishing and strengthening durable relations between refugees and members of the host society', the Migrants Hub certainly was a good example of a project that established interfaces between organisations that would have ordinarily not collaborated. Fourth, a number of projects work in or with existing communities, referring either to communities of refugees or asylum seekers, or to 'local communities' in a neighbourhood or village. This differs from the previous category, in the sense that it focuses less on interfaces between organisations. For a fifth type, community development is not a direct aim, but rather a side effect. Many projects focusing on basic services for refugees result in community integration by establishing connections between refugees and volunteers from the host society, for instance. In short, practitioners and policy-makers may consider a wide range of options of new, networked ways of dealing with refugees locally.

Something similar applies to self-organisation. Next to 'ideal typical examples', of fully independent citizens' initiatives and refugee groups, we also found initiatives, projects or organisations with a 'degree of self-organization', such as independent refugee groups operating in the context of a professional organisation, initiatives that refugees and members of the host society take together, citizen initiatives that partly fulfil a task for which they receive governmental subsidy, etc. It makes sense to not be rigid about definitions and examine where initiatives and new forms of organisation arise. They are likely to show unmet social needs and shortcomings in existing services. Moreover, they show the need to change the way services are organised, for instance with regard to involvement of the private sector and of refugees in the governance of new activities. New self-organisations also point to a desire to be more spontaneous and agile than offerings by some traditional public sector organisations and larger NGOs. These large organisations are crucial, however, for the basic services that they offer. If their services are limited by austerity, it leaves a void that is hard to fill. While a diminished service level can lead to new initiatives, the decay of a support infrastructure for refugees is thoroughly regretted by those involved.

Notes

1. We would like to thank all who made important contributions to the ITSSOIN project deliverable that formed the basis for this chapter: Van den Berg, E., Eger, C., Navratil, J., and Placier, K.
2. Based on a query ("community development" AND (refugee* OR "asylum seeker*")) on the Web of Science portal, October 4, 2016, generating a sample of 22 articles. Additional queries, using terms like "community integration", "community capacity building" and "community organizing" provided a few more relevant results.
3. Municipality of Utrecht 2010: Note 'Shelter and integration of asylum seekers and refugees in Utrecht, Evaluation, January 2010' [Opvang en integratie van asielzoekers en vluchtelingen in de gemeente Utrecht, Evaluatie, Januari 2010]. Municipality of Utrecht (2011): Human Rights in Utrecht; How does Utrecht give effect to international human rights treaties? An urban quest for social justice, www.utrecht.nl/fileadmin/uploads/documenten/2.concern-bestuur-uitvoering/Internationaal/2015-10-Human-Rights-Utrecht.pdf.
4. An ethnic minority significantly endangered by social exclusion.
5. http://vle.wolvcoll.ac.uk/reporter/celebration-of-birmingham-as-a-city-of-sanctuary-for-refugees-and-asylum-seekers/, website visited August 2016.

References

Altchouler, Y., Baba Ali, G., Goudappel, A., Medema, N., & Sangin, L. (2008). *Dans tussen macht en marge. Vluchtelingenorganisaties in Nederland.* Amsterdam: Vluchtelingen-Organisaties Nederland.
Bakker, J., Denters, B., Oude Vrielink, M., & Klok, P. J. (2012). Citizens' initiatives: How local governments fill their facilitative role. *Local Government Studies,* 38(4), 395–414.

Bhattacharyya, J. (1995). Solidarity and agency: Rethinking community development. *Human Organization, 54*(1), 60–69.

Böcker, A., & Havinga, T. (2011). *Een eeuw opvang van Europese oorlogsvluchtelingen in Nederland.* Working Paper Series. Nijmegen: Nijmegen Sociology of Law

Calloni, M., Marras, S., & Serughetti, G. (2012). *Chiedo asilo. Essere rifugiato in Italia [I ask for asylum. To be a refugee in Italy]* Milan: Università Bocconi Editore.

Cantle, T. (2001). *Community cohesion: A report of the independent review team.* London: Home Office.

Craig, G., & Lovel, H. (2005). Community development with refugees: Towards a framework for action. *Community Development Journal, 40*(2), 131–136.

ČSÚ. (2016). *Foreigners in the Czech republic.* Prague: Czech Statistical Office.

ČSÚ. (2017). *Foreigners in the Czech republic.* Prague: Czech Statistical Office.

Engbersen, G., Dagevos, J., Jennissen, R., Bakker, L., Leerkens, A., Klaver, J., & Odé, A. (2015). *WRR-policy brief 4. Geen tijd verliezen: van opvang naar integratie van asielmigranten.* Den Haag: Wetenschappelijke Raad voor het Regeringsbeleid/Sociaal en Cultureel Planbureau/WODC.

Galaskiewicz, J., Bielefeld, W., & Dowell, M. (2006). Networks and organizational growth: A study of community based nonprofits. *Administrative Science Quarterly, 51*(3), 337–380.

Gestnerová, A. (2014). Význam sdružení cizinců ze zemí subsaharské Afriky a bývalí Jugoslávie v průběhu integračního procesu. *Český lid, 101*(2), 171–178.

Hall, P., Kettunen, P., Löfgren, K., & Ringholm, T. (2009). Is there a Nordic approach to questions of democracy in studies of network governance? *Local Government Studies, 35*(5), 515–538.

Home Office. (2000). *Full and equal citizens: A strategy to integrate refugees into the United Kingdom.* London: Home Office.

Huisman, C. (2016, April 27). Primeur: Utrecht gaat vluchteling al op dag één aan de stad binden. *de Volkskrant.*

Kalir, B., & Wissink, L. (2016). The deportation continuum: Convergences between state agents and NGO workers in the Dutch deportation field. *Citizenship Studies, 20*(1), 34–49.

Kneebone, S. (2014). The Bali process and global refugee policy in the Asia—Pacific Region. *Journal of Refugee Studies.* doi:10.1093/jrs/feu015

Korac, M. (2005). The role of bridging social networks in refugee settlement: The case of exile communities from the former Yugoslavia in Italy and the Netherlands. In P. Waxman & V. Colic-Peisker (Eds.), *Homeland wanted* (pp. 87–107). New York, NY: Nova Science Publishers.

Kos, S., Maussen, M., & Doomernik, J. (2015). Policies of exclusion and practices of inclusion: How municipal governments negotiate Asylum policies in the Netherlands. *Territory, Politics, Governance,* 1–21.

Lenette, C., & Ingamells, A. (2015). Mind the gap! The growing chasm between funding-driven agencies, and social and community knowledge and practice. *Community Development Journal, 50*(1), 88–103.

McGehee, N. G., & Santos, C. A. (2005). Social change, discourse and volunteer tourism. *Annals of Tourism Research, 32*(3), 760–779.

McLennan, S. (2014). Networks for development: Volunteer tourism, information and communications technology, and the paradoxes of alternative development. *PoLAR: Political and Legal Anthropology Review, 37*(1), 48–68.

Mensink, W., Van den Berg, E., Navrátil, J., D., Š., Bauer, A., Ricciuti, E., & Ferlisi, M. (2015). *Field description in community development*. Part 2 of deliverable 7.1 of the project: "Impact of the Third Sector as Social Innovation" (ITSSOIN), European Commission—7th Framework Programme. Brussels: European Commission, DG Research.

Ministry of the Interior of the Czech Republic (2005). *Conception of the Foreigners integration in 2005*. Prague: Ministry of the Interitor of the Czech Republic.

Ministry of the Interior of the Czech Republic. (2011). *Conception of the Foreigners integration: Living together*. Prague: Ministry of the Interitor of the Czech Republic.

Ministry of the Interior of the Czech Republic. (2016). *Conception of the Foreigners integration: In mutual respect*. Prague: Ministry of the Interitor of the Czech republic

Mitchell, J., & Correa-Velez, I. (2010). Community development with survivors of torture and trauma: an evaluation framework. *Community Development Journal, 45*(1), 90–110.

Moulaert, F., Swyngedouw, E., Martinelli, F., & Gonzalez, S. (2010). *Can neighbourhoods save the city? Community development and social innovation*. Abingdon: Taylor & Francis.

Murray, R., Caulier-Grice, J., & Mulgan, G. (2010). *The open book of social innovation*. London: National Endowment for Science, Technology and the Art.

Nah, A. M. (2016). Networks and norm entrepreneurship amongst local civil society actors: Advancing refugee protection in the Asia Pacific region. *The International Journal of Human Rights, 20*(2), 223–240.

Nair, Y., & Campbell, C. (2008). Building partnerships to support community-led HIV/AIDS management: A case study from rural South Africa. *African Journal of AIDS Research, 7*(1), 45–53.

Pitkänen, M. (2014). Since I am here, I scream. *Tijdschrift voor Genderstudies, 17*(3), 229–243.

Sheaff, R., Windle, K., Wistow, G., Ashby, S., Beech, R., Dickinson, A., & Knapp, M. (2014). Reducing emergency bed-days for older people? Network governance lessons from the 'Improving the Future for Older People'programme. *Social Science & Medicine, 106*, 59–66.

Skovdal, M., Magutshwa-Zitha, S., Campbell, C., Nyamukapa, C., & Gregson, S. (2013). Community groups as 'critical enablers' of the HIV response in Zimbabwe. *BMC Health Services Research, 13*(1), 195.

Stewart, J. (2012). A tale of two communities: Divergent development and embedded brokerage in postwar Guatemala. *Journal of Contemporary Ethnography*. doi:10.1177/0891241612442215

UNHCR. (2006). *Tavolo sull'asilo. Per una futura legge organica in materia d'asilo [Table on Asylum. For a future organic law on Asylum]*. Retrieved May 20, 2018, from www.unhcr.it/wp-content/uploads/2015/12/Tavolo_sull_Asilo.pdf

Van den Berg, E. (2016). Making human rights the talk of the town: The role of civil society in the Netherlands. In B. Oomen, M. Davis, & M. Grigolo (Eds.), *Global urban justice: The rise of human rights cities*. Cambridge: Cambridge University Press.

Van den Berg, E., & Oomen, B. M. (2014). *Towards a decentralization of human rights: The rise of human rights cities*. In T. Van Lindert & D. Lettinga (Eds.), *The future of human rights in an urban world: Exploring opportunities, threats and challenges* (pp. 11–16). Amsterdam: Amnesty International.

Van der Leun, J., & Bouter, H. (2015). Gimme Shelter: Inclusion and exclusion of irregular immigrants in Dutch civil society. *Journal of Immigrant & Refugee Studies*, *13*(2), 135–155.

TK. (2013/2014).Vaststelling van de begrotingsstaten van het Ministerie van Binnenlandse Zaken en Koninkrijksrelaties (VII) voor het jaar 2014, 33750 VII, Tweede kamer (2013/2014).

Verstecgt, I., & Maussen, M. (2012). *Contested policies of exclusion: Resistance and protest against asylum policy in the Netherlands.* Amsterdam: Amsterdam Institute for Social Science Research, University of Amsterdam.

Weiler, R., & Wijnkoop, M. (2011). Jullie hebben de klok, wij hebben de tijd 60 Jaar vluchtelingenbescherming: de Nederlandse praktijk en VluchtelingenWerk als maatschappelijke beweging. In A. B. Terlouw & K. Zwaan (Eds.), *Tijd en asiel. 60 jaar vluchtelingenverdrag.* Deventer: Kluwer.

Zetter, R., Griffiths, D., & Sigona, N. (2005). Social capital or social exclusion? The impact of asylum-seeker dispersal on UK refugee community organizations. *Community Development Journal*, *40*(2), 169–181.

Zetter, R., & Pearl, M. (2000). The minority within the minority: Refugee community-based organisations in the UK and the impact of restrictionism on asylum-seekers. *Journal of Ethnic and Migration Studies*, *26*(4), 675–697.

Interviews

Acronym	Organisation	Interview date
	The Netherlands	
NL1	African Sky	September 2016
NL2	New Dutch Connections	April 2016
NL3	Ubuntu House	May 2016
NL4	Villa Vrede ('Peace Villa')	May 2016
NL5	'Get down to work' (Project of Pharos, Dutch Centre of Expertise on Health Disparities)	May 2016
NL6	Welcome to Utrecht	April 2016
NL7	Plan Einstein (Refugee Launch Pad) (Utrecht Municipality)	June 2016
NL8	Mexaena Foundation	May 2016
NL9	Doenja Language coaching	May 2016
	Italy	
IT1	Comune di Milano (Social Policies Department)	March 2016
IT2	ATS (Local Health Authority)	June 2016
IT3	Fondazione Progetto Arca	March 2016
IT4	Cooperativa Farsi Prossimo	April 2016
IT5	Save the Children (Italy)	May 2016
IT6	ISF (Informatics Without Borders)	June 2016
IT7	GMI (Young Muslims of Italy)	June 2016
IT8	Cambio Passo	July 2016
	United Kingdom	
UK1	Lifeline Options	May 2016

UK2	Humanitarian and Business Development Consultancy— Consortium	June 2016
UK3	St. Chad's Sanctuary	July 2016
UK4	STAR-NETWORK	May 2016
UK5	Piers Road New Communities Association	June 2016
UK6	City of Sanctuary	June 2016
UK7	British Red Cross	August 2016
	Czech Republic	
CZ1	Nesehnutí	April 2016
CZ2	Islamic Foundation	April/May 2016
CZ3	Department of Social Care, Brno City Municipality	April 2016

Part III

Synthesis

Social Innovation Conditions

11 Results

The Comparative Analysis

*Gorgi Krlev, Helmut K. Anheier, and
Georg Mildenberger*

Setting the Scene

Our research presented in this book has developed an inventory of recognised social innovation streams in seven fields of activity (general settings in which more particular strategic action fields form): Arts & Culture; Social Services; Health Care; Environmental Sustainability; Consumer Protection; Work Integration; and Community Development. These have each been studied across three to four European countries to arrive at pathways of their emergence and in order to identify the involvement and contribution of third sector organisations, firms and public agencies or political institutions therein. In other words they have been used to identify actor involvement and actor traits. The social innovation streams have furthermore been embedded into and examined as regards the influence of field/context conditions on actor involvement in the innovation and the transformative capacity of the stream (profoundness, scope of change occurring, etc.) overall.

More broadly speaking, however, the research of ITSSOIN was also a continuation of work conducted previously in another project funded by the European Commission and called TEPSIE (The Theoretical, Empirical and Policy Foundations of Social Innovation in Europe). More precisely, our research related to TEPSIE's model of national social innovation environments that focussed on a cyclical process of (social) entre- or intrapreneurial activity embedded in framework conditions consisting of (1) available resources (financial and non-financial); (2) formalised and rigid institutional structures, which often have a long tradition and which may refer to the landscape and funding of welfare provision, governmental social welfare regimes and social structure, or principles directing national political economies; (3) less formalised politics and policies, including agendas and discourses that may remain at that level but also shape future legislation and institutional structures; and (4) the societal climate and discourses in the broadest sense, which include normative discussions of the 'good life' and who is responsible for shaping it, which are therefore often fuzzy and indistinct (see Figure 11.1).

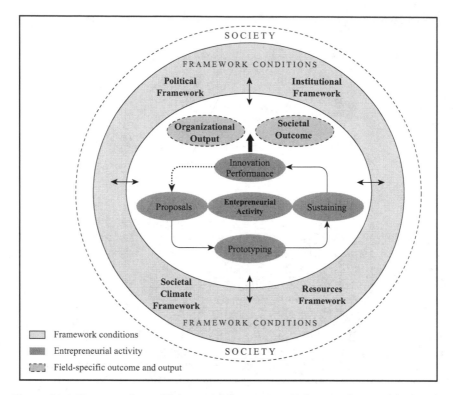

Figure 11.1 Framework model for social innovation (Krlev, Bund, & Mildenberger, 2014)

The focus in the part of our research presented here lay on the 'inner circle' of the model and its interaction with the 'outer circle'. We are not going into detail in the analysis of each of the frameworks, which are probed more deeply elsewhere by means of the analysis of policies, media reporting and citizen perceptions; all constructing arenas within fields shaping the action going on in relation to the SI stream itself (Krlev, Anheier, & Mildenberger, forthcoming).

In relation to engaged actors and their characteristics we had developed rationales on which traits would matter for social innovation before going into the investigation, while (as will be seen later) these were refined or complemented by others in the process. One of our pre-held suppositions was that social innovation would increase with a higher number of contacts to multiple and diverse stakeholders. Furthermore, we suggested that the diversity, not merely the quantity, of resources available to the actors would increase their social innovation potential. By resources we refer to financial sources as well as human capital (such as access to voluntary work, expertise and knowledge). Finally, we assumed a high importance of value sets to social innovation capacity. Through them, actors would increase their potential of connecting to others with the aim of driving social mobilisation and the dissemination of the social innovation.

As we were particularly interested in assessing the influence of such organisational aspects on the development of social innovations, a methodological transition from macro to meso and micro levels of analysis had to be performed. By the application of field theory (Fligstein & McAdam, 2012) as a theoretical lens we were capable of integrating all three levels. Our analysis moved in two ways as regards the levels. On the one side we moved from broad field descriptions to streams to actors and potentially to individuals. On the other side the probing of organisational traits, practices and strategies enabled us to give a thick description of factors that led to the emergence of the SI stream. Field theory was additionally useful for incorporating a high, diverse number of research objects and for maintaining a high degree of empirical openness. The research object 'social innovation' served as the basis for field construction.

As outlined initially, field theory makes several assumptions about environmental influences on fields as well as the structure and dynamics within them. Its main idea is that actors such as third sector organisations, social entrepreneurs, social movements, policy makers or firms each focus on their objects of interest and accordingly shape a field to exert influence. Firms in online education for alternative financial services, for instance, mainly engaged for reputational reasons in the Czech Republic, while civil society action in the field emerged out of a longer tradition in advocating for consumers' rights originally covering areas other than finance. Thereby, actors avail themselves of resources such as intrapreneurship and management, or mobilise new capabilities, e.g., through entrepreneurship or through mobilising volunteers. The latter played a role in the financial services field throughout, but in particular in Denmark, where volunteers with financial and/or legal expertise provided advice in face-to-face settings as a result of (and contributing to) the 'offline manifestation' of the SI stream there.

During this process, interests among actors may rival or contradict field structures. For example, a social innovation might stand in conflict with welfare or economic structures. A good example for such a situation is self-organised community development with refugees, which by many of the actors was not seen as an innovation but a reaction provoked by budget cuts and lack of state or municipal resources. At the same time, new approaches might come up and result in innovative approaches despite substantial investment in an area. This was the case for cross-sector partnerships in Work Integration in Germany, where despite a magnitude of previous efforts, CSPs were seen as a more effective means of bridging a transition from joblessness into the labour market. By empirically describing such processes and constellations, field theory enabled us to address the micro level of relations among actors as well as to draw a conceptual picture of the institutional settings and power relations that shape the field.

Following the concept of field theory, cases were designed in such a way that they allowed answering key questions, such as: Who are and were the relevant actors for the social innovation in question? What are the interests these actors have with regard to the social innovation? What actions did and do the field members undertake to meet these interests and which resources did and do they dedicate to these tasks? To address the inherent temporal dimension in these questions, we used process tracing as a methodological approach.

We did not start off from individual and thus potentially particular and isolated organisational practices. Instead, we identified one 'innovation stream' (recognised, cross-national phenomena that have gained 'some tradition', that is existed for some time) found among a selection of dominant innovations in each of the ITSSOIN fields of activity, and with the promise of high explanatory potential as to the preceding questions. A move from the consultation of 'external experts' to 'internal experts' was realised through snowball sampling, resulting in a detailed description of the relevant actor landscape and the conditions it was embedded in. In addition to enabling this research process per field-country combination, the scaffolding provided by process tracing enabled us to maintain consistency and comparability across the sub-sample of countries for each field as well as across fields of activity—visible not least in the joint structure of the empirical chapters.

Process tracing, originally used in the analysis of policies or legislation in political science (Ford, Schmitt, Schechtman, Hults, & Doherty, 1989; Tansey, 2007), served to add a dynamic perspective to the analysis, since we were able to identify temporal shifts in conditional factors that had spurred or impeded social innovation in a field. When analysing these innovation streams in more detail, we turned to the relevance of the context structure and characteristics of the organisations involved in the development of the innovations. In addition to an aggregated testing of necessary and sufficient conditions by means of qualitative comparative analysis (QCA; Krlev, Anheier, Behrendt, & Mildenberger, 2017), the empirical chapters highlight that we generated exploratory insights with a high degree of granularity as regards SI actors' characteristics. As a reminder, all observations relate to the social innovation streams displayed in Table 11.1. We studied a multitude of aspects and were looking at actors' motivation, their images of innovation and their expectations regarding the innovations' impact, only part of which could be presented in this book. The following sections serve to present highlights from the qualitative case work and discuss and compare them to each other regarding the relevance of those organisational traits which appear to have been influential on the development of the social innovation streams in each of the analysed fields.

Table 11.1 ITSSOIN social innovation streams

Field of activity	SI stream
Arts & Culture	Arts for spatial rejuvenation
Social Services	New governance arrangements to reach marginalised groups
Health	The recovery approach to mental health
Environmental Sustainability	Promotion of bicycle use in urban contexts
Consumer Protection	Online financial education
Work Integration	Cross-sector partnerships
Community Development	Self-organised integration of refugees

Actor Traits and Interaction

We move from meso level categories such as sector affiliation to the micro level of organisational traits and the role of individuals in organisations in driving the social innovation streams. While we explicitly and exclusively focus on sector affiliation in the first section, it continues to play a role in relation to organisational traits. When it comes to the set of actor characteristics we review, we relate back to our introductory reasoning of factors promoted in the (social) innovation literature as relevant. These comprise (1) actor provenience; (2) actor motivations (needs and values); (3) actor positioning (openness, links and embeddedness); (4) actor resources (financial and human, including volunteering); and (5) action capacity (multi-level action and freedom to act). We outline whether and how they have been exhibited by the social innovation actors and how the traits have contributed (or not) to the social innovation stream.

Actor Provenience and Constellations

The first group of findings relates to *sector affiliation* as a factor in driving social innovation. Across almost all fields that we analysed by means of case studies, we observed a high relevance of the third sector. Especially in the fields of Community Development with refugees and Consumer Protection, the third sector seems to play the most prominent role in fostering social innovations. In the field of Community Development with refugees, for instance, almost all formal entities exert only a marginal influence on community organisation, while (informal) third sector and civic initiatives were most active in promoting the innovation. This is not trivial, since community development was not per se an informal activity but performed as such due to the retreat of state actors and the relative indifference of market actors, curiously with the exception of the hub in Milan where corporations engaged profoundly. In the field of Consumer Protection the third sector played an important role too. Here, even though there was involvement of actors from other sectors, the contribution of third sector organisations to online financial education was especially high in the sense that their advocacy and legitimising functions enabled the engagement of other actors. One exception of this was found in the field of Consumer Protection in the Czech Republic, where financial service providers were engaged substantially, often for reputational reasons.

Next to the instances of third sector dominance we saw cross-sector collaboration constellations or less formalised, cooperative arrangements between actors from different sectors. The field of Community Development with refugees can be mentioned here again, since in addition to individual civic initiatives we found examples of the third sector receiving direct public support, supposedly as a compensatory device to hedge decreasing activity of public authorities. In particular local governments often actively sought partnerships with third sector organisations to improve the situation of refugees. The field of Environmental Sustainability also frequently displayed such cooperation. Here, both sectors have been influential in the opening of public spaces for bike use. Predominance of the state, however, was detected with regard to the creation of context factors, such as traffic planning, that allow innovative efforts to take root. In the field of Social Services, cross-sector collaboration as a new governance device was so prominent in Spain that a substantial amount of the analysis was dedicated to these interactions. The arrangements were mostly set up to realise the mobilisation of organisational resources and leverage joint capabilities in order to provide social services to vulnerable groups in society.

If it had to be allocated to one of the actor constellations identified in our research, the recovery approach in mental health would largely match the pattern of engagement of third sector actors with some support of state actors. However, it needs to be mentioned that this case was remarkable as being among the only one where actors on the individual level played a greater role than organisation types and affiliations. This applied to both the influence of volunteers and that of professionals. With regard to the latter, there were health care pioneers acting in a supportive way for the innovation on the one side and professionals interested mainly in preserving their professional power on the other.

In all of the fields mentioned so far, private commercial organisations played a lesser role throughout. Our findings differed from this in the field of Arts & Culture. Although cross-sector cooperation was of relevance there too, they were mostly formed between commercial and public actors. Especially in the Netherlands and Italy, such collaborations played an important role in providing grants as well as in the targeted promotion of cultural entrepreneurship initiatives to rejuvenate places by means of the arts. In Spain and France, the other two countries in which we investigated the SI stream, we could not find a single sector (coalition) or logic (bottom-up or top-down) to be most effective in driving the SI stream. The countries showed a degree of variation in this regard that made condensation difficult.

The one field where cross-sector interaction was most pronounced, by default, was the one of CSPs for Work Integration, where formalised engagement of actor coalitions was identified as one of the main innovations. How the coalitions came about and which roles actors took in them, however, depended strongly on the institutional setting they were embedded in. It was peculiar to note that in the supposedly stronger welfare state environment of Germany, market players were more reluctant to act on the Work Integration challenge than in Spain, where businesses had been the driving force. It is worth noting that this coincidence of weaker institutional structures—speaking of voids would be exaggerated—and business activity could also be observed in the Czech online education for consumer protection in AFS. This suggests that such structures, along with the challenges they provoke (bad reputation in Czech AFS provision; labour shortage in a tense economic situation in Spain), make firms act. In other circumstances, which might affect firms less or where others can step in and take action, firms generally seem to rely on the innovation capacities of others.

Actor Motivations

Social needs orientation, a key element in the very definition of social innovation, was confirmed to play an important role for the contributions actors were able to make towards driving the social innovations. The 'social' in social needs refers to issues that are shared by society at large and which it feels responsible to act upon. The 'need' in social needs thereby refers to the necessity to act, since these issues have previously been inadequately addressed and are therefore 'needy', that is, they depend on support from inside or outside the system they are placed in. In that sense social needs are defined by context.[1] Social needs have to be differentiated from societal needs. The latter may include almost anything that is regarded as necessary to fulfil the aggregate desires and requirements of a society's individuals, much of which however can be achieved by the individuals themselves given appropriate framework structures, for instance a market in which private goods can be acquired. While 'societal' serves as a purely descriptive/analytic category comprising all of society, 'social' contains the normative dimension of 'what society has to take care of, since it is lacking or neglected'. In short, organisations are social needs oriented when they address social issues that are recognised in society as in need of action and that are to the direct benefit of the needy target group(s).

The match between the very definition of social innovation and the relevance of social needs orientation at the organisational level as a finding is far from trivial. It calls into question other concepts, such as shared value (Porter & Kramer, 2011), which proclaims major leaps in social progress could be achieved if only firms realised that they can enhance their commercial value alongside or through employing their core competencies in a socially productive way. Our finding suggests that it might not be that easy and that an orientation at social needs must top commercial return seeking and not the other way around to ensure substantial contributions to social innovation. As suspected, social needs orientation was especially strong among third sector actors. It was particularly prominent across the fields of Work Integration, Arts & Culture and Consumer Protection. However, especially in the fields of Work Integration and Consumer Protection, firms were found to pursue social needs to some extent. Thus, the occurrence of social needs orientation does not follow a simple sector dichotomy of being present in one sector and absent in the other and by means of that observation makes actors from one sector relevant or irrelevant to social innovation. Occurrence and influence of social needs orientation was more complex.

While, for example, in the field of Work Integration the third sector was described as the driving force in establishing the social innovation due to its strong social needs orientation (which firms and the state started to follow in Germany and Spain), a focus on social needs—regardless of sector affiliation—was observed in the Czech Republic. France instead had a more rational and policy driven approach in which CSPs were meant to enhance the capacity of the ecosystem of WISEs that had existed for some time, instead of being directed explicitly at unfulfilled social needs.

The explanatory value of social needs orientation is further enhanced when linking it to the question of whether *pro-social values*—that is, virtues of, for example, 'care' and 'solidarity' (including the notion of caring for the environment) as another potential motivating factor to substantially engage in social innovation—were equally important. Pro-social values are to be differentiated from other motives of activity such as the earning of profits or the reliable and dutiful execution of one's mandate. Value sets are likely to be reflected in mission statements. There, action based on religious or ethical motives can be differentiated from motives of commercial professionalism such as customer satisfaction or product excellence, or a more technocratic understanding of improvement through increases in the efficiency or effectiveness of provision systems (see our previous remarks on WISEs in France). Social needs orientation increases the likelihood of having pro-social values and vice versa, but there are no clear directional associations. Social needs may, for instance, be addressed with the hope of benefiting from the improved situation of a needy target group. This is discussed as one of the motives for 'base-of-the-pyramid business activity' (Prahalad & Hammond, 2002). Such activity might thus be social needs oriented (and it might not), but it would rather certainly not be motivated by pro-social values. At the same time pro-social value actions might provide care for needy target groups but miss addressing their immediate social need. This is the case where food banks provide immediate remedy to hunger but might lower individuals' ability to sustain themselves.

We encountered very different constellations with regard to pro-social values. Picking up the French Work Integration context, we can say that while social needs orientation was weakly pronounced, pro-social values were altogether insubstantial, which is in line with the primary aim of increasing existing structures' efficiency and effectiveness. The constellation in Environmental Sustainability was similar, and in fact across countries. Here, actors stated that social needs (including the enhancement of the capacity of the local transportation environment) were in fact an orientation shared by all involved; however, the corresponding value sets, including ecological aspects, did not appear to be a driving force behind the SI. None of the actors, neither public nor private, claimed pro-social values to be central to their work, although some higher importance of the latter could be observed in public institutions than in business actors. Besides this, the precise outline of value sets in this field differed a lot, especially among third sector organisations, with some being primarily motivated by ecological reasons whereas others were trying to promote civic initiative.

In contrast to the detachment or controversial links between social needs and pro-social values in the preceding fields, we detected a symbiosis of both in the SI streams of Community Development with refugees, Social Services, and Health Care. In the latter, for example, all organisations that had implemented the recovery approach shared a strong focus on 'caring'. This is of course spurred by the fact that the activity in the three fields related to vulnerable, excluded and/or minority groups of people. Focussing on them mostly entails some value orientation, which makes it difficult to assess the exact influence of social values on the SI. The fact that they were not unanimously strong in the case of online financial education in AFS, however, also shows that values might be rather inconsequential despite the fact that disadvantaged people represent the target group of the intervention.

Actor Positioning

Another hypothesised factor driving social innovation and simultaneously a trait of the third sector—thus driving our supposition that the latter would play a prominent role—was *organisational openness*, necessary for detecting signals from outside but also for engaging stakeholders inside the organisation. Thereby, open organisational culture is internally oriented and refers to the ways and means by which members of an organisation can shape or participate in the creation of structures and processes. We therefore also refer to it as internal openness. An open organisational culture is participatory and grants employees a high degree of co-determination in strategy formation or other issues. While not mainly determined by organisational structure but by processes, a very hierarchically organised entity would be unlikely to have a very open culture. External organisational openness instead refers to how receptive an organisation is to influences from the outside. An organisation with a high degree of openness holds a great number of intense stakeholder contacts and invites them (regularly) to engage with the organisation or actively takes part in other forms of exchange. The latter may be embodied by participation in membership organisations, involvement in open policy dialogue or the use of customer feedback platforms. As shall be seen later both relate to, but are different from, organisations' social capital, including the aspect of context embeddedness.

Regarding the factor of *internal organisational openness*, i.e., hierarchies and other aspects of organisational culture, the case studies revealed that the level of such characteristics among those actors most influential on the SI stream strongly varied across countries and fields as well as in relation to the different sectors involved. For example, in Italian Social Services it was mainly third sector organisations that exhibited an open organisational culture, while in Sweden this trait was predominantly featured in public organisations. In Spain a high territorial decentralisation was more important than openness with regard to organisational culture. Some cases rather unmistakably suggested a favourable influence of low institutionalisation within the organisation on the SI. This was particularly so for Community Development with refugees in the Czech Republic, where many initiatives started off as informal groups almost without any hierarchical structure and moved only slowly to some but with a limited degree of formalisation. Formalisation included the establishment of defined positions and roles within the organisations. Those were important in applications for subsidies or when attempting to achieve a legal status. They were less important in other situations and almost all experts agreed on the inhibiting effects of 'closed' and static organisational structures and processes.

This was mirrored in other fields too, for instance that of Health Care. The rather rigid organisational cultures of psychiatric institutions, for example,were not of any support to the SI in focus. The contrary is true. They were seen as the biggest barrier to the dissemination of the recovery approach in all of the countries analysed. Furthermore, actors from the UK and Spain in the field of Social Services lamented the lack of participation, information exchange and organisational learning as a consequence of vertical management structures and claimed it slowed down innovation processes. In contrast to the other fields, our case work in Work Integration and Consumer Protection did not suggest a strong link between internal organisational openness and social innovation at all. It was also not a central aspect in Environmental Sustainability, where the degree varied strongly in particular between third sector and public sector actors with the latter being far more formalised. However, external openness and informal interaction between actors was seen to be very important by almost all actors in the field.

Aspects of *external organisational openness* proved to be a strong driver of social innovation across the different fields and countries. The clearest account of positive effects of external organisational openness on SI was found in the case of online financial education. All involved actors, regardless of their national context or sector affiliation, were strongly open to their external environment, disposing of a high number of stakeholders and intense or at least frequent relations with them. Comparable tendencies were found in the field of Social Services, where actors from all three sectors and in between turned out to currently focus on extending their relationships with external stakeholders. Only in the UK was external openness clearly much more pronounced in third sector organisations engaging in the provision of telecare than in other organisations. Much exchange had been detected between different groups of third sector actors and boundaries between them seemed to be kept at a minimum level. In a similar way, third sector actors in the field of Environmental Sustainability were found to be more actively engaged in mutual exchange than those from the public sphere.

Despite the general tendency of external openness being important, and more so than internal openness, there were some instances of irrelevance or counter-productive effects. In Work Integration, for example, we could not identify a uniform pattern of external openness contributing to social innovation. Results from the field analysis in Community Development with refugees even suggest that active participation in stakeholder exchange might hinder innovative approaches. This happens when people in cases of conflict or deficiency move to different partner organisations and thus cause inefficiency in their original organisation. In particular, in the Czech Community Development case, actors furthermore stated that external openness might increase competitiveness and the fear of losing funds, both of which might contribute to lowering social innovation capacity.

Analysing the effects of the social capital available to actors across fields revealed a picture quite similar to the one concerning external organisational openness. *Social capital* describes the network of organisations and refers to the number *and* intensity of contacts of the organisation to their stakeholders. It is also closely related to the level of trust which others ascribe to an organisation as a result of or prerequisite for being embedded in such a network. Stakeholders include other organisations, employees, customers/beneficiaries, policy makers, etc. An organisation with a large number of contacts, that is a network with many nodes, which are however only superficial, may have a lower degree of social capital than an organisation with a limited network, but one in which it engages intensely—the latter being likely to additionally result in a higher degree of trust into the second organisation than into the first. Both organisations just described might have a similar degree of openness though. Thus, social capital in this regard is not about the mere degree of closure and interaction but also about the intensity of embeddedness within a context.

As with openness, sector provenience was not always a good predictor of high social capital or embeddedness. Instead we found many instances in which the aim was the creation of broad and heterogeneous networks, spanning a range of organisations with different foci and capacities for further relationship building. In the field of Arts & Culture such networks were used to establish links to local residents and to foster social cohesion at the level of the target groups. The most important moderating factor was not so much the size of networks but the quality of contacts. This aspect was also of high relevance in online education for AFS, where all actors showed strong embeddedness in society and local communities. We also found cooperative constellations promoting bike use in the field of Environmental Sustainability. A high level of inter-organisational trust was characteristic across countries for many organisations involved, particularly those belonging to the third and public sector. A different situation was observed in the field of Social Services, where the sector affiliation of actors with high social capital mattered and varied. While in Spain it was the third sector that exhibited the highest embeddedness in the local context and pulled together a network of actors to enable the provision of telecare, the public sector was taking on that position in the UK. In Italy, in turn, the highest amount of social capital was found for business organisations acting as founders/funders and intermediaries of the emerging social investment market.

Variance across fields was also visible in the way that social capital plays out for each of the organisations possessing it. In Work Integration, for example, high social capital of some third sector organisations, e.g., in Spain and France but also in Germany, was one of the aspects leading to the set-up of cross-sector partnerships, i.e., to the formation of the SI in the field. Cooperating partners here became interested in the partnership due to the potential profits of acquiring social legitimacy through the cooperation. Societal legitimacy with regard to social innovation occurs where the innovation is broadly recognised and accepted—possibly not in all of society but in a societal sub-sphere. The ultimate acceptance of an innovation manifests in legislation of a democratically elected authority but also, though to a lesser extent, in positive citizen attitudes, media perceptions, or policy discussions of the innovation (see Krlev, Anheier, & Mildenberger, forthcoming). To say it in relation to Kant's categorial imperative, a social innovation is fully accepted and on its way to becoming main stream when the new type of action is considered a rightful basis for passing legislation to address a social problem.

In other fields the relevance of social capital depended on the main objectives and core competencies of each of the organisations analysed. For example, organisations in the field of Health Care that held strong contacts to local actors were more strongly focussed on offering local and direct service related support, while organisations that had an emphasis on advocacy or capacity building paid more attention to establishing links with other organisations in the same field regardless of geographical proximity. Some fields literally required social capital as part of the social innovation. This was the case for example in self-organised integration of refugees, where the SI is supposed to establish and strengthen durable relations between refugees and members of the host society. Social capital, therefore, can be considered an essential part of the SI itself. However, and surprisingly, promoting local embeddedness was not of major relevance since most organisations engaged in the SI were already well-established at the local level. Neighbourhood and local contacts were also not the prime base of support for the innovative initiatives and projects studied. What was needed to realise the innovation instead were networks spanning local context. In other words, it was the cross-setting connectivity that mattered rather than the within-setting embeddedness.

Actor Resources

The diversity of resources was another factor initially introduced to have a supposedly positive influence on the social innovativeness of actors. Concerning *financial resources*, third sector organisations turned out to draw on the most varied cash inflows, e.g., combining membership fees with public funding and donations, while the public sector itself was marked by low resource diversity. This situation can be observed in several fields such as Environmental Sustainability, Work Integration, and to some extent in part of the countries analysed in Social Services. It was also mainly in these fields that the third sector drew on the most varied resources in terms of expertise and knowledge (*human resources/capital*). This was clearly stated in the field of Environmental Sustainability, while the distribution seemed to be less uniform and also less relevant to CSPs for Work Integration in two of the analysed countries (France and the Czech Republic). In Social Services, in turn, we found the highest diversity in human resources with both public authorities and service provides (rather than advocates), irrespective of them being third sector or business entities. In contrast to this, third sector organisations active in the field of Consumer Protection in the Czech Republic and in Spain were characterised by less heterogeneity than market actors, especially with regard to professional experience and academic background.

Overall, resource diversity turned out not to be a useful explanatory factor for social innovation. Across all of the fields and countries analysed, we could not draw a clear pattern of the overall degree of diversification of the funding structure or the diversity of human resources, and thus it was not possible to make a concise statement on the overall relevance of this organisational trait for the streams of social innovation.

Volunteering as a particular resource factor turned out to be both, a more coherent factor to analyse and a more relevant influencer of social innovation than diversity per se. In assessing the relevance of voluntary engagement for the SI streams in the various fields two poles were identified. One is constituted by those fields and organisations that involve a high degree of voluntary engagement. Examples of these fields are Health Care and Community Development with refugees. In Health Care, the case studies revealed that voluntary engagement, often in the form of peer support as part of the recovery approach, was an essential part of the work performed by all of the third sector organisations. Voluntary engagement in this setting served as a bridge between those currently and those formerly affected by mental health issues to enhance self-healing. Volunteers with 'lived experience' provided a unique resource. In Community Development, volunteering served a compensatory function instead. Here, although most organisations active with the SI received some sort of funding, financial in security often was a serious issue. When national governments retreated from the field, the effective continuity of the SI depended on local or European subsidies, private foundations or donations. The lack of financial resources was partly compensated by recruiting volunteers, whose numbers in some cases were far greater than those of paid staff.

In addition to variations across fields, we found variations in fields across countries. In Consumer Protection, for example, voluntary engagement appeared to be a relevant factor for social innovation in Spain and Denmark, while in the Czech Republic even third sector organisations mostly did not have volunteers. A similar situation was observed in the field of Social Services, where voluntary engagement was found to be high in the Spanish third sector whereas Italian and Swedish organisations involved volunteers only to a minimal extent. This leads us to the opposite pole, namely where the voluntary engagement played no or only a marginal role. An example of such a field is Work Integration. Here, very few volunteers were engaged or informally active in the cross-sector partnerships. Another relevant setting in this regard is Environmental Sustainability, where volunteers participated in the realisation of public events to promote bike use, such as 'bike nights', but where they had no substantial influence on the organisations or the SI stream as driving actors. This seemed to differ in Arts & Culture, where the influx of new ideas through volunteer engagement was regarded highly by organisations, but these still represented a minority influence (potentially with the exception of the Dutch case, where civic cultural action was prominent), making volunteers less important than other factors.

Action Capacity

Finally, we are relating back to one of the core traits of third sector organisations, namely the *combination of service provision and advocacy*. While we were able to confirm that third sector organisations appeared more apt to successfully tie together the two functions than other actors, we did not find a clear indication that this capacity enhanced social innovativeness. With regard to the recovery approach in Health Care, we saw how third sector organisations were able to integrate the two functions with synergies arising, probably making the SI take ground more easily but not considered a major factor by the consulted experts. Similar situations were found in Environmental Sustainability and in Consumer Protection.

In self-organised integration of refugees within Community Development we found that organisations, although to some extent engaged in advocacy, were generally more focused on service delivery. Some organisations stated the two functions to be interlinked; however, it became clear that advocacy and awareness raising were mainly pursued to change the conditions for service delivery and to support the identification of needs. Particularly interesting in the UK was that the provision of funding from the private sector allowed non-profits performing the actions to also engage in lobbying, which would have been impossible if funding had come under the more authoritative auspices of the state. In Work Integration and in Social Services, the situation appeared to vary considerably across countries. Work Integration actors in Spain and Germany almost completely lacked advocacy efforts, while in France the key actors were marked by pursuing that function. In the field of Social Services in Italy, advocacy was also not very prominent (despite the aim being to promote a social investment market), whereas in the UK both public and for-profit organisations tried to combine both functions to enhance the provision of telecare. A similar situation could be found in Spain, but with advocacy playing a lesser role. Swedish organisations in turn engaged profoundly, and across sector borders, in advocating with the aim of capacity building for volunteer centres.

External pressures turned out to be important for the social innovation streams we studied in our case work. However, the connection between pressures (or their absence) was not unidirectional in the sense that their absence was always positive with regard to the development of the SI.

On one side there were instances in which we saw a link between the absence of pressures and greater innovation. Our work on biking showed how gradual changes in public opinion and political will turned out to be crucial for socio-cultural and socio-political developments favouring the SI. For traffic planning being a state regulated field, the liberties of engaged third sector or market actors depended substantially on the diversity of their funding sources and thus their effective independence from the state in this regard. Common among all market actors in the field was the feeling of exposure to pressures from competitors in the provision of bike sharing systems, which might have contributed to stymieing the impact on the innovation of this particular activity in the promotion of bike use. All of this held across country contexts. External pressures experienced by actors in the field of Consumer Protection appeared to be differing across countries. The highest independence from external pressures was observed in Spain, while in the Czech Republic and in Denmark external pressures were high with some counter-productive effects on the provision of online financial education. High economic, competitive and regulatory pressures shaped the field of Social Services independent of the specific governance leverage of the innovation (technology for telecare, human resources for volunteer centres and financial resources for social investment) and have contributed to keeping dynamism in the respective contexts at a fairly low level to date.

On the other side, dynamics in the field of Community Development with refugees showed how pressures can be productive. Here, the policy context was crucial to understand the emergence of self-organised activities, since the past decade had been characterised by austerity and restrictive policy which had severely hindered innovative approaches. On these grounds, the work of many organisations studied in the field can be seen as a particular coping mechanism to changes in the policy framework. Other external pressures can be interpreted as acute triggers to the development of the SI. For example, a greater number of refugees led to greater pressure on the system of dealing with the situation and at the same time increased public awareness for their situation. Similarly, public opinion in the form of criticism in local areas encouraged municipalities to develop better services to both refugees and inhabitants of the neighbourhood, making way for the SI to originate.

Finally, the field of Work Integration gave a good illustration of the way in which external pressures may both spur and block the unfolding of an SI. In this field exogenous shocks, such as the one caused by financial crisis, were identified to have propelled the CSPs into developing. It is interesting to note that while in Spain the social innovation evolved despite, or maybe because, the state was disengaged, the emergence of CSPs was strongly dependent on state support in Germany. However, our case work also revealed how pressures in the form of negative public opinion, restraints in funding and competition for market shares or for resources have weakened social innovativeness. What we learn from this is that dynamics between pressures and innovation should not be considered per se but always need to be assessed against a set of context conditions.

Condensed Field Level Insights

Finally, to sum up the conditions that turned out to be particularly driving the SI stream in the different fields, we present some condensed insights based on the preceding synthesis. While we studied three SI streams in which actors' traits and coalitions seemed to matter most (Arts & Culture, Health Care and Consumer Protection), the other four depended more on (shifts) in context factors (Social Services, Environmental Sustainability, Work Integration and Community Development).

For driving arts-based spatial rejuvenation within Arts & Culture, organisations needed a strong orientation at meeting social needs and were characterised by high external openness. Heterogeneous actor contacts thereby had to be paired with a high amount of social capital, in particular in relation to the local setting and active engagement in collaborative projects. A social innovation that proved to have taken very different trajectories across countries was that of online financial education for Consumer Protection. Only one common feature stood out in the analysis, which in congruence with Arts & Culture was that the SI stream was always nurtured through collaborations across sector borders. In the field of Health Care, our findings suggest that in all four countries the recovery approach was initiated and driven by pioneer actors on the national level and consequently taken up and implemented by other individuals. The transmission to the local level happened through social entrepreneurs who initiated what became leading service-user and political movements to disseminate the SI, which eventually influenced organisational practices more broadly. With regard to all three fields, the 'inner circle' of the entrepreneurial activity, to speak in terms of the TEPSIE framework initially referred to, was most important.

Almost no general statement can be made regarding new governance arrangements to reach out to the most vulnerable in the field of Social Services, except that the actors needed strong social needs orientation, and in contrast to Arts & Culture organisations, had to be motivated by pro-social values. Otherwise the heterogeneity of embodiments of the SI stream and the different levers used to enhance governance only allow us to state that the roles actors played relative to their context were more important than sector provenience. This last aspect underscores why the driving actors of telecare in the UK were public authorities, while third sector actors prevailed in Spain. Similarly, regarding the promotion of bike use in the field of Environmental Sustainability, the aspect that turned out to be most influential was not an organisational trait as such but a gradual change in national societies' mind-sets in favour of alternative means of transportation and healthy lifestyles. Furthermore, investments in infrastructure have helped strengthening the SI stream across all countries. In contrast to changes 'within the system' or strategic action field, and as discussed regarding external pressures, the factors that seem to have contributed most strongly to the development of CSPs in the field of Work Integration have been the challenges posed by the economic crisis and the increased number of refugees. A similar influence has occurred in Community Development when it comes to self-organised integration of refugees. However, the effects of the 'external shock' depended greatly on pre-existing positive or negative inclinations towards helping refugees. In contrast to Work Integration where stakeholders engaged largely in a reactive fashion, third sector actors, or rather individual and informal civil society action, was key in shaping public perceptions, partly against pre-dispositions in government and policy. In this regard it was interesting to note that collaboration and exchange spanning geographical boundaries was important for an innovation that is locally bound by definition.

The situation in all these fields relates mainly to what we described as institutional and political frameworks in the cases of Social Services, and to the societal climate in the case of Environmental Sustainability and Community Development. The latter in combination with Work Integration are special in the sense that temporal dynamics triggered by 'external events' had a major influence on the development of the SI stream.

Contributions to Social Innovation Research

Inspired by the experience made in the case work presented in this book, the next section sets out to highlight some of the learnings that emerged from the cases beyond the main lines of inquiry and in relation to our supposition of a particularly high social innovativeness in third sector organisations.

Generalisation on the Innovation Rather Than on the Field of Activity

First of all, throughout the research process we noted, in contrast to initial expectations, that a generalisation of results is hardly possible across fields. The social innovations investigated in the ITSSOIN project were very different in character and the evolution, notions or logics underlying a field turned out to be relevant factors shaping the studied innovations—yet not always to the same extent and in the same fashion. We have seen that some SI streams were more driven by organisational action and others more by context conditions or external events. Contextual aspects in turn are harder to capture and more difficult to compare than organisational action, in particular in view of the inchoate state of social innovation research.

The difficulties arising partly stem from our exploratory research approach in which we went to pursue the social innovation streams most prominent and most promising in terms of explanatory potential rather than focus on a predefined set of innovations that are similar in character. In other words, we traded neat comparability against representativeness and relevance. The variety that came with this decision is outlined in Table 11.2.

Table 11.2 Traits of the social innovation streams

Social innovation stream	Specificity of the stream	Geographic scope	Innovation objects
Arts for spatial rejuvenation	Medium	Local	Action principle
New governance arrangements	Low	National	Governance mechanism in service delivery
The recovery approach to mental health	High	National	Action principle (in service delivery)
Promoting public spaces for bicycle use	Medium	Local	Advocacy effort
Online financial education	High	National	Advocacy effort (and service)
Cross-sector partnerships	High	Local/regional	Formal actor constellation
Self-organised integration of refugees	Low	Local	Informal actor constellation

To do that we can look at the traits of the SI streams in three dimensions: (1) the specificity of the SI stream, which refers to the ability to clearly delineate the innovation by a neat set of definitional criteria; (2) the geographic scope; and (3) the innovation object, specifying the character and 'embodiment' of the innovation.

In relation to the specificity, we worked on SI streams whose delineation was rather easy and clear, either because of pre-existing definitional criteria (recovery) or such that we worked out in the research (CSPs), or because the innovation was bound to a particular organised structure (online financial education via web platforms). Other streams were of medium specificity, since while they were composed of some common elements their effective realisation entailed significant variations, some of which were strongly path dependent (arts-based spatial rejuvenation and the promotion of bike use). Finally, we also had SI streams that were much harder to pin down, either since the innovation itself contained a high degree of fuzziness and defied formalisation (self-organisation), or because the mechanisms studied to exemplify the innovation differed across countries (new governance through tapping new technology, human resources or financial resources).

SI streams also differed as regards location. Four needed to be studied at the local level since extending geographic reach beyond it would have made any analysis not only impracticable but also meaningless. This was either due to high place specificity (urban spatial rejuvenation, promotion of bike use in cities and self-organised integration of refugees in neighbourhoods), or due to restrictions of geographic action ranges (CSPs). Three others were located at the national level, either since the innovation would have a uniform appearance nationally (recovery), or provision systems were regulated at that level (new governance arrangements in social services), or the innovation in itself was not locally bound (online financial education).

We also looked at innovation objects, and while these objects show some striking relation to the conceptualisation of fields composed in Chapter 3 as regards advocacy and service provision, this congruence became visible only at the stage of reflection across fields rather than being embedded in the selection of streams. Overall we see three generic innovation objects emerge.

First, we have three innovations that come in the form of action principles or variations thereof. Arts as a means to rejuvenate urban places is one of them. A shift from therapy to the self-healing capacities of patients and the lived experience of ex-patients is another. The new governance arrangements in Social Services are similar in that they refer to the application of mechanisms to increase capacity, including technology for telecare, volunteer centres to enhance human resources or the build-up of social investment market to increase financial resources. While the action principles in Health Care and Social Services lead to how action principles aid service provision, in Arts & Culture they may relate to a service but also to how advocacy is performed or how civic action and discourses are shaped and directed on a much more abstract level.

Second, we have two SI streams that represent advocacy efforts both in the promotion of bike use and the provision of online financial education. While advocacy and the shaping of people's behaviour is at the core of both, they are also tied to the provision of infrastructure (biking) or the provision of a service (the counselling of AFC customers). So neither are exclusive advocacy innovations, but the SI stream in Consumer Protection is more service oriented in the classical sense than the one in Environmental Sustainability.

Third, we see social innovation embodied in particular organisational forms or actor constellations, either in a formalised way (CSPs) or in a very informal and more process-oriented one (self-organised integration).

The baseline is that the insights we created relate much more to a specific social innovation stream than the larger field of activity. Despite this we have referred to fields of activity in our comparative discussion to aid readability and to span the introductory and concluding chapters of this book. And despite the preceding variety and specificity of the research we have still been able to condense certain actor traits and context conditions that were central in shaping the social innovation streams. In consequence we are also able to identify the most potent actor (constellations) for promoting social innovation as well as to qualify the specific role of the third sector, all of which we highlight in the following sections.

Importance of Collaboration and (Cross-sector) Networks

Despite the heterogeneity outlined previously and the challenges that come with it, some overall conditions turned out to be characteristic across all cases and fields analysed. One of them, and maybe the most remarkable one, is the importance of heterogeneous networks as a source of innovation. We hardly found any single actors driving the SI stream on their own. Mostly social innovation was shaped and carried out by multiple actors at a time, who contributed to it in various ways, based on their individual capabilities.

Furthermore, the identified networks shared certain characteristics, which turned out to be crucial to the viability and spread of an SI stream. For example, actors engaged in those networks often stemmed from different sectors, or sector affiliation was blurred. Cross-sector engagement was a typical trait of collective entrepreneurial efforts, which were not always free of conflicts though. Especially in the collaboration between formal and informal actors, where different logics were at play, it wasn't always easy to arrive at a shared understanding of goals and ways to achieve them. However, the commitment to collaboration and an openness of organisations towards external influences often helped to find solutions in the longer term. Although collaboration trespassed sector boundaries, organisations which shared similar values were more likely to work together. Relevant values came in different shapes, ranging from pro-social values (e.g., in Community Development) to a shared 'business' mind-set, for instance, an orientation towards cost effectiveness in meeting social needs within the field of Social Services.

Third Sector Organisations as 'Hubs' and 'Brokers' and Initiators of Social Innovation

Within the denoted networks, in many cases we could identify one or several organisations that acted as 'brokers' and managed to bring together actors from different spheres, both in terms of sector provenience and specific skills or expertise. Due to their traits, third sector organisations seemed to take on this role very readily. Favourable for taking this role were, among others, their proximity to target groups, their long or specialised expertise in working with those groups, a sense of devotion to a cause, their trustworthiness, openness and high degree of social capital, in particular embeddedness in local settings. Such non-profit 'hubs' frequently invited partners to contribute and thereby acted as a bridge into a collaborative constellations. The 'connective action' of third sector organisations, which often seemed to even go beyond their ability to perform 'collective action', deserves closer attention, in particular as regards its specific function in social innovation processes.

In addition to their role as brokers and hubs, third sector organisations' influence was found to be particularly strong in the early phases of the investigated SI streams. Third sector organisations were not only the ones to spot a need for action but also those to take initial action. However, after this initial phase it often took other actors and their respective competencies to bring in further resources or scale the innovation. External shocks were found to act as triggers to multi-actor engagement, galvanising informal, isolated or loosely coupled initiatives into an alliance. It is to be remarked though that such alliances do not only have positive effects. Third sector organisations, for instance, often collaborated with governments. This created relations of dependency, letting formerly independent actors become cautious when it came to advocacy or political activism. Such dynamics in alliances, which are often more subtle and fluid than contracted public-private partnerships, yet with material consequences, need more detailed inspection.

Solutions to Social Problems in Times of Austerity: Social Innovation or Substitution?

Finally, a debate which frequently came up during the ITSSOIN research centred on the impact of austerity measures and the (mis-)interpretation of a substitution of public engagement in the respective field and the taking over of state responsibilities by other actors as social innovation. We indeed often found that third sector organisations' engagement in a field was driven by the ambition that the government should eventually take over the created activities. While those activities were clearly novel, we sometimes observed a reluctance of third sector actors to label them as 'innovations', since they feared this would provide an argument for keeping them out of the competencies and responsibilities of the state. In some cases, respondents actively stressed that certain activities would be better positioned in the public sector. At the same time, financial constraints and thus a lack of public commitment to tackling the social problem in question had important and often restraining effects on the social innovation process.

This underpins the importance of putting more emphasis on finding 'better solutions' than on finding solutions that are merely 'new', and strengthens the normative dimension in social innovation research. Activities that had previously been performed by the state and then merely taken over or substituted by others due to cuts in public spending and a forceful termination of previous activities, clearly wouldn't satisfy the 'better' criterion. This brings us back to our definition of social innovation and social innovativeness, which has laid the ground for our testing and further development of social innovation theory throughout ITSSOIN, and which we hope will be fruitfully translated into new and ever more tailored research.

Conclusions

At present general statements abstracting from the specific SI streams, on fields of activity or across the latter, on the typical processes of social innovation development and capacity are still hard to make. Yet, we have provided valuable insights on actors, their traits, roles and constellations as well as context conditions. Both the methods we applied and the insights we generated have highlighted promising lines of inquiry, which should be taken onward in future research. The latter needs to produce more work in similar settings to confirm or relativise our findings. It can link neatly to the work we performed and enrich it by studying other fields or countries. Based on what we have found, certain aspects deserve more attention in such endeavours than others. What these are is going to be is highlighted in the concluding chapter of this book.

Note

1. Example: Extending the coverage of medical treatment is not a social need in most Western countries, whereas it clearly is in many remote places of developing countries. Mobile health interventions (addressing transport or data transmission) are therefore addressing a social need in these countries, whereas they would mostly be inappropriate or redundant in many Western countries. This may change with provision gaps in rural areas due to urbanisation.

References

Fligstein, N., & McAdam, D. (2012). *A theory of fields*. Oxford, New York, NY: Oxford University Press.

Ford, J. K., Schmitt, N., Schechtman, S. L., Hults, B. M., & Doherty, M. L. (1989). Process tracing methods: Contributions, problems, and neglected research questions. *Organizational Behavior and Human Decision Processes, 43*, 75–117.

Krlev, G., Bund, E., & Mildenberger, G. (2014). Measuring what matters-Indicators of social innovativeness on the national level. *Information Systems Management, 31*(3), 200–224.

Krlev, G., Anheier, H. K., & Mildenberger, G. (forthcoming) Symposium: Social innovation and the third sector—policies, media images and citizen perceptions. *Nonprofit and Voluntary Sector Quarterly*.

Krlev, G., Anheier, H. K., Behrendt, C., & Mildenberger, G. (2017). The who, what and how of social innovation: A qualitative comparative analysis. *Academy of Management Proceedings, 1*, 14266. https://doi.org/10.5465/AMBPP.2017.14266abstract

Porter, M. E., & Kramer, M. R. (2011, January–February). Creating shared value: How to reinvent capitalism—and unleash a wave of innovation and growth. *Harvard Business Review*, 2–17.

Prahalad, C. K., & Hammond, A. (2002). Serving the world's poor profitably. *Harvard Business Review, 80*(9), 48–57.

Tansey, O. (2007). Process tracing and elite interviewing: A case for non-probability sampling. *Political Science and Politics, 40*(4), 765–772.

12 Conclusions and Implications for Research, Policy and Practice

Gorgi Krlev, Helmut K. Anheier, and Georg Mildenberger

Future Research Themes and Areas

In this book, we looked at the phenomenon of social innovation less in terms of measurable impact than as a source of mostly incremental and sometimes discontinuous attempts at problem-solving and improvements. The sum of such innovative acts increases the capacity of fields and entire societies to adapt to current and future challenges, and, hence, in the longer-term leads to sustainability and greater prosperity. Here we first highlight our main findings, then discuss open questions for future research.

Main Findings: Context and Actor Constellations

The context of social innovations matters. This is not a new insight, of course, and has long been highlighted across the social sciences, e.g., in social network analysis (Friemel, 2008), in social media marketing (Vaynerchuk, 2013), or in studies of international business and leadership (Chakravorti, 2003). We have used welfare regimes (Esping-Andersen, 1990), varieties of capitalism (Hall & Soskice, 2001) and social origins (Salamon & Anheier, 1998) as approaches to assess these conditions and social origins proved most useful as a predictor of social innovativeness, pointing at the relevance of third sector size and civic engagement (see Anheier, Krlev, Behrendt, & Mildenberger, 2017, for more details). The importance of third sector organisations is further underscored by the fact that in our 'open sampling,' guided by independently identified social innovation streams rather than starting with a pre-defined organisational sample, the majority of identified actors were from the third sector. *State prevalence along with third sector prevalence* emerged as stronger driving forces for social innovation at the field level than market prevalence, calling into the question claims that social problem-solving would emerge from seizing market opportunities alone (Porter & Kramer, 2006, 2011), at least in Western contexts.

Even more important moderators of social innovation than these relatively rigid institutional structures were policies and in particular perceptional frames, paving the way for or blocking an innovation's way, for instance perceptions relating to ecology and lifestyles (with an influence on biking) or solidarity (with an influence on attempts of self-organisation by and for refugees). We have performed work presented elsewhere which shows that the hopes of policy makers at the national level in social innovation are high, but the ideas of who is supposed to do what are underdeveloped (Krlev, Einarsson, Wijkström, Heyer, & Mildenberger, forthcoming). At the same time we have seen across fields and countries how *local policy making in particular can enhance social innovation* (green city parliaments) or severely inhibit stakeholders' action capacity (fiscal cut-backs on financial resources in community development or social services).

An overarching theme affecting context on all levels was the impact of austerity and crises on social innovation. *Exogenous shocks* in specific fields, such as the economic crisis or the refugee crisis, often triggered the dispensation of resources, financial and otherwise, and thereby enabled action. Or they created a surge of needs and pushed actors towards fulfilling their social responsibilities, as, for instance, demanded in public discourse. While crises thus partly promoted social innovation, budget cuts usually had stymieing effects on social innovation, especially when it came to taking successful pioneering approaches onward. We often encountered reluctance among innovators to call their actions innovations, motivated by the fear that this would prevent their incorporation into standard provision by the state. A recurrent theme was that social innovation should not be used as a reason to substitute state welfare.

One of the main insights emerging from the research was the *central role of (cross-sector) networks and collaborations in the governance of social innovation*, from its emergence to its diffusion. Third sector organisations seem to take two distinct roles within these networks. First, they are particularly active in paving the way for social innovation, being the ones who not only care about social needs but actively try to tackle them in new ways. However, they often need other actors, with distinct capabilities, to come in at later stages. Based on this we can assesses the social innovativeness of third sector organisations, whereby we defined social innovativeness as more lasting, more frequent and more substantial involvement in the evolution of the SI stream. We can confirm our claim of high social innovativeness in third sector organisations in particular in terms of early stage and lasting engagement, but also need to relativise it with regard to the frequency and substantiality of the involvement, where others might be stronger.

Second, even more so than 'collective' action, *third sector organisations performed 'connective' actions*, bringing formerly detached or isolated actors together and establishing a link to target groups. This is an argument which supports the aspect of a high degree of substantiality in third sector influence on social innovation. Field theory (Fligstein & McAdam, 2012) served as a potent theoretical lens for sketching out the landscape of involved actors and the relations and interactions between them; in other words, the strategic action field surrounding the social innovation. This came in addition to its usefulness when moving down from the level of the individual field of activity to the identification of our eventual unit of analysis, the social innovation stream, in relation to which an understanding for the strategic action field could evolve. When it comes to studying specific, potentially formalised, actor coalitions pushing social innovation in future research, actor network theory could be another promising lens to apply, especially when the focus on micro level interactions and the question of 'what is assembled' in such social systems (Latour, 2008) is strong. When the focus is on the enabling of broader 'transitions' instead, potentially spanning decades and thus supposedly trespassing the span of time that is easily dealt with through process tracing, multi-level perspectives can help (Geels, 2002, 2005). While initially applied to study shifts in socio-technological regimes, they have found recognition in the historically oriented study of social innovation processes (Schimpf, Scheuerle, Mildenberger, Haindlmaier, & Giesecke, 2017).

Overall, there was *not one single formula that determined organisations' social innovativeness*. On the contrary, we found that conditions enabling social innovation varied significantly across fields. Yet, there are some *organisational traits* that emerged against others. Most prominent among them are *social needs orientation, external organisational openness and local embeddedness, and also but less uniformly pro-social values and voluntary engagement*. All the aforementioned proved more important than, for instance, variables of organisational structure (e.g., age or size), resource diversity or the ability to combine advocacy and service provision.

Although it has just been mentioned as mostly relevant as an organisational trait, we have dived deeper into volunteering as a micro level practice within organisations. This was based on the supposition that volunteers may bring openness and produce new ideas within organisations, suggesting that volunteering has an impact on social innovation in motives, organisational forms or outcomes. It was not always easy to locate individuals providing prompts for the emergence of social innovation, since new ideas are often incidental rather than produced by deliberate actions. What we also saw is that while volunteers came up with new ideas, it was mostly professionals who initiated and channelled innovations. *The innovative potential of volunteering thus largely depends on establishing a system of productive collaboration between volunteers and staff.*

Open Research Questions

As regards context conditions we have learnt that while third sector prevalence and civic engagement are important, these factors alone are far from sufficient for producing social innovation. Instead, and in line with previous social innovation research (Nicholls & Murdock, 2012), actor collaboration across sector borders was a significant enabler of social innovation. Thus, the *links between context conditions and social innovation would need to be tested further* and alternative conceptual approaches should be considered to better understand nations' or regional contexts' capacity of producing social innovation. An important role therein is the *establishment of a time dimension*, a call we have recently seen pronounced in institutional studies more generally (Greenwood, Raynard, Kodeih, Micelotta, & Lounsbury, 2011), which proved helpful to get a better grasp of the streams' development through tracing the underlying process.

Another important contextual factor highlighted in our findings is place, which has found recognition in previous social innovation studies (Evers, Ewert, & Brandsen, 2014; Moulaert, Martinelli, Swyngedouw, & Gonzalez, 2005). Yet, place as mere geographic scope is unlikely to add much to the insights we can generate. We have seen how shared conditions of emergence for the social innovation streams could be spotted independent of locality, for instance, boundary-spanning actor coalitions in arts-based place rejuvenation and in online financial education. What we need instead is a *concept of 'contextualized space'* that takes a magnitude of influences into account, including that of societal discourses. Our further works on media reporting on social innovation or citizen perceptions (Krlev, Anheier, & Mildenberger, forthcoming) can serve as sources of inspiration here, which for reasons of capacity were however only placed at the national level, and therefore mainly used as hints in the screening of fields and the identification of the social innovation stream rather than its contextual analysis.

Societal discourse, that is the societal and policy climates, have come out as a third essential factor. The reoccurring issue of a tension between innovation and cutbacks in state welfare connects to studies that have examined the 'social enterprise' agenda of policy makers. Nicholls and Teasdale (2017), for instance, show how while interpreted as a new and more effective form of solidary action, reflected in the terminology applied such as that of 'Big Society' in the UK, the concept has mostly remained closely tied to neoliberal ideas of increasing citizen responsibility in return for decreasing provision by the state. More needs to be understood about the *enabling and inhibiting dynamics caused by such directed, yet fluctuating, policy shifts over time* and by the supposedly *more chaotic transformations triggered by events of crisis.* This is another instance where sequential analysis of social innovation processes that acknowledges different phases (Murray, Caulier-Grice, & Mulgan, 2010), including iterative loops often neglected in such models, would prove useful to further specify (shifts) in actors' roles. *Time oriented studies of organisation* more generally could prove useful in providing a repertoire of viewpoints and analytic approaches (see, for example, Goodman, Lawrence, Ancona, & Tushman, 2001 or Lee & Liebenau, 1999).

The understanding for what such spaces and processes look like can be advanced tremendously by research such as that produced in ITSSOIN. What we refer to is research that acknowledges and embraces complexity in exploring social realities but at the same time works within a common framework that allows for rigorous testing of claims and propositions throughout.

When it comes to the special role taken by third sector organisations within social innovation processes, drawing on the literatures of brokerage in the context of technological innovation studies should add value (Fleming, Mingo, & Chen, 2007). Using those would also speak to the network aspects identified in our research as well as the procedural dimension that needs to be advanced in conceptualising action towards social innovation, both of which it seems to have in common with technological innovation (see Obstfeld, 2016, 2017 on brokerage in innovation and Obstfeld, Borgatti, & Davis, 2014 on brokerage as a process). A very open question is: *Do third sector organisations in social innovation settings possess similar properties as technology brokers? And is there any resemblance in the process of brokerage performed at all, or do we need alternative conceptualisations?* Other concepts of brokerage, including political brokerage with a stress on power positions, mediation or agenda setting (Stovel & Shaw, 2012) might prove more accurate representations of what we see with regard to brokers in social innovation processes. There is reason to think this could go in both directions, since we also found that the *conditions for technological innovation and social innovation overlap in some areas while they differ in others.* For example, organisational openness was important for both (Crossan & Apaydin, 2010), while tinkering and freedom from pressures is seen as relatively important for technological innovation (Saxenian, 1994), but took a more ambiguous role with regard to social innovation that sometimes emerged in the absence, sometimes due to the presence of pressures.

Finding a diversity of innovation actors, in combination with the fact that organisational structure embodied in organisation size or age proved relatively inconsequential for contributions to social innovation, spurs the critical discussion about the search for hero entrepreneurs to tackle social challenges (Nicholls, 2010). Future research should try to *confirm or call into question those traits that have come out as significant and uniform enablers of social innovation* (in particular needs orientation, openness and embeddedness), and *develop insights into those that generally have an enabling function*, but not in all contexts (pro-social values and volunteering). It should also give *specific consideration to those occurring with ambiguous effects*, such as resource diversity or independence from external pressures.

Finally, despite the favourability of civic engagement and volunteering implied by our findings, very little is understood about the particular role of volunteers in creating social innovation and there is some evidence that current practice is not fully up to harnessing its existing potential. On the micro level of involved actors, future research will need to refine the first insights on the *interplay between volunteers and professionals in the creation of innovative practices* and the management of social innovation processes within organisations. ITSSOIN research going beyond what could be presented here may provide guidance for the composition of future studies on this issue (see de Wit, Mensink, Einarsson, & Bekkers, 2017).

Implications for the Policy and Practice of Social Innovation

From the perspective of policy making we learned that when it comes to *institutional structures*, it is the more flexible aspects that seem to matter more for social innovation than those that are near impossible to change in the mid-term. We could show that a strong third sector with productive links to the state and a high share of volunteering were beneficial conditions for social innovation. These can all be promoted to a larger extent than the macro conditions of welfare regimes can be changed.

When it comes to shaping *social innovation policies* they can be enhanced in three different ways relating to (1) the level of policy making; (2) the specificity of social innovation agendas; and (3) data availability as regards perceptions of social innovation. First, we identified bottom-up engagement and the focus on local development as more beneficial than structures imposed top-down. The link here is more tentative than the one with regard to institutions and further investigation of the stimulating effects of targeted policies is needed. Nonetheless it contains strong impetus to *foster social innovation policy making in particular at the local and regional level.* Second, our findings suggest that policy makers at the national level can actively engage in creating favourable conditions by drafting policy agendas and initiatives that are *mindful of their potential effects on the social innovation climate,* that is, do not evoke high hopes but remain vague on potential actor roles and contributions. Third, despite the fact that, social innovation is embraced and promoted as a concept (in particular at the EU level), it proved hard to assess discourses and citizen perceptions around social innovation and the actors engaged in it other than building singular stories based on our extensive set of qualitative data. Policy makers should think about integrating such and related aspects with regard to *citizen perceptions into national statistical accounts,* which would better enable them and practitioners to understand the climate in which they are acting and harness or work towards changing it.

When it comes to *innovators and fields of innovation,* networks between diverse actors turned out to be key to driving social innovation. Those who are particularly social needs oriented, externally open and locally embedded, take on central or 'hub' positions in such networks. Third sector organisations often inhabit this role. However, they cannot solve challenges on their own, but need dedicated partners with shared value sets. The formation of such networks can be steered by policy only to a degree. In some instances political steering is counter-productive, since informal and fluid structures are needed. Policy makers need a deep understanding of the dynamics and logics underlying certain fields of activity, sometimes even more specifically of certain innovation domains and objects, to decide on whether or not the state should engage and how. Although we found instances of pressures and restrictions promoting innovation, the existence or creation of spaces for actors to meet or contexts in which first informal collaboration is possible proved central to social innovation. We propose some kind of *observatory for social innovations in Europe*, charged with the task to monitor what kind of policy intervention would be most appropriate and beneficial. Recommendations could range from regulatory action and financial support schemes to the formal convening of parties and more informal consultations.

We also looked at the micro level of individual actors from another angle, namely that of *volunteering*. We found that volunteers are only innovative where they are encouraged to employ their individual experience or expertise (professional competencies acquired in their job, 'lived experience', etc.). While the management of such engagement and the targeted recruitment of volunteers is more challenging, volunteering when interpreted as a mere 'helping hand', albeit important, is unlikely to produce innovation. *A focus on distinct individual competencies and how to best employ them* would have to be implemented *in the design of organisational and policy initiatives promoting volunteering* that aim at producing social innovation.

In conclusion, the main message is that much social innovation happens on a day-to-day basis. It is the result not of fragmented activities but of multi-actor initiatives that add up to major social innovation streams, which produce (some) answers to the current challenges of our time, including sustainable financial markets, social inclusion, environmental sustainability, health and social services provisions for vulnerable persons, livable communities, employment, competitiveness, etc. Saying that social innovations can and should be replicated clearly counteracts the essence in our findings. What we want to express instead is: There are some general principles, such as the ones we worked out, that act as triggers in promoting or slowing down social innovation and thereby moderate socioeconomic impact. While social innovation is hard to replicate or scale in the classical sense, these principles should be adopted to drive innovation. We still need to understand better how to operate these triggers, but the preceding recommendations can inform policy making and engaged action right now.

References

Anheier, H. K., Krlev, G., Behrendt, C., & Mildenberger, G. (2017). *Findings: The who, what and how of social innovation.* A deliverable of the project: "Impact of the Third Sector as Social Innovation" (ITSSOIN). Brussels.

Chakravorti, B. (2003, December 11). An unexpected lesson from Mandela: Why context matters. *Harvard Business Review.* Retrieved from: https://hbr.org/2013/12/an-unexpected-lesson-from-mandela-why-context-matters.

Crossan, M. M., & Apaydin, M. (2010). A multi-dimensional framework of organizational innovation: A systematic review of the literature. *Journal of Management Studies, 47*(6), 1154–1191.

Esping-Andersen, G. (1990). *The three worlds of welfare capitalism* (Pbk. ed.). Cambridge: Polity Press.

Evers, A., Ewert, B., & Brandsen, T. (2014). *Social innovations for social cohesion: Transnational patterns and approaches from 20 European cities.* Retrieved from www.wilcoproject.eu/downloads/WILCO-project-eReader.pdf

Fleming, L., Mingo, S., & Chen, D. (2007). Collaborative brokerage, generative creativity, and creative success. *Administrative Science Quarterly, 52*(3), 443–475. https://doi.org/10.2189/asqu.52.3.443

Fligstein, N., & McAdam, D. (2012). *A theory of fields.* Oxford, New York, NY: Oxford University Press.

Friemel, T. (Ed.). (2008). *Why context matters: Applications of social network analysis* (1st ed.). VS research. Wiesbaden: VS, Verl. für Sozialwiss.

Geels, F. W. (2002). Technological transitions as evolutionary reconfiguration processes: A multi-level perspective and a case-study. *Research Policy, 31*(8–9), 1257–1274. https://doi.org/10.1016/S0048-7333(02)00062-8

Geels, F. W. (2005). *Technological transitions and system innovations: A co-evolutionary and socio-technical analysis.* Cheltenham, UK, Northampton, MA: Edward Elgar Publishing.

Goodman, P. S., Lawrence, B. S., Ancona, D. G., & Tushman, M. L. (2001). Introduction: Time in organizations. *Academy of Management Review, 26*(4), 507–511. https://doi.org/10.5465/AMR.2001.5393884

Greenwood, R., Raynard, M., Kodeih, F., Micelotta, E. R., & Lounsbury, M. (2011). Institutional complexity and organizational responses. *The Academy of Management Annals, 5*(1), 317–371. https://doi.org/10.1080/19416520.2011.590299

Hall, P. A., & Soskice, D. W. (Eds.). (2001). *Varieties of capitalism: The institutional foundations of comparative advantage.* Oxford, New York, NY: Oxford University Press.

Krlev, G., Anheier, H.K., & Mildenberger, G. (forthcoming) Symposium: Social innovation and the third sector—policies, media images and citizen perceptions. *Nonprofit and Voluntary Sector Quarterly.*

Krlev, G., Einarsson, T., Wijkström, F., Heyer, L., & Mildenberger, G. (forthcoming). The policies of social innovation—a cross-national analysis. *Nonprofit and Voluntary Sector Quarterly.*

Latour, B. (2008). *Reassembling the social: An introduction to actor-network-theory* (Reprint). Clarendon lectures in management studies. Oxford [u.a.]: Oxford University Press.

Lee, H., & Liebenau, J. (1999). Time in organizational studies: Towards a new research direction. *Organization Studies, 20*(6), 1035–1058. https://doi.org/10.1177/0170840699206006

Moulaert, F., Martinelli, F., Swyngedouw, E., & Gonzalez, S. (2005). Towards alternative model(s) of local innovation. *Urban Studies, 42*(11), 1969–1990.

Murray, R., Caulier-Grice, J., & Mulgan, G. (2010). *The open book of social innovation* Social Innovator Series: Ways to design, develop and grow social innovation. London: The Young Foundation.

Nicholls, A. (2010). The legitimacy of social entrepreneurship: Reflexive isomorphism in a pre-paradigmatic field. *Entrepreneurship Theory and Practice, 34*(4), 611–633.

Nicholls, A., & Murdock, A. (2012). The nature of Social Innovation. In A. Nicholls & A. Murdock (Eds.), *Social innovation: Blurring boundaries to reconfigure markets* (pp. 1–32). Houndmills, Basingstoke, Hampshire, New York, NY: Palgrave Macmillan.

Nicholls, A., & Teasdale, S. (2017). Neoliberalism by stealth? Exploring continuity and change within the UK social enterprise policy paradigm. *Policy & Politics*, *45*(3), 323–341. https://doi.org/10.1332/030557316X14775864546490

Obstfeld, D. (2016). Social networks, the tertius iungens orientation, and involvement in innovation. *Administrative Science Quarterly*, *50*(1), 100–130. https://doi.org/10.2189/asqu.2005.50.1.100

Obstfeld, D. (2017). *Getting new things done: Networks, brokerage, and the assembly of innovative action*. Stanford, CA: Stanford Business Books, an imprint of Stanford University Press.

Obstfeld, D., Borgatti, S. P., & Davis, J. (2014). Brokerage as a process: Decoupling third party action from social network structure. In D. J. Brass, S. P. Borgatti, D. S. Halgin, G. Labianca, & A. Mehra (Eds.), *Research in the sociology of organizations: vol 40. Contemporary perspectives on organizational social networks* (pp. 135–159). Bingley: Emerald Group Publishing Limited.

Porter, M. E., & Kramer, M. R. (2006, December). Strategy & society: The link between competitive advantage and corporate social responsibility. *Harvard Business Review*, 2–17.

Porter, M. E., & Kramer, M. R. (2011, January–February). Creating shared value: How to reinvent capitalism—and unleash a wave of innovation and growth. *Harvard Business Review*, 2–17.

Salamon, L. M., & Anheier, H. K. (1998). Social origins of civil society: Explaining the nonprofit sector cross-nationally. *VOLUNTAS: International Journal of Voluntary and Nonprofit Organizations*, *9*(3), 213–248.

Saxenian, A. L. (1994). *Regional advantage: Culture and competition in Silicon Valley and Route 128*. Cambridge, MA: Harvard University Press.

Schimpf, G-C., Scheuerle, T., Mildenberger, G., Haindlmaier, G., & Giesecke, S. (2017). *Comparative report on historic examples and similar recent social innovations in an early stage*. CRESSI Working Paper 35/2017. Brussels: European Commission.

Stovel, K., & Shaw, L. (2012). Brokerage. *Annual Review of Sociology*, *38*(1), 139–158. https://doi.org/10.1146/annurev-soc-081309-150054

Vaynerchuk, G. (2013). *Jab, Jab, Jab, right hook*. New York, NY: Harper Collins.

Wit, A. de, Mensink, W., Einarsson, T., & Bekkers, R. (2017). Beyond service production: Volunteering for social innovation. *Nonprofit and Voluntary Sector Quarterly*, *43*. https://doi.org/10.1177/0899764017734651

Index

Note: Page numbers in *italic* indicate a figure and page numbers in **bold** indicate a table on the corresponding page.

Taylor & Francis Group
an **informa** business

Taylor & Francis eBooks

www.taylorfrancis.com

A single destination for eBooks from Taylor & Francis
with increased functionality and an improved user
experience to meet the needs of our customers.

90,000+ eBooks of award-winning academic content in
Humanities, Social Science, Science, Technology, Engineering,
and Medical written by a global network of editors and authors.

TAYLOR & FRANCIS EBOOKS OFFERS:

A streamlined
experience for
our library
customers

A single point
of discovery
for all of our
eBook content

Improved
search and
discovery of
content at both
book and
chapter level

REQUEST A FREE TRIAL
support@taylorfrancis.com

Routledge
Taylor & Francis Group

CRC Press
Taylor & Francis Group